750

**Democracy
in the
United
States**

Democracy in the United States: Promise and Performance

Robert A. Dahl
YALE UNIVERSITY

Second Edition

RAND McNALLY & COMPANY · Chicago

Rand McNally Political Science Series

Advisory Editor
MORTON GRODZINS
Late of the University of Chicago

Second Printing, 1972

Second Edition

Copyright © 1967, 1972 by Rand McNally & Company
All rights reserved
Printed in U.S.A. by Rand McNally & Company
Library of Congress Catalog Card Number: 78-187576

To Kit
and his generation,
the inheritors

Preface to the Second Edition

The most immediately apparent change in this edition is in the title. In the interval since the first edition, it has become more and more clear to me that the words *pluralist democracy* in the original title caused more readers than I had expected to misunderstand some aspects of that book. I had intended the term *pluralist* to have a narrower and more definite sense than some readers imputed to it. I have since come to realize that 'pluralism' has so many different meanings and to many people carries so many connotations and assumptions I do not share that using it only obscures my own particular intentions and assumptions. Among political scientists the word now seems to mean whatever any writer chooses it to mean. One consequence is that despite precautions taken to define the term narrowly, some readers are bound to give it their meaning, which will be different from mine. So I have abandoned it.

Although I have kept it in the title, the term *democracy* seems hardly better off. In writing the first edition, I had too readily taken for granted the facility of readers to maintain consistently the distinction authorized by dictionary usage and ordinary language between democracy as (1) an ideal system and (2) a class of actual, concrete political systems to which the term is conventionally applied in the everyday language of journalists, politicians, political scientists, philosophers, and other ordinary citizens. The relationship between the ideal and concrete systems with certain characteristics has long seemed to me both interesting and highly problematical and I had thought that the distinction contained in ordinary language would allow me to express myself unambiguously enough. I was wrong.

Some years ago C. E. Lindblom and I introduced the term *polyarchy* to apply to concrete systems that are 'democracies' according to dictionary usage and everyday language. Since our new use of an old word has not yet made it a household term, I was reluctant to use it in a book which for many readers might be their introduction to political science. Yet all my experience in the interval points to the desirability of reducing confusion by using one term to designate the ideal and a different term to designate these concrete, real-world systems. In this edition, therefore, *democracy* refers to an ideal system, *polyarchy* to a class of actual systems. This usage immediately calls attention to the fact that the ideal and the reality are different, requires one to specify the characteristics of each, raises the question of how the two are related, and invites us to appraise the actual by the standards of the ideal. Unfortunately, we often find that the performance falls far short of the promise.

If the change in title and the introduction of the term *polyarchy* are the most visible changes, a more important one is a substantially new set of chapters that comprise Part 1, Democracy as an Ideal and as an Achievement. These seven chapters help to make explicit what was at best only implicit in the first chapter of the previous edition. They have also enabled me to take advantage of some clarifications and developments in my own thinking about polyarchies, and serve to place the American polyarchy in comparative perspective.

This edition also gives me the opportunity to correct an omission in the first. I had intended to write a final evaluative chapter for that edition. But to evaluate any highly complex political system has always seemed to me a task which, if it is to be done responsibly, would require about as much space as the task of description and explanation that forms the core of this book. So in the end, I decided against the chapter in the first edition. Yet its omission left me dissatisfied, as perhaps it did some readers, and in the intervening years my dissatisfaction has grown. I have therefore concluded this edition with such a chapter, though I am only too keenly aware that what is a final chapter here might better form an introductory chapter of a much larger effort, one which you will, I hope, be challenged to undertake yourself.

Another important feature of this new edition is the increased emphasis on Part 3, The Major Institutions: Design and Performance. In direct response to critics of the first edition, I have greatly expanded my discussion of the presidency, the Congress, the Supreme Court, the many state and local governments, and political parties, since these institutions are the basis of American government. Naturally, I have also rewritten other parts of the book as well, adding some new sections, eliminating others, and wherever possible introducing newer data from the constant flow of research going on in the social sciences, and not least, in political science.

As these comments suggest, in describing, explaining, and appraising the American political experiment, this book is deliberately and enthusiastically eclectic. No single approach, or even several approaches, can deal adequately with the major questions created by democracy as an ideal and the American polyarchy as an incomplete achievement. Consequently, where I have felt it appropriate I have drawn freely on history, political philosophy, empirical theory, institutional description, political behavior, and comparative studies. The student whose first look into political science is through the windows of this book will, I hope, not only add to his knowledge of American political institutions but also to his understanding of American political development, the philosophical foundations of democratic ideas, the ways in which the American system differs from other 'democracies,' a sense of how and why American performance falls short of democratic promise, and a perspective from which to evaluate the gap between promise and performance.

One who writes a book with as broad a coverage as this incurs innumerable intellectual debts to fellow scholars, debts going well beyond the laconic acknowledgments in footnotes. I particularly want to record my thanks to Mrs. Nancy Hoskins for the efficiency, accuracy, and cheerfulness with which she helped me to convert my drafts into readable manuscript and to acknowledge the work of Stella Jenks of Rand McNally in editing the manuscript for publication. I also want to express my appreciation publicly to Lawrence Froehlich, Christopher Harris, and Thomas Milch for their indispensable assistance in providing the most recent data available for the tables and figures.

Robert A. Dahl

North Haven, Connecticut, 1971

Acknowledgments

I wish to thank the following for permission to reprint copyrighted material:

Figure 13.2 from *Mass Politics* by Erik Allart and Stein Rokkan, copyright © 1970 by the Free Press; quotations from *Ideology and Discontent* by David E. Apter, copyright © 1964 by the Free Press of Glencoe; quotation from *Political Ideology* by Robert Lane, copyright © 1962 by the Free Press of Glencoe; and Figure 9.1 from *Political Life* by Robert Lane, copyright © 1959 by the Free Press; all reprinted by permission of The Macmillan Company.

Table 17.8 from *The Civic Culture: Political Attitudes and Democracy in Five Nations* by Gabriel A. Almond and Sidney Verba, copyright © 1963 by Princeton University Press, published for the Center of International Studies, and reprinted by permission of Princeton University Press.

Quotation from *The New American Right* by Daniel Bell, copyright © 1955 by S. G. Phillips, Inc., and reprinted by permission.

Quotations from *President and Congress* by Wilfred E. Binkley, copyright © 1937, 1947, by Wilfred E. Binkley, and reprinted by permission of Alfred A. Knopf, Inc.

Figure 19.6 from "The End of American Party Politics" by Walter Dean Burnham, copyright © December, 1969, by Transaction, Inc., New Brunswick, N. J., and reprinted with their permission.

Table 22.15 and quotations from *The American Voter* by Angus Campbell, Philip E. Converse, Warren E. Miller, and Donald E. Stokes, copyright © 1960 by John Wiley & Sons, Inc., and reprinted by permission.

Quotations from *Elections and the Political Order* by Angus Campbell, Philip E. Converse, Warren E. Miller, and Donald E. Stokes, copyright © 1966 by John Wiley & Sons, Inc., and reprinted by permission.

Tables and figures from *Congress and the Nation* and *Congressional Quarterly Weekly Report,* copyrighted by Congressional Quarterly, Inc., and reprinted with their permission.

Quotations from *His Majesty's Opposition 1714–1830* by Archibald S. Foord, copyright 1964 and used by permission of the Clarendon Press, Oxford.

Table 22.4 and quotations from *Public Opinion and American Democracy* by V. O. Key, Jr., copyright © 1961 by V. O. Key, Jr., and reprinted by permission of Alfred A. Knopf, Inc.

Quotations from *Democracy in America* by Alexis de Tocqueville (Reeve/Bowen/Bradley trans.), copyright © 1945 by Alfred A. Knopf, Inc., and reprinted by permission of the publisher.

Table of Contents

Tables and Figures

Democracy
As An Ideal
And
As An
Achievement

part

Conflict and Cooperation: The Primal Task

Like other forms of life on this planet, human beings confront a primal task: to deal satisfactorily with their conflicts and thereby secure the advantages of community and cooperation. Unlike other forms of life, human beings are endowed with capacity to reflect on this task and to search for better solutions by conscious thought and deliberate choices.

The primal task of overcoming conflicts and achieving community and cooperation arises because human beings are unable and unwilling to live in complete isolation one from another. Much as we yearn for solitude and enjoy its blessings when we are lucky enough to have them, one characteristic of mankind for the last ten thousand years, and no doubt the last hundred thousand, is a marked preference for living together in some kind of community, however small or rudimentary. The advantages of cooperation and community life are so numerous and so obvious that they must have been evident to man from earliest times. By now, our ancestors have closed off the choice; for most of us the option of total isolation from a community is, realistically speaking, no longer open.

Nonetheless, however strongly human beings are driven to seek the company of one another, and despite millennia of practice, they have never discovered a way in which they can live together without conflict, that is, without creating situations in which one individual wishes to follow a line of action that would make it difficult or impossible for someone else to pursue his own desires. Conflict seems to be an inescapable aspect of the community and hence of being human. Why conflict seems inescapable is a question that has troubled many people: philosophers, theologians, historians, social scientists, and doubtless a great many ordinary people who have not recorded their musings. James Madison, who perhaps more than any other single individual gave shape to the American constitutional system, held that conflict was built into the very nature of man. Men have diverse abilities, he wrote in *The Federalist,* and these in turn produce diverse interests:

> . . . As long as the reason of man continues fallible, and he is at liberty to exercise it, different opinions will be formed. . . . A zeal for different opinions concerning religion, concerning government, and many other points, as well of speculation as of practice; an attachment of different leaders ambitiously contending for pre-eminence and power; or to persons of other descriptions whose fortunes have been interesting to the human passions, have, in turn, divided mankind into parties, inflamed them with mutual animosity, and rendered them much more disposed to vex and oppress each other than to co-operate for their common good. . . . A landed interest, a manufacturing interest, a mercantile interest, a moneyed interest, with many lesser interests, grow up of necessity in civilized nations, and divide them into different classes, actuated by different sentiments and views.[1]

Whatever the explanation for conflict may be, and Madison's is but one among many, its existence is one of the prime facts of all community life. Yet if this were the only fact, then human life would truly fit that famous pattern described by the English political philosopher, Thomas Hobbes, in his great and controversial book, *Leviathan* (1651). Hobbes describes mankind in a state of nature:

> In such condition, there is no place for industry; because the fruit thereof is uncertain; and consequently no culture of the earth; no navigation, nor use of the commodities that may be imported by sea; no commodious building; no instruments of moving, and removing, such things as require much force; no knowledge of the face of the earth; no account of time; no arts; no letters, no society; and which is worst of all, continual fear, and danger of violent death and the life of man, solitary, poor, nasty, brutish, and short.[2]

But life is not so dismal. A condition of totally unregulated conflict is, as Hobbes himself argued, obviously incompatible with community life. Along with the deep human need for living in communion with fellow men, and alongside the inevitable conflicts that are generated whenever human beings try to live together, as far back into man's past as one can pry, there have also been traces of a search for ways by which human beings can cooperate and conflicts within a community can be settled without extensive violence and bloodshed, according to standards of justice, held, at the very least, among those who enforce the rules. We cannot pause to probe the mystery; but the evidence is so great that we can safely accept it as a fact.

1. Alexander Hamilton, John Jay, and James Madison, *The Federalist* (New York: Modern Library, n.d.), pp. 55–56. Madison's famous passages in *The Federalist,* too long to include here, are worth reading in full.
2. Thomas Hobbes, *Leviathan* (New York: Macmillan, 1947), p. 82.

Thus man's existence as a social being—a social animal, if you prefer—is conditioned by a set of contradictory tendencies that, taken altogether, make him a member of some political system:

1. His need for human fellowship and the advantages of cooperation create communities.
2. But he is unable to live with others without conflict.
3. *Hence,* communities search for ways of adjusting conflicts so that cooperation and community life will be possible and tolerable.

The third stage in this dialectic is the turning point from man as a social animal to man as a political animal. For if conflicts are to be settled, somewhere in the community there must be individuals or groups with enough authority or power to secure—if need be to compel—a settlement: to make sure that the parties to a conflict abide by the judgment of the ruler, the will of God, existing rules, their own agreement, or law. At any rate, human communities do not seem ever to have existed without some such powers—without, that is, political institutions.

WHAT GOVERNMENT IS BEST? To say that political institutions—governments—seem to be inevitable is not to say that they are invariably good. Unlike other animals, human beings can and do ask themselves whether things might not be better than they are. This concern for betterment impels some persons to search for standards by which to judge what is better. Thus when people become aware of their political institutions and the possibility of improving them, some begin to ask: What form of government is best?

It is impossible to say when men first became conscious of their political institutions. We know that for at least two thousand years before the first settlers came to America there had been in the Western world a distinct consciousness of political systems and an awareness of differences between them. During these twenty centuries men asked questions about politics, particularly during eras of great change and crisis when old systems confronted new ones. It is not a great step from becoming keenly aware that communities do have and probably must have governments—institutions for settling conflicts, enforcing rules, and perhaps even making rules—to the question, "What form of government is 'best'?" Because this question—like many other questions about politics—is likely to come to the fore in times of political disturbance and change, it was one of the most important questions that confronted the Founders gathered in Philadelphia in 1787 to discuss constitutional problems. As we shall see they were by no means agreed on an answer. For they reflected, among other influences, the history of ancient controversies, controversies that still persist in our own day and will not die, I imagine, as long as men continue to ask questions.

Although they were very far from agreed on many questions, most of the men at the Constitutional Convention appear to have believed that they were establishing a good government in the United States. They asserted as much in that famous Preamble which every American schoolchild is supposed to learn, even if he never learns anything else about our political system.

Nearly two centuries later, it is still as proper as it was then to ask what kind of political system would be best for the American people, and whether what has actually evolved in this country measures up satisfactorily to appropriate standards. That, in fact, is a central concern in this book.

Unfortunately, evaluating a political system is an enterprise of extraordinary difficulty. Consequently I would not want anyone to expect to find anything like a definitive answer here. Nonetheless, in what follows I want to explore these questions:

1. What standards or goals can we reasonably apply to the American political system? What obstacles to achieving these goals can we expect to arise?

To answer these questions is the task of Part I.

2. How does the American political system operate, and why?

The answer to this question is the substance of this book, and comprises Parts II, III, and IV.

3. Given the way the American political system operates, and the causes, how can citizens influence the conduct of the government?

This question is dealt with in Part V.

4. How does the operation of the American political system measure up to the standards discussed in Part I?

In the concluding chapter, I offer what is unavoidably a rather personal answer. It is hardly to be expected that every reader will agree with my appraisal. Even one who agrees that the descriptions and explanations offered in Parts II, III, and IV are essentially valid might arrive at a different judgment on the achievements of the American political system. Yet if we agree that the standards I am about to discuss are appropriate criteria for judging the American polity, then it is less likely, I think, that we shall disagree widely in our appraisal.

Two Principles:
Equality and Consent

2

Given the inevitability of conflict and the desirability of cooperation, what form of government is best? In particular, what kind of government is best for Americans?

Despite all the enormous changes affecting the American people and the world in which they live, the answer to this question that was most widely accepted by Americans during and after the American Revolution is still relevant today—and offers standards that have not yet been met in this country or elsewhere. This is the view that the government of a state is legitimate only if it derives its authority from the people. Behind the idea of government by the people lie beliefs in political equality and consent—as we can see in the words that have become so much a part of the catechism of American schoolchildren as to be nearly devoid of specific meaning:

> We hold these truths to be self-evident, that all men are created equal, that they are endowed by their Creator with certain inalienable Rights, that among these are Life, Liberty and the pursuit of Happiness. —That to secure these rights, Governments are instituted among Men, deriving their just powers from the consent of the governed.

A commonplace objection to the principle of political equality—and to the famous phrase in the Declaration of Independence—is that men are not, in fact, equal. I do not think this is a lethal thrust, however, for even if the language of the Declaration is ambiguous, the principle is best understood not as a strictly factual proposition but as a moral or ethical assertion.[1] So interpreted, it does not imply that men are identical or equal in intelligence, strength, cunning, or many other

---

1. John Locke, who was a prime source of much of the political philosophy of the Founders, was explicit on this point: "Though I have said above . . . 'That all men by nature are equal,' I cannot be supposed to understand all sorts of 'equality.' Age or virtue may give

respects. As a moral principle, its meaning might be summed up in this way: Human beings are entitled to be treated as if they were equal on all matters important to them. It is up to people who accept this moral principle to see to it that everyone has the minimal resources needed to make the principle workable in practise.

Nor is the objection fatal that no government—certainly none involving a large population—has ever managed to live up to the principle nor quite likely ever will. Ethical principles are intended as criteria against which to judge achievement. We do not abandon standards of personal honesty, love, or justice merely because no one seems to be perfectly honest, loving, or just.

Why, you might ask, should one accept the principle of political equality? The authors of the Declaration seem to have gotten by with the extravagant assertion that the principle is self-evident. It was convenient to assume so, for a consideration of the arguments for and against the principle of political equality would take us far beyond the limits of this book. Yet some of the reasons are worth mentioning here; since they also relate to the idea of consent, we can treat the two ideas together.

If political equality was "self-evident," Americans also fell into the habit quite early, as the Declaration shows, of asserting that the government of a state ought to rest on the consent of the people subject to it. Two years earlier, the First Continental Congress had already insisted

> that the inhabitants of the English colonies in North America, by the immutable laws of nature . . . are entitled to life, liberty and property: and they have never ceded to any foreign power whatever, a right to dispose of either without their consent.

The preamble of practically every state constitution adopted during the next several decades contained words to the general effect that the power of government derives from the people and depends upon their consent. Revolutionary in their time, the words, if not the ideas themselves, gradually became exhausted from sheer overwork. By now they come so easily to the lips of an American that few ever pause to ask *why* governments should or *how* they can rest on the consent of all.

There are at least four reasons, however, for insisting that governments ought, ideally, to derive their just powers from the consent of

---

men a just precedency. Excellency of parts and merit may place others above the common level. Birth may subject some, and alliance or benefits others, to pay an observance to those to whom Nature, gratitude, or other respects, may have made it due; and yet all this consists with the equality which all men are in in respect of jurisdiction or dominion one over another, which was the equality I there spoke of as proper to the business in hand, being that equal right that every man hath to his natural freedom, without being subjected to the will or authority of any other man'' (*Of Civil Government, Two Treatises* [London: J. M. Dent, 1924], p. 142).

the governed, considered as political equals. First, government without consent is inconsistent with personal freedom. To the extent that I am compelled to obey man-made rules that do not have my moral approval, I am not a free man. To be sure, personal freedom is an exacting demand; complete personal freedom is probably impossible to achieve. Nonetheless, one who believes in the value of individual freedom may reasonably hold that so far as possible no adult human being should ever be governed without his consent.

Second, government without one's consent can be an affront to human dignity and respect. We see this most vividly in extreme cases—the hapless victim in a concentration camp, who is subjected to the utmost humiliation, degradation, deprivation, and torture, loses thereby a part of his humanity.

Third, one may demand solely out of self-interest that a government rest on consent and equality. For one might reason as follows: Certainly I do not want the government to act without *my* approval. But since I am not nor am I likely to be a dictator or even a member of a ruling oligarchy, perhaps the safest way to insure that the government will have *my* approval is to insist that it must have the approval of *everyone*. Reasoning from self-interest is not generally thought to be quite as noble as reasoning from general principles of freedom and dignity. Nonetheless we should rejoice, I believe, whenever freedom and dignity are supported by widespread self-interest; for nothing is quite so strong a buttress to social institutions as a firm foundation in self-interest.

Finally, one may insist on consent and equality because one thinks that governments "deriving their just powers from the consent of the governed" are more likely to be stable and durable. There are innumerable reasons why one may want stable government, including the fact that revolutions are very uncertain affairs; with a few exceptions, among which, happily, the American Revolution may be counted, those who start the first fires of a revolution are consumed in the holocaust. To control the course of a revolution is almost as difficult as to direct the path of a tornado. Whatever the reasons why one may want stability in a government, it is reasonable to suppose that a government is less likely to create hostility, frustration, and resentment—sentiments that breed revolution—if it acts with the approval of its citizens than if it does not. Common sense and modern history both lend substance to this judgment; in the past century the most durable governments in the world have rested on widespread suffrage and other institutions for popular control.

Nonetheless, to erect and maintain a political system that meets standards of political equality and consent to some reasonably satisfactory degree is an undertaking of very great difficulty. Let me mention five problems:

☐ Consent: How can *continuing* and not merely *past* consent be assured?
☐ Equality: How can gross inequalities be kept from undermining the principle of political equality?
☐ Conflict: How can a political system that is consistent with consent and political equality overcome conflicts?
☐ Competence: Can ordinary people govern themselves wisely?
☐ Effectiveness: Can they create and operate a government that is effective in solving the problems they want it to handle?

Five Questions
About Equality and Consent

3

1. ARE CONSENT AND POLITICAL EQUALITY TO BE CONTINUOUS?

Today the term *consent* has the flavor of the eighteenth century. It calls to mind the effort—successful, as it turned out—to destroy the legitimacy of monarchies by denying that they rested on the "consent of the people." In this perspective, you merely give or deny your consent to a person or government. To a particular government, you may perhaps give your consent once and for all.

Beyond this rather passive view, however, lies the notion that when certain decisions are made you ought to be able to express your deepest preferences, desires, or goals, and have them taken fully into account. If we also invoke the principle of political equality, your preferences as to the outcome ought to be weighed equally along with everyone else's: no more, no less; one man, one vote.

Considered as a continuing and active process, then, consent and political equality seem to require that every full citizen must have unimpaired opportunities:

1. To figure out, discover, and formulate his goals: to find out what he really wants.
2. By acting individually or in concert, to indicate his preferences to his fellow citizens and to the government.
3. To have his preferences weighted equally in the conduct of the government—that is, weighted with no discrimination because of *what* he wants or *who* he happens to be.

How much lag or delay is reasonable between the time you formulate a goal and it is taken into account in decisions? Must institutions insure that your preferences are *immediately* taken into account? Is a year's delay reasonable? Two? Four? Longer? What about constitutional arrangements? Should not the system of government itself be more difficult to change than the specific policies of the government? If so, how difficult should it be to change or throw off a constitution?

For example, the fact that some people may have voted in the distant past to accept the Constitution of the United States—as a rather small proportion of the population did in 1787–8, and as the people or their representatives did in the territories prior to entering the Union—is surely no reason why we, today, should feel bound to accept their verdict: not, at any rate, if we demand continuing 'consent' to the processes of government. Ideally, it seems, every new generation must be free to refuse its consent to the old rules and to make new ones. The Declaration of Independence contains these ringing phrases:

> That whenever any Form of Government becomes destructive of these ends [Life, Liberty, and the pursuit of Happiness], it is the Right of the People to alter or to abolish it, and to institute a new Government, laying its foundation on such principles and organizing its power in such form, as to them shall seem most likely to effect their Safety and Happiness.

Seventy years later, confronted by secession, and on the eve of war, in his inauguration speech, Lincoln reaffirmed the same principle:

> This country, with its institutions, belongs to the people who inhabit it. Whenever they grow weary of the existing government, they can exercise their constitutional right of amending it, or their revolutionary right to dismember or overthrow it.[1]

But "the people" is an ambiguous phrase. Do these famous words mean that whenever a majority is discontented with the government it should be free to change it? If they are not permitted to do so, then can we say that they have given their approval, in any realistic sense, to the processes of government? Yet if every majority must be free to alter the rules of government, what is the significance of a "Constitution"? How can a constitution be more binding than ordinary law? Is there no legitimate way by which groups smaller than a majority can receive guarantees that the rules they agree to abide by will be more or less permanent and will not change at the whim of the next legislature? This leads directly to the problem of minority rights.

2. CAN SUFFICIENT EQUALITY BE MAINTAINED?

Political equality must surely be one of the most exacting demands ever placed on a government. Certainly it has never been attained in the United States, or, for that matter, elsewhere.

There are three persistent causes of political inequalities. First, some persons manage to acquire more political resources, influence, and

---

1. Carl Sandburg, *Abraham Lincoln, The War Years*, vol. 1 (New York: Harcourt, Brace, 1939), p. 133.

power than others because of what appear to be *individual* characteristics: matters of temperament, interests, skills, and specific endowments.

Second, independent of individual characteristics, *social* arrangements generally create some inequalities in political resources, influence, and power. Thus an enormous source of inequality in the United States has been racial discrimination against American Indians and Afro-Americans. So far as I am aware, no other country with continuing institutions of representative government (that claim to rest on equality and consent) has had such an appalling record of mistreatment of racial minorities. As we shall see, the tension between the effort to maintain a democratic republic and yet deny political equality to Afro-Americans has dominated political life in this country from the Constitutional Convention to the present day. Racial discrimination, however, is by no means the only source of unequal political resources. There have also been large and persistent differences in education, income, wealth, access to communications, and so on.

Third, among any collection of people larger than a few thousand, not everyone can participate equally in all aspects of decision-making. Even if there were no other limitations, people rarely, if ever, have an unlimited amount of time to spend on making decisions. At a meeting of ten thousand people, only a tiny minority can have an opportunity to speak; where citizens number in the millions, the opportunities must necessarily be even more restricted. In situations where everyone cannot be granted the right to participate fully, the principle of political equality itself dictates the need for a system of *representation.*

The criterion of equality might still be met if everyone could participate equally in choosing and influencing representatives, if the representatives were mere agents of their constituents, and if all were equal in influencing decisions. In practise these conditions are never wholly satisfied. For example, it appears to be very nearly impossible for a large collection of people to elect representatives who are nothing more than agents of their constituents. In practise, representatives invariably acquire an additional increment of power; they are not simply ordinary citizens expressing the collective will of their constituents. Among other causes are these: questions of policy are often highly complicated; citizens sometimes have no clear-cut views; if they do, they disagree among themselves; they often fail to keep in touch with their representatives; they find it hard to do much more than vote; they leave decisions pretty much to the person elected.

It is not surprising, as we shall see in the next chapter, that some critics contend that what is called a representative government is largely a facade behind which a cohesive elite actually rules. The argument, to be sure, often gains support by confusing the undeniable existence of inequalities in political resources, influence, and power, with the existence of a *ruling* elite. Yet whatever the correct assessment may be, the existence of serious inequalities poses a problem for a system that claims to adhere to the principle of political equality.

3. CAN CONFLICTS BE HANDLED SATISFACTORILY?

Like any other government, a government by the people must somehow cope with the primal task of overcoming conflict.

In an impressive and justly famous analysis (that foreshadowed the remarks quoted above from *The Federalist*), James Madison, during the second week of the Constitutional Convention, expressed a concern that must have been widely shared among the other delegates:

> All civilized Societies would be divided into different Sects, Factions, & interests, as they happened to consist of rich & poor, debtors & creditors, the landed, the manufacturing, the commercial interests, the inhabitants of this district or that district, the followers of this political leader or that political leader, the disciples of this religious Sect or that religious Sect.[2]

Madison took it for granted, then, that cleavages could occur in many ways; economic relationships, geographical location, religious feelings, even loyalties to particular leaders, all could lead to conflict. And what would restrain one faction in its struggles with another? Honesty? Reputation? Conscience? Religion? In Madison's view, all limits to faction that depend, like these, on the willingness of an individual or a group to exercise self-restraint are bound to be inadequate.

Like most of the other delegates, Madison was more inclined to stress the dangers that could arise from a willful or tempestuous majority than from a minority; for he assumed that in a republic a majority could more easily have its own way. But he was not unmindful of the possibility that minority factions might also threaten a republic.

> . . . According to the Republican theory indeed, Right & power being both vested in the majority, are held to be synonimous. According to fact & experience, a minority may in an appeal to force be an overmatch for the majority. 1. If the minority happen to include all such as possess the skill & habits of military life, with such as possess the great pecuniary resources, one third may conquer the remaining two thirds. 2. one third of those who participate in the choice of rulers may be rendered a majority by the accession of those whose poverty disqualifies them from a suffrage, & who for obvious reasons may be more ready to join the standard of sedition than that of the established Government. 3. where slavery exists, the Republican Theory becomes still more fallacious.[3]

2. From "Debates in the Federal Convention of 1787 as reported by James Madison," in *Documents Illustrative of the Formation of the Union of the American States,* selected, arranged, and indexed by Charles C. Tansill (Washington: Government Printing Office, 1927), p. 162 (hereafter cited as *Documents*).

3. *Ibid.,* p. 230.

The Dangers of Faction

Precisely what are the dangers of faction that preoccupied the Founders? Curiously enough, none of the men at the Convention ever seems to have stated exactly what he had in mind. On this question even the clearest minds, like those of Madison and Wilson, gave forth cloudy answers. When the delegates descended from vague generalities to concrete cases, the examples they chose generally involved attempts to change the distribution of property. In fact, a careful reading of the record of debates suggests the cynical answer that when the delegates at the Constitutional Convention spoke of the dangers of faction they were usually thinking of attacks on property—their own. Here, for example, is what Madison said at one point:

> . . . No agrarian attempts have yet been made in this Country, but symptoms, of a leveling spirit, as we have understood, have sufficiently appeared in certain quarters to give notice of the future danger. How is this danger to be guarded agst on republican principles? How is the danger in all cases of interested coalitions to oppress the minority to be guarded agst?[4]

With the aid of the experience that has accumulated since 1787, perhaps today we can see the problem of faction more clearly than the delegates to the Convention were able to do. We have learned some hard lessons. When someone says he opposes factions and parties, what he usually means, it seems, is that he opposes every faction, every party, every interest—except his own. If one believes that policies proposed by others will deprive him of something he values, or if he so strongly believes his own policies are right that he would impose them on other people no matter what they prefer, he finds it easy to define what the others wish to do as tyranny and what he himself wishes to do as obvious justice.

Many of the concrete concerns of the Founders were, I believe, of this kind. To some extent, they elevated their own privileges into universal matters of abstract and universal right; groups who might interfere with their privileges were, in their eyes, dangerous factions. In this respect they carried partisan attitudes into the Convention, yet were usually unaware that they did so. They were not necessarily cynical, merely human. (Does one have a right to expect more from men simply because they make a constitution?)

Yet it is too facile to jump to the conclusion that the fear of faction expressed by the Founders represented nothing more than sordid self-interest. Whatever their motives and biases may have been, whatever the extent to which they were influenced by their own socioeconomic positions and ideological perspectives, the problem they confronted was genuine, important, timely, persistent, and worthy of the concern they

---

4. *Ibid.*, pp. 280–281.

gave it. For the problem of faction is simply the mirror image of the problem of gaining consent—of governing with the consent of the governed. Goals of personal freedom, human dignity, enlightened self-interest, and political stability all justify a serious concern for gaining consent, and hence for keeping conflict within bounds, so that in the best of circumstances all citizens will feel that what they hold most dear is respected and protected by the government—while even in the worst of circumstances they will feel that the laws are at least tolerable, and do not encourage disloyalty, violence, or civil wars.

As practical men, the Founders were concerned lest conflicts get out of hand. Faction had been the bane of previous republics; faction was a worrisome fact of recent experience; and faction would be a standing danger to the new republic.

> . . . In Greece & Rome the rich & poor, the creditors & debtors, as well as the patricians & plebians alternately oppressed each other with equal unmercifulness. What a source of oppression was the relation between the parent cities of Rome, Athens & Carthage, & their respective provinces: the former possessing the power, & the latter being sufficiently distinguished to be separate objects of it? Why was America so justly apprehensive of Parliamentary injustice? Because G. Britain had a separate interest real or supposed, & if her authority had been admitted, could have pursued that interest at our expense. We have seen the mere distinction of colour made in the most enlightened period of time, a ground of the most oppressive dominion ever exercised by man over man. What has been the source of those unjust laws complained of among ourselves? Has it not been the real or supposed interest of the major number? Debtors have defrauded their creditors. The landed interest has borne hard on the mercantile interest. The Holders of one species of property have thrown a disproportion of taxes on the holders of another species.[5]

The Inevitability of Conflict

Yet, being realists, they also knew that conflict is inevitable. Conflict, as Madison said, is sown in the nature of man. An autocratic government might suppress the symptoms of conflict, as modern dictators have succeeded in doing; but even an autocracy cannot eliminate the causes. By establishing a republic in which citizens would enjoy a large measure of personal freedom, the Founders were bound to make it easy for conflict to erupt. How, then, was conflict to be managed? How could it be moderated so that it would not wreck the new republic? How could government be effectively carried on with something like the general consent of the people?

Since political philosophers, like architects, sometimes conceal their failures behind a handsome facade, the unwary may conclude that the solution would be clear if he only understood the philosophers better.

---

5. *Ibid.*, pp. 162–163.

In this case, however, modesty may be misplaced; although political philosophers have long wrestled with the problem, the disagreeable fact remains that they have not been able to prescribe a perfect solution except under certain highly improbable circumstances.

Solution: Eliminate Conflict

The obvious way out, of course, is to eliminate conflict. This happy solution is characteristic of many literary utopias, where social life is downright inhuman in its lack of conflict. Utopianism of this genre appears in unsuspected places: Karl Marx was a militant critic of the utopian socialists of an earlier generation, yet he evidently thought that his famous dialectic—"All history is the history of class conflict"— would for all practical purposes come to an end in a communist society: there would be no need for a state because there would be no significant conflicts.

Agreement on Policies

If one concludes that complete agreement is a hopeless objective and not necessarily a very desirable one, then one must search else- where for a solution. A second way out is to search for specific policies that every citizen approves of, even though he may have disagreed, initially, with his fellow citizens. It is not absurd, surely, to suppose that conflict can sometimes be transmuted into decisions that have the approval of everyone. Perhaps all of us have had experiences of this kind, particularly when we try to arrive at decisions within some group where everyone else shares our fundamental values, even though we may differ on specific questions.

There is something of this idea behind Rousseau's much disputed notion of a General Will that bespeaks more truly what we believe than we always do ourselves. Yet the difficulty with all solutions along these lines is that decisions rarely do receive unanimous approval. Do I consent to decisions with which I disagree? Who is a better judge than I of what my 'will,' my policy, really is? Should anyone else have the authority to proclaim that a policy really has my consent? Although a distinction can be made between what I really believe is best and what I momentarily think or say is best, a good deal of experience suggests that to allow someone else to make this distinction for me is very dangerous.

A tyrant might insist that he has my consent for all he does, though I deny it, because he knows better than I what I really want. When an individual says he disapproves of the policies of the government, even when these policies have the blessings of an enlightened dictator or an enlightened majority, the safest course in practise, I believe, is to postulate that he knows his own mind. Otherwise, government by consent is likely to degenerate into a mere ritualistic formula.

Agreement on a Process

Even if people cannot always agree on specific policies, however, a third solution is to gain their consent for a *process.* It is perfectly reasonable of me to say that I approve of the process by which certain kinds of decisions are made, even if I do not always like the specific results. Thus the consent of the governed may be interpreted to mean their approval of the processes by which decisions are arrived at and their willingness to abide by these decisions even when they seem wrong.

But what kind of a process shall I require? If I hold that no one can, as a general matter, know my goals and values better than I myself, then no doubt I will insist that the process of making decisions must provide me with a full opportunity to make my views known; and even if I am willing to leave details to experts, I do not want anyone else to have more power over the decision, in the last say, than I do. A solution along these lines might well appeal to me as the best attainable, given the inescapable conditions mentioned earlier: that my need for human fellowship impels me to live in a society, that I cannot live with others without sometimes disagreeing with them, and that I must therefore find some way to adjust to our conflicts that will appeal to all of us as fair.

One familiar process that is widely thought to meet these requirements is majority rule. In the next chapter we shall explore this solution, and some difficulties with it.

4. CAN THE PEOPLE GOVERN WISELY?

If the best government is one where all persons who are subject to a government's decisions must, somehow, give their active and express consent to those decisions, then clearly we will have—must have—rule by the people. Yet no government has ever tried to secure the active consent or participation of *all* the people. To take one example, persons under some rather arbitrary age like 18 or 21 are excluded everywhere from voting in elections. Why? Because they are assumed (by those beyond this threshold) to be, on the average, not yet competent enough to be allowed to participate in the government of the state.

Aha! one might say, isn't it possible that a lot of people over 18 or 21, or whatever age you may choose, are also incompetent to govern themselves? In fact, may not the people, taken as the general adult population, be incompetent to govern? If so, shouldn't the people *be* governed by those among them who are *best* qualified to govern?

The belief that the best government is necessarily one controlled by a small elite of the most qualified persons is an ancient and powerful objection to rule by the people. One set of alternatives to rule by the people, then, consists of political arrangements that call for government by an aristocracy, a meritocracy, an elite. The argument for meritocracy has never been more brilliantly nor more persuasively set out than by

Plato in *The Republic.* Plato argued that government should be in the hands of those who because of their exceptional virtues and knowledge are best qualified to govern. A crucial element in his argument is the assumption that the number of people properly qualified to govern is, in any community, almost certain to be a minority. The contrary view holds that everyone should govern since, ideally, no adult should be governed without his consent; that political virtue and wisdom are not lodged exclusively in any identifiable group of persons; and that if consent is to mean anything, every adult must be quite free to participate in all political decisions without fear or favor.

The debate between those who espouse these conflicting doctrines would not have endured so long if each viewpoint did not have a good deal to be said for it—and each runs into some rather serious problems.

Meritocracy, the aristocratic or elitist solution (which has nothing intrinsically to do with birth) is frequently used, even by those who reject it for governing the state, for governing other organizations where superior skills are crucial to success and where, it is supposed, these superior skills can be more or less definitely defined and identified. The perennial appeal of the doctrine of meritocracy or aristocracy, then, is that it focuses directly on the problems of *fitness* to rule and stresses the importance of having good leadership, of giving authority to *skillful, wise,* and *virtuous* men (or women). Leadership is a persistent problem in all political systems.

Yet it is one thing to govern a family, a ship, an army, a business firm, or a government bureau, and quite another to govern a community or a nation. As a matter of fact even in those institutions where 'aristocratic' solutions are supposed to work best, they have often produced notoriously incompetent leaders. Whatever may be the justification for the aristocratic solution for providing leadership in certain situations, there are four major objections to applying the aristocratic doctrine to the political system of an entire community.

First, the standards of skill, wisdom, and virtue required are unclear. Men of great learning are not always virtuous, and men of virtue are not always learned. After nearly twenty-five centuries, almost the only people who seem to be convinced of the advantages of being ruled by philosopher-kings are . . . a few philosophers. Though indispensable as advisers and occasionally skillful in politics, scholars, as a group, have not greatly impressed others with their competence as rulers. The skills of the businessman or military leader are highly specialized, and very different from those required in government: Ulysses S. Grant, a great general, and Herbert Hoover, a great businessman, were not great presidents. In sum, it is easy to propose in the groves of academe that the skillful, wise, and virtuous should rule; but it is difficult to establish practical criteria for identifying persons with superior skill, wisdom, and virtue in politics. There seems to be a very strong and very human tendency to solve the problem by defining skill, wisdom, and virtue in the image of one's own self, group, or class. Was it by chance that Plato, a philosopher, concluded that the best rulers would be contemplative men rather like himself?

In the second place, even if the criteria were much clearer than they are, how are these criteria to be applied? How are the rulers to be selected? In a mad scramble for power, the wise and virtuous are likely to be trampled to death. Popular election would turn the whole process upside down. Hereditary aristocracies have always been subject to the great gamble of genetics and early environment; there is no guarantee that the first-born son of a wise and virtuous father may not be a dullard, or a scoundrel, or both. One might propose that the rulers should be chosen by the wise and virtuous. But of course this only pushes the problem one stage farther back: Who is wise and virtuous enough to choose the wise and virtuous men who will choose the rulers?

Third, can a process designed to select only the wise and virtuous also insure that the leaders so chosen have widespread consent for their government? If it is said that surely the wise and virtuous would have general consent for their rule, then why not adopt the democratic solution and allow the people to choose their leaders? If, on the other hand, one objects that the people might not choose wise and virtuous leaders, then, since they are not the choice *of* and *by* the people, must they be imposed *on* the people? If so, would not the attempt to impose leaders on the people degenerate into a trial by battle in which the strongest, not the wisest and most virtuous, would win?

Finally, even if the skillful, wise, and virtuous could somehow be chosen as rulers, how can we be sure that they will not be corrupted by power? Lord Acton's famous proposition about power corrupting is, surely, an overstatement;[6] wags have sometimes proposed that it be amended to read: "Power corrupts, and the absence of power corrupts absolutely." Nonetheless, the dangers created by the mysterious alchemy of power are too familiar to be laughed aside.

For anyone convinced by these objections to meritocracy, the main alternative in the United States ever since colonial times has always been popular government. In the eyes of one who believes in equality and consent, no one group can be found with such clearly superior talent and virtue to entitle it to rule. With the proper conditions—and it is the job of one who advocates these goals to foster and maintain these conditions—practically everyone has sufficient knowledge and virtue to share, directly or indirectly, in the task of governing. In any

---

6. See the analysis of Arnold Rogow and Harold D. Lasswell, *Power, Corruption and Rectitude* (Englewood Cliffs: Prentice-Hall, 1963).

case, even though I may lack technical knowledge as to the best or most efficient means, is anyone else likely to know better than I what end or goals are best for me?

Nonetheless, the problem is troublesome and real. Even if the ordinary citizen may be counted on, by and large, to know what ends are best for him, what about the excruciatingly difficult problems of means? For example, most of us could not possibly decide intelligently what pharmaceuticals should be sold freely, or prohibited, or issued only by prescription. Clearly, then, there are decisions that require me to *delegate* authority to others. One solution is to delegate some authority to elected representatives; but if I delegate, may I not, in practise, end up with a kind of aristocracy of experts, or even false experts? As we shall see in the next chapter, some critics of representative government argue that this is exactly what happens.

5. WILL THE GOVERNMENT BE EFFECTIVE?

Can a government that tries to honor the ideas of consent and political equality be effective in dealing with the matters that the people regard as important?

Once again, the heart of the problem is the existence of disagreements over the ends that a government should seek or the means most appropriate to achieving particular ends. A process that requires a search for policies that will satisfy everyone may be interminable. Because of the opposition of a minority, policies advocated by a substantial part of the people may be blocked for years or decades, or even indefinitely put off. Yet if minorities can be easily overridden, the government may be able to act with dispatch, but how effective will it be from the point of view of the minorities? It may not solve *their* problems. And what happens to *their* consent? Like the problem of conflict itself, the problem of governmental effectiveness is so intimately tied up with the solution of majority rule and alternatives to it that we must now turn to that solution and the problems it generates. But first let me summarize the argument so far.

SUMMARY

In the first two chapters, we saw that:

1. The benefits of human fellowship and cooperation impel human beings to seek ways of handling conflicts so that cooperation and community life will be possible and tolerable.

2. A conscious concern for this task generates the question: What government is best?

3. One answer, singularly important for Americans, is that the best government for a state is a government of the people based on political equality and the consent of all.

In this chapter we have seen that an attempt to establish and maintain a government that will satisfy the principles of equality and consent encounters five major problems: continuing consent, inequalities, the primal problem of conflict, competence, and governmental effectiveness. In the next three chapters, we shall examine three very general types of solutions.

First Answer:
Majority-Rule Democracy

4

Can a government be established and maintained that will surmount the challenges discussed in the last chapter and achieve rule by the people based on consent and political equality?

Probably the best known answer is something like this: The requirements of consent can be satisfied if the citizens all approve of the principle of majority rule, according to which all conflicts over the policies of government are settled, sooner or later, by a majority of citizens or voters—either directly in a public assembly or in a referendum, or indirectly through elected representatives. That this consent will be freely given, and not coerced, can be insured by legal and constitutional protection of basic rights to speak, write, publish, organize, oppose the government, vote, be a candidate, and the like. If these basic rights are protected for everyone, then political equality will also be attained.

There are, however, some problems concealed in this attractive answer. Let me mention a few.

WHAT PEOPLE? When one says he favors government by the people, the question immediately arises: what people? In practise, what we assume to be a *people* for purposes of self-government consists of a particular collection of human beings whose identity as a "people" or a nation has already been established, often by bitter controversy, violence, compulsion, and, as in the case of the American people, civil war.

Notice that by conceding to every human being claims to his consent and his political equality you do not answer the question: what people? You simply require that an answer be found. For unless all the people of the world are to govern themselves in a single, unitary world state, the human species has to be separated into political communities within each of which self-government can take place.

When the term *democracy* was first used by the Greeks, they assumed that a "people" could not be more numerous or more hetero-geneous than the citizens of a small city-state. By the beginning of the nineteenth century advocates of democracy pretty generally assumed that the citizens of a nation-state could constitute a "people." Yet the boundaries of nation-states are mainly products of struggle and violence. Do the persons incorporated within these boundaries, perhaps by force, necessarily form a "people"? If residents of a nation-state disagree as to whether they should form a single people or separate into two or more countries, are there general principles to which we may look for guidance? This much may be said: if there are general principles, they are obscure, difficult, controversial, and command so little agreement that when such issues arise, in practise force seems more likely to prevail than reasoned discussion and peaceful settlement.

Even if we were to agree that some particular collection of human beings—Americans, let us say—ought to constitute a single people for purposes of governing themselves according to the principles of consent and political equality, two further problems would remain. First, even the most ardent advocate of democracy does not mean that consent and political equality should apply literally to *all* the people. For full political equality will be denied to some part of the people, and their consent will be thought unnecessary, because they are held to be incompetent on grounds of immaturity. No one seriously contends that the suffrage should be extended to five-year-old children, for example. Thus "a majority of the people" really means, at most, "a majority of adults."

Second, suppose that a "people" such as the Americans, the Swiss, or the Canadians want to form themselves into a single self-governing unit for some purposes and at the same time into smaller units—states, provinces, cantons, cities, towns, etc.—for other purposes. If so, a majority of the people for some purposes must necessarily be different in size and composition from a majority for other purposes. In fact, a majority of adult citizens in the whole country may even be thought to have no right to overrule the majority of the smaller unit on some matters. We have now plunged deeply into the problem of *federal* states, to which it is difficult and sometimes impossible to apply simple democratic ideas formed on the model of the small city-state.

MAJORITY RULE VERSUS MINORITY RIGHTS   The straightforward application of the principle that the majority should be sovereign on *all* questions of public significance is, as a practical matter, not likely to receive everyone's continuing approval—except under unusual circumstances. While a citizen may make certain allowances for majority decisions that displease him, the more frequently he expects to be in a minority, the less likely he is to accept the principle of majority rule. One can, perhaps, accept calmly the prospect of being in a minority so long as the issues are trivial. But the more important the issues, the more difficult it is to accept defeat by a hostile majority. The more I expect that majorities are going to insist on policies that conflict with my most cherished values, the more likely I am to oppose the principle of majority rule. Surely few people would be so loyal to the abstract principle as to approve of it even if they expected it to lead regularly to repugnant policies. At some point even the most convinced adherent of majority rule will give up in despair. In a nation of convinced anti-Semites and religious bigots, a modern Jefferson might be compelled to oppose the principle of the sovereign majority. In short, continuing and universal approval of the principle of majority rule requires a high degree of consensus among all the citizens as to what the policies of government should be.

It seems reasonable to conjecture that the more diverse the beliefs held among a body of people, the less likely it is that they will approve of the idea of making decisions by majority rule. To the extent that this conjecture is valid, it is a severe restriction on the principle of rule by a sovereign majority, particularly in heterogeneous societies. For it seems entirely reasonable to hold that diversity of beliefs is likely to be greater the larger the number of citizens, the bigger the territory over which they are spread, and the greater the distinctions of race, ethnic group, regional culture, occupation, social class, income, property, and so on. Some advocates of rule by the sovereign majority have therefore argued, as Rousseau did, that majority decisions would be acceptable only among very small and highly homogeneous bodies of people, groups no larger perhaps than a town or a very small city. According to this view, nations, even as small as Norway and certainly as large as the United States, are unsuitable for rule by the people.

One possible way to maintain homogeneity would be to eliminate all dissenting minorities who would object to the decisions of a majority. In Athens the Ecclesia—the sovereign town meeting composed theoretically of all adult citizens—had the power of *ostracism,* by which it could banish an unpopular citizen from Athens for ten years. Rousseau evidently believed that homogeneity would be maintained if dissident citizens had the right to emigrate—presumably to a more sympathetic community. Another possibility, a painful one to Americans, is secession. Yet all of these solutions entail serious practical and moral difficulties, particularly in the modern world. Emigration, for example, can be a staggering price to pay simply for being in a minority; must the price of one's beliefs depend solely on the numbers who happen to share them? Yet if emigration is purely optional, who would emigrate? Many dissenters would remain to deny the legitimacy of majority rule as it applies to them. Shall we then expel these dissenters in order to maintain consensus? To expel an individual from a community is not difficult; American communities have often done so, sometimes with the aid of tar and feathers. But to expel a significant minority that does not choose to depart in peace can mean civil war. It might be said that a discontented minority can be permitted to separate amicably by the simple expedient of redrawing the boundary lines and thus creating a new and independent state. But should every minority that wishes to do so be allowed to secede in full possession of the territory in which they happen to reside, even if this has been so integrated into the economy, transportation system, defenses, and sense of nationhood of the larger country that its loss would be a serious blow? Such forbearance and generosity are unlikely. In any case, what is to be the fate of a minority within a minority, as in the case of blacks in the South? And of minorities that are not geographically separated but intermixed, like Jehovah's Witnesses?

For Americans these questions are more than rhetorical; here, secession was proposed and rejected as a practical solution by a civil war. Lincoln's first inaugural address pierced the logic of secession:

> Plainly, the central idea of secession is the essence of anarchy. A majority held in restraint by constitutional checks and limitations, and always changing easily with deliberate changes of popular opinions and sentiments, is the only true sovereign of a free people. Whoever rejects it does, of necessity, fly to anarchy or to despotism. Unanimity is impossible; the rule of a minority, as a permanent arrangement, is wholly inadmissible; so that, rejecting the majority principle, anarchy or despotism in some form is all that is left.[1]

But even civil war did not finally settle the debate about the proper scope and limits of rule by majorities in the United States.

MAJORITY DECISIONS: HOW? Even when a collection of people can agree to combine for purposes of self-government, and to construct their government faithfully according to the principles of consent, equality, and majority rule, *how* are they to do so?

Although the question raises a host of practical and theoretical problems, I wish to allude here only to one mentioned in the last chapter: representation. If the people are few in number (a key assumption of all classical democratic theory), then the principles of consent, political equality, and majority rule can be satisfied if the people directly govern themselves in an assembly open to all citizens. Here we have a key

---

1. Sandburg, *Abraham Lincoln, The War Years*, p. 132.

conclusion of all classical democratic theory. However, the greater the proportion of adults who are excluded from citizenship and hence the right to participate in the assembly, and the greater the proportion of citizens who fail to exercise their rights to participate, the less persuasive is the classical solution. And the more numerous the people are, of course, the less valid the solution; for the more numerous the citizens, the more the right to participate must be reduced simply to voting. The more that *full* participation—presenting proposals, discussion, advocacy, etc.— is necessarily confined to a few, the more that equality requires that the few who govern should be *representative*. Representative how and in what respects?

For example, if laws are made not by the people themselves but by their elected representatives, then is it not possible that laws passed by a majority of representatives may differ from the laws preferred by a majority of the people? Should this possibility be avoided at all costs? If so, how? There are a host of problems here, and no obviously right solutions.

Clearly, however, the *system of election* will have a bearing on the extent to which a majority of representatives correspond with the views of a majority of citizens. In practise, different countries have chosen significantly different kinds of election systems. Later on, we shall consider the effects of several main types of election systems. Meanwhile, the point to be kept in mind is that there seems to be no agreement as to what kind of system of election and representation is most nearly in accord with the principles of consent, equality, and majority rule.

POLITICAL EQUALITY AND INEQUALITY?

There is, finally, the problem posed in the last chapter. How, if at all, can sufficient equality be maintained? For if it is not, then political equality will become a mere formality.

From Aristotle in the fourth century B.C. to Montesquieu, Rousseau, and Jefferson, for over 2,000 years, practically everyone who advocated popular rule also insisted on the need for a relatively even distribution of resources such as property. Yet to maintain enough equality in resources to insure genuine political equality has proved to be an exceptionally intractable problem. In fact, one view of political reality is that anything remotely approaching political equality is bound to be a chimera. This view forms the basis of the second general answer to our question, to which we turn in the next chapter.

SUMMARY

The solution of majority-rule democracy thus runs into serious theoretical and practical problems:

1. If individuals disagree as to whether they constitute a single

people for purposes of self-government—as Americans disagreed in 1861—must the matter be settled finally by force, as Americans did? If not, must we grant to every minority the right to secede and establish its own government?

2. How can majority-rule democracy be applied in a federal system or in any other decentralized system in which certain territorial minorities are guaranteed certain rights to govern themselves? According to what principles are we to solve conflicts between the wishes of a majority of citizens in a state or province and a national majority?

3. More generally, how are minority rights to be secured, if not by placing restraints on the authority of majorities?

4. Since laws and policies will ordinarily be made by elected leaders and not by the assembled people, how can we insure that the leaders' decisions reflect majority preferences?

5. How, if at all, can sufficient equality of resources be maintained so that political equality is an actuality and not a mere formality?

Second Answer: Rule by Elites

5

Can a government be established and maintained that will surmount the obstacles discussed in Chapter 3 and achieve rule by the people based on consent and political equality?

The second important answer is a straightforward *no.* Such a government, it is said, cannot be established; for no matter what the forms may be, in practise every political system is ruled by an elite.

Unlike the argument for aristocracy or meritocracy, which asserts that a well-qualified minority *ought* to rule, this argument purports merely to describe what happens *in fact.* Advocates of meritocracy insist that rule by the people is undesirable. Spokesmen for the view that "rule by the people" means oligarchy insist only that the people do not and probably cannot rule. If the people cannot rule, it is silly to discuss whether they *ought* to rule, just as it is silly to discuss whether they ought to be able to live without food and water. If oligarchy is inevitable, the moral arguments for rule by the people are plainly irrelevant.

MOSCA, PARETO, MICHELS Perhaps it is no accident that those who equate all politics with oligarchy turn out to be observers whose initial enthusiasm for democracy in its most pure form turns into disappointment and disgust when they discover how widely political reality departs from their democratic utopia. Probably the best statements of the perspective under consideration are by a disillusioned liberal, Gaetano Mosca (1858–1941), a disillusioned radical, Vilfredo Pareto (1848–1923), and a disillusioned socialist, Robert Michels (1876–1936).

Thus Mosca advanced the idea of a ruling class in 1896:

> In all societies . . . two classes of people appear—a class that rules and a class that is ruled. The first class, always the less numerous, performs

all political functions, monopolizes power and enjoys the advantages that power brings, whereas the second, the more numerous class, is directed and controlled by the first. . . .[1]

In 1909, Pareto defined "the elite" as "the totality of qualities promoting the well-being and domination of a class in society." "This elite," he went on to say, "exists in all societies and governs them even in cases where the regime in appearance is highly democratic."[2]

Two years later, with due acknowledgment to Mosca and Pareto, Michels concluded that "the majority of human beings, in a condition of eternal tutelage, are predestined by tragic necessity to submit to the domination of a small minority, and must be content to constitute the pedestal of an oligarchy."[3] He summed up his theory in his famous "iron law of oligarchy":

> It is organization which gives birth to the domination of the elected over the electors, of the mandataries over the mandators, of the delegates over the delegators. *Who says organization says oligarchy.*[4] (Italics added.)

Not everyone who equates "rule by the people" with rule by an elite is as pessimistic as these three men. Optimists believe that the ruling class may one day be forced to make way for rule by the people. Thus in *The Communist Manifesto* (1848), Marx and Engels asserted that "the history of all hitherto existing society is the history of class struggles." In the nineteenth century "the bourgeoisie has at last . . . conquered for itself, in the modern representative State, exclusive political sway. The executive of the modern State is but a committee for managing the common affairs of the whole bourgeoisie." Yet the increasingly more numerous proletariat would one day seize power "in the interest of the immense majority. The proletariat, the lowest stratum of our present society, cannot stir, cannot raise itself up, without the whole superincumbent strata of official society being sprung into the air."

The idea that representative institutions conceal a ruling elite has long been popular in the United States among observers disillusioned by the visible shortcomings of the American political system. Americans with unconventional and unpopular views who feel thwarted in their efforts to change 'the system' sometimes attribute their defeats to a half-hidden ruling class. Thus Socialists and Populists have thought the country to be run by Wall Street bankers. Many extreme conservatives believe that a small Eastern Liberal Establishment dominates communications, education, religion, finance, the State Department, and

1. Gaetano Mosca, *The Ruling Class*, trans. Hannah D. Kahn (New York: McGraw-Hill, 1939), p. 50.

2. *Vilfredo Pareto: Sociological Writings*, ed. S. E. Finer (New York: Praeger, 1966), p. 155.

3. Robert Michels, *Political Parties*, trans. Eden and Cedar Paul (New York: Collier Books, 1962), p. 354.

4. *Ibid.*, p. 15.

indeed government generally. In recent years, the position of a dominant elite has often been assigned to "the military-industrial complex."

SOURCES OF THE TENDENCY TO OLIGARCHY

The view that in practise rule by the people means oligarchy draws a good deal of its strength from certain general characteristics of political life. For example, Michels seems to have been outraged to discover that his own Socialist party preached democracy but practiced oligarchy. How was it possible that parties dedicated to democratic ideals could be so undemocratic in their own internal government? Some of his chapter headings provide his answer: the need for organization; mechanical and technical impossibility of direct government by the masses; the need for leadership felt by the mass; the political gratitude of the masses; the cult of veneration among the masses; superiority of the professional leaders in respect to culture, and their indispensability; the formal and real incompetence of the mass; financial power of the leaders and of the party; bureaucracy; psychological metamorphosis of the leaders, etc.

Probably the strongest aspect of this theory—and as we shall see its weakest, too—is its focus on persistent inequalities in power and influence that can be seen in every political system, including "democratic" systems. Thus the theory fastens on a problem that, as we have already seen, is definite and serious.

CAUSES OF INEQUALITIES

In the last two chapters we saw that equality and consent are threatened by persistent inequalities. We noted that among the causes of political inequalities are social arrangements, individual characteristics, and in representative governments, the very process of representation itself. These factors in turn help to produce differences in political *resources, skills,* and *incentives.*

Resources

Political resources consist of all the means available to one for influencing the behavior of other people. In this country, political resources include access to money, hence wealth, income, and credit. They also include control over jobs; the ballot; popularity, friendships, reputation, and esteem in the eyes of others; knowledge or access to knowledge; control over mass media and other means of communication; and many other things.

One important political resource easily lost sight of is *time.* If you have no time left over from your other affairs to try to change the conduct of government, you are unlikely to be in a position to exercise much influence over it. Conversely, the more time you have available, the better your chances. Time is one of the most critical resources that professional politicians have; by hook or crook they manage to spend almost full time at the game of politics, while most of us devote only a few hours out of the year.

Still another resource which is unevenly distributed—inevitably so —is *officiality*. Constitutional rules, law, and practise allow officials to do things that ordinary citizens cannot. A major difference between the policeman and the man he arrests is that the office of the policeman entitles him to make arrests, using force if necessary. Official position invariably allocates to officials some resources that are denied to others; thus only judges can decide legal cases and only legislators can pass laws. By conferring officiality on the winner and denying it to the loser, elections award extra resources to the winner. In 1876, one electoral vote—a rather dubious one at that—was enough to confer the presidency on Rutherford B. Hayes rather than on Samuel J. Tilden; even in that age of weak presidents, the presidency gave important legal authority to Hayes, such as the veto, that was denied to Tilden.

Allied to officiality as a resource, but not identical with it, is *legitimate authority*: the widespread view that an individual or an office ought to be obeyed. Thus the president is powerful not only because of what the Constitution authorizes him to do but also because of what history and tradition authorize him to do.

Except perhaps for the ballot, and that only recently, all these resources are unequally distributed among adult American citizens. Hence it should not be too surprising if various citizens exert unequal influence on the conduct of government.

Skills

Even if two individuals had practically identical resources, they might, nonetheless, be unable to exercise equal influence over the conduct of government if one of them were politically more *skillful*. (Political skill might be considered, of course, as a special kind of resource, but it seems more illuminating to think of it as a capacity for using one's resources efficiently.) Although almost all political observers agree with Niccolò Machiavelli (1469–1527) that differences in political skills exist and are important, like military, entrepreneurial, artistic, and scientific skills, political skills are hard to pin down and not well understood.

Incentives

Even if two individuals had identical resources and skills, one might exercise more influence over government than another simply because he *wanted* to influence the government and the other did not. If you do not care what the government is doing, you probably will not use your resources and skills to influence it; the more you care, the more of your resources you will be willing to invest and the harder you will try to acquire the necessary skills. Thus, your influence is partly dependent on your goals and estimates of the best strategies for obtaining them. We might call this third factor *incentives* for acquiring political skills and for employing resources to influence the conduct of government.

While some causes of political inequalities can be reduced or removed, others seem ineradicable. Can we ever—indeed should we try to—get rid of all differences in political incentives? Will differences in incentives not inevitably lead to differences in skills? Will not appointed and elected officials to whom authority is delegated inevitably have access to more political resources than ordinary citizens?

Extreme advocates of the view that all political systems are dominated by a ruling class argue that so much inequality in resources, skills, and incentives is bound to persist as to make rule by the people impossible and rule by a particular class, stratum, or elite inevitable. However, to leap from the premise of inequality to the conclusion that all political systems are ruled by an elite entails some highly questionable assumptions.

THE FALLACY OF DICHOTOMOUS THINKING

In fact to equate all politics with oligarchy is to fall into the fallacy of dichotomous thinking. Dichotomous thinking is characterized by a tendency to divide phenomena into two mutually exclusive categories: good-bad, we-they, saints-sinners, Americans-foreigners, democracy-dictatorship.

Most of us know that outside the domain of politics things can often be thought about as if they were located on a *continuum.* Thinking in *continuities* is more supple and more subtle than dichotomous thought. Most of us would agree, I think, that it is not necessary, and for many purposes is unprofitable, to divide human beings, for example, into just two groups: tall-short, lean-fat, blond-brunette, healthy-sick, nice-vicious, etc. We all recognize that while it is convenient for some purposes to dichotomize, for others it is senseless. Imagine an insurance company that divided applicants for life insurance into young-old; a judicial system that knew only the categories guilty of murder or innocent; an educational system in which students were categorized as either idiots or geniuses!

Yet for many people it evidently seems reasonable to believe that if a country is not an ally, it is an enemy; if a political system is not a democracy, it is a dictatorship. And if the people do not rule, there must be a ruling elite.

The difficulty with dichotomies like these is that they often rob us of important distinctions. Even if the people do not rule, and political equality and consent are by no means fully achieved, are there not significant differences in political systems? Would it not make sense to say that while no country has a truly "democratic" political system, some systems are *significantly more* democratic than others? An alternative interpretation, which answers in the affirmative, is the theory of polyarchy.

SUMMARY   1. An important line of thought, best represented by Mosca, Pareto, and Michels, argues that rule by the people is impossible and in practice every political system, whatever its forms, is ruled by an elite.

2. This line of argument draws strong support from the observable facts that (a) inequalities in power and influence seem to persist in all associations and societies, despite their professed ideals, and (b) some of the causes of these inequalities seem extremely difficult, perhaps impossible, to remove.

3. However, the premise that inequalities in power and resources exist does not warrant the conclusion that a ruling class exists.

4. If we are to avoid the fallacy of dichotomous thinking, we need to consider the possibility that even if the people do not rule and political equality and consent are by no means fully achieved, there may, nonetheless, be significant differences in the extent to which these goals are achieved in different political systems.

Third Answer: Polyarchy

6

A third answer to the question posed at the beginning of Chapter 4 holds that:

☐ All political systems fall considerably short of achieving rule by the people based on consent and political equality.
☐ However, some systems approach these goals considerably more than do others.
☐ These systems are not democracies in the ideal sense, yet they contain democratic components. Nor are they dominated by a cohesive elite, yet elites and leaders play powerful parts.
☐ These systems, a mixture of elite rule and democracy, are called polyarchies.

Like democratic theories, the theory of polyarchy assumes that political systems can and should be distinguished and judged, among other criteria, according to the extent to which they achieve rule by the people, political equality, and consent. Like elitist theories, the theory of polyarchy holds that all human organizations contain strong tendencies toward the development of inequalities and the emergence of powerful leaders. Yet while it incorporates these assumptions from both approaches, the theory of polyarchy also advances a critique of ideas advanced in majority rule and elitist theories, and offers an alternative interpretation of politics in 'democratic' systems.

DEMOCRACY: AN AMBIGUOUS TERM

So far I have usually managed to avoid using the term *democracy*. I have done so because no political term is more ambiguous, nor more productive of fruitless controversy. The term is not only ambiguous, it is thoroughly impregnated with connotations of goodness; practically everyone except outright advocates of meritocracy insists that democracy is good, that he, of course, advocates it—and that what he advocates is, naturally, true democracy.

One elementary source of ambiguity stems from the fact that our language permits democracy to be used both for (1) an ideal political system, which may not actually exist anywhere, and (2) a number of actual systems that do exist in our world of experience. Ever since the Greeks began presenting their ideas about politics more than two thousand years ago, a common practice among philosophers has been to set out the characteristics of an ideal, complete, or perfect polity, including a democratic polity. Simultaneous with this usage, actual systems have also been called democracies, even though they have always fallen far short of the ideal. Thus it is perfectly consistent with usage, and not logically contradictory, to say both that the United States *is* a democracy (actual) and that it is *not* a democracy (ideal).

While the language of the dictionary, politician, street, newspaper, TV commentator, and classroom fully authorize one to use the term *democracy* in both ways, to do so creates an enormous amount of confusion. It is amazing, indeed, how much controversy is produced by a difference in usage that every American must surely be aware of by the time he leaves high school. Yet while most of us calmly recognize that a ham in a meatmarket is not the same as a ham in a theatre, and ordinarily find no difficulty in grasping which usage a speaker intends, the distinction between (ideal) democracy and (actual) democracies is a source of endless confusion and controversy, even, alas, among scholars. This is why the theory of polyarchy adopts a simple terminological distinction: the term *democracy* is reserved exclusively for an ideal state of affairs. Actual systems that appear to approach this ideal state of affairs more closely than others, at least along some dimensions, are called *polyarchies*. The theory of polyarchy assumes that all polyarchies fall short of democracy by a considerable and significant margin. Unlike some theories of elite rule, however, it offers grounds for believing that the gap can be narrowed. Yet unlike some theories of democracy, it does not say that unlimited extension of majority rule is the best or most feasible way of closing that gap. Moreover, it leaves open—as a practical problem to be solved pragmatically in specific circumstances—just how and how much the gap between democracy and polyarchy can actually be closed.

POLYARCHIES AS SYSTEMS ON A CONTINUUM In order to avoid the fallacy of dichotomous thinking, it is helpful to think about polyarchy as a collection of points on a continuum. Imagine that we could measure the amount of "democracy" in a political system. Imagine further that our measurements could be reduced to a single dimension stretching from ideal democracy at one end to its negation at the other. For convenience, call the negation of democracy autocracy or hegemony.

Autocracy (—) _____(+) Democracy

Now suppose that we measure the amount of "democracy" in a set of political systems. These might be the political systems of two dozen different countries. When we locate these systems on our dimension, suppose we find that they cover a wide spread, thus:

Autocracy • •• •• •••• • •• ••• •• •• • ••• • Democracy

Suppose we discover a fairly distinct cluster of countries lying closer than the others to the democratic end of the continuum. We shall then call these polyarchies.

Polyarchies
Autocracy • •• •• •••• • •• ••• •• ••• • ••• • Democracy

That is all very well as a mental exercise, you might say, but can we really do anything like this in practise? It appears that we can, though imperfectly.

THE CONDITIONS OF DEMOCRATIC GOVERNMENT RESTATED

In Chapter 3 we saw that if consent and political equality are to be active and continuing, every full citizen would have to possess unimpaired opportunities

☐ to formulate his goals,
☐ to indicate his goals or preferences to other citizens and the government, and
☐ to have his preferences weighted equally with those of other citizens in the conduct of the government.

What would be required in order to insure these opportunities? Evidently a set of institutions:

1. In order to know what he wants, a citizen needs access to the best possible information. The worst situation would be one in which a single elite with interests and ambitions of its own controlled the major sources of information. At a minimum, then, it would be important to have access to alternative sources of information not under the control of any one elite.

2. To know what one wants and to indicate it to others, one needs the right to express himself freely without fear of punishment, particularly by leaders.

3. In order to indicate one's preferences and have them taken into account in the conduct of government, one must be able to vote in elections.

4. To have one's preferences actually taken into account effectively, and weighted equally, elections must be free and honest, and also fair, in the sense of adherence to the general principle of one man–one vote.

5. To insure that elected leaders actually pay attention to one's preferences, it helps if leaders compete with one another for one's support, including one's vote.

6. In case no candidate is willing to advance one's ideas, one would need to be able to run for public office.

7. In order to explore one's preferences with others, to indicate them effectively, and to have them taken into account, one needs to be able to form and join organizations, including organizations formed for the purpose of competing in elections and advancing policies and programs in representative bodies.

8. Since all the previous requirements would come to naught if the officials who actually made the policies of government were unresponsive to elected officials and did not depend in any way on the outcome of elections, it is essential to have arrangements for insuring that government policies depend on votes and other expressions of preference by citizens. Thus the officials effectively determining policies must be dependent on the outcome of free and fair elections. These requirements are summarized in Table 6.1.

A SURVEY OF POLYARCHIES

To avoid the trap of thinking dichotomously about these eight institutional guarantees, we might consider each one as if it were a hypothetical dimension extending from complete attainment of the guarantee to its complete absence or negation. It would then be reasonable to expect that (1) while no country fully provides these guarantees, (2) countries vary significantly in the *extent* to which each of the guarantees is present.

Surprising as it may seem, political scientists have begun only recently to assemble and process the kinds of data needed to determine the extent to which guarantees like these are present. Unfortunately, data are still often crude and unreliable. Nonetheless, it is possible to distinguish a very large number of countries, at least in a rough way, by the extent to which they provide these guarantees.

Thus in a recent study of political opposition, the eight institutional guarantees were assumed to indicate the extent to which opponents enjoyed opportunities to contest the conduct of the government. A number of indicators proved more or less satisfactory for measuring the extent to which the institutional guarantees were present. It turned

Table 6.1
Some Conditions of
Democratic Government

To satisfy the principles of:	Every citizen must have unimpaired opportunities to:	In order for these opportunities to exist, the following institutional guarantees are required:
1. Consent 2. Political equality	1. Formulate his preferences 2. Signify his preferences 3. Have his preferences weighted equally in the conduct of the government	1. Alternative sources of information 2. Freedom of expression 3. The right to vote 4. Free and fair elections 5. Competition among political leaders for votes and other support 6. The right to run for public office 7. Freedom to form and join organizations, including political parties 8. Institutions for making government policies depend on votes and other expressions of preference

out, in fact, that the indicators could be satisfactorily consolidated into a single, overall measure. This overall measure of the extent of opportunities available to political opposition to contest the conduct of the government was then joined with another dimension, the percent of adult citizens eligible to vote in national elections. The results are shown in Table 6.2.

The thirty-two countries in the upper right corner of Table 6.2, where the adult citizens eligible to vote in national elections is over 90 percent and the greatest opportunities exist for political opposition to contest the conduct of government, represent the fullest attainment of the eight institutional guarantees in Table 6.1. They were, therefore, polyarchies in 1971. The thirty-two countries are listed in alphabetical order in Table 6.3. You will notice that because of restrictions on the suffrage resulting from residence requirements and discrimination against voting by blacks in the South that did not begin to disappear until after the passage of the Civil Rights Acts of 1964 and 1965, the United States must be regarded as a somewhat marginal member of the group of polyarchies. As we shall see, throughout most of its history the United States has had a dual political system: polyarchy among whites, hegemony for Southern blacks. This peculiar effort to maintain hegemony vis-à-vis a racial minority and polyarchy among the overwhelming majority has played such a prominent part in shaping American political

Table 6.2
Political Regimes in
114 Countries, circa 1971

| | | Extent of opportunities open to political oppositions to contest the conduct of government.[a] | | |
		Least	Medium	Greatest
Percent of adult citizens eligible to vote in national elections	Over 90%	16	16	32[b]
	20%–90%	1	4	—
	Under 20%	—	1	—
	No elections held	16	5	—
	Uncertain, transitional, etc.[c]	4	13	6
	Total (114)	37	39	38

[a]Based on the eight indicators of institutional guarantees listed in Table 6.1.

[b]The list contains six countries where until the 1960s there had existed significantly greater restraints on the suffrage or on other institutional guarantees than in the remaining 28 countries. These special cases are: *Ceylon*, which underwent a period of disorders culminating in the assassination of the prime minister in 1959, and in the 1960s steady charges by the government of attempted right-wing coups. In 1971 an uprising was put down by force. *Chile*, where a literacy requirement for voting had restricted the suffrage to less than 90 percent of the adults until the late 1960s. *Colombia*, which after a decade of widespread violence from 1948 to 1958, managed relatively peaceful elections throughout the 1960s under a constitutional provision dividing membership in Congress equally between the two major parties and requiring that the presidency alternate between the two major parties and the membership of Congress be divided equally between them. The provision expires in 1974. *Switzerland*, which did not grant women the right to vote in federal elections until 1971. The *United States*, where residency requirements and discrimination against blacks in the South prior to the passage of the Civil Rights Acts of 1964–5 had restricted the suffrage to less than 90 percent of the adults. *Venezuela*, which except for a three-year period had for generations prior to 1958 been ruled by severely repressive dictatorships.

[c]Includes countries where a constitutional government or elections have been superseded or nullified at least once since 1960, the constitution has been suspended, a state of seige declared, or massive civil violence has occurred.

life that we shall have to pay attention to it again and again in the chapters that follow.

POLYARCHY AND MAJORITY-RULE DEMOCRACY

How do polyarchies deal with the difficulties in majority-rule democracy mentioned in Chapter 4?

What People?

As we have seen, democratic theory seems to provide no definite answer to the question: What constitutes a *people* for purposes of self-government? In practise, then, countries with polyarchic regimes use force, just as other regimes do, to repel threats to the integrity of the national territory. Consequently, as in other regimes, secession is, as a practical matter, usually either impossible or extremely costly. (Colonies thought to lie outside the territory of the "nation" may, of course, be granted independence.) To a considerable extent, then, large minori-

Table 6.3 Polyarchies circa 1971	**Fully inclusive polyarchies:**	
	1. Australia	17. Italy
	2. Austria	18. Jamaica
	3. Belgium	19. Japan
	4. Canada	20. Lebanon
	5. Ceylon[a]	21. Luxembourg
	6. Chile[a]	22. Netherlands
	7. Colombia[a]	23. New Zealand
	8. Costa Rica	24. Norway
	9. Denmark	25. Philippines
	10. Federal Republic of Germany	26. Sweden
	11. Finland	27. Switzerland[a]
	12. France	28. Trinidad and Tobago
	13. Iceland	29. United Kingdom
	14. India	30. United States[a]
	15. Ireland	31. Uruguay
	16. Israel	32. Venezuela[a]

[a]See footnote [b], Table 6.2.

ties are virtually 'compelled' to remain within the territorial limits of the nation. To make compulsory citizenship tolerable, great efforts are made to create and sustain a common sense of nationhood, so that minorities of all kinds will identify themselves with the nation. Hence secession or mass emigration are not usually thought of as practical alternatives.

Majority Rule versus Minority Rights

In practise, the effective scope of majority rule is limited in all polyarchies in at least three ways:

First, many matters of policy—religious beliefs and practises, for example—are effectively outside the legal authority of government. Sometimes, as in Britain, they are placed beyond the legal authority of government through understandings and agreements widely shared and respected. In many cases, as in the United States, these understandings and agreements are expressed in written constitutions that cannot be quickly or easily amended by a simple majority vote. Such a constitution is regarded as peculiarly binding; and ordinary laws that run counter to the constitution will be invalid, or, at the very least, subject to special scrutiny.

Second, a great many questions of policy are placed in the hands of private, semipublic, and local governmental organizations such as churches, families, business firms, trade unions, towns, cities, provinces, and the like. These questions of policy, like those left to individuals, are also effectively beyond the reach of national majorities, the national legislature, or indeed any national policy-makers acting in their legal and official capacities. In fact, whenever uniform policies are likely to be costly, difficult, or troublesome, in polyarchies the tendency is to find ways by which these policies can be made by smaller groups of like-minded people who enjoy a high degree of legal independence.

Third, whenever a group of people believe that they are adversely affected by national policies or are about to be, they generally have extensive opportunities for presenting their case and for negotiations that may produce a more acceptable alternative. In some countries, many minorities may have enough power to delay, to obstruct, and even to veto the attempt to impose policies on them. Probably there are a few such minorities in every polyarchy.

Majority Decisions: How?

Although polyarchies restrict the scope of majority rule in the three ways just mentioned, there are significant variations in the extent to which a single party or a single unified coalition can acquire the authority to translate its proposals into government policy by winning a majority of votes in a national election. It may help to consider two hypothetical extremes.

At one extreme, only two political parties compete in elections; the party that wins a majority of votes acquires a majority of seats in the legislative body; as a consequence it forms a cabinet which, together with its legislative majority, is able to convert the party's program into government policies. The opposition party may criticize the administration and hope to win its own majority in the next election; but until then it cannot prevent the majority party from governing as it pleases—within, to be sure, the three general kinds of limits mentioned above. Elections, then, are *completely decisive.* Although this extreme type does not fully exist in any country, a few approach it much more closely than others. Britain represents one of the closest approximations.

At the other extreme, many parties compete in elections. No party wins a majority of votes or seats. Cabinets are formed from *all* the parties; thus the basic principle of the system is not majority rule, but unanimity. Nothing that is strenuously opposed by any significant minority can become government policy. Elections, then, are *not decisive.* Again, no country actually embodies this extreme type, but one of the countries that comes closest to it is Switzerland.

As we shall see in the next chapter, the political system of the United States seems to lie somewhere between the two extremes, but perhaps somewhat closer to Switzerland than to Britain.

Political Equality and Inequality

An essential difference between polyarchies and hegemonic regimes, as we have stressed, is the existence in polyarchies of effective institutional guarantees that protect the bulk of the population in the exercise of a broad range of elemental rights. For anyone who places a high value on these rights, the difference is decisive. I shall return to this point shortly.

Yet in spite of these institutional guarantees, differences in political resources, skills, and incentives produce in polyarchies, too, marked inequalities in influence. In this respect, polyarchies are a long way from the pure theory of majority-rule democracy, where all officials are mere agents of the people. For example, in a later chapter we shall see that the president of the United States is very far indeed from being merely the agent of the American people. In fact his extraordinary power and authority create a serious challenge to the future of the American political system.

Polyarchy, then, appears to be significantly different from **majority-rule** democracy. Is it significantly different from autocratic or hegemonic rule by an elite?

POLYARCHY AND HEGEMONIC ELITE RULE

Differences

Polyarchy differs from hegemonic rule by an elite in at least three ways:

1. Opposition. As we have already seen, in polyarchies the barriers against opposition are much lower than in hegemonic regimes. In polyarchies, opponents can contest the conduct of the government by speaking out against it, publishing and distributing newspapers, pamphlets, brochures, magazines, books and other writings, holding meetings, organizing opposition parties, running candidates in elections, winning seats, and even displacing the incumbent administration. Although non-polyarchies vary over a broad range, from brutally repressive autocracies to relatively tolerant mixed systems, in all of them the barriers to opposition are higher than in polyarchies. At the extreme, in fully hegemonic dictatorships critics are denied all opportunities to contest the conduct of the government and opposition in any form is ruthlessly repressed.

2. Elite conflict and competition. No political system, no matter how repressive, ever seems able to eliminate every vestige of competition and conflict among its leaders. But in highly hegemonic regimes, whether modern dictatorships or centralized monarchies of the seventeenth century, the range of permissible competition and conflict is extremely narrow, and much of that must be concealed from public view, so in such regimes competition is often reduced to little more than subordinates vying for the favors of the ruler. Woe to the subordinate who displeases the autocrat!

Whenever the barriers to opposition are lowered, leadership invariably splits into opposing cliques, factions, or parties competing for control of the government. Opposing cliques may have nothing nobler in mind than acquiring patronage, incomes, and wealth. Yet however narrow and selfish their aims may be, their infighting is often bitter, sometimes lethal. In their struggle to gain the upper hand, factions search for additional resources. Their need for resources often compels them to compromise with other factions. Thus coalitions of factions with similar but not identical interests develop within the governing stratum.

When institutional guarantees are extended to a point where the executive becomes dependent on winning a majority in the legislature, the legislator's vote becomes one of his resources. Factional leaders must now negotiate for these votes by offering something in return: flattery, recognition, offices, access, graft, policies. As the institutional guarantees are extended to broader and broader segments of the population outside the legislature, the same process repeats itself. To gain the support of voters, leaders of cliques, factions, or parties must now offer rewards to voters, whether flattery, recognition, offices, access, graft, or policies. These developments can be clearly seen in the slow transformation of many European centralized monarchies into narrow oligarchies, then into polyarchies.

3. Elections. The third and most visible difference between polyarchies and hegemonic rule, then, is the periodic occurrence of local and national elections which are contested by competing political parties offering rewards to voters. Leaders actively seek to gain popular support and thus the right to hold office and participate in governing.

Perhaps no institution is more critical to the differentiation between polyarchies and non-polyarchies than competitive elections. And perhaps no testimony to the importance of competitive elections is more impressive than the implacable resistance of ruling elites in hegemonic regimes to the introduction of fully protected national elections in which opposition parties would be effectively protected in their opportunities to compete for popular support. Even regimes that have reduced other barriers to opposition almost to the level of polyarchies are generally unwilling to cross this last, dangerous threshold to polyarchy. For once the threshold has been crossed, an elite's capacity to rule will almost certainly be drastically impaired—as no one knows better than a ruling elite protected from the threat of being displaced in an election.

Because elections open to contests by opposing political parties are bound to menace a ruling elite in a hegemonic system, the advocates of hegemony in one form or another typically denigrate the importance of elections and seek to show that elections actually permit an elite to dominate the country—the wrong ruling elite, of course. In order to substitute good rulers for bad, they are likely to argue, competitive elections must be suspended or abolished.

Do the Differences Matter?

Even if the institutional guarantees of polyarchy lower the barriers to opposition, produce conflict and competition among leaders, and make leaders dependent to some degree on winning the support of nonleaders in elections, it is reasonable to ask whether these differences really matter. In the end, a follower of Mosca might argue, polyarchies and non-polyarchies are pretty much the same in their essential consequences; the people do not rule, he might say, elites do.

Yet it is a highly revealing and often neglected fact that the father of modern elite theory concluded in his later years that polyarchies were not only significantly different from dictatorships, they were also better.

Mosca's conclusion. Mosca lived long enough to witness the emergence of modern dictatorships, including Fascism in his native Italy. In 1923, when Mussolini had already come to power and was beginning to consolidate his Fascist dictatorship in Italy, Mosca brought out a revised and enlarged edition of the *Elements of Political Science,* in which he had advanced the theory of the ruling class more than a quarter of a century earlier. Since Mosca left no doubt where he now stood, his words are worth quoting at some length.

> Confining oneself to the political field, one has to admit the great benefits which constitute the undying glory of the nineteenth century as a result of the very illusions that guided it. To be sure, majority government and absolute political equality, two of the mottos that the century inscribed on its banners, were not achieved, because they could not be achieved, and the same may be said of fraternity. But the ranks of the ruling classes have been held open. The barriers that kept individuals of the lower classes from entering the higher have been either removed or lowered, and the development of the old absolutist state into the modern representative state has made it possible for almost all political forces, almost all social values, to participate in the political management of society.
>
> This development, it should be noted, has divided the political class into two distinct branches, one issuing from popular suffrage, and the other from bureaucratic appointment. This has not only permitted a better utilization of individual capacities; it has also made it possible to distribute the sovereign functions, or powers, of the state, and that distribution, whenever social conditions are such as to make it effective, constitutes the chief virtue of representative systems. It is the chief reason why they have given better results than any of the many others that have so far been applied

to great political organizations. Rousseau set himself an unattainable goal when he tried to show that the only form of legitimate government was one that was founded upon the express consent of the majority of citizens. Montesquieu stated a much more practical and profound idea when he maintained that if a nation is to be free, in other words governed according to law and not according to the arbitrary will of its rulers, it must have a political organization in which authority arrests and limits authority, and in which, therefore, no individual and no assembly has the power to make laws and at the same time the power to apply them. To make that doctrine complete, one need add that a controlling and limiting political institution can be effective only when it represents a section of the political class that is different from the section represented by the institution to be limited and controlled.

If, again, we take due account of the individual liberties that protect the citizen from possible arbitrary acts on the part of any or all of the powers of the state, especially of liberty of the press, which, along with liberty of parliamentary debate, serves to call public attention to all possible abuses on the part of those who govern, one readily sees the great superiority of the representative system.[1]

This was a remarkable concession. But the advance of Fascism was to wring from Mosca one more anguished declaration. For Mosca was not only a theorist; from 1908 onward he had also been a member of the Italian Parliament, first as a deputy, later as a senator. In 1925, Mussolini presented to the Italian Senate a bill that would strip the parliament of its right to initiate legislation and would make the prime minister independent of both king and parliament. As everyone knew, the bill symbolized the legalization of the dictatorship and the final end of the parliamentary regime. On Christmas Day, 1925, Mosca rose in the Senate to pronounce his obituary for parliamentary government:

> [He spoke, he said,] with a certain emotion because, let us be frank, we take part in the funeral rites of a form of government. I should not have thought possible that I would be the one to deliver the funeral oration on the parliamentary regime. . . . I, who have always taken a harsh attitude toward it, am today obliged to lament its departure. . . . A form of government [he went on] can be judged only in one way: by comparing it with both its predecessor and successor. To speak of the latter would be premature. As to the predecessor: it was such that one may say in all sincerity: the parliamentary regime was better.[2]

SUMMARY In this chapter we have briefly explored the theory of polyarchy, which incorporates certain aspects of both democratic and elitist theories, presents a critique of both, and offers an alternative way of understanding politics in different systems, particularly systems ordinarily

---

1. Mosca, *The Ruling Class*, pp. 474–475.

2. Gaetano Mosca, in *The Myth of the Ruling Class*, James Meisel (Ann Arbor: University of Michigan Press, 1958), pp. 225–226.

called "democratic." The argument of the theory of polyarchy can be summarized as follows:

1. The theory of polyarchy assumes:

□ A hypothetical continuum extending from pure or ideal democracy to its complete negation, autocracy or hegemony. Democracy and autocracy are purely theoretical entities, not fully realized in the world of experience.
□ At a minimum, in an ideal democracy consent and political equality would be active and continuing, not merely passive and intermittent.
□ For consent and political equality to be active and continuing would, in turn, require that every full citizen have unimpaired opportunities to formulate and indicate his preferences and have them weighted equally in the conduct of the government.
□ The existence of these opportunities requires at least eight kinds of institutional guarantees.

2. Political systems that provide these guarantees to a higher degree than other systems (even though incompletely) are called polyarchies.

3. Reasonably satisfactory (if imperfect) indicators for the presence of these eight guarantees make it possible to rank the systems of one hundred and fourteen countries. Thirty-two systems that provided the fullest opportunities for opposition in the late 1960s and had extended the suffrage to cover 90 percent of the adults are classified as polyarchies.

4. Polyarchies modify, amplify, or supplement the usual assumptions of majority-rule democracy in dealing with the problems of

□ Who constitutes "the people."
□ How and what rights are guaranteed to minorities.
□ The extent to which electoral and other arrangements facilitate government by representatives of majorities.
□ Reducing inequalities.

5. Polyarchies differ from hegemonic rule by elites in

□ The extent of opportunities available to opposition to contest the conduct of government.
□ The amount of open conflict among political leaders and open competition for support of nonleaders, particularly by votes in elections.
□ The periodic occurrence of local and national elections contested by competing political parties.

The American Polyarchy:
Four Characteristics

7

Everyday language authorizes one to call the American political system a "democracy," as we saw in the last chapter. No matter what term is used in this book, doubtless most Americans will go on referring to their political system by that familiar term.

Yet it is perfectly clear, and will become clearer as we proceed, that in the United States as in other countries called democracies the political system departs pretty far from the characteristics of an ideal democracy. This is not merely a matter of marginal differences, like a tiny blemish on a lovely face. It would be silly to contend, for example, that adult American citizens are even approximately equal in their influence on governmental decisions. The American polity contains an important element of democracy, but it is not, certainly, fully democratic.

In order not to blur the distinction between ideal and actual democracy, in this book the American system is called a polyarchy. For the United States is among thirty or so countries in which the eight institutional guarantees described in the last chapter exist more fully than in the remaining countries of the world.

Although by definition polyarchies all have certain characteristics in common, they vary in their concrete institutions and practises. In fact, as political scientists have become more familiar with a larger number of polyarchies in recent years, they have discovered that polyarchy is a system with great individual variation. The unique history and conditions of each country tend to make every polyarchy different from the rest in its overall patterns.

Thus although the American polyarchy by definition shares a number of characteristics with other polyarchies, it also differs from others in some ways. Taken altogether, its characteristics form a uniquely American pattern of polyarchy.

DISCRIMINATION AGAINST RACIAL MINORITIES

From colonial times onward, a distinct aspect of American life has been its harsh treatment of Indians and inhabitants of African racial stock. In particular the presence of a black minority constituting about 10 percent of the population, who first lived here mainly as slaves and later were nominally free citizens, had a profound influence on the emergent characteristics of the American polity. I have called that polity a polyarchy, yet until the late 1960s Southern blacks were excluded from the opportunity to participate in the American polyarchy. In effect, the United States developed a kind of dual system, a polyarchy for whites and a hegemony for blacks. In this century Northern urban blacks gained admission to the polyarchy; but it was not until after the passage of the Civil Rights Acts of 1964 and 1965 that the hegemonic suppression of the blacks by Southern whites, operating among themselves within a peculiar system of polyarchy, began to end.

In the depth and extent of discrimination practised against racial minorities, the United States appears to be unique among the polyarchies of the world. To be sure, its uniqueness in this respect is no doubt largely a product of the fact that no other polyarchy contains such a large and distinguishable racial minority as blacks have formed in the United States. Whatever the explanations may be, it is the fact and its consequences that are of primary concern here.

Consequently, just as the theme of racial discrimination runs like an ugly thread through the pattern of American history, so it constitutes an underlying theme in this book. Because racial discrimination has contributed mightily to the peculiar shape and character of the American polyarchy and to the pattern of its conflicts and compromises, we shall observe its effects again and again. Moreover, you should keep constantly in mind that a good deal of what follows applies to the American polyarchy and persons permitted to participate in it—whites, for the most part—and not to those excluded from it, mainly blacks, or to the hegemonic system used in the South (often with the tacit consent of the North) to deny influence to blacks.

WIDE ACCEPTANCE OF AMERICAN INSTITUTIONS

Keeping this important qualification in mind, one feature that makes polyarchy in America different from polyarchy in some countries is the relatively wide acceptance of their institutions among Americans—white Americans, at any rate. Throughout most of their history as an independent country, a high proportion of Americans seem to have accepted a belief in the desirability of democracy in general and their political system in particular. Few Americans, to say the very least, openly contest this belief. Even the economic and social institutions of the country have, over long periods of time, been less severely criticized and challenged than in many other countries.

One may like or dislike the complacency or enthusiasm Americans have displayed toward their institutions; but the fact itself, as we shall see in the next chapter, seems pretty much beyond dispute. This widespread acceptance has had important consequences. For one thing, political movements openly hostile to the political system, or even to the prevailing social and economic institutions, have always encountered massive difficulties. Throughout the history of the United States, political life has been almost completely blanketed by parties, movements, programs, proposals, opinions, ideas, and an ideology directed toward a large mass of convergent 'moderate' voters. The history of radical movements, whether of right or left, and of antisystem parties, as they are sometimes called, is a record of unrelieved failure to win control over the government. Even moderate democratic socialist parties have been unable to acquire much of a following, whereas in Europe they have usually played major parts.

Yet it would be a mistake—one both Americans and foreigners often make—to assume that this ideological convergence eliminates serious conflicts over the conduct of the government. The American Civil War should stand as a warning against glib interpretations.

In later chapters we shall see how a comparatively high degree of ideological convergence came about, what its limits are, how it affects conflict, and how serious conflicts do arise nonetheless.

EXTREME PARTITIONING OF POLITICAL AUTHORITY

One of the most striking characteristics of the American polyarchy, perhaps the one most often singled out for praise by its advocates and for condemnation by its critics, is the extent to which political authority is partitioned among a variety of actors each somewhat independent of the others.

As we saw in the last chapter, polyarchies vary widely in the extent to which they allow the leaders of a party or coalition to acquire the authority to translate their proposals into government actions by winning a majority of votes in a national election. In Britain elections have relatively decisive consequences for governmental decisions. In the United States, elections are less decisive. In this country it is difficult and rare for leaders of a single party or coalition to acquire the amount of authority that, for example, leaders of the majority party in the British House of Commons are ordinarily able to exercise over a fairly broad range of decisions. In this country, as we shall see, the president can exercise, or at any rate in recent decades has exercised, a rather decisive authority over decisions involving military actions, as with President Roosevelt's control over war policies during World War II, President Truman's decision to intervene in Korea, and in the decisions of his successors about intervening, expanding, and contracting the war in Vietnam. Outside this key area, however, the president and other leaders rarely form a coalition cohesive enough to exercise decisive influence over a large variety of decisions.

The fact that elections are relatively less decisive and political authority more fragmented in the United States than in Britain and several other polyarchies can be attributed to two main sets of factors.

First, the *political institutions.* These were originally designed, not to make elections decisive or to facilitate the formation of a powerful majority coalition but with precisely the opposite purpose in mind: to prevent the concentration of authority in any single set of government officials. As the institutions developed, they have largely fulfilled the original purpose of making it difficult for officials to operate as a cohesive governing coalition. In Parts II and III, we shall examine in more detail why the institutions were originally designed with this purpose in mind and how their development has achieved it.

Second, the normal *pattern of cleavages and conflicts.* At the Constitutional Convention of 1787, James Madison predicted that if this country were large enough, the very diversity and variety of political interests and conflicts would create a barrier to the cohesion of national majorities. Madison has been proved substantially correct, at least for the United States. In Part IV we shall see how the normal pattern of cleavage and conflict in the United States renders the task of forming a cohesive and powerful governing coalition extremely difficult. We shall also see that the normal or usual pattern does not always hold. In the extreme instance it was displaced by a degree of polarization that helped to produce a civil war.

INCREMENTAL PERSPECTIVES ON POLITICAL ACTION

Most people who participate actively in political affairs in the United States appear to behave most of the time as if they were acting on three assumptions:

☐ That problems are more or less *divisible* or *independent,* not inextricably interrelated. The assumption is that you do not have to solve every important problem in order to solve one important problem.

☐ That problems can usually be dealt with satisfactorily by *incremental* or piecemeal adjustments of the existing state of affairs. The process of piecemeal adjustments can go on indefinitely.

☐ That satisfactory compromises can ordinarily be found that do not drastically damage the interests of anyone or at least of any 'important' group of participants. From this perspective it is usually thought to be both possible and desirable to limit the scope of conflict to the particular issue at hand, to cooperate with others in seeking solutions, and to accept compromise solutions.

These assumptions are, of course, highly debatable. Many critics of American society deny one or more of them. Some critics argue, in effect, that many evils result directly from the inability or unwillingness of leaders, activists, and the public to believe that most problems are really indivisible, cannot be dealt with satisfactorily by piecemeal changes, cannot be solved without severely damaging some of the most fundamental interests of those who benefit from the status quo, and hence necessarily entail severe, polarizing conflicts.

You might well decide, then, to reject one or more of the three assumptions listed above as a foundation for your own political strategies. Yet even if you adopt different assumptions, you would still need to take into account what is, I think, the fact: that for better or worse incrementalist perspectives have prevailed among most political activists in this country practically all the time and are therefore not likely to change abruptly.

What makes these perspectives even more difficult to change is that they probably result in part from the two characteristics of the American polyarchy just described:

1. Because an ideological convergence reflecting a wide acceptance by Americans of their institutions makes it extraordinarily difficult (and, up to now, impossible) to gain a big public following for a movement that openly seeks comprehensive, radical, or revolutionary changes in a large number of American institutions, and because, in any case, most political activists hold views similar to the rest of the population on these matters, political activists are prone to believe that whatever problems the country confronts are not inherent in the fundamental character of the institutions themselves, but rather are specific, concrete, and separable from one another. Political activists who believe the existing system does not need to be profoundly transformed are likely to feel also that for this very reason satisfactory changes can be brought about by piecemeal alteration. And since, in this view, no basic institutions have to be destroyed to solve the problems confronting American society at any given time, no really fundamental interests are threatened. Hence it ought to be possible to narrow the scope of conflict to the particular problem, and to work out mutually acceptable solutions by cooperation and compromise.

2. Extreme partitioning of political authority creates seemingly insuperable barriers to any movement that wants to use the government to bring about comprehensive, root-and-branch alterations in policies and institutions. As we shall see, partitioning creates innumerable strongholds where comparatively small groups can successfully resist attempts to bring about policies they regard as adverse to their interests. Partitioning encourages those who seek change to avoid attacking all these strongholds at once, to follow instead the tactics of divide-and-

conquer, to reject policies that could only succeed if the fragmented and sprawling nationwide structure of political authority were coordinated as tautly as the actions of a professional football team or ballet group.

SUMMARY   Although by definition polyarchies have certain features in common, every polyarchy also seems to possess a combination of characteristics that to some degree distinguish it from others. The combination of characteristics that, taken together, tend to make the American polyarchy somewhat different from other polyarchies are:

1. American polyarchy has been shaped by a long history of severe discrimination against two racial minorities, Indians and Afro-Americans. The South, in fact, developed a dual system: polyarchy among whites, hegemony over blacks.

2. American political, social, and economic institutions have tended to be rather widely accepted by Americans over rather long periods of time. Political movements highly critical of these institutions have rarely made much headway (as discussed in Part II).

3. For at least two reasons, political authority is extremely partitioned:

☐ Because the political institutions were successfully designed to partition authority (as discussed in Part III).

☐ Because the normal pattern of conflicts and cleavages makes it difficult to form cohesive governing coalitions (as discussed in Part IV).

4. Partly because of the last two characteristics, most people who participate actively in political affairs in the United States seem to adopt incrementalist perspectives; that is, they seem to believe that problems are separable, can be dealt with satisfactorily by piecemeal adjustments, and can be solved by limiting the scope of conflict, cooperating with others in searching for solutions, and accepting compromises. Although incrementalist perspectives are roundly criticized as inadequate, they appear to be such an enduring characteristic of the American polyarchy that any person who wishes to bring about changes would have to take them into account in formulating his own strategies (as discussed in Part V).

How And Why A Polyarchy Emerged On The American Continent

part

2

How Decisions in 1787
Shaped the American Polyarchy

In every polyarchy, contemporary political life is powerfully shaped by the overarching arrangements and understandings that make up its constitution. With a few exceptions, Britain being the best known, these superordinate arrangements and understandings are to a great extent prescribed in a single written document held to be more binding than ordinary law—a written constitution. In polyarchies with written constitutions, making and modifying the basic document are actions of singular importance.

To understand, then, how American political institutions came to be widely accepted and why the partitioning of authority is so marked in American political life, we must turn to certain key choices made at the American Constitutional Convention of 1787.

As every American child learns in grade school, the American Constitution, except for amendments, was formulated by fifty-five men gathered at a constitutional convention held in Philadelphia in 1787. Our school child may not realize, of course, that American political life is by no means governed entirely by that document. Political parties, for example, are nowhere mentioned in the Constitution, much less provided for. Nonetheless, the Constitution has probably contributed more than any other single factor to the special features, the peculiarities of form, substance, and process that differentiate the American from other polyarchies. Even if political parties go unmentioned in the Constitution, the American party system takes its shape from certain elements in the Constitution.

The Constitution proposed by the men at the Convention was both an end and a beginning. It was the culmination of a slow, steady, and gradual growth in America of institutions, practises, and ideas favorable to popular government. It was the beginning of a new period in which these institutions, practises, and ideas were to be tested and vigorously expanded.

The men at the Constitutional Convention did not create a polyarchy. They helped one to emerge. No group of men can create popular government unless the people and their existing institutions are ripe for it. By 1787 Americans were ready for polyarchy; so much so that sooner or later, one is tempted to conjecture, a polyarchy would surely have grown up. The men who worked in Philadelphia through the summer of 1787 did not—could not—give final shape to the American political system, nor even to the constitutional foundations. The shape of our system was bound to be influenced by other men, by social and economic conditions, by the beliefs and attitudes of Americans, by events beyond the control of the handful of men in Independence Hall meeting week after week in the face of summer's heat and flaring tempers.

Yet if it is easy to exaggerate the work of the Convention, or of any constitutional convention, it would be wrong to minimize the consequences of that Convention. For the framework of government proposed by the men in Philadelphia, and in due course accepted by the states and the people, was a unique framework. Once it was put into effect, it was bound to influence the specific ways in which popular government would or could develop in the new United States. If the American political system today is different in some important respects from any other system, this is, at least in part, a result of the *particular* pattern of polyarchy that grew out of the beliefs, the proposals, the matters of agreement and conflict, the discussions, and the compromises of the Convention. As we shall see in the next chapter, it is a result, too, of the fact that Americans of later generations continued to value, and so to preserve, many of the major aspects of the pattern shaped at the Convention.

WERE THE FOUNDERS CONSERVATIVES OR REVOLUTIONARIES?

The Constitutional Convention, curiously enough, has been described both as a revolutionary body and as a conservative one. There is truth in both views.

Until the year 1787, the entire history of mankind had never witnessed a single case of a successful and enduring representative republic over a large area. This was a fact of which every man at the Convention was well aware. If a delegate did not happen to know it when he arrived in Philadelphia, he learned it soon enough, for it was on the minds and lips of all the greater leaders of the Convention. Some of the men who came to Philadelphia—most of them, as it turned out—had in view something that had never been done before. Rule by the people, though rare, was not new. But to expand representative government over a vast domain—that would be a new and revolutionary undertaking.

Although the Founders were uncertain as to how many people there were in the thirteen states, they evidently assumed that the total population was something between 2.5 and 3 million. One compilation used at the Convention counted 2.6 million whites and a half million blacks. (These were conservative estimates: the federal census of 1790 showed a total population just under 4 million.) Already the number of free white male citizens was fifteen to twenty times as large as in Athens at the time of Pericles. As Charles Pinckney of South Carolina pointed out in the early weeks of the Convention, "The United States include a territory of about 1500 miles in length, and in breadth about 400."[1] The state of New York alone was larger than the whole Greek mainland, larger than the entire Swiss Confederacy, larger than the Dutch Confederacy. And the men in Philadelphia took it for granted that in both population and territory the United States would expand—ultimately, perhaps, into a country of unbelievable vastness.

Revolutionaries Without Precedents

All the experience furnished by history seemed to foredoom an attempt to establish a national government on republican principles over such a great domain.

More than twenty centuries earlier, the citizens of many Greek city-states—especially Athens—participated in political decisions to an extent that probably has never existed since. Athenian politics was virtually a permanent town meeting. Yet the Greeks, for all their political genius, failed to create a federal system that would link one city with another in a representative republic. Indeed, they seem always to have held fast to their belief that citizenship was meaningless unless it provided for direct participation and control over political decisions. Their inability to develop a wider sense of citizenship and to create a larger Hellenic state in which the perennial wars of Greek against Greek would be eliminated led in time to their subjugation, first by the Macedonians and then by the Romans.

More than any other people before, and more than most since, the Romans learned the complex arts of managing a single government

---

1. Most of what we know about the debates is found in Madison's detailed, full, and apparently scrupulous "Notes of Debates," which he wrote down each day but which he did not revise until after he retired from the presidency in 1817, and which were not finally published until 1840. The official record was little more than a list of votes taken. In addition to Madison, six other delegates kept notes, but none were as detailed as his. All of these notes are collected in *Documents.* This quotation is at p. 805.

A shorter collection of materials, including an extensive though incomplete selection from Madison's notes, may be found in *The Federal Convention and the Formation of the Union of the American States,* edited, with an introduction by Winton U. Solberg (New York: Liberal Arts Press, 1958). Saul K. Padover has arranged Madison's report on the debates according to topics (and has excluded some material) in *To Secure These Blessings* (New York: Washington Square Press, Ridge Press, 1962). This is the most convenient arrangement of the debates available.

over a large area. The Republic of Rome endured for nearly five centuries. The history of that Republic was as familiar to the men at the Convention as our own national history is to us, for their education had typically included a study of the classics; and they were always quick to cite Roman experience. They knew, then, that the Republic had been initially a city government, and that the Romans had been generous in extending the privileges of citizenship throughout the Italian peninsula, and that they had attempted (being a conservative people) to adapt the institutions of the city to the government of the new and greater Rome. Yet the Founders also knew that the Romans never did create an effective system of representation.

The Founders also knew that some of the cities of medieval Italy were, like Florence, republics. But Italy had never developed a national government; in *The Prince,* Machiavelli had concluded pessimistically that Italy was incapable of a republic and that only a vigorous and even tyrannical leader could ever bring peace and unity to Italy. Before the eighteenth century, the most extensive development of popular government had occurred among the rural cantons of Switzerland, which of all modern countries can rightly claim to have had a lengthier experience with democratic institutions than the United States. In 1787, however, Switzerland was still a confederacy in which the cantons were sovereign states; their central 'national' assembly, the Diet, had virtually no power. If the men at the Convention had wanted such a confederacy, they need not have come to Philadelphia at all. The Articles of Confederation already provided at least as much of a central government as the Swiss then enjoyed. Yet it was precisely because they were discontented in various degrees with the weak confederacy of the Articles that these Americans had assembled. The Swiss example, like Greece, told a good deal about the prospects of popular government on a small scale. But it did not provide a model for a representative republic in a new and extensive nation. Nor, in this respect, was the Netherlands any more useful; for there, too, the oligarchic republics in the provinces were for all practical purposes wholly sovereign.

What the Founders proposed to do, then, had never been done before. More than that, a fair reading of a familiar body of historical experience would suggest that their efforts were more likely to fail than to succeed. You can have republican government in a canton, a city, or perhaps even a small state, historical experience seemed to say, but you cannot have it over a large area. Republics can link themselves into a confederacy with a weak central government; but if you want a strong central government you cannot have a republic. The Founders—with some fears, to be sure—rejected this dilemma and proposed to establish the first great republic. In this perspective, then, the Founders were indeed revolutionaries.

Conservatives?

Yet as revolutionaries they seem oddly out of place. They were, it is true, a youthful group. Nearly 40 percent were not over forty years old, and three-quarters of them were under fifty. Some of the most vigorous leaders at the Convention were surprisingly young. James Madison was thirty-six, Gouverneur Morris was thirty-five, Alexander Hamilton was thirty-two, and Charles Pinckney was twenty-nine.

Nonetheless, most of them had already had extensive and often even distinguished public careers. Many had acquired experience and reputation during the Revolutionary War. With few exceptions they were substantial and well-known figures in their states; some were respected throughout all thirteen states; and the fame of a few, like Franklin and Washington, extended to Europe. Most of them were moderately well-to-do: a few were exceedingly wealthy by the standards of the time. John Rutledge and Pierce Butler of South Carolina were big planters and could be counted on to defend the interests of the planting and slaveholding aristocracy of that state. Gouverneur Morris of Pennsylvania was a wealthy financier and a conservative aristocrat. Although Nathaniel Gorham of Massachusetts had started his business career as an apprentice to a merchant, by 1787 he was one of the leading businessmen in his state.

They were, then, a respectable group. Sixty percent of them were lawyers; an incredibly high proportion for those times—nearly half—were college graduates.

Although they may have seemed revolutionary to Europeans, in their American setting they were not so daring. To be sure, a national government constructed on republican principles was a new experiment for Americans and for the world, but by 1787 representative governments were already well established at the state level. The long period of colonial rule, extending over a century and a half, had given the people in the colonies considerable training in the skills required to operate a representative government. Despite the myths that have since grown up, the colonies had enjoyed an astounding measure of self-government. One house of a colonial legislature was invariably elected by the voters; the second house was sometimes appointed by the first; and in two states, Connecticut and Rhode Island, the governor was elected by the voters. Where the governor was appointed by the King, conflicts between governor and legislature contributed to the development of the art of managing representative institutions. Since the legislature usually controlled the pursestrings and voted the governor's salary, even a royal governor could sometimes be outmaneuvered.

Just how many people were eligible to vote in colonial elections has been a matter of debate. For many years it was assumed that property requirements restricted the vote to a small and wealthy minority;

but recent research indicates that in most of the colonies from half to three-quarters of the white adult males must have been eligible to vote in the years before the Revolution.[2] In Massachusetts, possibly as many as 95 percent of the adult males could vote.[3]

Counterrevolutionaries?

How did the men at the Convention look upon this strong tide of political equality? Some scholars have argued—implicitly or explicitly—that the Constitution was the work of a small group of wealthy aristocrats who wished to stem the rapid advance of equality in the states by constructing a strong national government that would protect the economic interests of large planters, speculators, financiers, merchants, and shippers from their natural enemies, the small farmers, who made up the overwhelming majority of the population of the United States, and the mechanics and artisans in the cities, who, though still a small minority, nevertheless were a potential threat to the well-to-do.[4]

In recent years, however, this view of the Convention and its fruits has been subjected to extensive criticism. Although a fair assessment of this controversy is impossible in a short space, the criticisms cannot easily be turned aside. If the Founders were engaged in an anti-democratic counterrevolution, how did it happen that the Constitution was approved by eleven states within the following year? The answer had once been that a large part of the adult males were disfranchised by property requirements; hence the conventions held in the various states to approve or disapprove the Constitution were easily rigged by the same aristocratic minority whose representatives had drafted the Constitution. But more recent evidence, as we have just seen, seems to indicate that suffrage was in fact rather widely held in most of the states. If the small farmers who comprised the overwhelming bulk of the population were opposed to the Constitution, they must have been very apathetic or confused, because they evidently did not turn out in large numbers to vote against it.

In the second place, in a surprisingly short time, the arrangements provided for in the Constitution seemed to have acquired very widespread approval among the general population. In fact, one of the most

---

2. Chilton Williamson, *American Suffrage from Property to Democracy, 1760–1860* (Princeton: Princeton University Press, 1960), ch. 2.

3. Robert E. Brown, *Middle-Class Democracy and the Revolution in Massachusetts, 1691–1780* (Ithaca: Cornell University Press, 1955), pp. 49–50.

4. The famous pioneering study in this vein was Charles Beard, *An Economic Interpretation of the Constitution* (New York: Macmillan, 1913). Many later historians adopted, expanded, or developed views implicitly contained in Beard's analysis. See, particularly, Merrill Jensen, *The Articles of Confederation* (Madison: University of Wisconsin Press. 1940), and his *The New Nation* (New York, Knopf, 1950). Beard was severely attacked by Robert E. Brown, *Charles Beard and the Constitution* (Princeton: Princeton University Press, 1956); and in turn defended by Lee Benson, *Turner & Beard, American Historical Writing Reconsidered* (New York: Free Press of Glencoe, 1960). A succinct and judicious evaluation of the debate is contained in Edmund S. Morgan, *The Birth of the Republic, 1763–89* (Chicago: University of Chicago Press, 1956).

influential people at the Convention, James Madison, was soon to be-come the main leader in Congress of the very forces—the small farmers—who, according to the theory, were defeated at the Convention by the aristocratic counterrevolution. Yet Madison, like Jefferson, was a staunch supporter of the Constitution, and there is no persuasive evidence that their supporters, the small farmers, were less so. In fact, it was not the small farmers or artisans who displayed the most opposition to the Constitution during the following generation, but a wealthy minority who distrusted democracy and disliked the power given to the people under the new republic.

Finally, on a number of key issues, including the issue of democracy versus aristocracy, the men at the Convention were not of one mind. Although most of them agreed on the need for a stronger central government, they disagreed—as we shall see—on the extent to which a strengthened central government should be under the influence of the people. If the framework of government they finally proposed showed what the Founders could agree on, it also reflected their disagreements and conflicts.

Pragmatic Reformers?

Indeed, as one reads Madison's reports of the debates at the Convention, one senses two rather different levels of debate. At one level there were practical problems of designing a system of govern-ment that would not only have the approval of the delegates and of the states but would work well enough to endure: Should there be one executive or three? How many representatives should there be in the legislative body? What specific powers should be given to Congress?

But underlying and greatly influencing the debates on practical matters, there were agreements and disagreements over political objec-tives that seemed to reflect more general political ideas and ideology.

AGREEMENTS: THE NEED FOR COMPROMISE One principle which most of the delegates seemed to take for granted—particularly those who lasted the course—was that politics, including the politics of constitution-making, required compromises. Madison and Wilson, who were among the most principled men at the Convention, were finally driven to accept equal state representation in the Senate despite their belief, which they never altered even in later years, that this feature of the Constitution could not be justified by any acceptable political principle except the principle that in politics compromise is sometimes more virtuous than purity.

Were men like Madison and Wilson right to have entered into a compromise that violated their principles? Should they have left the Con-vention in indignation, like Lansing, Yates, and Luther Martin? Should they have refused to sign the document because they did not subscribe to everything in it, as Randolph and Gerry did? Should they have refused to support it because, as some delegates concluded, the Constitution had been formed too secretly, with too little popular participation and consultation?

Questions like these are easy to answer if one has very weak principles of conduct—or very strong ones. To the man of weak principle, compromise is an easy path so long as one gains even a little in the bargain. To the man of rigid morality, the answer is equally obvious: it is better not to agree at all than to agree to an imperfect bargain.

But the problem is not just a personal affair, a matter of private morality. Since the way a political leader answers these questions may greatly affect the rest of us, the problem is also a public affair.

Lying between the simple extremes of unprincipled politics and rigid morality is a domain of action that has been called *the ethics of responsibility:* meaning by this term an attempt to weigh the consequences of each alternative as intelligently as possible, and then to choose the best available. Acting according to the ethics of responsibility, a political leader cannot enjoy the luxury of rejecting an imperfect compromise, even a highly imperfect compromise, so long as that compromise represents the best possible alternative presented by the world as it happens to be. Irresponsibility, in this view, consists not in making concessions, but in making unnecessary concessions; not in making imperfect bargains, but in failing to make the best possible bargains; not in adhering strictly to principles, but in holding rigidly to one principle at excessive cost to other principles. One may be irresponsible, then, not merely from a want of principles but also from a want of intelligence and knowledge of the real world; in the ethics of responsibility it is important not only to know what one wants but also to know exactly what one must do to get it, and what it will cost, not merely in money but in other values.

What is sometimes called the Anglo-American political tradition has, at its best, accented the ethics of responsibility. If that tradition has rejected wholly unprincipled and unscrupulous politics as an aim unworthy of the political calling, it has also rejected fanaticism and rigidity as too simple for the complex world of political decisions. If sheer opportunism is ignoble, rigid morality in politics is dangerous and inapplicable.

The men at the Convention were English (Wilson was a Scot) before they were American. Whatever else they were, they were not fanatics. Nor were they mere opportunists. They were above all realists, who knew or believed they knew the rough boundaries of the politically possible: yet they were principled realists who sought to achieve their aims with the imperfect materials at hand. When the committee appointed to examine the thorny question of equal representation in the Senate reported back to the Convention, Mason probably expressed the sentiments of most of the delegates when he said:

> . . . There must be some accommodation on this point, . . . however liable the Report might be to objections, he thought it preferable to an appeal to the world by the different sides, as had been talked of by some Gentlemen. . . . He would bury his bones in this City rather than expose his Country to the Consequences of a dissolution of the Convention without any thing being done.[5]

The Founders took for granted one of the key assumptions of the incrementalist perspective on political action: that it was morally responsible to search for, and in American circumstances it would be possible to discover, satisfactory compromises for specific problems, compromises that would not drastically damage the interests of any important group of participants.

Thus the men at the Convention bequeathed more than a Constitution. In what they did there, and in what they did in public life in later years, they also helped to shape a way of entering into political decisions and evaluating political institutions that is as much a part of the American political system as the Constitution.

THE NEED TO PARTITION AUTHORITY   Had the Founders not seen some virtues in compromise, they would hardly have designed the Constitution the way they did. For without a readiness to compromise, their framework of government would have been totally unworkable. Its unworkability in the absence of compromise stems from a second general principle on which the Founders were substantially agreed and which entered into practically everything they did at the Convention: *Governmental power and authority must always be partitioned among several centers and never concentrated in a single center.*

Instead of a single center of sovereign power, then, they had to insure the existence of multiple centers of power, none of which (whether representing a majority of the people or a minority) would be wholly sovereign. Although like their successors they agreed that the only legitimate sovereign is the people, they also agreed, and later generations of Americans seem to have concurred, that even the people ought never to be an absolute sovereign; consequently no part of the people, such as a majority, in this view ought to be absolutely sovereign.

Why this axiom? Those who accept it tend to assume, as I see it, that the existence of multiple centers of power, none of which is wholly

---

5. *Documents*, pp. 329–330.

sovereign, will help (may indeed be necessary) to tame power, to secure the consent of all, and to settle conflicts peacefully:

☐ Because one center of power is set against another, power itself will be tamed, civilized, controlled, and limited to decent human purposes, while coercion, the most evil form of power, will be reduced to a minimum.

☐ Because even minorities are provided with opportunities to veto solutions they strongly object to, the consent of all might be won in the long run.

☐ Because constant negotiations among different centers of power are necessary in order to make decisions, citizens and leaders will perfect the precious art of dealing peacefully with their conflicts, not merely to the benefit of one partisan but to the mutual benefit of all the parties to a conflict.

In considering the importance in American political life of this belief in the need to partition power and authority, it is useful to keep four points in mind.

First, the impact of the belief stems not only from the thrust it gave to the decisions of the Founders but also from the fact that later generations of Americans have tended, albeit unconsciously, to adopt the same belief. They have also tended to accept as desirable the particular arrangements for, and the degree of, partitioned authority that help to distinguish the American political system from polyarchy in other countries.

Second, in applying their belief to the design of the Constitution, the Founders went much further in partitioning authority than those who later drafted the constitutions that govern today in many other polyarchies. A belief in the need for such an elaborate system of checks and balances is much less widely shared outside the United States than most Americans seem to be aware of.

Third, one reason the Founders went so far in applying their faith in the virtues of partitioned authority is that they faced a wholly novel task. In one sense they were conservatives, but in a longer perspective, they were revolutionaries. They confronted a new problem: in a large country, too large for the people to assemble, how, if at all, could you insure the sovereignty of the people and at the same time avoid tyranny? A few years after the Constitutional Convention, events in France demonstrated what has been shown many times since: a solution is neither simple nor self-evident.

Fourth, the Founders may also have adopted an extreme pattern of partitioned authority because the doctrine itself is an incomplete guide to action. It is, in fact, more an orientation, perspective, or hunch than a political philosophy. Certainly it does not constitute a philosophy

of democracy, a theory of polyarchy, or a complete strategy of constitution-making.

DISAGREEMENTS   Among other things, the assumption that power ought to be partitioned
provides no specific answer to three questions the Founders had to
answer:

☐ Should the Constitution establish democracy or instead provide for
some kind of meritocracy or aristocracy of talents?
☐ Who were the American people and how were they to govern themselves? As a confederacy of thirteen different peoples, as a single
people, or both?
☐ If the principle of political equality was to be respected, did it imply
equality among individuals or among political units?

The men at the Convention disagreed sharply on these matters. And
disagreement on the answers to these questions did not end when the
Founders completed the writing of the Constitution, nor when the Constitution was adopted by the states and put into effect. On the contrary,
conflicting answers continued to reappear in American politics. Nearly
all of the great conflicts that have wracked the country since 1787 have
raised these questions anew. In fact, the differences in viewpoint expressed during the Convention continue to appear in American politics
right down to the present day.

DEMOCRACY OR   Thanks to a rule of secrecy that was adopted by the Convention at the
ARISTOCRACY?   third meeting, the delegates were free to ventilate their opinions with
unusual candor. Probably they would not have spoken so frankly outside
the closed doors of Independence Hall. Fortunately, then, the records
of the Convention enable us to learn something about the real beliefs
of the delegates. Secrecy was, no doubt, of particular value to those
delegates who distrusted popular government and yearned for some kind
of aristocratic republic in which the rich and the wellborn would occupy
a special place. These delegates might not have dared to admit in public
what they were willing to affirm in private.

The Case for Aristocracy

The most articulate spokesmen for an aristocratic republic were
Gouverneur Morris of Pennsylvania, Rufus King of Massachusetts, and
of course Alexander Hamilton of New York (whose influence was greatly
reduced, however, by his extreme proposals and his fitful attendance).
One of the delegates from Georgia, William Pierce, contributed little to

the Convention but left a good deal to posterity, for he made some vivid sketches of the delegates, from which we learn that

> Mr. Gouverneur Morris is one of these Genius's in whom every species of talents combine to render him conspicuous and flourishing in public debate: —He winds through all the mazes of rhetoric, and throws around him such a glare that he charms, captivates, and leads away the senses of all who hear him. With an infinite streach of fancy he brings to view things when he is engaged in deep argumentation, that render all the labor of reasoning easy and pleasing. But with all these powers he is fickle and inconstant, —never pursuing one train of thinking, —nor ever regular. He has gone through a very extensive course of reading, and is acquainted with all the sciences. No Man has more wit, —nor can any one engage the attention more than Mr. Morris. He was bred to the Law, but I am told he disliked the profession, and turned Merchant. He is engaged in some great mercantile matters with his namesake Mr. Robt Morris. This Gentleman is about 38 years old, he has been unfortunate in losing one of his Legs, and getting all the flesh taken off his right arm by a scald, when a youth.[6]

Morris's views on the Senate are a good example of his attitudes. Although he did not maintain a consistent position as to how the senators should be chosen, he was unvarying in his views as to the proper role of the Senate:

> . . . It is confessed, on all hands, that the second branch ought to be a check on the first—for without its having this effect it is perfectly useless. —The first branch, originating from the people, will ever be subject to *precipitancy, changeability,* and *excess.* Experience evinces the truth of this remark without having recourse to reading. This can only be checked by *ability* and *virtue* in the second branch. On your present system, can you suppose that one branch will possess it more than the others? The second branch ought to be composed of men of great and established property— *an aristocracy.* Men, who from pride will support consistency and permanency; and to make them completely independent, they must be chosen *for life,* or they will be a useless body. Such an aristocratic body will keep down the turbulency of democracy. But if you elect them for a shorter period, they will be only a name, and we had better be without them. Thus constituted, I hope they will show us the weight of aristocracy.[7]

Hamilton was a great admirer of the British Constitution as it existed (or rather as he believed it to exist) in the eighteenth century. "In his private opinion," Madison reports him as saying, "he had no scruple in declaring . . . that the British Gov^t was the best in the world: and that he doubted much whether any thing short of it would do in America."[8] Accordingly, Hamilton proposed to emulate the British system as closely as possible in designing a new construction for Americans. An assembly elected by the people would take the place of the House of Commons.

---

6. *Ibid.,* pp. 101–102.

7. *Ibid.,* p. 838. The quotation is from the notes of Robert Yates, a delegate from New York.

8. *Ibid.,* p. 220.

Corresponding to the House of Lords—"a most noble institution"—he proposed a Senate elected for life "or at least during good behaviour." The absence of a monarch was annoying. "As to the Executive, it seemed to be admitted that no good one could be established on Republican principles. . . . The English model was the only good one on this subject. . . . Let the Executive also be for life."[9]

The Case for Popular Control

The most consistent spokesmen at the Convention in behalf of popular control were James Wilson of Pennsylvania, George Mason of Virginia, and James Madison.

Of these, Wilson seems to have had the deepest confidence in popular government and the most clear-cut vision of what a democratic republic should and would be. Wilson was a Scot, who had attended the University of Saint Andrews before emigrating to America where he had taken up the practise of law. He was described by Pierce as follows:

> Mr. Wilson ranks among the foremost in legal and political knowledge. He has joined to a fine genius all that can set him off and show him to advantage. He is well acquainted with Man, and understands all the passions that influence him. Government seems to have been his peculiar Study, all the political institutions of the World he knows in detail, and can trace the causes and effects of every revolution from the earliest stages of the Grecian commonwealth down to the present time. No man is more clear, copious, and comprehensive than Mr. Wilson, yet he is no great Orator. He draws attention not by the charm of his eloquence, but by the force of his reasoning. He is about 45 years old.[10]

Early in the Convention, Wilson announced that "he was for raising the federal pyramid to a considerable altitude, and for that reason wished to give it as broad a basis as possible. No government could long subsist without the confidence of the people. In a republican Government this confidence was peculiarly essential."[11] Wilson urged that not only the lower house but also the Senate and the president should be chosen by the people.[12]

Disagreements

Wilson represented at best a small minority. At the other extreme, the ardent aristocrats were also a rather tiny group. Although decisions on specific questions were often influenced by considerations that had little to do with a delegate's preference for democracy or aristocracy,

---

9. *Ibid.*, pp. 221–222. In the plan he submitted on June 18, the Senate and the executive were to serve "during good behaviour," which ordinarily would mean for life (pp. 224–225). The notes kept by Yates of New York confirm Madison's account, see pp. 781–782; for various texts of Hamilton's plan of government, see pp. 979, 988.

10. *Ibid.*, p. 101.

11. *Ibid.*, p. 126.

12. *Ibid.*, pp. 209–211.

Table 8.1
Three Issues in the
Constitutional Convention

	Limited Term for President	Limited Term for Senators	A Constitution without Restrictions on Suffrage
Wilson	Yes	Yes	Yes
Mason	Yes	Yes	Yes
Madison	Yes	Yes	Yes[a]
Hamilton	No	No	?[b]
G. Morris	No[c]	No	No[d]

[a] Madison's views are not entirely clear. On July 26 he opposed restricting the suffrage to freeholders. On August 7 he seemed to lean in that direction. Cf. *Documents*, pp. 489, 935.

[b] Hamilton was absent during these discussions.

[c] At first Gouverneur Morris strongly supported a motion to give the executive tenure "during good behavior." "This is the way to get a good Government," *ibid.*, p. 396. A week later, he seemed to have doubts, p. 447. But he generally opposed efforts to limit the term of the president, e.g., pp. 453, 458.

[d] Favored restricting the suffrage to freeholders, *ibid.*, pp. 489, 935.

there were several issues on which the differences showed up most clearly. These were whether either the president or members of the Senate should have a limited term or hold office for life or good behavior, and whether the right to vote should be constitutionally restricted to free holders or property owners of some sort. On these issues, Wilson, Mason, and Madison took a democratic position, while on all three of them Morris favored the aristocratic view (Table 8.1).

It falsifies history, then, to assume that the delegates at the Convention were in substantial agreement on the alternatives of a democratic republic versus an aristocratic republic. Clearly they were not. Yet it is also easy to exaggerate the extent of their differences. Although some delegates advocated a democratic republic and others an aristocratic republic, most of them were probably ranged somewhere between Wilson at one pole and Morris or Hamilton at the other. Mason, who stood with Wilson on the three issues listed in Table 8.1, frequently took less advanced positions on other issues. Madison, perhaps the most conservative of the three men, was evidently near the midpoint of the Convention. If he was as democratic as Wilson on some issues, on others, such as limiting the suffrage to freeholders or advocating definite constitutional protections for wealth and property, he was conservative enough to maintain the confidence of pro-aristocratic delegates like Morris.

Agreements

Some elements of popular government. On two important questions involving democracy, nearly all the delegates were in agreement. First, with only a few exceptions, they believed that the new national government should contain an important element of popular government. Even Morris and Hamilton wanted one branch chosen by the people. To be sure, a few delegates, like the South Carolinians Pierce Butler and Charles Cotesworth Pinckney, went so far as to oppose the election of the lower house by the people; they wanted even this choice to be filtered through the state legislatures. But their views do not seem to have had much influence on the Convention.

Partitioned authority. Second, evidently every delegate was firmly opposed to a national government in which the representatives elected by the voters would have full constitutional authority to enact any laws whatsoever. A follower of Rousseau might have said, "Let there be no constitutional restrictions on what the people (or, in practise, a majority of their representatives) can do." An unusually doctrinaire follower of Rousseau might have added, "for the people can do no wrong." A more moderate follower might have said, "The people or their representatives from time to time may—nay, probably will—pass bad laws. But it is better that the people should have the chance to learn from their errors than that they should be prevented from acting in ways they think best. After all, men who frame constitutions are also human, and times do change. By putting restrictions into a constitution the framers may prevent not only a bad law today but also a good law tomorrow."

No delegate to the Convention ever advanced arguments remotely like these. If one had, his arguments would have fallen on deaf ears. One reason was purely practical. The task, as the delegates saw it, was to enlarge the powers of the national government; yet there was much opposition to a more powerful national government. The defenders of the Articles of Confederation would undoubtedly put up a very stiff fight against the new Constitution. To give unlimited powers to a majority of elected representatives was exactly equivalent to giving unlimited constitutional authority to the national government. But an unlimited national government in any form would surely be turned down in every state. The most that the Convention could do, therefore, would be to frame a national government with definitely circumscribed authority.

Suspicion of power. In addition to this practical reason, there were others of a more philosophic cast. Whether democrats or aristocrats, the men at the Convention shared a hard-headed, unsentimental, skeptical view of man's ability to withstand the temptations of power. They took it for granted that men are easily corrupted by power; to any man with great power, they might have said, self-restraint is a fragile dike. The best way to prevent the abuse of power, then, was not to trust in human character but to limit the legal authority allocated to any person and to set one power over against another.

"Men love power," said Hamilton. "Give all power to the many, they will oppress the few. Give all power to the few, they will oppress the many. Both therefore ought to have power, that each may defend itself ag^st the other."[13] "The Rich," Gouverneur Morris said, and well he knew, "will strive to establish their dominion & enslave the rest. They always did. They always will. The proper security ag^st them is to form them into a separate interest. The two forces [the rich and the poor] will then controul each other."[14] Mason announced that "he went on a principle often advanced & in which he concurred, that 'a majority when interested will oppress the minority.' "[15] Wilson, that unwavering advocate of a democratic republic, said:

> Despotism comes on Mankind in different Shapes, sometimes in an Executive, sometimes in a Military, one. Is there no danger of a Legislative despotism? Theory & practice both proclaim it. If the Legislative authority be not restrained, there can be neither liberty nor stability. . . . In a single House there is no check, but the inadequate one, of the virtue & good sense of those who compose it.[16]

Three principles. It was not enough, then, to construct a national government with definite but limited legal authority. The potential abuse of power had somehow to be checked. How was this to be accomplished? The answers that came from the Convention can be summarized in three principles derived from their belief in the need to partition authority:

1. *The principle of limited authority.* Since the virtues and wisdom of men are not powerful enough to prevent their abusing their power, no person, official, or group—whether a minority or a majority— should ever be allowed to have unlimited legal authority. In other words, legal authority should always be strictly limited.
2. *The principle of balanced authority.* Since purely legal or even constitutional restraints, standing by themselves, are sure to prove inadequate, whenever authority is allocated by law or constitution to one official or body—whether representing a minority or a majority— that authority must be counterbalanced (to some degree) by allocating authority to some other official or body.
3. *The principle of offsetting social power.* Since even legal and constitutional arrangements will be subverted if some citizens or groups of citizens gain disproportionate opportunities for power in comparison with other citizens, the potential power of one citizen or group must be offset by the potential power of other citizens.

Applications. From the first two principles it followed that the legal authority of the proposed national government should be carefully de-

---

13. *Ibid.*, pp. 217, 221.
14. *Ibid.*, p. 319.
15. *Ibid.*, p. 587.
16. *Ibid.*, pp. 212–213.

fined and limited, and that the authority allocated by the Constitution to one branch or body should be offset by authority allocated to another.

The Constitution reflects these two principles in a great variety of ways:

- □ It preserves the states as fixed elements in a federal system.
- □ It yields to the Congress specific, not unlimited, legal powers (Article I, Section 8).
- □ It specifically denies to the Congress legal authority of some kinds (Article I, Section 9).
- □ It provides for a Congress consisting of two separate and rather independent branches, whose members have somewhat different qualifications and were, until 1913, chosen by different means (Article I, Sections 1, 2, 3).
- □ It forbids members of Congress from holding executive offices during the period for which they are elected, thus making it difficult for the president to influence them by appointing them to high offices in the Executive Branch (Article I, Section 6).
- □ It provides for a president elected for a fixed term independently of Congress and bars Congress from shortening his tenure (except by impeachment) and from increasing or decreasing his salary during his four-year term (Article II, Section 1).
- □ It assigns to the president definite but limited legal authority, including a veto of laws passed by Congress (Article II, Section 2).
- □ It provides for a Judicial Branch substantially independent of both president and Congress (Article III).
- □ It makes amendments to the Constitution difficult by requiring approval of two-thirds of the members of each house, and of three-fourths of the states (Article V).

Moreover, when in 1791 the Bill of Rights filled one of the great gaps in the Constitution, it amplified these principles by imposing further specific restraints on the Congress, by guaranteeing a number of individual rights, and by reemphasizing (in the Tenth Amendment) the limited and federal character of the political system.

The third principle, offsetting social power, is more vague and more difficult to execute than the others. It draws strength less from the Constitution than from 'politics,' less from laws than from social and economic forces, less from officials than from citizens. Its application, therefore, does not depend as much on what the Convention did as on what the country that existed outside the Convention has done; and less on the delegates than on the generations to come. Nevertheless the formulation of the principle goes back to the Convention, and specifically to Madison who, in a brilliant analysis during the second week of the Convention, sought to meet head-on the charge by the aristocratic faction that a democratic republic would open the door to oppression by the majority:

> . . . The lesson we are to draw [Madison admitted] . . . is that where a majority are united by a common sentiment, and have an opportunity, the rights of the minor party become insecure. In a Republican Gov^t the Majority if united have always an opportunity. The only remedy is to enlarge the sphere, & thereby divide the community into so great a number of interests & parties, that in the 1st place a majority will not be likely at the same moment to have a common interest separate from that of the whole or of the minority; and in the 2^d place, that in case they sh^d have such an interest, they may not be apt to unite in the pursuit of it. It was incumbent on us then to try this remedy, and with that view to frame a republican system on such a scale & in such a form as will controul all the evils wch have been experienced.[17]

A CONFEDERACY OR A NATIONAL REPUBLIC?

A month after the delegates got down to business, one of them, Dr. William Johnson of Connecticut, observed,

> The controversy must be endless whilst Gentlemen differ in the grounds of their arguments; Those on one side considering the States as districts of people composing one political Society; those on the other considering them as so many political societies.[18]

Johnson (whom Pierce described as "a character much celebrated for his legal knowledge . . . [who] . . . possesses a very strong and enlightened understanding") had put his finger squarely on one of the central issues of the Convention. Were Americans in the process of becoming a single people? Or were they thirteen separate peoples? Were they one nation—or several nations? Would they be served best by a new and vigorous national government—or by a confederation of state governments united by a relatively weak central government?

Nearly every delegate, to be sure, professed to be in favor of a federal system. But the word *federal* was no more than a label. The trouble was that they did not agree on what a 'federal' system was or should be. "Great latitude," Hamilton told the delegates, "therefore must be given to the signification of the term."[19]

The National Federalists

On the one side were a number of the most distinguished delegates at the Convention—Madison, Wilson, Hamilton, Gouverneur Morris, Rufus King—who wanted to create a strong national government.

> . . . Bad Govern^{ts} [said Wilson] are of two sorts. 1. that which does too little. 2. that which does too much: that which fails thro' weakness; and that

17. *Ibid.,* p. 163.
18. *Ibid.,* p. 297.
19. *Ibid.,* p. 216.

which destroys thro' oppression. Under which of these evils do the U. States at present groan? under the weakness and inefficiency of its Govern[t]. To remedy this weakness we have been sent to this Convention.[20]

This group of delegates—one might call them National Federalists —had three distinct objects in mind. First, they sought a definite and considerable increase in the powers of the national government. Since practically everyone at the Convention agreed that the national government should be strengthened, the differences among the delegates on this score were a matter of degree. But matters of degree are extraordinarily important: after all, the difference between jumping into a hot bath, an icy lake, or a tub of boiling water is only a matter of degree.

In the second place, the National Federalists wanted a central government that had legal authority over individual citizens. To National Federalists it was a fatal flaw in the Articles of Confederation that the Congress had no authority over individuals; that Congress could act only through the states themselves. Clearly it is one thing to compel an individual to obey laws passed by the national government; but it is quite another to compel a state. The disobedience of individuals can generally be met by police, by courts, by fines and imprisonment; the disobedience of a state creates the terrifying choice of governmental impotence or civil war.

Finally, the National Federalists wanted a national government that directly represented individual citizens and not simply the states. The central government, in their view, should be responsive to the citizens of the United States, not just to the states. To them, "the people" were the people of one United States, not thirteen different people in thirteen different states.

The State Federalists

Some of the delegates—the State Federalists, let us call them— were very strongly opposed to all these objectives of the National Federalists. One of the State Federalists, Lansing of New York, announced during the fourth week:

> I am clearly of opinion that I am not authorized to accede to a system which will annihilate the State governments and the Virginia plan [i.e., the plan supported by the National Federalists] is declarative of such extinction. . . . Can we expect that *thirteen* States will surrender their governments up to a national plan?[21]

In fact, Lansing and his fellow New Yorker, Yates, left the Convention not long after, protesting that state sovereignty would be destroyed under a national government.

---

20. *Ibid.,* p. 308.
21. *Ibid.,* p. 787. This comment is found in the notes of delegate Yates, which were later transcribed by Lansing himself.

Luther Martin of Maryland presented the most extensive case for State Federalism, ". . . that the General Gov[t] was meant merely to preserve the State Govern[ts]: not to govern individuals: that its powers ought to be kept within narrow limits; . . . that the States like individuals were in a State of nature equally sovereign & free."[22] "This," Madison added in one of his rare editorial comments, "was the substance of the residue of his discourse which was delivered with much diffuseness & considerable vehemence."[23] Like Lansing and Yates, Martin quit the convention and fought bitterly in Maryland against the adoption of the Constitution.

Most of the delegates agreed with the State Federalists on two points. First, the states had to be preserved as constituent and important elements in a federal system. In this sense, almost everyone was a 'Federalist.' Hamilton, as usual, was a lonely exception; of all the National Federalists, he was the most extreme, for he was quite willing to see the states abolished.[24] But Hamilton's views found little support. As Johnson of Connecticut dryly remarked: "A gentleman from New York, with boldness and decision, proposed a system totally different . . .; and though he has been praised by every body, he has been supported by none."[25]

Second, there was the age-old conviction that a republic could not function over a large area. Madison had tried to blunt this point by arguing, as we have seen, that size was less a vice than a virtue. Yet the worry about size continued. "The largest states," Ellsworth of Connecticut observed, singling out Virginia and Massachusetts for special attention, "are the worst Governed."[26] Although the delegates from these states denied the specific charge, the general point was admitted even by the most enthusiastic National Federalists:

[Hamilton, on July 16] The extent of the Country to be governed, discouraged him. . . . This view of the subject almost led him to despair that a Republican Gov[t] could be established over so great an extent.[27]

[Wilson, on June 25] When he considered the amazing extent of Country— the immense population which is to fill it, the influence which the Gov[t] we are to form will have, not only on the present generation of our people & their multiplied posterity, but on the whole Globe, he was lost in the magnitude of the object.[28]

22. *Ibid.*, pp. 287–288.

23. *Ibid.*, p. 290.

24. See his discussion and his plan in *Documents*, pp. 215 ff., and his subsequent remark quoted in Madison's notes: "As *States*, he thought they ought to be abolished. But he admitted the necessity of leaving in them, subordinate jurisdictions" (*ibid.*, p. 238).

25. *Ibid.*, p. 791.

26. *Ibid.*, p. 276.

27. *Ibid.*, pp. 219–220.

28. *Ibid.*, p. 274.

[Gouverneur Morris, on July 19] It has been a maxim in Political Science that Republican Government is not adapted to a large extent of Country, because the energy of the Executive Magistracy can not reach the extreme parts of it. Our Country is an extensive one.[29]

Because they had no relevant experience to go on, the delegates continued throughout the Convention to express worries like these. They saw that they were fleeing from known evils toward dangers both known and unsuspected. But had they given less weight to the existing disadvantages and more to the dangers in a cloudy future, they would never have drafted a new constitution.

The confirmed and intransigent State Federalists were a small minority among the delegates. Although the Articles of Confederation had many supporters outside the Convention, obviously the ardent State Federalists were not well represented there. Many of the leading opponents of radical change did not attend. Rhode Island, a stronghold of State Federalism, did not even send a delegation, and she refused to ratify the Constitution until 1790 (when it was already in effect). Delegates like Yates and Lansing left in anger, and subsequently fought the ratification of the Constitution in their own states.

The National Federalists were evidently much closer to the main body of the delegates than were the extreme State Federalists. National Federalism cut across the other principal cleavages and united men who disagreed on other questions. Thus the aims of National Federalism were shared by the leaders of both the democratic faction and the aristocratic faction. The principal spokesmen for National Federalism were Wilson, Mason, and Madison, who supported a democratic republic, and Gouverneur Morris, Hamilton, and King, who supported an aristocratic republic. National Federalism was not, as is sometimes supposed, exclusively an aristocratic aim nor an aristocratic doctrine: it was, and continued to be, advocated by those who believed in a democratic republic. Andrew Jackson and Abraham Lincoln did not have to invent National Federalism; they simply took it ready-made from the doctrines that prevailed at the Convention. The State Federalists, by contrast, were not only a minority at the Convention; if they were not already a minority in the nation—a question much disputed by historians—they were soon to become so, and they have remained a dissenting minority ever since.

Nor was the conflict between National Federalists and State Federalists, as is often thought, simply a mirror image of the contest between large states and small. New York, the fourth largest state, was represented not only by Hamilton, perhaps the most extreme National Federalist in the Convention, but also by Lansing and Yates, who were so

29. *Ibid.,* p. 408.

extreme in their support for State Federalism that they left the Convention and opposed the Constitution. The fifth largest state, Maryland, sent both Luther Martin, an extreme State Federalist, and Daniel Carroll, a National Federalist. The three smallest states were Delaware, Rhode Island, and Georgia. Delaware, the smallest, was represented by (among others) Read, who agreed with Hamilton that the states "must be done away."[30] Rhode Island, the second smallest, sent no delegates. The third smallest, Georgia, sent Pierce, a National Federalist.

Victory of the National Federalists

In the end, the National Federalists won a clear-cut victory. The Constitution contains all three of their principal objectives.

First, the new national government was endowed with a set of broad legal powers. Two of these, the power to tax and to regulate interstate commerce, were very comprehensive—or at least they could be so interpreted. The Congress, said the Constitution,

> . . . shall have Power To lay and collect Taxes, Duties, Imposts and Excises, to pay the Debts and provide for the common Defence and general Welfare of the United States. . . .
>
> To regulate Commerce with foreign Nations, and among the several States, and with the Indian tribes (Article I, Section 8).

As legislation of a later century was to show, these two powers were ample enough to permit extensive regulation of the economy. Under the first, for example, the production and sale of agricultural products would one day be so minutely controlled that a tobacco grower in North Carolina could not bring to market more than his allotted quota of tobacco. Under the second, even strikes by elevator operators in New York City would someday fall under the jurisdiction of the national government.

The new central government was given exclusive constitutional authority to coin money and issue currency. It could borrow money on its own credit. It could regulate bankruptcies. For all practical purposes, it had exclusive control over foreign relations, over the military establishment, over the declaration and conduct of war. It could establish a national judiciary with jurisdiction over all cases arising under the Constitution, laws of Congress, or treaties, and over a number of other matters as well. In a sweeping grant (as if to leave no doubts), the Congress was authorized "to make all Laws which shall be necessary and proper for carrying into Execution the foregoing Powers, and all other Powers vested by this Constitution in the Government of the United States, or in any Department or Office thereof" (Article I, Section 8).

In the second place, all of these powers gave the national govern-

30. *Ibid.*, p. 299.

ment legal authority over individual citizens. The president and the Congress would not have to work through the agency of state governments; they could deal directly with the individual citizens of the United States. To avoid all doubt on this crucial point, the Founders took pains to spell it out:

> This Constitution, and the Laws of the United States which shall be made in Pursuance thereof; and all Treaties made, or which shall be made, under the Authority of the United States, shall be the supreme Law of the Land; and the Judges in every State shall be bound thereby, any Thing in the Constitution or Laws of any State to the Contrary notwithstanding (Article VI).

Finally, the National Federalists insured that American citizens would be directly represented in the national government. They beat off all attempts to have the members of the lower house appointed by the state legislatures, and spelled out their victory in these words:

> The House of Representatives shall be composed of Members chosen every second Year by the People of the several States, and the Electors in each State shall have the Qualifications requisite for Electors of the most numerous Branch of the State Legislature (Article I, Section 2).

The manner in which the president was to be chosen (as we shall see in Chapter 10) was one of the most difficult practical problems that confronted the Convention. Though they changed their minds several times, in the end they decided that even the president would be chosen by the people of the United States, though in a manner that seemed somewhat more indirect to the delegates than it ever proved to be in practise (Article II, Section 1).

The states were represented, then, only in the Senate. After lengthy and often bitter controversy, it was finally agreed that the senators should be chosen by the state legislatures (Article I, Section 3). As it turned out, however, even this solution proved impractical, for it merely succeeded in converting the elections to the state legislatures into indirect senatorial elections. Nonetheless, the anomaly remained until 1913, when the Seventeenth Amendment provided for the direct election of senators by the people.

EQUAL STATES OR EQUAL CITIZENS? Although the Declaration of Independence unambiguously affirmed the principle of political equality, the men at the Convention were far from united in accepting that principle or, insofar as they did accept it, the conclusions they drew from it. Does political equality mean—as most democratic theorists have affirmed—that individual citizens are to count equally in making decisions? Or does it mean that (as in the General Assembly of the United Nations) aggregates of citizens called states, not individuals, are to be assigned equal weights? Clearly one contradicts the other, if states vary in the number of citizens. For if individuals are weighted equally, then small states must have less weight than large; but if states are weighted equally, then a citizen of a large state will have less weight than a citizen of a small state.

More concretely, if there were to be a strong national government (as the National Federalists proposed), how should the various states share their control over the new government: Equally, as under the existing Articles? By wealth or taxes, as had sometimes been proposed? Or according to population? This question provoked the bitterest controversy at the Convention, and perhaps the most pointless.

The story of this famous conflict and the final compromise has been told many times. Right at the beginning, on May 29, John Randolph of Virginia introduced a plan of government that favored National Federalism. This proposal, which quickly gained the name of the Virginia Plan, had the backing of the National Federalists, the advantage of a head start, and at once became the basis of nearly all the later work of the Convention. The second item in the Virginia Plan provided "that the rights of suffrage in the National Legislature ought to be proportioned to the Quotas of contribution [i.e., taxes], or to the number of free inhabitants, as the one or the other rule may seem best in different cases."[31] On the basis of taxes, Virginia might have had sixteen representatives to one for Georgia.[32] On the basis of population, the disparity would have been less—about seven to one.[33] Naturally delegates from some of the small states objected. On June 15 they made their countermove through Paterson of New Jersey, who presented a rival plan that would have left the existing system of equal state representation untouched.[34]

Although Paterson's New Jersey Plan was soon rejected, the conflict over representation remained to plague the Convention. At times, indeed, it looked as if the problem could not possibly be solved. The issue came up repeatedly; summer came on; tempers grew frayed; and delegates talked angrily of ending the Convention, going home, leaving the country with nothing but the old Articles. There were even hints and veiled threats of disrupting the existing Confederation. Some delegates from small states threatened their opponents from the large states by alluding to the possibility of foreign intervention. In a menacing outburst Bedford of Delaware clashed with Rufus King of Massachusetts.

31. *Ibid.*, p. 116.

32. Based on a congressional recommendation for tax quotas in 1785. See Solberg, *Federal Convention*, p. 407.

33. The delegates used various population estimates, all differing by some margin from the subsequent census of 1790. Moreover, the question whether slaves were to be counted would affect the representation of the Southern states. For population estimates, see *Ibid.*, Appendix II, pp. 407 ff.

34. *Documents*, pp. 204–207.

Bedford: . . . We have been told with a dictatorial air that this is the last moment for a fair trial in favor of a good Governm!. It will be the last indeed if the propositions reported from the Committee go forth to the people. I am under no apprehensions. The Large States dare not dissolve the Confederation. If they do the small ones will find some foreign ally of more honor and good faith, who will take them by the hand and do them justice. . . .

King: . . . I can not sit down, without taking some notice of the language of the honorable gentleman from Delaware. It was not I that uttered . . . dictatorial language. This intemperance has marked the honorabl gentleman himself. It was not I who with a vehemence unprecedented in this House, declared myself ready to turn my hopes from our common Country, and court the protection of some foreign hand. This too was the language of the Honbl member himself. I am grieved that such a thought has entered into his heart. I am more grieved that such an expression has dropped from his lips. The gentleman can only excuse it to himself on the score of passion. For myself whatever might be my distress, I would never court relief from a foreign power.[35]

Delegates from the large states in turn drew dismal pictures of the sad fate of small states if the United States were to dissolve. Both sides were intransigent. A delegate from Delaware had reminded the Convention at the end of its first week that should there be any change from the existing system of representation—that is, any departure from an equal weight for each state—"it might become their duty to retire from the Convention."[36] If the states were not given equal weight in the new government, Paterson of New Jersey warned, "N. Jersey will never confederate. . . . She would be swallowed up. He [Paterson] had rather submit to a monarch, to a despot, than to such a fate. He would not only oppose the plan here but on his return home do every thing in his power to defeat it there."[37] The other side seemed equally committed. It was his "firm belief," said Rufus King, "that Mas^{ts} would never be prevailed on to yield to an equality of votes" in the Senate.[38] Madison "entreated the gentlemen representing the small States to renounce a principle wch was confessedly unjust, [and] which c^{d} never be admitted."[39]

Compromise

On June 29, the advocates of equal representation of states suffered their first defeat. On that day, by a vote of six states to four, the delegates rejected the principle of equal state representation in the lower house (Table 8.2). From this time forward, the question centered on the Senate. On July 2, over a proposal by Ellsworth of Connecticut that each state should have one vote in the Senate, the Convention split

---

35. *Ibid.*, pp. 316–317. In the original, Madison puts these speeches in the third person.
36. *Ibid.*, p. 123.
37. *Ibid.*, p. 183.
38. *Ibid.*, p. 378.
39. *Ibid.*, p. 300.

States	In the House June 29	In the Senate July 2	In the Senate July 7
Solid "Yes"			
Connecticut	Yes	Yes	Yes
New York	Yes	Yes	Yes
New Jersey	Yes	Yes	Yes
Delaware	Yes	Yes	Yes
Solid "No"			
Virginia	No	No	No
Pennsylvania	No	No	No
South Carolina	No	No	No
Waverers			
Maryland	Divided	Yes	Yes
North Carolina	No	No	Yes
Massachusetts	No	No	Divided
Georgia	No	Divided	Divided
Yes	4	5	6
No	6	5	3
Divided	1	1	2
	11*	11*	11*

*Rhode Island sent no delegates. Those from New Hampshire arrived later.
Sources: *Documents,* pp. 303, 324, 340.

in two. Five states supported Ellsworth's motion, five opposed it, and one was divided (Table 8.2). The Convention, split asunder, agreed to appoint a committee. The committee, consisting of one member from each state, reported back three days later with the recommendation "that in the 2ᵈ branch each State shall have an equal vote."[40] On July 7 the decisive vote was taken on the committee report. Among the delegations that had fought against this principle, only Virginia, Pennsylvania, and South Carolina held firm to the last. North Carolina now swung to the other side. The vote of Massachusetts was lost because the delegates from Massachusetts were split. Georgia was also divided. Six states favored the compromise (Table 8.2). Thus, the issue was put to rest by a compromise that had little to be said for it except for one extremely important virtue: its acceptability.

A Principle or a Bargain?

Though equal state representation has sometimes been hailed as a great constitutional principle, Hamilton's judgment of the controversy was not far off the mark: "The truth is," he said, with the cruel candor of youth that made him both feared and admired, "it is a contest for

40. *Ibid.,* p. 324.

power, not for liberty."[41] Because the conflict was dramatic and dangerous, and because it had the happy ending Americans firmly believe in,
it has been given an importance by later generations out of all proportion
to its intrinsic significance. For the advocates of equal representation of
the states were defending a principle that events were to make obsolete.

Men like Madison and Wilson foresaw this with considerable clarity.
"Can we forget for whom we are forming a Government?" Wilson asked.
"Is it for *men,* or for the imaginary beings called *States?*"[42] Madison
asked:

> Was a combination to be apprehended from the mere circumstance of
> equality of size? Experience suggested no such danger. The journals of
> Cong^s did not present any peculiar association of these States in the votes
> recorded. . . . Experience rather taught a contrary lesson. . . . The States
> were divided into different interests not by their difference of size, but by
> other circumstances.[43]

Madison proved to be right. There has, in fact, never been a significant
conflict between the citizens of small states and the citizens of large
states. Or, to put it another way, there has been no important controversy in the United States that has not cut squarely across the people
in both small states and large.

Nonetheless, equal representation of states in the Senate was firmly
written into the Constitution (Article I, Section 3). And those delegates
like Madison and Wilson who had so vigorously opposed a bad principle
preferred compromise to a dissolution of the union, swallowed their
bitterness, and accepted defeat—though they always refused to concede
that the outcome was anything more exalted than an unprincipled
bargain that had to be accepted, not because it was just, but merely
because the alternatives were still more unpleasant.

THE UNCOMPLETED
AGENDA
As the years passed, and the Constitution took an exalted place in the
American creed alongside a faith in the virtues of democracy, the
Founders came to be treated less as men than as gods. More than a
century later, when critics like Charles Beard punctured the myth by
showing that they were not gods but only men, and men with invest-
ments, it came to be intellectually fashionable to hold that the Founders
really carried through a kind of aristocratic counterrevolution that somehow was converted, nonetheless, into a democratic republic as time
wore on.

A more exact interpretation than either of these would surely be:
The Founders could not create either a polyarchy or an oligarchy. What-

---

41. *Ibid.,* p. 301.
42. *Ibid.,* p. 307.
43. *Ibid.,* pp. 292, 310.

ever their intentions were—as we have seen they did not agree on these—what they did was to create a framework of government which, once it had been accepted, might become either a polyarchy or a kind of aristocratic or oligarchic republic. Which it was to be depended not on what any group of men could do in three or four months at a Convention in Philadelphia, but on what was to happen later, over years and decades and perhaps centuries, among men outside the Convention and generations still unborn. And what these men, these Americans then living and yet to be born would do, in turn depended on many factors— factors that no one at the Convention could control or even predict, some of which are even today little understood.

One thing is perfectly clear now, even if it was not so clear at the time: given the right conditions, the framework of government they had created could become a polyarchy.

SUMMARY   1. The Founders were both revolutionary and conservative:

☐ They were revolutionary insofar as they attempted to establish a national government on republican principles over a great domain; for prior experience, conventional wisdom, and political science asserted that a republic could exist only in a small unit, such as a city-state.

☐ In the American setting, however, they were for the most part building on existing institutions, practises, traditions, and already dominant social forces, rather than instituting radically new and unfamiliar political, social, or economic relationships.

2. Older interpretations that portrayed the Founders as a unified group of counterrevolutionaries who defeated the aspirations for democracy and equality of the small farmers, the overwhelming majority of the American people at the time, are rendered implausible because:

☐ Evidence that has become available since the older view was proposed shows that the suffrage was in fact rather widely dispersed in most states. Yet despite their opportunity to do so, voters did not turn out to vote down the proposed Constitution.

☐ In a very short time the Constitution seems to have acquired very wide approval among the general population, including particularly the small farmers. In fact, those who became the main leaders of the small farmers, like James Madison, helped to draft the Constitution and supported it strongly.

☐ The Founders were by no means united on certain basic matters.

3. They were generally agreed on:

☐ The need to compromise
☐ The need to partition authority.

4. Nonetheless, they disagreed over:

☐ Democracy versus aristocracy
☐ A national republic versus a confederacy
☐ Whether political equality applied to individuals or to states.

5. As to democracy versus aristocracy:

☐ They disagreed over whether the president and members of the Senate should have a limited term or hold office for life or good behavior, and whether the right to vote should be constitutionally restricted to free holders or property owners of some sort.
☐ They agreed, however on:
The need for an important element of popular participation in the national government.
The need to partition authority so as to prevent full majority rule.
Mistrust of power.
The principles of limited authority, balanced authority, and balanced social power.
☐ These agreements influenced the Constitution in important ways.

6. As to a confederacy versus a national republic, the National Federalists won a clear-cut victory.

7. As to equal states or equal citizens, in order to have an acceptable document, those like Madison who held that the states should be represented entirely by population were finally compelled to compromise with those who held out for equality of state representation. The compromise was equal state representation in the Senate.

8. The Founders themselves did not establish polyarchy. Their framework of government could have been adapted to polyarchy, as events were to prove, or had American conditions and dominant beliefs been less favorable to the development of polyarchy, to an aristocratic or oligarchic republic.

How American Conditions
Favored Polyarchy

9

In 1835 an English visitor to the United States, Harriet Martineau, paid a visit to James Madison, who was then 84 and within a year of his death. "Mr. Madison remarked to me," she wrote later, "that the United States had been 'useful in proving things before held impossible'."[1]

This view of the American experience was not uncommon in the nineteenth century. It attracted foreigners like Alexis de Tocqueville and Miss Martineau to the United States in order to unravel the mystery.

> . . . The experiment of the particular constitution of the United States may fail [Miss Martineau went on to say]; but the great principle which, whether successfully or not, it strives to embody, —the capacity of mankind for self-government, —is established for ever. It has, as Mr. Madison said, proved a thing previously held impossible.[2]

Today, polyarchy is no longer a novelty. Nearly three dozen countries, as we have seen, operate under systems of polyarchic government. Some sixteen or seventeen of these countries have done so for more than half a century (if we except a few periods of foreign occupation in the First and Second World Wars).

Although polyarchy is not novel, it nonetheless remains comparatively uncommon. Only about one-fifth of the countries of the world have polyarchies, and in some of these countries polyarchy is new and shaky. Why polyarchy develops and endures in some countries and not in others is a question that is still surrounded by a good deal of uncertainty and conjecture.

Polyarchy not only developed first in the United States, but it has proved highly durable there. Throughout the nineteenth century Ameri-

1. Harriet Martineau, *Society in America*, ed. S. M. Lipset (Garden City: Anchor Books, 1962), p. 57.
2. *Ibid.*, p. 58.

cans and foreigners were often fascinated—and sometimes repelled—by the existence of a 'democracy' in this country. Its mere presence seemed to offer visible proof that 'democracy' in a large country was not a wholly utopian idea. Yet the proof generated a mystery: What was required for such an experiment to succeed? What was it about this country that created a congenial soil for the rapid evolution of this new political form? How was it that the Americans were able to prove "a thing previously held impossible"?

The answer—at the very least, an important part of the answer—lies in three general conditions that facilitated the rapid development of polyarchy. These were:

☐ The pervasiveness of equality
☐ The convergence on a democratic belief system
☐ The constitutional framework.

Yet each of these favorable conditions had an unfavorable counterpart that could—and as it happened, would—create troublesome problems for the American polyarchy.

FIRST CONDITION: With few exceptions, Europeans who came to the United States during
EQUALITIES the first half of the nineteenth century were struck by the degree of political, social, and economic equality among Americans. Tocqueville made this observation the very kernel of his famous analysis of American democracy. Some foreign visitors were charmed, some were offended, but all agreed that the prevalence of equality was truly astounding.

Even when considered in the most cautious light, Tocqueville's conclusion appears to be correct: the world had never before witnessed so much equality of condition as existed in America. In everything that one says on this topic, of course, one is bound to except the Afro-Americans, particularly the great bulk who were slaves in the Southern states. This is no slight exception, but rather, as I indicated in Chapter 7, a basic feature that distinguishes polyarchy in America from polyarchy elsewhere. It is well to keep in mind, then, that I speak at the moment only of the free white population. Among these there was not only a fair approximation of universal male suffrage, but evidently an amazing degree of social and economic equality as well. At the Convention, Charles Pinckney had portrayed Americans in words that were to be echoed two generations later by Tocqueville:

> . . . Among [Americans] there are fewer distinctions of fortune & less of rank, than among the inhabitants of any other nation. . . . Equality is . . . the leading feature of the U. States.[3]

---

3. *Documents.*, pp. 267, 270.

And Pinckney, like Tocqueville, pointed to the principle reason, the availability of land:

> ... this equality is likely to continue, because in a new Country, possessing immense tracts of uncultivated lands, where every temptation is offered to emigration & where industry must be rewarded with competency, there will be few poor, and few dependent.[4]

If Pinckney's statement stood alone, we could count it as the kind of exaggerated rhetoric about equality that Americans seem to enjoy hearing themselves say to one another. But Pinckney's observation in 1787 was also Tocqueville's in 1832. *Democracy in America* begins with:

> Among the novel objects that attracted my attention during my stay in the United States nothing struck me more forcibly than the general equality of condition among the people. I readily discovered the prodigious influence that this primary fact exercises on the whole course of society; it gives a peculiar direction to public opinion and a peculiar tenor to the laws; it imparts new maxims to the governing authorities and peculiar habits to the governed. I soon perceived that the influence of this fact extends far beyond the political character and the laws of the country, and that it has no less effect on civil society than on government; it creates opinions, gives birth to new sentiments, founds novel customs, and modifies whatever it does not produce. The more I advanced in the study of American society, the more I perceived that this equality of condition is the fundamental fact from which all others seem to be derived and the central point at which all my observations constantly terminated.[5]

Economic equality. Unfortunately the kinds of statistical information one would need in order to make these observations more precise is lacking.[6] Yet one fact is beyond argument: during the first half century of experience under the new Constitution, the United States was a country of farmers. Until 1840, seven out of ten workers were engaged in farming; in the two decades before the Civil War the proportion fell, but even in 1860, six out of every ten were in agriculture. Americans were, therefore, a rural people. In 1790, only 5 percent of the population lived in places with 2,500 inhabitants or more. In the 1830s, when Tocqueville and Harriet Martineau visited the United States, the proportion was about 10 percent. As late as 1860, it was only 20 percent.[7]

Unfortunately we can only guess at the distribution of property ownership. But observers agreed that among this vast farming popula-

4. *Ibid.,* p. 267.

5. Alexis de Tocqueville, *Democracy in America,* 2 vols. (New York: Vintage Books, 1955), vol. I, p. 3. On this general point and its bearing on American development, see Louis Hartz, *The Liberal Tradition in America* (New York: Harcourt, Brace, 1955).

6. See, however, Ralph L. Andreano, "Trends and Variations in Economic Welfare in the United States before the Civil War," in *New Views on American Economic Development,* ed. R. L. Andreano (Cambridge: Schenkman, 1965), pp. 131–167.

7. *Historical Statistics of the United States, Colonial Times to 1957,* prepared by the Bureau of the Census, with the cooperation of the Social Science Research Council (Washington, D.C.: U.S. Government Printing Office, 1960), p. 9, Series A 34–50; p. 72, Series D 36–45.

tion, property was, thanks to the availability of land, widely diffused. Tocqueville and Martineau found few rich and few poor, even though frontier families sometimes lived under the most miserable conditions, particularly during their first years. Because land was plentiful in relation to the population, labor was relatively scarce; society put a premium on a man's labor. In the towns and cities, wages were relatively high. In the countryside, sons of farmers found it possible to acquire their own farms. The European practise of keeping landed estates intact by passing them on to the eldest son was uncommon; even among the land-rich Patroons of New York, Miss Martineau reported, the practise was disappearing.[8]

Equality extended in other directions, too. In a nation of farmers, there was no peasantry, and not even any tradition of peasantry in the European sense. Large landed estates existed, to be sure, particularly in the South; but it was extremely difficult to keep free white farm labor from leaving. "The people of the United States," Miss Martineau observed, "choose to be proprietors of land, not tenants."[9] The large governmental establishments of the centralized European monarchies scarcely existed in the United States of 1831; in a population of over 13 million only 11,491 persons were employed by the federal government—and of these, nearly 9,000 were in the Post Office[10] and therefore dispersed throughout the country. The vast private corporations created by industrial capitalism had not yet arrived; the giant factories, the great financiers, the urban proletariat, the army of clerks and white-collar workers—these were still unknown. Nearly everyone, according to Tocqueville, had at least a modest education; though he encountered few great scholars in his travels, he also found few wholly uneducated people. In fact, though illiteracy was high among Negro slaves, among the whites it was exceedingly low for the time; between 1840 and 1860, the U.S. Census reported that among white people 20 years of age or over, only about one in ten could not read and write.[11]

Social equality. Given the substantial degree of equality that prevailed in property, incomes, wealth, control over economic enterprise, and education, it is not surprising that there was also a remarkable degree of equality in social relations among Americans. Europeans were frequently struck by the comparative weakness of social barriers among Americans, particularly outside the Eastern cities, and most notably in the agricultural West. Even servants did not give the deference to which an Englishman or European was accustomed. Yet Miss Martineau, per-

8. Martineau, *Society in America*, p. 264.

9. *Ibid.,* p. 179.

10. *Historical Statistics,* p. 710, Series Y 241-250.

11. *Ibid.,* p. 206.

haps too generously, insisted that "the manners of the Americans [in America] are the best I ever saw."[12] Indeed, among Americans then, as now, even family relationships were conducted with an astonishing amount of equality. The lack of strong parental domination, the tendency of parents to rely more on persuasion than severe punishment, and the free and easy ways of American children were as evident to Tocqueville and Harriet Martineau in the 1830s as they are to foreign visitors today. "For my own part," said Miss Martineau, "I delight in the American children"; but (it is only fair to add) what she found charming, many others saw as insolence and lack of proper deference toward adults. Both Tocqueville and Miss Martineau concluded that the family was a kind of miniature training ground in 'democratic' attitudes.

Beliefs in equality. Just as striking to the foreigner as all other aspects of equality was the extent to which Americans seemed to believe that equality was a virtue. No doubt there was a good deal of rhetoric, muddleheadedness, and hypocrisy in the widespread emphasis by Americans on the virtues of equality. But thoughtful foreigners like Tocqueville and Harriet Martineau held that the American belief in equality went far deeper than mere cant; to a greater extent than in any other society up until that time, it seemed to them, Americans, taken in the large, believed that in essential value as a human being, one person was very much like another. Sixty years after Tocqueville and Martineau, another famous observer from abroad, James Bryce, emphasized the same point in a happy metaphor:

> . . . In America men hold others to be at bottom exactly the same as them-
> selves. If a man is enormously rich . . . or if he is a great orator . . . or a
> great soldier . . . or a great writer . . . or a President, so much the better
> for him. He is an object of interest, perhaps of admiration, possibly even of
> reverence. But he is deemed to be still of the same flesh and blood as other
> men. The admiration felt for him may be a reason for going to see him and
> longing to shake hands with him. But it is not a reason for bowing down to
> him, or addressing him in deferential terms, or treating him as if he was
> porcelain and yourself only earthenware.[13]

Qualification: Inequalities

Since so much of all that has just been said about equality in agrarian America has long since passed into American mythology to provide us with gilt aplenty for our Golden Age, it might have been superfluous to emphasize the matter so strongly, except for one thing: Unlike many other American myths, this particular one seems to have been substantially true. And unless we realize how extensive was the

---

12. Martineau, *Society in America*, p. 272.
13. James Bryce, *The American Commonwealth*, 2 vols. (London and New York: Macmillan, 1889), vol. II, p. 606.

equality of condition among Americans—to use the phrase of both Pinckney and Tocqueville—in the first half century or so after the men at the Convention completed their labors, we shall not be able to understand why polyarchy took root so readily in this soil and survived through some hard times.

However, if equality prevailed among Americans to a degree that had not been matched anywhere up to that time (and perhaps has not been matched since even in the United States), there were nonetheless important exceptions, and these the myth-makers usually forget to mention. Some of these exceptions were to threaten the system at its foundations; not even in our time have we seen the last of them.

Social status. In the first place, if social classes in the harsh European fashion were absent in America, rudimentary forms of social stratification existed among the white population, most markedly in the old cities along the eastern seaboard and in the South. Harriet Martineau had some strong words to say about the snobbery she encountered among

> those who consider themselves the aristocracy of the United States: the wealthy and showy citizens of the Atlantic ports. . . . I was told a great deal about "the first people in Boston": which is perhaps as aristocratic, vain and vulgar a city, as described by its own "first people," as any in the world.[14]

Were these rudimentary social classes merely a legacy of the past—or, worse, a foreshadowing of the future? Was equality only a fleeting aspect of American life? Would 'equality of condition' become more and more a myth, a dream about a vanished Golden Age? And would the new American aristocrats look with disdain on the political institutions of a democratic republic? Harriet Martineau was, as usual, optimistic:

> . . . Such an aristocracy must remain otherwise too insignificant to be dangerous. It cannot choose its own members, restrict its own numbers, or keep its gentility from contamination; for it must be perpetuated, not by hereditary transmission, but by accessions from below. Grocers grow rich, and mechanics become governors of States; and happily there is no law, nor reason, nor desire that it should be otherwise. This little cloud will always overhang the republic, like the perpetual vapour which hovers over Niagara, thrown up by the force and regularity of the movement below.[15]

Business. To the extent that social equality reflected a general equality in property, wealth, and control over economic enterprise, the pervasive equality that seemed to be so characteristic of American agrarian society rested upon a transitory phenomenon—the fact that Americans were predominantly a nation of farmers in a country where there was a vast supply of cheap land. But if Americans became a nation of businessmen

14. Martineau, *Society in America*, p. 260.
15. *Ibid.*, p. 263.

and employees, what then? In 1800 about 10 percent of the people in the labor force were employees. In 1860 the number had grown to 60 percent. By 1960, 90 percent would be working for others.[16] What would happen when agrarian capitalism gave way to business capitalism? One answer was at least suggested by those parts of the United States where this had already occurred.

For urban business enterprise—commerce, banking, manufacturing —provided the second important source of inequalities. To be sure, business enterprise was still small; it was confined to a few cities. But it was exactly in the cities that the consequences were evident: disparities of wealth, the sharper delineation of social 'classes,' greater possibilities of political corruption. This was why men like Jefferson and Madison often argued that the United States should, if possible, remain a nation of farmers and that business enterprise should not be encouraged; for they held that the equality of condition necessary to a democratic republic could not be maintained in a society that was based on business rather than on small farmers.

Was there any ground for the Jeffersonian dream of an agrarian democracy or for the fear that business enterprise and manufacturing would endanger democracy? Farmers are not necessarily more knowledgeable, upright, or more civic-minded than city dwellers,[17] and a nation of landlords and peasants would surely be no Eden for democrats. Yet a country made up exclusively of small farmers is likely to be a country where equality prevails. The kernel of truth in the myth, then, was this: A nation of small farmers would almost automatically preserve a high degree of economic, social, and political equality. By contrast, the development of commerce, industry, manufacturers, and banking on a large scale was bound to generate inequalities—in wealth, income, control over economic enterprise, social status, knowledge, skill, and, because of these, in power too. Although Jefferson and Madison did

16. Stanley Lebergott, "Labor Force Mobility and Employment," in Andreano, *New Views on American Economic Development*, pp. 362–376, at p. 369.

17. In fact, whenever measurable differences in the performance of civic duties can be found, American farmers tend to come off rather badly in comparison with city dwellers. Whether this was true in the early nineteenth century, we cannot say. In recent times, farmers seem to have been less interested in politics, felt less involved, and been less likely to vote than urban residents; among city people, only the unskilled workers show so little interest, involvement, and participation. Compared with city people today, farmers do not write or wire their congressmen or senators as often; they are less likely to be asked by others to express their political views; they express a weaker sense of citizen duty; they feel less confident and effective in politics; they are less likely than white-collar workers to have opinions on international and domestic issues, and have no opinions about as frequently as blue-collar workers. Nor can the differences be explained by educational inequalities, for even when we compare citizens with the same general level of education—grade school, or high school, or college—the differences tend to remain. In general, on all the measures, farmers trail behind professional people, businessmen, and white-collar workers and usually a bit behind skilled workers; the only urban group they often exceed, and not by much, are the unskilled laborers. For evidence, see Robert A. Lane, *Political Life* (Glencoe: Free Press, 1959), pp. 68, 91; V. O. Key, Jr., *Public Opinion and American Democracy* (New York: Knopf, 1961), pp. 326, 329, 333; and Angus Campbell, Philip E. Converse, Warren E. Miller, and Donald E. Stokes, *The American Voter* (New York: Wiley 1960), p. 411.

Table 9.1
Negro Population in the
United States, 1800 to 1860

| | Total Population | Negro | |
		Total	Slave
	(000)	(000)	(000)
1800	5,297	1,002	894
1810	7,224	1,378	1,191
1820	9,618	1,772	1,538
1830	12,901	2,328	2,009
1840	17,120	2,874	2,487
1850	23,261	3,639	3,205
1860	31,513	4,442	3,954

Source: *Historical Statistics*, p. 9, Series A 34-50; A 59-70. For 1800 and 1810, figures used for Negroes are for nonwhites.

Table 9.2
Negro Population in the
South, 1800 to 1860

| | Total Population | Negro | |
		Total	Slave
	(000)	(000)	(000)
1800	2,622	918	857
1810	3,461	1,268	1,160
1820	4,419	1,643	1,508
1830	5,707	2,162	1,980
1840	6,950	2,642	2,428
1850	8,983	3,352	3,117
1860	11,133	4,097	3,838

Source: *Historical Statistics*, p. 12, Series A 95-122.

not accurately foresee the shape of the future, they were right in their conjecture that the expansion of commerce and industry would create a serious obstacle to achieving a high degree of democrary in America—in the cities of the eastern seaboard, in fact, it had already done so in their own day.

Blacks. The third exception to the prevalence of social, economic, and political equality was, as I have already said, the Afro-American. Whether he was free or slave, he discovered that the prevailing practises of the white man placed him in a position of social, economic, and political subordination. Yet blacks were no trifling minority; from 1800 to 1860 they were 15 to 20 percent of the population of the United States; in the South, one out of every three persons was a slave (Tables 9.1, 9.2).

In a society that preached equality and to a surprising extent practised what it preached, slavery was an anomaly; and everyone knew it. It had been a sore issue at the Constitutional Convention. Yet no one wanted to face the issue squarely, then or later, for everyone knew it was explosive. When Harriet Martineau entered the United States in 1834,

. . . there was an absolute and almost ominous silence in Congress about slavery. Almost every leading man told me in conversation that it was the grand question of all; that every member's mind was full of it; that nearly all other questions were much affected, or wholly determined by it; yet no one even alluded to it in public.[18]

In 1836, the House of Representatives even went so far as to adopt a Gag Rule, as it came to be called, preventing the House from considering "all petitions, memorials, resolutions, propositions, or papers relating in any way or to any extent whatever to the subject of slavery or the abolition of slavery."[19]

The subjection of the blacks, a monument to inequality, cast a dark shadow over the prospects of democracy in America. For one thing, an ideology that justified slavery was difficult to reconcile with an ideology that made virtues of equality, liberty, and democracy. Yet the barefaced contradiction was too much to live with. There began, as a result, that strange effort to construct an ideology that justified both democracy and slavery, a task (carried on most enthusiastically but not exclusively in the South) that proved to be one long travail of tortured logic and denial of humanity to the Negro—whatever the cost to fact, reason, and sentiments of humanity.

Political participation. Another set of differences that contributed heavily to political inequality among Americans were the elemental causes of inequality mentioned in Chapter 5—differences in political skills and incentives. In every political system, some citizens are much less interested and active in politics than others. Apathetic citizens disfranchise themselves; active citizens gain influence. Among Americans, as among other peoples, these differences are pronounced.

Thus a recent survey confirms a long accumulation of depressing findings on levels of political participation among Americans (Table 9.3). Although seven out of ten citizens in the sample had voted in a recent presidential election, less than half said they voted regularly in local elections. About a quarter tried to persuade others how to vote during campaigns or had ever worked for a party. About one out of five had attended political rallies or had initiated a contact with officials. Only one out of eight had contributed money in a political campaign and only one out of twelve reported being a member of a political organization. More encouraging was the relatively higher level of cooperative political activity: about a third said they had worked with a local group to deal with a social problem and a third reported being active members of an organization engaged in community activities.

Is this only a recent development? Were the early years of the

---

18. Martineau, *Society in America*, pp. 78–79.
19. Richard B. Morris, *Encyclopedia of American History* (New York: Harper & Bros., 1953), p. 179.

Table 9.3

Participation in Various Political Activities in the United States

	Proportion Active[a] %
A. Taking Part in Campaign Activities	
Persuade others how to vote	28
Ever worked for a party	26
Attended political rallies	19
Contributed money in a political campaign	13
Member of a political club or organization	8
B. Voting	
Voted in 1964 presidential election	72
Voted in 1960 presidential election	71
Votes regularly in local elections	47
C. Cooperative Activities	
Worked through local group	30
Helped form local group	14
Active member of organization engaged in community activities	32
D. Contacting Officials	
Contacted local officials	20
Contacted extralocal officials	18

[a]For a simpler presentation, we have collapsed some of the multiple categories into dichotomies. In generating linear statistics, however, we have used the full range of variation if such variation represented an underlying continuum and if bivariate relations among such variables were approximately linear.

Source: Sidney Verba, Norman H. Nie, and Jae-on Kim, "The Modes of Democratic Participation: A Cross-National Comparison," *Sage Professional Papers in Comparative Politics* (Beverly Hills: Sage Publications, 1971), vol. 2, no. 01-013, p. 20, by permission of the publisher, Sage Publications, Inc.

republic, as our myth-makers tell us, a political Golden Age when citizens were far more interested, knowledgeable and active in politics than they are today? Although we do not have nearly enough or the right kinds of data to permit us to speak with confidence, the myth does not seem to survive a critical examination. Unfortunately, Tocqueville, a shrewd observer of many things, contributed to the myth by describing the American as extraordinarily concerned with politics. "To take a hand in the regulation of society and to discuss it is his biggest concern and, so to speak, the only pleasure an American knows."[20] Tocqueville's observations, however, ran counter to those of Harriet Martineau, who was in the United States at almost the same time and for a longer period. In fact she wrote a special section on "Apathy in Citizenship."[21] Half a century later, another Englishman, James Bryce, came to the same conclusion:

> The citizen has little time to think about political problems. Engrossing all the working hours, his avocation leaves him only stray moments for this fundamental duty. . . . He has not leisure to do it for himself, and must

20. Tocqueville, *Democracy in America*, vol. I, p. 260.

21. Martineau, *Society in America*, pp. 106–108.

Figure 9.1
Percent of Total Population
Voting in Presidential
Election, 1824-1968

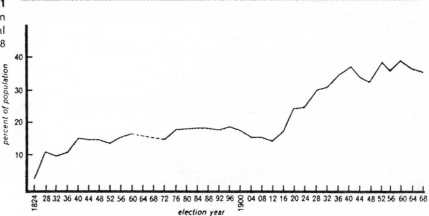

Sources: Robert Lane, *Political Life*, p. 20; and *Statistical Abstract of the United States, 1970*, U.S. Bureau of the Census (Washington, D.C.: U.S. Government Printing Office, 1970), p. 5, Table 2; p. 354, Table 535.

practically lean upon and follow his party. It astonished me in 1870 and 1881 to find how small a part politics played in conversation among the best educated classes and generally in the cities.[22]

These are impressions. An examination of the number of people who have voted in presidential elections indicates several conclusions. First, the percentage of the total population voting in presidential elections rose rapidly until 1840 and then remained rather stable until the Civil War. After the Civil War the proportion increased slightly, no doubt because of the newly enfranchised Negroes. From 1896 to 1912, the proportion declined; with the general enfranchisement of women in 1930, the proportion rose to new heights (Figure 9.1). Thus the percentage of the total population voting in presidential elections has actually increased over the whole period.

However, over against the rising percentage of voters in the population there was also a countertrend: for the number of persons eligible to vote seems to have increased more rapidly than the number of persons who actually voted (Figure 9.2). Thus the proportion of the electorate that does not bother to go to the polls has been higher in the twentieth century than in the nineteenth. However, the data are shaky, for it is difficult to arrive at reliable historical estimates of the numbers actually eligible to vote in all the states. One cannot be entirely sure, then, that

22. Bryce, *American Commonwealth*, vol. II, p. 249.

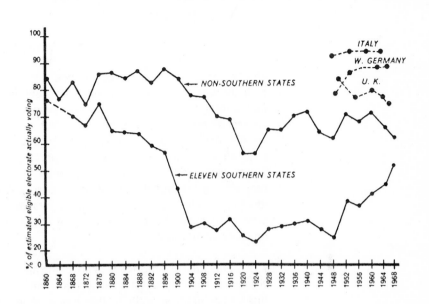

Sources: Walter Dean Burnham, "The Changing Shape of the American Political Universe," *American Political Science Review*, 59 (March, 1965), 11; *Statistical Abstract 1970*, pp. 368, 371; and Stein Rokkan and Jean Meyriat, eds., *International Guide to Electoral Statistics* (The Hague: Mouton, 1969).

the myth is false; but it is not sustained by the evidence now at hand. In any case, it is quite clear that then, as now, only a small percentage of citizens gave much time to politics; only a few were willing to make a career out of politics; and it was these professional politicians who, then as now, organized and controlled those vital instruments of polyarchy, the political parties.

SECOND CONDITION: IDEOLOGICAL CONVERGENCE

For a polyarchy to survive, political equality is not enough. Political equals may quarrel: quarreling may bring civil strife. The policies of a majority may seem oppressive to a minority: the minority may revolt. Consent, you may remember, has a practical side: if the laws passed by the representatives of a majority fail to gain the tacit 'consent' of a large minority, a polyarchy is likely to be ripped apart.

In this case, too, destiny seemed to favor polyarchy in America, for during the first half century under the new Constitution, there were powerful forces uniting Americans, forces strong enough to overcome centrifugal tendencies toward disintegration. Among these was the rapid growth of a comparatively high degree of ideological agreement on a number of key aspects of their society.

Equality and democracy. Unfortunately, we have no more than impressionistic evidence to go on; despite many learned attempts to do so, no one can say with much confidence what the content of these beliefs actually was. However, judging from contemporary descriptions, and particularly from Tocqueville, most Americans seemed to affirm the virtues of equality and democracy. Not all, to be sure, were equally fervent; nor was public utterance always the same as private belief; and practise did not necessarily correspond perfectly with belief. Both Tocqueville and Martineau found skepticism and cynicism about democracy among the wealthy strata of the population. Nonetheless no sharp ideological cleavage between supporters and opponents was visible, simply because the opponents were too few and too fearful of the opinions of the rest.

The Constitution. Americans also came to agree very quickly on the virtues of their constitutional system. The reverence of Americans for the Constitution, an attitude that has at different times puzzled, astonished, amused, and irritated foreign observers, evidently developed rapidly. Within an unbelievably short time, hardly more than a decade, Americans no longer debated seriously whether their constitutional system was good or bad; it appeared to be a postulate almost universally subscribed to that the American Constitution was a good one, if not in fact the best in the world. Americans ceased to be divided over questions of constitutional structure. There was, however, one aspect of the Constitution on which Americans did not wholly agree, and that was the full nature of the powers granted to the federal government. Yet even in this case the debate was not so much over the virtues of the Constitution, per se, as whether this or that interpretation of the Constitution was the correct one. Very early, therefore, a familiar semantic device appeared in American politics that continues down to the present time. To question the Constitution itself was taboo; one argued instead over what the Constitution 'really' meant. In this it was possible to isolate the Constitution from political debate.

Compromise. Not only Tocqueville but also the political practises of that time suggest that Americans also tended to agree on the virtues of political compromise. Tocqueville remarked on the self-restraint of Americans, on their reluctance not to push a good point too far.

Nationhood. With exceptional speed, Americans also developed a sense of nationhood. If it is difficult to be sure what the content of American beliefs is or has been, it is even harder to determine the exact nature of American national feeling. That such a nationalism exists is, however, beyond doubt, and evidently it came about surprisingly soon. Foreigners and Americans alike began to observe from the time of the Revolution onward that Americans seemed to feel themselves more and more to be a distinct people, a unique people, not Englishmen now, nor Canadians, nor Frenchmen, nor Mexicans, nor any other people but Americans. Americans soon gained a reputation among Europeans for being touchy about the virtues of the United States and even for a sort of national vanity. Traveling abroad, blowhard Americans often alienated foreigners, as they have done ever since; while on this side of the Atlantic, the visitor who implied that the United States had any blemishes was likely to stir up a resentful counterattack.

Tocqueville's description. There is perhaps no more vivid description of this unity of beliefs than Tocqueville's summary:

> The observer who examines what is passing in the United States . . . will readily discover that their inhabitants, though divided into twenty-four distinct sovereignties, still constitute a single people; and he may perhaps be led to think that the Anglo-American Union is more truly a united society than some nations of Europe which live under the same legislation and the same prince.
>
> Although the Anglo-Americans have several religious sects, they all regard religion in the same manner. They are not always agreed upon the measures that are most conducive to good government, and they vary upon some of the forms of government which it is expedient to adopt; but they are unanimous upon the general principles that ought to rule human society. From Maine to the Floridas, and from the Missouri to the Atlantic Ocean, the people are held to be the source of all legitimate power. The same notions are entertained respecting liberty and equality, the liberty of the press, the right of association, the jury, and the responsibility of the agents of government.
>
> If we turn from their political and religious opinions to the moral and philosophical principles that regulate the daily actions of life and govern their conduct, we still find the same uniformity. The Anglo-Americans acknowledge the moral authority of the reason of the community as they acknowledge the political authority of the mass of citizens; and they hold that public opinion is the surest arbiter of what is lawful or forbidden, true or false. The majority of them believe that a man by following his own interest, rightly understood, will be led to do what is just and good. They hold that every man is born in possession of the right of self-government, and that no one has the right of constraining his fellow creatures to be happy. They all have a lively faith in the perfectibility of man, they judge that the diffusion of knowledge must necessarily be advantageous, and the consequences of ignorance fatal; they all consider society as a body in a state of improvement, humanity as a changing scene, in which nothing is, or ought to be, permanent; and they admit that what appears to them today to be good, may be superseded by something better tomorrow. I do not give all these opinions as true, but as American opinions.

Not only are the Anglo-Americans united by these common opinions, but they are separated from all other nations by a feeling of pride. For the last fifty years no pains have been spared to convince the inhabitants of the United States that they are the only religious, enlightened, and free people. They perceive that, for the present, their own democratic institutions prosper, while those of other countries fail; hence they conceive a high opinion of their superiority and are not very remote from believing themselves to be a distinct species of mankind.[23]

The Persistence of Ideological Convergence

The early tendency toward a widely shared set of beliefs has persisted throughout American history. However, a word of warning may be useful at this point: It is easy to exaggerate, as foreigners often do after visiting this country, the extent to which Americans agree. As we shall see, Americans do disagree among themselves; sometimes these disagreements lead to severe conflict; in one case they led to civil war.

Keeping in mind that there are dissenting minorities on every proposition and that once in every generation or thereabouts Americans engage in severe conflicts, the evidence from surveys[24] indicates that until recently:

☐ It was very nearly impossible to find an American who said that he was opposed to democracy or favored some alternative—at least for the United States. On the contrary, nearly everyone professed to believe that democracy is the best form of government.[25]

☐ Although substantial numbers of citizens approved of proposals for specific constitutional changes, the broad elements of the system were widely endorsed.[26]

---

23. Tocqueville, *Democracy In America*, vol. I, pp. 409–410.

24. An exceptionally useful source for anyone interested in a profile of recent American political attitudes is Lloyd Free and Hadley Cantril, *The Political Beliefs of Americans: A Study of Public Opinion* (New Brunswick: Rutgers University Press, 1967). The best summary of survey evidence on political attitudes of young people, with numerous citations to specific surveys, is Seymour Martin Lipset, "Youth and Politics," in *Contemporary Social Problems*, eds. R. K. Merton and Robert Nisbet (New York: Harcourt Brace Jovanovich, 1971), pp. 743–791. A useful comparison of college youth, noncollege youth, and adults is contained in Daniel Yankelovich, Inc., *Generations Apart*, a study conducted by Daniel Yankelovich, Inc., for the Columbia Broadcasting System (New York: Columbia Broadcasting System, 1969). Additional information can also be found in: Clyde Kluckhohn, "The Evolution of Contemporary American Values," *Daedalus*, 87, no. 2 (Spring, 1958), 78–109; Robert Lane, *Political Ideology, Why the American Common Man Believes What He Does* (New York: Free Press of Glencoe, 1962); Gabriel A. Almond and Sidney Verba, *The Civic Culture, Political Attitudes and Democracy in Five Nations* (Princeton: Princeton University Press, 1963); Key, *Public Opinion*; Herbert McClosky, "Consensus and Ideology in American Politics," *American Political Science Review*, 58, no. 2 (June, 1964), 361–382.

25. James W. Prothro and C. W. Grigg, "Fundamental Principles of Democracy: Bases of Agreement and Disagreement," *Journal of Politics*, 22 (Spring, 1960), 276–294.

26. Thus 61 percent said they would favor changing the terms of members of the House of Representatives from 2 years to 4 years; 24 percent were opposed; 15 percent expressed no opinion. There was little difference by region or party (AIPO release, Jan. 14, 1966). 50 percent said they would favor limiting U.S. Senators to two 6-year terms; 38 percent were opposed; 12 percent had no opinion (AIPO release, Jan. 26, 1966). The evidence for wide support for the main elements in the Constitution is indirect; e.g., "Should the Constitution be made easier to amend?" No, 69 percent (AIPO, March 1, 1937, in Hadley Cantril, *Public Opinion 1935–1946* [Princeton: Princeton University Press, 1951], p. 939). "Do you think the Constitution of the United States should ever be changed in any way?" No, 54 percent; Yes, 34 percent; Don't know, 12 percent (NORC, Nov., 1943, *Ibid.*).

□ There was substantial agreement that if defects existed in the laws and the Constitution they should be cured by traditional legal and political processes of change.[27]

□ Most people continued to believe in the virtues of compromise.[28]

□ Most Americans also continued to display complacency about their economic institutions. Proposals for extensive reconstruction did not enjoy much support. The great corporations, it appears, had gained rather wide acceptance. A minority held that corporations should be more severely regulated; a smaller minority held that they should be nationalized. The trade unions were somewhat more unpopular than the corporations; many wanted them more severely regulated by the government, but a few said that they would like to see trade unions done away with altogether.[29]

□ Although a majority of Americans seemed willing to place themselves in the 'working class,' their sense of 'class' was obviously weak. The key word seems to be 'working,' not 'class.' Few believed that 'class lines' divide Americans into hostile camps.[30]

□ Most Americans continued to profess a strong confidence in the possibilities of personal achievement in the American milieu. A great many continued to believe that personal success was attainable by hard work and skill.[31]

□ Thus Americans tended to express satisfaction rather than discontent with their lot. Most Americans claimed that life in the United States

27. One study provides as evidence for the point the percentages of "political influentials" (N=3020) and "general electorate" (N=1484) agreeing to the following statement: "There are times when it almost seems better for the people to take the law into their own hands than wait for the machinery of government to act." Political influentials 13 percent; general electorate 27 percent (McClosky, "Consensus and Ideology," p. 365). In 1965 only 10 percent of a national sample said that they had "ever felt the urge to organize or join a public demonstration about something" (AIPO release, Nov. 17, 1965).

28. In 1969, the following percentages said they personally believed that "compromise is essential for progress": college youth, 80%; noncollege youth, 88%; parents of college youth, 82%; parents of noncollege youth, 85% (Yankelovich, Generations Apart, p. 5).

29. On business, see Big Business from the Viewpoint of the Public, Survey Research Center, Institute for Social Research (Ann Arbor: University of Michigan, 1951), pp. 18, 20, 26, 44, 56. In the midst of the Great Depression, responses to the question, "Should the government attempt to break up large business organizations?" were: No, 69 percent; Yes, 31 percent (= 100 percent), no opinion, 10 percent (AIPO, July 19, 1937, in Cantril, Public Opinion 1935–1946, p. 345).

On government ownership, see ibid., Polls 14 and 16, p. 345; Polls 53, 54, and 59, p. 349; and Poll 73, p. 351. The percentages of Americans who say they approve of labor unions has varied from 60 to 76 percent for three decades; Gallup figures are: 1936, 72 percent; 1941, 64 percent; 1953, 75 percent; 1961, 63 percent; 1965, 71 percent. However, in recent years more people have said that the laws regulating labor unions were not strict enough than have said they were right or too strict (AIPO release, February 14, 1965). See also Free and Cantril, Political Beliefs of Americans, pp. 129–133.

30. See V. O. Key's analysis, "Occupation and Class," ch. 6 in Public Opinion and American Democracy; also Robert R. Alford, Party and Society (Chicago: Rand McNally, 1963), ch. 8.

31. The hypothesis that there has been a decline in the motivations for personal achievement is highly dubious. See the discussion in Seymour Martin Lipset, The First New Nation: The United States in Historical and Comparative Perspective (New York: Basic Books, 1963), "A Changing American Character?" ch. 3; the data cited in Key, Public Opinion, fn. 2, 4, p. 47, and fn. 5, p. 48; Fred I. Greenstein, "New Light on Changing American Values: A Forgotten Body of Survey Data," Social Forces, 42 (1964), 441–450; and Free and Cantril, Political Beliefs of Americans, pp. 114–115, 193–194.

was the best they could attain anywhere in the world; few wanted to emigrate.[32] They expected that their own material conditions would improve, and that for their children life would be much better, provided there is no war.[33]

QUALIFICATIONS: DIFFERENCES IN DEPTH AND DISTRIBUTION

How deeply these attitudes continue to run, how firmly they are held, and how they are shared among Americans are questions on which historical data shed almost no direct light, and modern survey data only a little more. Survey data do, however, lend some support for the following hypotheses:

1. If Americans are agreed on abstract general propositions about popular government, the Constitution, the virtues of individual liberty, and so on, an attempt to apply these generalities to concrete problems is likely to produce extensive disagreements.[34]
2. Statistically speaking, the more formal education an American has, the more likely he is to express support for the general views just described. The greater his income, the more likely his support—though we cannot be sure about the very rich, who are too small a group to show up in surveys. Support also increases with the status or social prestige of one's occupation; it is higher among professional people, for example, than among skilled workers. Again, it is not possible to be sure about small categories—corporate executives, or Wall Street brokers, for example. Finally, the more active and involved one is in political affairs, the more likely he is to support these views.[35]
3. On all these matters there are dissenting minorities and sometimes they are quite large. Moreover, there is reason to think that during the second half of the 1960s the size of these minorities began to

32. The proportion has, however, increased markedly since the 1950s. In 1971 a Gallup survey asked respondents in nine countries: "If you were free to do so, would you like to go and settle in another country? What country?" Twelve percent of the American respondents said yes, with a preference for Australia, Canada, Britain, and Switzerland. This percentage, Gallup reported, was twice as large as in 1959 and three times what it was soon after World War II. It still remained lower than in any of the other countries, where the percentages who wanted to emigrate were: Britain, 41%; Uruguay (Montevideo only), 32%; West Germany, 27%; Greece, 22%; Finland, 19%; Sweden, 18%; Brazil (Sao Paulo, Rio), 17%; Netherlands, 16% (*The New York Times*, March 21, 1971, p. 27).

33. In 1965, white persons in a national survey said overwhelmingly that they were satisfied with their family income (69 percent); housing (77 percent); the work they did (87 percent); the education their children were getting (77 percent). Among nonwhites, however, the proportions who were dissatisfied were: on income, 64 percent; housing, 66 percent; on the work they did, 38 percent; and on the education their children were getting, 46 percent (AIPO release, September 1, 1965). See also William Buchanan and Hadley Cantril, *How Nations See Each Other* (Urbana: University of Illinois Press, 1953), p. 53; and Free and Cantril, *Political Beliefs of Americans*, p. 107.

34. The best evidence is found in Prothro and Grigg, "Fundamental Principles of Democracy"; McCloskey, "Consensus and Ideology"; and Samuel A. Stouffer, *Communism, Conformity and Civil Liberties* (Garden City: Doubleday, 1955).

35. See the survey data reported and analyzed in Fred I. Greenstein, *The American Party System and the American People*, 2nd ed. (Englewood Cliffs: Prentice-Hall, 1970), ch. 3, pp. 18–42; Seymour Martin Lipset, *Political Man* (Garden City: Doubleday, 1960), "Working Class Authoritarianism," ch. 4, pp. 97–130. See also Stouffer, *Communism, Conformity and Civil Liberties*.

	Youth		Parents of	
	college	noncollege	college youth	noncollege youth
"There is too much concern with equality and too little with law and order."	%	%	%	%
Strongly agree	17	48	42	59
Partially agree	40	35	37	31
Strongly disagree	43	17	20	9

Source: Yankelovich, *Generations Apart*, pp. 24, 26.

increase, particularly among young people, and most of all among college students and educated young people.[36] By the beginning of the 1970s, dissenting perspectives had become an important factor in American political life. The Yankelovich survey in 1969 found many young people and their parents agreeing, fully or partially, with such criticisms of American society as "business is overly concerned with profits and not with public responsibility," "economic well-being in this country is unjustly and unfairly distributed," and "basically, we are a racist nation," etc.[37] On most criticisms, there were no significant differences between college youth and the rest of the population, but there was a marked difference in opinions about equality (Table 9.4).

4. Yet dissenters rarely rejected the traditional democratic values of popular rule, political equality, and consent. On the contrary, they generally affirmed these values; but they also held that American life and institutions had developed in ways inconsistent with democratic values, and demanded changes which, they evidently believed, would move the country closer to attaining these values. And even among college youth, where dissent was most strongly concentrated, preponderant majorities preferred the path of compromise and peaceful, nonviolent change, as shown in Table 9.5 where youth responded to the question, "Which of the following statements do you strongly agree with, which do you partially agree with, and which do you strongly disagree with?"[38]

---

36. "Freshman-to-senior changes in several characteristics have been occurring with considerable uniformity in most American colleges and universities, in recent decades. Declining 'authoritarianism,' dogmatism, and prejudice, together with decreasingly conservative attitudes toward public issues and growing sensitivity to aesthetic experiences, are particularly prominent forms of change" (Kenneth A. Feldman and Theodore M. Newcomb, *The Impact of College on Students* [San Francisco: Jossey-Bass, 1969], p. 326). See also the Yankelovich survey of youth, *Generations Apart.*

37. Yankelovich, *Generations Apart*, pp. 24–25.

38. Compare Table 9.5 with the analysis of survey evidence on attitudes of youth by Lipset, "Youth and Politics."

Table 9.5
Attitudes of Youth on
Political Goals and
Methods, 1969

	Total Youth %	College %	Noncollege %
A mass revolutionary party should be created			
Strongly agree	4	5	4
Partially agree	12	14	11
Strongly disagree	83	80	84
Disruption is preferable to discussing issues for changing our society			
Strongly agree	8	4	10
Partially agree	22	22	22
Strongly disagree	69	74	67
There are legitimate channels for reform which must be exhausted before attempting disruption			
Strongly agree	55	68	51
Partially agree	33	27	34
Strongly disagree	11	5	12
Today, rebuilding society is of less immediate importance than destroying it			
Strongly agree	29	19	31
Partially agree	15	13	13
Strongly disagree	58	68	55
Radicals of the left are as much a threat to the rights of the individual as are radicals of the right			
Strongly agree	52	54	51
Partially agree	34	36	33
Strongly disagree	11	10	11
The American system of representative democracy can respond effectively to the needs of the people			
Strongly agree	43	27	48
Partially agree	46	60	43
Strongly disagree	9	13	8

Source: Yankelovich, *Generations Apart*, pp. 23, 24.

5. The connection between the word and the deed is rather uncertain. In particular, to express disagreement with widely prevailing views does not at all mean that one will actually do anything more to act out his dissent. Many—perhaps most—Americans who express disagreement do not, it seems, try to change the attitudes of others by discussion, or bring about changes by joining dissident political movements or trying to secure the nomination and election of candidates favorable to their views. The reasons for inaction include

political apathy and indifference, lack of strong feeling, pessimism over the prospects of success, ignorance, and so on.[39]

Factors Facilitating Ideological Convergence

How can one account for the rapid development of a similarity of beliefs and attitudes that has impressed so many visitors to the United States?

Homogeneity. The social and economic similarities of Americans, together with their ethnic homogeneity and a common language undoubtedly helped a great deal: general ideas that appealed to one small farmer were very likely to have an appeal to another. Given a homogeneous population, similarities in beliefs were probably fostered also by physical isolation from Europe, by relatively firm boundaries to the east, north, and south, and by the existence of a unique political system that united Americans in a bold new experiment in self-government.

Conformism. Related to all these factors, there may be another, less flattering reason. A number of European observers, including Tocqueville and Martineau, were struck by the fear Americans displayed of seeming different from one another. To use the modern jargon, Americans often appeared to Europeans as strongly 'conformist' and 'other directed.' They worried about the opinions of their neighbors and were reluctant to express, or perhaps even to hold, unpopular views. Everyone seemed bent on converging around a common mean.

> . . . The time will come [Harriet Martineau wrote of Americans] when they will be astonished to discover how they mar their own privileges by allowing themselves less liberty of speech and action than is enjoyed by the inhabitants of countries whose political servitude the Americans justly compassionate and despise. . . . They may travel over the whole world, and find no society but their own which will submit to the restraint of perpetual caution, and reference to the opinions of others.[40]

Yet it is one thing to show how a certain unity of views happened to arise, and quite another to explain how it continued to exist when the United States ceased to be a nation of small independent farmers. By 1880 workers in nonfarm occupations exceeded those in farming. Thereafter the farmers were an ever smaller minority; by 1957 less than one out of ten persons in the labor force was in agriculture, and of these only about half owned their own farms.[41]

---

39. The evidence is indirect but strong. See Herbert McCloskey, "Conservatism and Personality," *American Political Science Review,* 52 (March, 1958), 27–45; Lane, *Political Life,* ch. 5, pp. 63–79, and ch. 12, pp. 163–181; Campbell et al., *The American Voter,* ch. 5, pp. 89–115.

40. Martineau, *Society in America,* pp. 249–251.

41. *Historical Statistics,* Series D 1–12 and K 8–52

Tradition. Probably the sheer inertia of an already venerable tradition helped the United States through periods of crisis. But the crises themselves may have helped even more. The inertial force of the traditional attitudes must have increased as each great challenge to the liberal democratic, individualistic, success-oriented ideology was turned back. Each challenge offered the possibility of a rival ideology—aristocracy, slavocracy, socialism, plutocracy. Yet in each case these potential rivals for the minds of Americans were defeated, and the older victorious ideology then became thoroughly intertwined with traditionalism. To attack the conventional ideas meant more and more to attack the whole course of American national history, to show that Americans had failed, long ago, to take the right path.

Yet these challenges might not have been successfully overcome if the "equality of condition" which Tocqueville had observed had vanished; if, in short, blatant contradictions had developed between the lives led by ordinary Americans and the aspirations offered in the dominant ideology. Despite increasing economic inequalities that accompanied industrialization, particularly in its early stages after the Civil War, evidently enough of the old "equality of condition" survived—if not in reality, at least in expectations—so that the old ideas won converts even among the very people who were worst off under industrial capitalism.[42]

Education. Two additional elements have helped to sustain the dominant traditional ideology in the twentieth century. One of these is the educational system, which from the primary grades through high school, and even in the universities, emphasizes the values and institutions expressed in the dominant liberal-democratic ideology. While the relationship between formal education and ideas is complex, most of all with any specific person, one simple and imposing statistical fact is that in survey after survey of political attitudes and ideas among Americans, the amount of formal education appears as a highly significant variable; more often than any other, indeed, education shows up as *the* most significant variable, even when the effects of socioeconomic status and occupation are cancelled out.[43] As we have already observed (and this is the important point) the greater one's formal education, the most likely

42. Comparative studies of rates of social mobility are still too few for confident conclusions. The view of S. M. Lipset and Reinhard Bendix that "the overall pattern of social mobility appears to be much the same in industrial societies of various Western countries" (*Social Mobility in Industrial Society* [Los Angeles: University of California Press, 1960], p. 13) appears, in the light of later studies, to be doubtful. Perhaps the most that one can say at this point is that social mobility is or has been relatively high in the United States, as compared with such European countries as Britain and the Netherlands, in some but not in all respects. See S. M. Miller, "Comparative Social Mobility: A Trend Report," *Current Sociology*, 9, no. 1 (1960), 1–5; Thomas Fox and S. M. Miller, "Occupational Stratification and Mobility," in *Comparing Nations*, eds. Richard L. Merritt and Stein Rokkan (New Haven: Yale University Press, 1966), pp. 217–237.

43. Key, *Public Opinion*, "The Educational System," ch. 13, pp. 315–343.

he was, at least until recently, to endorse the key propositions in the prevailing ideology.

The mass media. The other influence, that of the mass media—radio, television, newspapers, and mass circulation magazines—is harder to assess. Concrete data are few. Critics on the left argue that the great bulk of Americans are lulled by the mass media into a complacent acceptance of the values in the prevailing ideology—chiefly the emphasis on private property and personal success, and that these beliefs in turn protect the position of certain important elite groups, business leaders, men of wealth, and so on. Critics among the ranks of the radical right tend to view the mass media in much the same way; they see the mass media as major instruments (along with the educational system) by which the liberal 'establishment' acquires and retains its dominance over American institutions and attitudes.[44]

Both views probably exaggerate the direct, manipulative influence of the mass media on American attitudes. The opposition of three-quarters of the daily newspapers of the United States may have reduced the amount of support for Franklin D. Roosevelt, but it did not prevent him from being reelected three times. Or, to take a more recent example, differences in attitudes toward a highly controversial issue, like medical care was in 1956, related in a very weak way to the amount of exposure to the mass media. Moreover, some of the differences were the opposite of what one might expect from simple theories of the influence of the media on 'mass man.' Thus among persons with only a grade school education, both support for (76 percent) and opposition to (15 percent) a government program of medical care was higher among these *most* exposed to the mass media.[45]

The explanation is not mysterious. There is a good deal of evidence that the individuals and groups who might be most susceptible to positive influences from the media because of weak social, psychological, and political ties—'mass man'—also pay much less attention to the media; whereas the individuals who are most 'exposed' to the mass media are in general those with the strongest social, psychological, and political

44. The following quotation could as easily have come from a source on the Left as on the Right: ". . . the mass circulation media in this country have virtually closed their columns to opposition articles. For this they can hardly be blamed; their business is to sell paper at so much a pound and advertising space at so much a line. They must give the masses what they believe the masses want, if they are to maintain their mass circulation business; and there is no doubt that the promises . . . reiterated by the propaganda machine of the government, have made it popular and dulled the public mind to the verities of freedom." The source is, in fact, an editorial note in a right-wing publication, *The Freeman,* June, 1955, cited in Daniel Bell, "Interpretations of American Politics" in *The New American Right,* ed. Daniel Bell (New York: Anchor Books, 1964), p. 68, fn. 23. The editorial was attacking the mass media for lulling the public into socialism. The best known criticism from the Left, sounding many of the same themes, is in the late C. Wright Mills, *The Power Elite* (New York: Oxford University Press, 1956), "The Mass Society," ch. 13, pp. 298–324.

45. Key, *Public Opinion,* p. 398.

barriers between them and manipulative efforts.[46] The views of left and right also underestimate the extent to which the mass media themselves reflect stable values in the American culture; for better or worse, culture and media reinforce one another.

What is essentially correct, however, is that the amount of time and space devoted by the mass media to views openly hostile to the prevailing ideology is negligible.[47] An American who wishes to find criticism of the basic social, economic, and political structures can indeed find them; but he will have to search outside the mass media. And, naturally, the number who are strongly enough motivated to do so is relatively small. Hence the general effect of the mass media is to reinforce the existing institutions and ideology.[48]

A Persistent Ambiguity: Majority Rule

However successful the Founders may have been in resolving many of the practical problems they confronted, their inability to agree on the appropriate place of the majority principle and the extensive partitioning of public authority resulting from their work helped to create an important source of ambiguity that Americans have never resolved. It is not too much to say that *the great body of Americans has never agreed on any single, definite, widely understood rule for final, authoritative, legitimate decision-making in government.*

Neither the Constitution, constitutional doctrine, nor American ideology have ever treated all political institutions, national and federal, as components of an ordered hierarchy in which some constitutional units are invariably subordinate to others. Constitutionally speaking, the president does not dominate Congress; nor, on the other hand, is the president a mere agent of Congress; the Senate is not constitutionally superior to

---

46. Thus in explaining the unimportant effects of television on election turnout in the United States, Angus Campbell remarks: "If there is one dependable law in the world of mass communications, it is that those most likely to seek information are already the best informed. Thus we find that the people who follow the election campaigns most closely on television are precisely the same ones who read the most about them in the newspapers and magazines.

"It is among those at the other end of the scale, the quarter or third of the population that is generally uninvolved and uninformed, that television might have hoped to have its greatest impact. This is where the potential gains were greatest. But this group, alas, is very incurious about politics; its demands for information are exceedingly modest. Its members can apparently be induced to watch an occasional 'spectacular,' like the conventions or the debates, but their detachment from political matters is undisturbed" ("Has Television Reshaped Politics?" *Columbia Journalism Review* [Fall, 1962], 10–13).

A sophisticated and skeptical attempt to assess the influence of the mass media is in Key, *Public Opinion,* "Media: Specter and Reality," ch. 14, and "Media: Structure and Impact," ch. 15, pp. 344–410. On the general problem of manipulating attitudes, see also R. E. Lane and D. O. Sears, *Public Opinion* (Englewood Cliffs: Prentice-Hall, 1964), "Leaders' Influence on Public Opinion," ch. 5; and Elihu Katz and Paul F. Lazarsfeld, *Personal Influence* (Glencoe: Free Press, 1955).

47. "Extraordinarily few [American] journals, either daily newspapers or magazines, act as agencies of political criticism. They may dig to find the facts about individual acts of corruption, but the grand problems of the political system by and large escape their critical attention" (Key, *Public Opinion,* p. 381).

48. For a similar conclusion, see *ibid.,* p. 396.

the House, nor Congress and the president to the judiciary, nor the governors and state legislatures to the president and Congress.

Nor do Americans agree on a principle of majority rule that would provide a way of ordering these institutions into a lawful hierarchy. Majority rule? But which majority? How large? Operating in what institution? By what means? And anyway, what of minority rights? Given varying interpretations of political legitimacy possible within the American tradition, the extent to which a particular principle or institution is upheld often depends on whose ox is being gored. When the principle is invoked to support 'national' majorities (for example, as revealed in national elections), it is also used to support local, state, or regional majorities. This conflict over the legitimacy of 'national' versus 'local' majorities, as we saw in the last chapter, goes all the way back to the Constitutional Convention.

The American doctrine of partitioned authority, expressed at the Convention, implied in the Declaration of Independence, and traceable to Locke, holds that majorities lose their legitimacy if they infringe on natural rights or other absolute standards of political right or justice. Because there is always much dispute as to what these natural rights or absolute standards are and how far they extend, the boundary between majority rule and individual rights has been continually disputed throughout America's national history. Yet the doctrine that the right of a majority to govern is properly restricted by 'unalterable' rights is not widely challenged among Americans.

Since earliest times, doctrines of unalterable rights and of states' rights have both been invoked by defeated minorities to challenge the legitimacy or constitutionality of laws enacted or proposed by the president and Congress. Attacks on national law in the name of rights of individuals or states or both were expressed in the Virginia and Kentucky Resolutions of 1789–99, the declaration of the Hartford Convention in 1814, the South Carolina Resolutions in 1828, the "Exposition and Protest" accompanying them, the Ordinance of Nullification in 1832, and South Carolina's "Declaration of the Cause of Secession" in December, 1860. These principles were revived in the South from 1954 onward as the doctrine of 'interposition' to justify resistance to the Supreme Court's decisions on integration.

Specific institutions are admired or criticized by different groups at different times depending on the particular interests at stake; but the doctrine of partitioned authority itself is rarely rejected outright. In the 1930s, liberals attacked the Supreme Court and defended majority rule; in the 1950s and 1960s, the prestige of the Court among liberals had never been higher. During the early years of the New Deal, conservatives saw the Court as a bastion of freedom; in the 1950s some of them came to view it as rather tyrannical. During the New Deal and the Fair Deal, liberal Democrats frequently extolled the virtues (and political legitimacy) of a strong president; with the election of a Republican president in 1952 they began to discover new virtues in Congress; that theme was quickly muted after 1960, with the election of a Democratic president and revived again after Mr. Nixon's victory in 1968. Many conservatives insist that "power must be kept close to the people"; they praise the legitimacy of 'states' rights'; but they opposed attempts to bring power 'closer to the people' by reapportioning state legislatures or allowing blacks to vote.

To be sure, there is the belief in the final legitimacy of rule by the people; that "this country, with its institutions, belongs to the people who inhabit it," as Lincoln said. "Whenever they shall grow weary of the existing government, they can exercise their constitutional right of amending it, or their revolutionary right to dismember or overthrow it." Yet 'the people' have not chosen to amend the Constitution in order to establish a single hierarchy of authority in our political institutions. Quite the contrary: 'the people' have never shown the slightest interest in any of the schemes for doing so that are sometimes propounded by eager constitution-makers. Moreover, a *majority* of the people is not constitutionally sovereign even in amending the Constitution, unless that majority happens also to constitute a majority in three-fourths of the states. Indeed, in at least one respect, a unanimity of opinion in three-fourths of the states does not make 'the people' constitutionally sovereign even in its power to amend the Constitution; for the final words of Article V of the Constitution read: ". . . no State, without its Consent, shall be deprived of its equal Suffrage in the Senate."

To anyone searching for a single principle of legitimate decision-making, it is of little value to say that 'the people' may exercise "their revolutionary right to dismember or overthrow" the political institutions. Perhaps if Americans converge on a single principle, it would be this: unanimity, though unattainable, is best; institutions must therefore be so contrived that they will compel a constant search for the highest attainable degree of consent. But this leaves a vast area of decision-making open to conflict.

THIRD CONDITION: THE CONSTITUTIONAL FRAMEWORK

So powerful were the two conditions discussed so far that it is difficult to imagine that polyarchy would not have developed in the United States. Seen in this light, the contribution of the Constitutional framework looks pretty unimportant.

Such a view no doubt runs counter to what I take to be a belief common among Americans to the effect that "it was the Founders who created democracy in America." As we have just seen, however, the Constitutional Convention created an instrument of government that could have been adapted to either a relatively aristocratic republic, a meritocracy, or a more democratic republic, a polyarchy. The direction in which the new system was to develop was not wholly within the control of any constitutional convention. As Alexis de Tocqueville wrote in 1835,

> . . . Mexico, which is not less fortunately situated than the Anglo-American Union, has adopted these same laws [i.e., the federal Constitution] but is unable to accustom itself to the government of democracy. Some other cause is therefore at work, independently of physical circumstances and peculiar laws, which enables the democracy to rule in the United States.[49]

In recent times, too, we have relearned the ancient lesson that a constitution is a frail barrier along the path of an aspiring dictator who has a large and disciplined following.

Proper constitutional agreements are, obviously, necessary conditions for a polyarchy. One cannot have polyarchy if there are no elections, no legislatures, no legal rights to speak freely about politics, no courts to enforce these rights. But it is equally obvious that constitutional arrangements are not sufficient to insure polyarchy. For there must also be suitable social and economic conditions, and appropriate beliefs among the citizens. Thanks to greater experience with polyarchic government, the task of drafting a constitution for a polyarchy is, nowadays, very much easier than it was in 1789. But it is as difficult as ever to insure the proper socioeconomic conditions and beliefs.

Consider two problems: first, the problem of power. In order for a satisfactory approximation of democracy to exist, power over government must not be distributed too unequally among the citizens. One of the most important contributions to the wide diffusion of power over government is broad suffrage. But standing alone even universal suffrage is insufficient, for legal equality in the voting booth can be nullified by inequalities outside. Imagine an agricultural society, for example, where a tiny group of people owns all the land; where these people control the police, the military, the newspapers, the radio; and where the great bulk of the population consists of uneducated agricultural laborers dependent for their livelihood on the few landowners. Is it likely that the introduction of universal suffrage and a wide variety of constitutional guarantees would, by themselves, produce a durable polyarchy?

Second, there is the problem of unity and diversity, of consensus and conflict. Even if power were equally distributed, a polyarchy might nonetheless be destroyed from internal dissension. A minority, outvoted, might grow to prefer dictatorship to the prospect of obeying laws passed and enforced by the representatives of a hostile majority.

---

49. Tocqueville, *Democracy In America*, vol. I, p. 333.

As we have seen, for reasons with which the Founders had very little to do, conditions in the United States were unusually favorable for a solution to both these problems. In fact, then, what produced polyarchy in America was not so much the American Revolution and the Constitutional Convention as the underlying forces that facilitated a second, silent revolution. These were the forces that made for pervasive equality and widespread acceptance of American institutions.

In less favorable circumstances, the American experience might only have added new evidence that a thing previously held impossible was indeed impossible. For the Constitution might easily have been adapted to an aristocratic or oligarchic system of government. The Founders, as we saw, left the alternatives open. It was the second, silent revolution that settled the matter.

Most notably, the Constitution left open the question of how broad the suffrage was to be. It nowhere guaranteed against narrow suffrage. Senators, you will recall, were to be chosen by the state legislatures, representatives by "electors in each State [who] shall have the Qualifications requisite for Electors of the most numerous Branch of the State Legislature" (Article I, Section 2). The president was to be chosen by electors from each state appointed "in such manner as the legislature thereof may direct" (Article II, Section 1). Nor did the Bill of Rights guarantee a wide suffrage. Conceivably, then, the states might have limited the suffrage to a wealthy few. That was, after all, the situation in Britain, where only about 5 percent of the total population over 20 could vote in 1831. After Britain was shaken by a protracted political crisis over the successful battle to enlarge the suffrage in 1832, the percentage over 20 who could vote was still only 7 percent![50]

In the United States, however, the suffrage was already fairly widely diffused in most of the states in 1787, and in subsequent decades it was expanded, not contracted. The causes for this expansion were complex. They include, of course, the two conditions just described—equality and democratic beliefs. These insured that the framework of government designed by the Founders would have to prove itself capable of adapting to the impulse toward democratization or else be cast aside.

Yet in downgrading the contribution of the Constitution to the process of democratization, it is important to keep in mind that the framework was not, in fact, cast aside. It did not need to be. For even if the Constitution did not itself guarantee a broadly based republic, it was quite capable of adapting to such a republic. More than that: by requiring that the national government rest on elections and by making that government relatively powerful and important, it practically insured that

---

50. Dolf Sternberger and Bernhard Vogel, eds., *Die Wahl Der Parlamente*, 2 vols. (Berlin: Walter de Gruyter and Co., 1969), vol. 1, *Europa*, p. 632.

demands for broad participation would exist; by guaranteeing fundamental liberties in the Bill of Rights, the Constitution made it likely that
these demands would be expressed, heard, organized, channeled. Thus
because it was flexible enough to adapt to the pressures for democratization, the constitutional framework also gained acceptability, and
thereby contributed to the thrust toward ideological convergence and
the widespread acceptance of American institutions.

SUMMARY   How was it that Americans were able to prove "a thing previously held
impossible?" This chapter examined three conditions favorable to polyarchy. Yet each was qualified in a way that would leave a legacy of
unsolved problems:

1. The conditions of American life fostered equality and egalitarian
attitudes to a degree that astounded observers like Tocqueville. Yet the
United States also contained sources of inequalities. The most extreme
inequalities stemmed from slavery and racial discrimination, but other
sources included social status, business enterprise, and differences in
political skills and incentives.

2. Aided by their experiences and environment, Americans rapidly
converged toward a belief in a democratic ideology and in the major
American institutions. Yet this outward convergence conceals many
differences in the depth and content of the belief. It also leaves at least
one key matter, the proper place of majority rule, in a thoroughly
ambiguous state.

3. The constitutional framework was perhaps the least important
condition for the emergence of polyarchy in the United States. Nonetheless, because it left open the issue of aristocracy versus democracy,
made the national government important and its offices and policies
worth contesting, provided for elections to the main offices, and guaranteed a set of basic liberties in the Bill of Rights, it created a constitutional framework that not only could be democratized as demands arose
but stimulated and protected these demands. In addition, the adaptability
of the framework to demands for democratization helped to make political institutions widely acceptable to the American people, and thus
contributed to the convergence of beliefs that, as was suggested in
Chapter 7, has tended to be one of the pronounced characteristics of
American polyarchy.

Yet here, too, there is a legacy of unsolved problems. For the extreme
partitioning of authority and the ideas supporting it that were and remain
so basic a part of the American polyarchy have created certain persistent problems for the operation of polyarchy in the United States—

including, as we just saw, a certain ineradicable ambiguity about the legitimacy of majority rule itself.

Two sets of factors contribute to the extreme partitioning of authority in the United States: political institutions and patterns of cleavage and conflict. In the next part of this book we shall see how the first of these, the political institutions, contribute to the system of partitioned authority.

The Major
Institutions:
Design
And
Performance

part

3

The Presidency: Design

10

INTRODUCTION For many a fervent proponent of democracy, it is awkward to admit that a 'democratic' system needs leaders. For the admission seems to imply that the people are not wholly capable of governing themselves. Yet every political system with more than a handful of citizens has to provide for governmental functions that the whole people are unable or unwilling to perform individually or collectively. Among the most important of these functions are to work out specific proposals of policies that the government should adopt; to insure that these policies are properly executed; to undertake emergency actions, especially on matters of war and foreign affairs; and to perform certain kinds of symbolic functions—as symbolic head of the state for internal and for international purposes and as spokesman for and representative of unity. These functions are carried on in polyarchies (as in other systems) by political leaders.

In American life, far and away the most important political leader is, of course, the president. As a contribution to the art of politics, the American presidency is unique. The institution was not at the outset a copy of anything else; nor, despite a number of attempts, has it been successfully copied elsewhere.

What makes the American presidency unique is its particular and peculiar combination of characteristics. Except perhaps for the Supreme Court, no institution plays so important a symbolic role in American political life; particularly in times of crisis, the president symbolizes the nation. Yet a president is inescapably a partisan; he is the head of a political party and up to his ears in partisan politics. In the late 1960s a number of U.S. senators voiced the fear that on certain matters involving a mixture of military and foreign policy decisions, the presidency had become virtually out of control. Above all, they had the Vietnam war in mind. Yet President Johnson, who had used the powers of the presidency to expand that war, chose not to run for a second term because he felt he could no longer govern the country. Despite congressional and public criticism, President Nixon retained control over the speed at which our involvement in the war in Vietnam was to be lessened; yet he met stunning defeats on his legislative proposals and Supreme Court appointments.

AT THE CONVENTION: THE PAUCITY OF MODELS

To understand the presidency it is instructive to put ourselves briefly in the shoes of the men at the Convention. That some functions of leadership had to be performed in the political system for which they were designing a constitution, these men were both too practical and too versed in political experience to doubt. They knew they had to design the office of "national executive," "executive magistracy," "magistrate," or "executive," as they referred to it at various times.

Yet how were they to create an "executive magistrate" who would perform whatever functions the other institutions could not properly execute and who at the same time would not be a political monstrosity? In 1787, the problem was far more baffling than it would be today, because the alternatives we are familiar with today were unknown. A popularly elected president was a novelty; the chief alternative solution, a prime minister chosen by the parliament, had not yet emerged in its modern form even in Britain.

Every problem was unsolved, every proposal debatable, every solution risky. How many executives should there be: one or several? How should the executive be chosen? For how long? What should the qualifications be for executive office? What constitutional powers and limits were required? Whatever was written into the Constitution, what would be the real role of the executive in the new political system? The answers necessarily had to be highly speculative.

FOUR QUESTIONS IN SEARCH OF ANSWERS

How Many?

It is true that earlier republics furnished some experience, but republican executives had generally been collegial, consisting of several men, each of whom served as a check on the others. This was the famous solution of the Roman Republic. Although the plural executive is designed to solve one problem, it creates another. The plural executive may help to prevent any single man from gaining too much power; yet where one executive checks another, decisions may be paralyzed. That system must, therefore, avoid great emergencies, particularly those requiring decisive action in international affairs and war; or else, as in the Roman Republic, it must have some provision for a temporary 'dictator' armed with emergency powers.

Because of these disadvantages, the plural executive is rarely used in polyarchies. Switzerland has employed it most successfully—but Switzerland is small, maintains a vigorous neutrality, remains free of alliances and international organizations, and avoids war. In 1951, one of the few polyarchies of Latin America, Uruguay, shifted from a presidential executive to a nine-member council. Uruguay, like Switzerland, is small and peaceful; even so, in 1966, Uruguay decided to restore the single executive. No other nation has chosen the collegial form, though the cabinet system bears a superficial resemblance to it.

The idea of a plural executive had little support at the Convention. Randolph of Virginia

strenuously opposed a unity in the Executive magistracy. He regarded it as the foetus of monarchy. . . . He could not see why the great requisites for the Executive department., vigor, despatch & responsibility could not be found in three men, as well as in one man.[1]

But Randolph won few converts. After all, the Articles of Confederation had followed the pattern of the ancient republics; the only executive provided for in the Articles was a committee, appointed by Congress, "to sit in the recess of congress, to be denominated 'A Committee of the States,' and to consist of one delegate from each state." Not even Randolph wanted to duplicate that feeble system in the new Constitution. In their own constitutions, the states (except for Pennsylvania) had settled, nominally, for a single executive—though often he was so hedged around by a legislative council that the executive was in fact collegial. One famous republic, it is true, had in outward form a single executive: the Doge of Venice. That republic, the longest-lived republic in history, was after some seven or eight centuries approaching its final *coup de grace* at the hands of Napoleon. But the Doge was virtually all figurehead and no power; executive authority was in fact lodged in numerous councils, commissions, and officials.

Whatever the reasons, the proposal for a single executive was agreed to in the early days of the convention. It was almost the only question having to do with the presidency on which the Convention, having once made a decision, did not later change its mind.[2]

How Long?

In the absence of an appropriate model for a republican executive, the most visible alternative was the form that all members of the Convention knew best: a hereditary monarchy. Yet it was precisely because

---

1. *Documents*, p. 132.

2. No one except Randolph spoke against the single executive. Three states—New York, Delaware, and Maryland—voted against it on the decisive vote of June 4. Virginia voted for it, although the delegation was split down the middle: Madison, Washington, and two others favored the single executive; Randolph, Mason, and Blair opposed it (*Documents*, p. 132).

this solution was barred to them by their own beliefs and the attitudes of the country—". . . there was not a one-thousandth part of our fellow citizens who were not against every approach toward monarchy," said Gerry—that there existed the vacuum they had to fill. To Alexander Hamilton—if we can rely on Madison's notes—a republic was inherently a second-best form of government because, unlike a monarchy, it could provide no good solution to the problem of the executive:

> . . . As to the Executive [Madison reports Hamilton as saying on June 18], it seemed to be admitted that no good one could be established on Republican principles. Was not this giving up the merits of the question: for can there be a good Gov.ᵗ without a good Executive. The English model was the only good one on this subject. The Hereditary interest of the King was so interwoven with that of the Nation, and his personal emoluments so great, that he was placed above the danger of being corrupted from abroad—and at the same time was both sufficiently independent and sufficiently controuled, to answer the purpose of the institution at home. . . . What is the inference from all these observations? That we ought to go as far in order to attain stability and permanency, as republican principles will admit. Let one branch of the Legislature hold their places for life or at least during good behaviour. Let the Executive also be for life.[3]

One weak spot of Hamilton's argument was, as everyone knew, the simple matter of genes and the accidents of human personality. A great king may have a son less suited to kingship than his own fool. A king famed for his justice may beget a tyrant. To a king of intelligence, vision, courage, and resolution, the mysteries of genes and child-rearing may produce an heir, shortsighted, feckless, weak, and irresolute. Writing some years later, Jefferson reflected on the monarchs of Europe:

> While in Europe, I often amused myself with contemplating the characters of the then reigning sovereigns. . . . Louis XVI was a fool, of my own knowledge. . . . The King of Spain was a fool, and of Naples the same. They passed their lives in hunting, and despatched two couriers a week, one thousand miles, to let each other know what game they had killed the preceding days. The King of Sardinia was a fool. All these were Bourbons. The queen of Portugal, a Braganza, was an idiot by nature. And so was the King of Denmark. Their sons, as regents, exercised the powers of government. The King of Prussia, successor to the great Frederick, was a mere hog in body as well as in mind. Gustavus of Sweden, and Joseph of Austria, were really crazy, and George of England, you know, was in a straight waistcoat. There remained, then, none but old Catherine, who had been too lately picked up to have lost her common sense. . . . These animals had become without mind and powerless; and so will every hereditary monarch be after a few generations. . . . And so endeth the book of Kings, from all of whom the Lord deliver us.[4]

---

3. *Ibid.*, pp. 221–222.
4. *Thomas Jefferson On Democracy*, selected and arranged by Saul K. Padover (New York: Penguin Books, 1946), p. 26.

The Americans had thrown off one hereditary monarch; it was obvious to all—including Hamilton—that they would not tolerate another.

An executive for life might solve some of these problems; but such a system would create others. To give a man a lifetime in which to accumulate power is dangerous. A lifetime tenure might even be enough to establish a dynasty. Sickness, senility, degeneration, insanity have turned good leaders into evil ones; yet an executive appointed for life might not yield power gladly and might have too much power to be dispossessed without violence. The Roman emperors were the obvious model: they had held office for life. Yet while some of them, like Hadrian, were undoubtedly great leaders and ruled during times of great prosperity and peace, many were brutal tyrants: Caligula, Nero, Commodus, Caracalla.

An executive chosen for life had no support at the Convention. Even Hamilton, when he got down to his specific proposals, called for an appointment not explicitly for life, but "during good behavior." When James McClurg (a delegate from Virginia whose role at the Convention was brief and unimportant) moved that the executive hold office "during good behavior," the idea won little acclaim. That distinguished advocate of an aristocratic republic, Gouverneur Morris, briefly endorsed it but changed his mind a few days later.[5] Madison tactfully suggested that "respect for the mover entitled his proposition to a fair hearing & discussion."[6] Mason remarked:

> . . . He considered an Executive during good behavior as a softer name only for an Executive for life. And that the next would be an easy step to hereditary Monarchy. If the motion should finally succeed, he might himself live to see such a Revolution. If he did not it was probable his children or grand children would. He trusted there were few men in that House who wished for it. No state he was sure had so far revolted from Republican principles as to have the least bias in its favor.[7]

The proposal was turned down by a close vote—four states in favor, six against—which, according to Madison, grossly exaggerated the actual support the proposal had enjoyed at the Convention.

> This vote [he wrote in a comment on his own notes] is not to be considered as any certain index of opinion, as a number in the affirmative probably had it chiefly in view to alarm those attached to a dependence of the Executive on the Legislature, & thereby facilitate some final arrangement of a contrary tendency. The avowed friends of an Executive, "during good behaviour" were not more than three or four, nor is it certain they would finally have adhered to such a tenure.[8]

---

5. Cf. *Documents*, pp. 396, 447.
6. *Ibid.*, p. 398.
7. *Ibid.*
8. *Ibid.*, p. 399, fn.

Yet, while this proposal was disposed of fairly easily, the Convention twisted and turned like a man tormented in his sleep by a bad dream as it tried to decide just what term would be proper. On July 24, the Convention had a particularly trying day: Luther Martin proposed a term of eleven years; Gerry suggested fifteen; King, twenty years—"the medium life of princes"; Davie, eight years. After that day's work, the Convention adjourned without having decided anything at all.

The log of votes in the Convention on the length of term of the president reveals the uncertainty of the delegates:

June 1. Seven-year term, *passed,* 5 states to 4.

June 2. Ineligible for reelection after seven years, *passed,* 7–2.

July 19. Seven-year term, *defeated,* 5–3.

Six-year term, *passed,* 9–1.

Ineligibility for a second term, *defeated,* 8–2.

July 26. Seven-year term, with ineligibility for reelection, *passed,* 7–3.

Sept. 6. Seven-year term, *defeated,* 8–3.

Six-year term, *defeated,* 9–2.

Four-year term, *passed,* 10–1.

How Chosen?

But having settled on a four-year term, how was the executive to be chosen? On this question the Convention could never quite make up its mind. Almost to the end, it would move toward a solution and then, on second thought, reverse itself in favor of some different alternative. On no question was experience so uncertain a guide. If ultimately the Convention invented the popularly elected presidency, it would be excessively charitable to say that the men in Philadelphia foresaw what they were doing.

The most obvious solution in 1787 was the election of the executive by the legislature. This was the essence of the cabinet system that was evolving in Britain. Yet, in 1787, that evolution was far from complete; neither in Britain nor in this country did anyone quite realize how much the prime minister was ceasing to be the agent of the king and becoming instead the representative of a parliamentary majority. When one spoke of the British executive in 1787 one still meant the king, not the prime minister.

In the American states, too, under new or revised state constitutions, the governor was generally chosen by the legislature. Yet the experience of the various states suggested some of the disadvantages of that solution: If the executive were elected by the legislature, what was to prevent him from becoming a mere creature of that body? To some of the men at the Convention, this was exactly what was needed. Thus Sherman of Connecticut "was for the appointment by the Legislature, and for making him absolutely dependent on that body, as it was the will of that which was to be executed. An independence of the Executive on the supreme Legislature, was in his opinion the very essence of tyranny if there was any such thing."[9] Was Sherman thinking of his own state—one of the few in which the governor was popularly elected?

The main reason those who opposed election by the Congress gave for their opposition was a fear that the executive would be too weak. The chief spokesman for an aristocratic republic, Gouverneur Morris, joined with the spokesmen for the democratic republic, Madison and Wilson, in opposing election by the Congress. But to find an alternative was infinitely more difficult. If the executive were elected by the people, as Wilson proposed, would he not then be too dependent on the whims of popular majorities? And could the people possibly know enough to make a wise choice? Even to Mason, who usually favored the more democratic solutions, it seemed "as unnatural to refer the choice of a proper character for chief Magistrate to the people, as it would, to refer a trial of colours to a blind man. The extent of the Country renders it impossible that the people can have the requisite capacity to judge of the respective pretensions of the Candidates."[10]

Thus the argument went on. Every possible solution seemed fatally flawed. Should the president be chosen by the Congress? by the Senate only? by the people? by the state governors? by the state legislatures? by electors chosen by the people? As Madison wearily concluded in late July, "there are objections agst every mode that has been, or perhaps can be proposed."[11]

The United States came within a hairsbreadth of adopting a kind of parliamentary system. The Virginia plan had proposed that the executive be chosen by the national legislature. On July 17 this mode was unanimously agreed to. It won another trial vote, 6–3, on July 26. As late as August 24 the Convention voted against an attempt to substitute election by the people or by electors for choice by the legislature. Yet when a committee reported out on September 4—two weeks before the end of the Convention—it suggested the "electoral college" solution which was embodied in Article II of the Constitution. No one altogether knows what happened in the interval; perhaps many delegates who had earlier voted for election by the legislature were so unsure of their grounds, so weary of the dispute, and so fearful of further haggling and possible deadlock that they eagerly accepted the compromise suggested by the committee. Whatever the reasons, all who struggle today with the task of inventing new political institutions may be comforted by this record of the Convention's torment:

---

9. *Ibid.*, p. 134.
10. *Ibid.*, pp. 394–395.
11. *Ibid.*, p. 449.

June 2. Virginia plan (Randolph) proposes a national executive "to be chosen by the National Legislature." Discussed.

June 2. Wilson's proposal for presidential electors chosen by the people, *defeated,* 8–2.

June 9. Gerry's proposal that the executive be chosen "by the executives of the states," *defeated,* 9–0.

July 17. Wilson's proposal for election by the people, *defeated,* 9–1. Luther Martin's proposal for choice by electors appointed by state legislatures, *defeated,* 8–2.

Randolph's original proposal, "to be chosen by the National Legislature," *passed unanimously.*

July 19. Ellsworth's proposal that the national executive be chosen by electors appointed by state legislatures, *passed,* 6–3 (Massachusetts divided).

July 24. Houston's proposal that "the Executive be appointed by the National Legislature," *passed,* 7–4.

July 25. Ellsworth's proposal that "the Executive be appointed by the Legislature" except for reelection "in which case the choice shall be by Electors appointed by the Legislators in the States," *defeated,* 7–4.

July 26. A comprehensive resolution on the national executive proposing among other things that he be "chosen by the National Legislature," *passed,* 6–3 (Virginia divided, with Washington and Madison against). This article, as approved, referred to Committee of Detail.

August 6. Constitution as reported by Committee of Detail reads "he shall be elected by ballot by the legislature."

August 24. Carroll's proposal to strike out "by the legislature" and insert "by the people," *defeated,* 9–2.

G. Morris' proposal that the President "shall be chosen by electors," *failed,* 4–4 (Connecticut and Maryland, divided, Massachusetts absent).

September 4. Committee of Eleven, to which this and other sections had been referred, propose essentials of present Constitution: "Each State shall appoint in such manner as its Legislature may direct,[12] a number of electors equal to the whole number of Senators and members of the House of Representatives to which the State may be entitled in the Legislature."

September 6. This proposal *adopted,* 9–2.

September 17. Constitution signed; Convention adjourns.

What Powers and Functions?

It was in providing for the powers and functions of the president that the Founders were the least comprehensive and left the most to future

---

12. For further discussion of this matter, see p. 131.

developments. As a glance at Article II will show, only one-third of the article is devoted to the powers of the president. In fact, the grand edifice of the American presidency, the most powerful popularly elected office in the world, rests, in a narrowly legalistic sense, on barely three hundred words in the Constitution. What is more, of a dozen 'powers' granted in those three hundred words, only half are of really critical importance:

☐ The president is vested with "the executive power."
☐ "He shall take care that the laws be faithfully executed."
☐ He is commander in chief of the armed forces.
☐ He is vested with certain powers of appointment.
☐ "He shall have power, by and with the advice and consent of the Senate, to make treaties. . . . He shall receive ambassadors and other public ministers."

From a mere reading of these phrases in the Constitution it would be impossible to derive anything like an adequate understanding of the powers of an American president. As we shall see in the next chapter, the development of that edifice was more the work of those who occupied it than of those who originally designed it.

A Separate Head of State?

In deciding that a single executive elected for a specific term was to be vested with "the executive power" and the right to "receive ambassadors and other public ministers," the Founders in effect decided to endow the president with the ceremonial and symbolic functions of head of state. The Founders seem not to have considered the possibility of splitting off this role. They seem instead to have assumed without reflection that the president must be chief executive *and* symbolic head of state.

In uniting these two functions, the Founders adopted a solution that has been rejected in most other polyarchies. In a number of countries a hereditary monarch with virtually no executive power has been maintained for these purposes; it is an intriguing fact that these include countries where democratic ideas and the institutions of polyarchy are every bit as strongly supported as in the United States: Britain, Belgium, Denmark, the Netherlands, Norway, and Sweden. In most other polyarchies a separate official, a president or governor general, is ceremonial head while the actual chief executive is the prime minister.

Being virtually compelled to reject a monarch, evidently the Founders could not envisage the possibility that some of a monarch's functions might be vested in an office other than that of chief executive. If some among them conceived the possibility, probably they at once rejected it, fearing that out of such an office monarchy might grow. Two important consequences follow from their solution:

□ To the unbearable burden of his political and executive duties, the president must also add the crushing obligations of ceremony and ritual that fall on the head of state in any large and powerful country.

□ United in a single office are roles that are at times confusing and conflicting. The president's role as symbolic head of state and spokesman for the nation as a whole, especially in times of urgency, conflicts with his role as partisan political leader and advocate of specific policies. Moreover, presidents characteristically take advantage of their role as head of state to enhance their political influence.

THE UNFINISHED BUSINESS

Most modern polyarchies have rejected the Founders' solution. They have preferred the parliamentary system in which the chief executive is chosen by and is dependent on the confidence of the national legislature, and a hereditary monarch, president, or governor general is symbolic head of state. The difficulty foreseen by the critics of an executive chosen by the Congress—his weakness—has come to pass in some countries and not in others. In Britain, the prime minister gradually emerged as a powerful leader who could count on the disciplined majority that chose him in parliament. In the twentieth century few British cabinets have ever fallen through a vote of no confidence; the prime minister is nearly as secure in his five-year tenure as the president is in his four-year term. A number of other polyarchies have followed a similar path. However, in France under the Third Republic (1870–1940) and the Fourth (1946–58), the worst fears of men like Wilson and Madison were vindicated: the cabinet, dependent on parliament, was its creature; governments fell with appalling frequency—about every seven months on the average during the Fourth Republic. The Fifth Republic (1958–) granted great executive authority to its first president, General de Gaulle, and in 1962 a constitutional amendment providing for the direct popular election of the president was approved by nearly two-thirds of the voters in a national referendum. A number of other countries that have chosen the parliamentary-cabinet system have had an experience similar to that of France. Some, paradoxically, have had both experiences. In Sweden during the nineteen-year period from 1917–36, there were eleven governments; yet, since 1936, Swedish cabinets have been remarkably stable and have carried through comprehensive reforms.

If the Convention had adhered to the Virginia plan and thereby left the choice of the executive to the Congress, would the United States have developed a stable and powerful executive like the British prime minister—or, instead, a weak and unstable executive like that of France under the Third and Fourth Republics? It is difficult to say.

But, instead of speculating on that subject, let us take stock of what the Convention did and did not do.

The Convention

- Provided unity in the office of chief executive.
- Insured that the president would (short of impeachment or death) remain in office for a fixed four-year term. Thus there would ordinarily be continuity and stability in the executive office at least for four years.
- Provided the president with an electoral base, a constituency, independent of the Congress.
- Armed the president (Article II) with constitutional powers not dependent on the Congress, the president's electors, the people, or the states. Hence, both in his election and in his powers, the president could be to some degree independent of congressional majorities and of popular opinion.
- And placed no limit on the number of times he could be reelected. (The Twenty-second Amendment, providing that "no person shall be elected to the office of the President more than twice" was not enacted until 1951.)

On the other hand, the Convention

- Could not foresee how the election of the president by the method they chose at the ultimate hour would actually work. Would presidential electors tend to speak for aristocracy, and thus choose a man who would be a brake on the Congress and the people? Or would they themselves be agents of popular majorities and choose presidents who appealed to the populace rather than to elite groups?
- Did not provide for a method by which conflicts between the president and the other branches might be resolved, other than by the cumbersome and unlikely process of impeachment or, somehow, through elections. Conflict between executive and legislature was, in the eyes of most of the men at the Convention, not wholly undesirable; conflict was the essence of the rationale for partitioning of power. But would conflict between president and Congress lead to unproductive stalemate?
- Could not know how weak or powerful the president's office they had created would become in actual practise. Would his independence and unity be sufficient to keep him from being a mere weak creature of the Congress? Conversely, might he become so powerful that he would overweigh the 'balances' in the system? Was he, despite all the efforts they had made to prevent it, a potential tyrant? Would he be too powerful—or not powerful enough?

SUMMARY   1. Although the presidency is the main center of political leadership in the American polyarchy, it is less the result of a carefully thought-out design than of the lengthy and elaborate growth of an institution very loosely prescribed by the Constitution.

2. Handicapped by the absence of relevant models, after a display of great confusion and uncertainty the Founders managed to reach agreement on answers to three basic questions about the office of the chief executive: How many? How long? How chosen?

3. The answers to three other basic questions had to await future developments:

☐ How dependent would the president actually be on the votes of the people?
☐ How would conflicts between president and Congress be dealt with?
☐ How powerful would the office become, and on what kinds of questions?

These questions remained to be answered by the presidents themselves, and by the political forces of which they were a part.

The Presidency: Performance

The evolution of the presidency is the story of a frequent and cumulative increase in the role—or, better, the roles—that the president can play, and is expected to play, in the American political system, and, more recently, in the world. Every 'great' president has left the office somewhat altered and enlarged. The presidency is like a family dwelling that each new generation alters and enlarges. Confronted by some new need, a president adds on a new room, a new wing; what began as a modest dwelling has become a mansion; every president may not use every room, but the rooms are available in case of need.

THE CONTRIBUTION OF THE PRESIDENTS

Head of State: Washington

Washington's greatest legacy to future presidents was, perhaps, in creating and acting out superbly the symbolic roles that presidents have generally played ever since: as head of state for official, semiofficial, and popular functions; as a key spokesman for national unity; as a symbol of the obligation imposed on all officials, on all Americans, to obey the Constitution and to behave according to the spirit of constitutionalism. In playing the role of constitutional monarch to a republic, Washington was assisted both by his beliefs and by his practises. For he appears to have believed that the president could and should be free of partisan attachments. Yet he himself was a staunch Federalist who was prone to see 'the spirit of party' in others but not in his own administration. "He is to be blamed," a modern critic has written, "not for allying himself with a party, but for not knowing that he had done so, and for denouncing those opposed to his party as opposed to the government. He was most in the grip of party feeling at the time when he was being represented as being above it.'"[1]

It was Washington's practises that helped rescue his image of himself as above partisanship. For in Alexander Hamilton, his secretary of the treasury, Washington had a lieutenant who came as close as any American cabinet member ever has to being a prime minister to the president. It was Hamilton who discharged many of the political duties that later presidents discharged themselves, and it was therefore Hamilton, not Washington, who became the prime target of the emerging opposition. It was Hamilton who developed the administration's major policies, Hamilton who struggled to build a durable presidential coalition, Hamilton who mobilized the Congress on behalf of presidential policies.

Party Leader: Jefferson

Under Jefferson, these roles—constitutional monarch and prime minister, chief magistrate and party leader, president of the country and head of a faction within the country—were fused.

If every president since Jefferson has played the role of party leader, none has ever performed it with more consummate skill. Before he became president, and as an important instrument in gaining the presidency, Jefferson and his staunch ally Madison had forged the Republican party (which in due time was to be called the Democratic-Republican, and finally the Democratic party) as a nationwide organization with many of the features of modern parties.[2] As president, Jefferson perfected the instrument he had helped to construct. Following the pattern of John Adams, who in the late moments of his presidency had sought to pack the courts with Federalists, Jefferson now initiated a policy of appointing only trustworthy Republicans to office; justified a policy of removing Federalists from office and replacing them with Republicans; worked closely with the congressional Republican leaders in gaining the support of Congress; and sought to strengthen the national and state party machinery.[3] He was perhaps as professional a party leader as has ever occupied the White House.

Yet if Jefferson saw himself as a spokesman both for the nation as a whole and for the majority (and the party) that elected him, he accepted the fact that he must work in and through the Congress, the only legitimate representative of the popular will. In this respect, Jefferson reflected the traditional republican doctrine expressed by men as unlike as Locke,

1. Joseph Charles, *The Origins of the American Party System* (New York: Harper Torchbooks, 1961), p. 44.

2. Charles, *Origins of the American Party System;* and Noble E. Cunningham, Jr., *The Jeffersonian Republicans In Power, Party Operations 1810–1899* (Chapel Hill: University of North Carolina Press, 1963).

3. Cunningham, *Jeffersonian Republicans In Power.*

Rousseau, and the delegates to the Constitutional Convention. This view —it has been called the Whig view—holds that the true representative of the people is the legislature; the task of the executive is to 'execute' the commands of the legislative body. In persisting as long as it did in its original decision to have the chief executive elected by Congress, the Convention was to some extent reflecting this deeply ingrained respect for the representativeness of the legislative body. When Sherman announced that "an independence of the executive on the supreme legislature was in his opinion the very essence of tyranny," he spoke for a powerful tradition. Not even Jefferson claimed that the president might be as representative of the popular will or of a national majority as the Congress.

Spokesman for National Majorities: Jackson

It was Jackson who proclaimed this role for the president and thereby justified his use of the veto against congressional majorities. Jackson and his followers formulated a revolutionary new concept of the democratic executive: because in the American system, the national leader elected by and responsible to the people was the only official elected by votes cast over the whole nation, he was therefore the most legitimate representative and spokesman, as no other official could be, for the majority of the nation.

As a result of gradual change in the method of electing the president, Jackson had, in fact, rather better grounds for claiming to be the elected spokesman of the nation than Jefferson had. You will recall that the Constitution directs that "each State shall appoint, *in such Manner as the Legislature thereof may direct,* a Number of Electors" who, in turn, choose the president (Article II, italics added). At first, in most states the legislatures themselves chose the presidential electors; when Jefferson was named president in 1800, the electors were chosen by the state legislatures rather than the people in ten of the sixteen states. By 1828, however, only two states out of twenty-four (Delaware and South Carolina) still followed the old practise, and when Jackson was reelected in 1832 the only state in which electors were chosen by the legislature was South Carolina—which, incidentally, stubbornly persisted in its anachronism until 1860.[4] Thus by Jackson's time the electoral college was already becoming an anomalous, quaint, but for the most part reliable way of designating the choice for president. Consequently, in Jackson's view, if there were a clash between president and Congress, the president had as much—if not more—right to speak for the people of the country, or a majority of them, as the Congress.

— —
4. For methods of electing presidential electors, 1788–1836, see *Historical Statistics,* p. 681.

In accusing him of breaking tradition, Jackson's enemies were correct, even if their language was characteristically intemperate:

> I look upon Jackson as a detestable, ignorant, reckless, vain and malignant tyrant [Chancellor Kent, the distinguished Federalist jurist of New York, wrote in 1834 to his equally distinguished Massachusetts friend, Joseph Story] . . . . This American elective monarchy frightens me. The experiment, with its foundations laid on universal suffrage and our unfettered press, is of too violent a nature for our excitable people. . . .

> We are in the midst of a revolution [said Clay] hitherto bloodless, but tending rapidly towards a total change of the pure republican character of the government, and to the concentration of all power in the hands of one man.[5]

If the passages seem familiar, even hackneyed, it may be because every strong president since Jackson has provoked similar rhetoric. Jackson's opponents chose to call themselves Whigs in order to emphasize their adherence to the traditional view that the legislature was the supreme representative agency in a republic. They professed to seek a restoration of Jeffersonian Republicanism. In 1840, a Whig newspaper thundered:

> If ever there was a genuine Republican party in the country it is that party which General Harrison now worthily leads and leads to victory. What are its objects and ends? To restore the Constitution, the charter of public liberty, to authority, to reduce the more the monarch's power of the President of the United States.[6]

Yet, though the Whig view of the presidency lingered on, and echoes of it are heard occasionally even now, it was Jackson's enlarged conception that has generally prevailed in practise. Jackson's own accomplishments as president were mainly negative; his success depended almost entirely on his use of the executive power and the veto to negate congressional policies rather than on leadership in creating new legislation; yet during his two terms in office he added a spacious new wing to the presidency. His conception of the role of president as a national leader with his own independent basis of legitimacy in a popular majority has won the support of all our most famous presidents; it has come to be widely accepted among political leaders and the public; and it has even shaped the development of our other elected chief executives in the state and municipal governments, the governors and mayors.

Jackson's presidency foreshadowed Lincoln's. When, in 1832, a special convention called by the state legislature of South Carolina adopted an ordinance nullifying the tariff acts of 1828 and 1832, and the state legislature passed laws to enforce this Ordinance of Nullification,

---

5. Both quotations are in the modern classic on the presidency: Edward S. Corwin, *The President, Offices, and Powers* (New York: New York University Press, 1948), pp. 21–22.

6. Quoted in Wilfred E. Binkley, *President and Congress* (New York: Knopf, 1947), p. 88.

Jackson issued a Proclamation to the people of South Carolina that described nullification as an "impractical absurdity," asserted the supremacy of the sovereign and indivisible federal government over the states, and denied the right of any state either to disobey federal laws or to leave the Union. Jackson asked for and received from Congress the authority to enforce revenue laws by military force. But force proved to be unnecessary, the crisis was resolved by a compromise on the tariff, and the questions at issue were postponed, to be confronted by Lincoln when he assumed office in 1861.

National Leader in Crisis: Lincoln

It was Lincoln who carried to the outermost boundaries the president's role as leader in times of national emergency. Two thousand years earlier the Roman Republic had provided for a short-term dictator to cope with great emergencies. At the Constitutional Convention, which was much concerned, as we have seen, with the danger of creating a tyrant, no one seems to have proposed a grant of 'emergency powers' to the executive—a constitutional lacuna that constitution-makers in other countries were later to fill by various devices, not all of them successful. American presidents have filled the gap, not by changing the letter of the Constitution but by adding invisible text between the lines.

Lincoln, to be sure, was not the first president to be confronted by a crisis. Jackson, as we just saw, had to meet South Carolina's threat of disobedience. Washington called out troops to put down an insurrection by farmers in western Pennsylvania (who objected to paying an excise tax on the manufacture of whiskey, a tax that fell heavily on backwoods farmers who disposed of their surplus grain by turning it into liquor). Jefferson faced a prolonged international crisis generated by the Napoleonic wars. Madison was president during the new nation's first war, the war of 1812–4 with Britain. A war with Mexico took place during Polk's administration.

All of these were modest crises compared with the breakup of the United States. History decreed that it would be Lincoln, a Whig before he was a Republican, who should stretch the Constitution to its very limits—or, to be candid, beyond them. As a Whig, Lincoln had espoused the narrow Whig doctrine on the president; yet Lincoln's inaugural address was no Whig statement: it could have been delivered by Jackson:

> . . . I hold that, in contemplation of universal law and of the Constitution, the Union of these States is perpetual. . . . It follows from these views that no State upon its own mere motion can lawfully get out of the Union; that resolves and ordinances to that effect are legally void; and that acts of violence . . . against the authority of the United States are insurrectionary or revolutionary.
>
> I therefore consider that, in view of the Constitution and the laws, the Union is unbroken and to the extent of my ability I shall take care, as the

Constitution itself expressly enjoins upon me, that the laws of the Union be faithfully executed in all the states. Doing this I deem to be only a simple duty on my part; and I shall perform it, so far as practicable, unless my *rightful masters, the American people,* shall . . . direct to the contrary.

The chief magistrate *derives all his authority from the people.* . . . His duty is to administer the present government, as it came to his hands, and to transmit it, unimpaired by him, to his successor.[7]

Lincoln's view that the president "derives all his authority from the people" created, for him, a source of authority even more exalted than the Constitution or the Congress; and his view that "the Union" was "perpetual" no doubt justified, to him, violations of the Constitution and disregard for congressional sentiment. "Was it possible to lose the nation," he asked in 1864, "and yet to preserve the Constitution?"

Perhaps few presidents have had less of the tyrant in their nature than Lincoln, as much charity, and as little will to dominate for the mere sake of domination. It is these qualities of the man himself, the mixture of great strength with great self-restraint, the compound of resolution and forebearance, that have helped to make him an all but mythical prototype of the great popular leader. And it is because of this, and the cruel choices he faced, that it is less than charitable to be harsh about his methods.

. . . Unquestionably the high-water mark of the exercise of executive power in the United States is found in the administration of Abraham Lincoln [a historian of the presidency has written]. No President before or since has pushed the boundaries of executive power so far over into the legislative sphere. No one can ever know just what Lincoln conceived to be the limits of his powers. Even a partial review of them presents an imposing list of daring adventures. Under the war power he proclaimed the slaves of those in rebellion emancipated. He devised and put into execution his peculiar plan of reconstruction. In disregard of law he increased the army and navy beyond the limits set by statute. The privilege of the writ of habeus corpus was suspended wholesale and martial law declared. Public money in the sum of millions was deliberately spent without congressional appropriation. Nor was any of this done innocently. Lincoln understood his Constitution. He knew, in many cases, just how he was transgressing and his infractions were consequently deliberate. It is all the more astonishing that this audacity was the work of a minority President who performed in the presence of a bitter congressional opposition even in his own party.[8]

MODERN   **Crisis Leader**
DEVELOPMENTS
If, after Lincoln's death, the Congress and the Whig view of the presidency reasserted themselves, the role of emergency 'dictator' that

7. The address is quoted in full in Sandburg, *Abraham Lincoln, The War Years*, vol. I, pp. 125–135, emphasis added.

8. Binkley, *President and Congress*, p. 127.

Lincoln had created could not be wholly forgotten. Lincoln had acted mainly under two clauses of the Constitution: "The President shall be Commander in Chief of the Army and Navy of the United States . . ." and "he shall take care that the laws be faithfully executed." During the two World Wars, the cold war that followed the Second World War, the Korean war (1950–52), American involvement in Vietnam from 1956 onward, during the Cuban missile crisis of 1962 when the confrontation between the United States and the Soviet Union brought the world to the very gates of the inferno, and through the escalation and deescalation of the Vietnam war—Presidents Wilson, Franklin Roosevelt, Truman, Eisenhower, Kennedy, Johnson, and Nixon all drew heavily on these constitutional sources. To constitutional authority, Congress added other powers by delegating through normal statutory law wide discretionary authority to the president, usually but not always for a fixed period. For example, under the Lend-Lease Act of 1940,

> . . . the President was empowered (even before the country was legally at war) to procure any "defense articles" and dispose of them on such terms as he saw fit to "any country whose defense the President deems vital to the defense of the United States." Allocation of material was authorized, price controls set up, plant seizure provided for—all within the discretionary control of the President. Where these and like dispensations were questioned in court, they were always sustained.[9]

Thus the president's war power is a mighty arsenal. Yet it is not unlimited. When Lincoln suspended the writ of habeus corpus (which Article I pretty clearly intended that only Congress could do) he asked rhetorically: "Are all the laws *but one* to go unexecuted, and the Government itself to go to pieces lest that one be violated?" Nonetheless, the Supreme Court has not always responded to a president's demand that military crisis allows him to stretch the terms of the Constitution. When President Truman, acting without statutory authority, seized the steel mills to forestall a strike during the Korean war, the Supreme Court denied that the constitutional powers of the chief executive went so far. Yet the Court was obviously troubled. Four of the nine justices dissented, and the five justices in the majority disagreed among themselves as to the grounds for their decision.[10]

Foreign Affairs

To the enormous role of the president as emergency head of the country in war, the exigencies of survival in the modern world have added yet another role of great compass: the nation's leader in foreign

9. Charles Black, *Perspectives in Constitutional Law* (Englewood Cliffs: Prentice-Hall, 1963), p. 73.

10. *Youngstown Sheet and Tube* v. *Sawyer*, 343 U.S. 579 (1952).

affairs. Starting from a rather modest base in the Constitution,[11] the president has become the dominant figure in foreign policy. Woodrow Wilson, who first developed the role in its modern form (and crowned his performance with failure), foresaw (four years before he became president, when the matter was still cloudy) that control over foreign policy would give the president great power as the United States moved from the wings to the center of the world stage.

> . . . One of the greatest of the President's powers [he wrote in 1908], [is] . . . his control, which is very absolute, of the foreign relations of the nation. The initiative in foreign affairs, which the President possesses without any restrictions whatever, is virtually the power to control them absolutely. . . . The President can never again be the mere domestic figure he has been throughout so large a part of our history. The nation has risen to the first rank in power and resources. . . . Our President must always, henceforth, be one of the greatest powers of the world, whether he act greatly and wisely or not. . . .[12]

After the outbreak of the First World War, Wilson virtually took control of foreign policy into his own hands—so much so that what was to have been his greatest triumph, the Peace Treaty and the League of Nations Covenant, became his greatest defeat at the hands of a hostile Senate. From 1938 onward, as the Second World War drew near, Franklin Roosevelt more and more dominated the foreign relations of the United States. Every president since Roosevelt has had to give a major part of his attention to foreign affairs; Congress, the courts, and the country have long since shown by word and deed that they expect the initiative on foreign policy to lie with the chief executive.

Policy Initiation

In this century the president has come to play still another role: the president, not the Congress, now initiates legislation, and a president now normally brings his skills, resources, and prestige to bear on the Congress in order to secure congressional support for his policies. He is often unsuccessful. Yet it is doubtful whether either the Congress or the electorate would now be content with a chief executive who adhered faithfully to the Whig view frequently heard in the nineteenth century; the view summed up by Lincoln, for example, when he was a Whig congressman: "Were I President, I should desire the legislation of the country to rest with Congress, uninfluenced in its origin or progress,

---

11. Article II. Section 1. "The executive Power shall be vested in a President of the United States of America. . . ." Section 2. "The President . . . shall have Power, by and with the Advice and Consent of the Senate, to make Treaties, provided two thirds of the Senators present concur; and he shall nominate, and by and with the Advice and Consent of the Senate, shall appoint Ambassadors, other public Ministers and Consuls. . . ." Section 3. "He shall . . . receive Ambassadors and other public Ministers. . . ."

12. Woodrow Wilson, *Constitutional Government in the United States* (New York: Columbia University Press, 1908), pp. 77–78.

and undisturbed by the veto unless in very special and clear cases."[13] Although Lincoln did not practise what he had preached, in the last half of the nineteenth century his successors generally followed the Whig ideal rather than Lincoln's. Even Cleveland, the first member of Jackson's party elected president since before the Civil War and a man whose historical reputation as a vigorous president is strangely unsupported by historical fact, held that it was enough to recommend legislation to the Congress and then to permit that body to go its way without pressure of any kind from the White House.[14]

Ever since McKinley and Theodore Roosevelt, however, presidents have taken a much bolder role in legislation. In 1908, Woodrow Wilson formulated a view of the president's role in policy-making that, if daring at one time, has become conventional in this century: "The Constitution bids him speak, and times of stress and change must more and more thrust upon him the attitude of originator of policies."[15]

Later, as governor of New Jersey, Wilson said: ". . . a new role, which to many persons seems a little less than unconstitutional, is thrust upon our executives. The people are impatient of a President or a governor who will not formulate a policy and insist upon its adoption."[16] As president, Wilson lived up to his conception; no president since Jefferson worked so closely with his party in Congress nor was more effective in gaining congressional support for his policies: tariff reform, the Federal Reserve Act, the Federal Trade Commission Act, the Clayton Anti-Trust Act.[17]

Wilson's successors, particularly Franklin Roosevelt, Truman, Kennedy, and Johnson, took for granted that they, not Congress, must originate legislation and must use every means at their disposal to secure its adoption by Congress. Thus in securing passage of most of the New Deal legislation, the preponderant influence was that of Franklin Roosevelt.[18] Although even as late as the New Deal, congressmen occasionally spoke as if the president's role in legislation was a usurpation of their own legitimate authority, objections of this kind have grown less and less audible. The death knell of the Whig view may have been sounded when Republican congressional leaders complained of Presi-

---

13. Cited in Corwin, *The President, Offices, and Powers*, p. 381, fn. 60.

14. Binkley, *President and Congress*, p. 178.

15. Wilson, *Constitutional Government*, p. 73.

16. Quoted in Arthur W. Macmahon, "Woodrow Wilson: Political Leader and Administrator," in *The Philosophy and Policies of Woodrow Wilson*, ed. Earl Latham (Chicago: University of Chicago Press, 1958), p. 100.

17. Lester V. Chandler, "Wilson's Monetary Reform," John Perry Miller, "Woodrow Wilson's Contribution to Antitrust Policy," and Richard P. Longaker, "Woodrow Wilson and the Presidency," in Latham, *Philosophy and Policies of Woodrow Wilson*.

18. See the tabulation in Lawrence H. Chamberlain, *The President, Congress and Legislation* (New York: Columbia University Press, 1946), p. 450. See also Chamberlain's comments, pp. 18–19.

dent Eisenhower's failure to present them promptly with a full legislative program.

Administrative Head

The most recent role in the now vast presidential repertoire is his responsibility as head—if sometimes only nominal head—of the extensive administrative structure that has developed for handling national affairs in this century. In 1901, the federal government had some 231 thousand civilian employees. By 1930 the number had reached 590 thousand. Under the impact of the New Deal and then the Second World War, civilian federal employment swelled to a total of 3.7 million in 1944, from which it receded to something over 2 million in the years that followed. Controlling this enormous establishment and meeting his constitutional obligation "to take care that the laws be faithfully executed" is a complex and time-consuming presidential task. Cabinet officers, bureau chiefs, commission heads are powerful men; and it is difficult indeed for the man in the White House to keep track even in a general way of what they are doing, or to secure their compliance with his own policies. Each president brings to this all but impossible task his own techniques and style. None discharges it without failures.

A SUCCESS? Thus the elastic framework the Founders created for the presidency has been filled out and expanded by the presidents. Today the presidency is a result of the forces that have played upon that office: the initial impetus received from the Convention, the men who have held the office, the situations and times in which they have acted, the responses of other leaders and of ordinary citizens.

Undeniably, what has emerged is one of the most influential offices in the world; considering the place of the United States in the world, it is no mere hyperbole to suggest that the American president today is, taken all around, the most important popularly elected official in human history.

But how successful is the presidency as an office in a polyarchy with aspirations toward democracy? To answer this question would require us to place the presidency in the perspective of other important elements in the American political system that bear heavily upon his power and his actions, particularly the Congress, the courts, elections, political parties, federalism, local governments. Description of these awaits later chapters. It is convenient and perhaps even necessary for clarity that we examine each of these major institutions separately; but like examining the organs of the human body one by one we might end with little sense of how they operate as a system. Nonetheless, it is not too soon to deal briefly with two questions that bear upon the success of the presidency as the chief magistrate of a polyarchy. First, given all the roles that the Constitution, the presidents themselves, and historical developments have thrust upon the president, is the office now too great for one man? If so, what if anything can be done about it? Second, does the office give the incumbent too much power measured by democratic standards—or not enough measured by the demands heaped upon him?

TOO MUCH TO DO? All the roles that have accumulated in the repertory of the president impose a burden that is appallingly difficult to discharge, and perhaps impossible to discharge well. A friendly critic can easily find serious deficiencies in the performance of all our twentieth century presidents. The presidency may have become a testing ground where failure is now the normal outcome. What human being *could* fulfill the awesome obligations of that great office?

Proposals are often made for reducing the burdens of the presidency. Yet workable or acceptable changes promise little relief; and changes that *would* reduce the scope of the office enough to matter seem unworkable or unacceptable. Thus it has been suggested that the president might give up his symbolic roles: his duties as head of state. But where are these duties to be lodged? As we have seen, a number of polyarchies solve the problem, at least in part, with a hereditary monarchy or an elected head of state who serves as a figurehead. Thus Britain, Sweden, Norway, Denmark, Holland, and Belgium have all retained their royal families for ceremonial purposes. Australia, Canada, and New Zealand each have a governor general. Switzerland, Germany, Austria, Italy, and India have a ceremonial president. These solutions have worked well. Yet a constitutional monarch is as unacceptable to Americans as it was in 1787. As for the other alternatives, if a special ceremonial office were to be created after nearly two centuries under the presidential system, it would probably not work in practise simply because the president's symbolic role is too important to him politically to make him willing to yield its advantages to a figurehead. Would he not, in fact, fight such a constitutional amendment tooth and nail? Moreover, what head of state, ambassador, member of Congress, or plain citizen would sit with a figurehead if he could meet with the real center of authority?

If the ceremonial burdens of the office cannot be lightened, what of the administrative load? It is sometimes suggested that the vice-presidency be turned into a kind of administrative chief-of-staff. But the president's burdens arise less from administrative details than from all the decisions he cannot delegate without abdicating his responsibilities. A vice-president who took over the burden of presidential decisions would in effect be another president; surely few presidents would tolerate such a rival. As for delegating work to subordinates, the president already has a White House staff of more than a thousand employees. He can, if he wishes, create a de facto chief-of-staff, as Eisenhower did with Sherman Adams. But the danger with a chief-of-staff is that the president may become too much his captive; most presidents are unwilling— rightly, I think—to allow one subordinate such a monopoly over access to him.

It has been suggested that the president make greater use of his Cabinet. Yet it is not clear how this would help. Cabinet officers are appointed for many reasons; they do not necessarily have great administrative skills; they may not always agree with the president on policy; indeed one task of the president, and no easy one, is to make sure that department heads follow his policies. The Cabinet is, in any case, a large and unwieldy collection.

Naive critics sometimes yearn for a president who would be 'above politics.' He could thus give up his role as party leader by yielding this presumably unworthy task to unworthy politicians. This seems to have been, at times, Eisenhower's view of the presidency: ". . . in the general derogatory sense you can say that, of course, I do not like politics."[19] Yet the result of not liking "politics" was that Eisenhower did not work at the job of party leader, and this in turn resulted, as it would for any president, in a considerable diminution of his authority with Congress.[20] A president who wants to persuade Congress to adopt his program will, above all, execute the role of party leader, as Jefferson, McKinley, Wilson, the two Roosevelts, Truman, Kennedy, and Johnson all did.

The presidency, then, is unquestionably too great for any man. No president can ever measure up to its obligations.

No one, then, is really qualified to be president of the United States, least of all now in the last part of the twentieth century. Yet in this period of history, could anyone assume this position who did not believe that it is the world's most important public office or sense, with at least a touch of awe, the rich traditions of an office inextricably intermingled with the history of the nation?

TOO MUCH POWER? The presidency has evolved into "the vital place of action in the system," as Woodrow Wilson described it.[21] The president is the energizer, the innovator; when energy, skill, and determination are missing in the White

19. Richard E. Neustadt, *Presidential Power, the Politics of Leadership* (New York: Wiley, 1960), p. 166.

20. For a concrete example, see the description of the congressional battle over renewing the Reciprocal Trade Act in 1955 in Raymond A. Bauer, Ithiel de Sola Pool, and Lewis A. Dexter, *American Business and Public Policy, The Politics of Foreign Trade* (New York: Atherton Press, 1963), ch. 5. See also Chapter 25 in this book.

21. Wilson, *Constitutional Government*, p. 73.

House, the system must coast along on past policies. New policies, new legislation depend almost entirely on the president.

What of the president's power? Is he too powerful? Or not powerful enough?

This innocent question, a favorite subject of discussion among those who contemplate the American presidency, is much more difficult to answer than it seems. It is difficult to answer in part because 'power' is not a simple concept, as it is often assumed to be, but an exceedingly complex and many-sided notion; there are, in practise, no ways of measuring power with satisfactory precision. Moreover, even for a crude answer, it is obviously important to specify the time in which the president's actions occur, the situation with which the country is confronted, and the subjects he deals with: what would be considered too much presidential power in peacetime might be too little in wartime. Finally, what criteria are we to use for determining 'too much' or 'too little'?

Variations among Presidents

Throughout the history of the presidency, there have been many fluctuations in the extent to which the president initiates policies and secures their adoption and enforcement by the national government. Lincoln, as we have seen, all but single-handedly determined policies bearing on the war and the South. On Lincoln's death a reaction against executive power set in, and from Grant's inauguration until McKinley entered the White House in 1897, the presidency was eclipsed by Congress. McKinley's presidency may be regarded as the beginning of a long-run increase in presidential control over policy-making. This secular increase in presidential power has been marked, however, by significant fluctuations caused both by the man and the circumstances. In emergencies such as the Great Depression and particularly in wartime, presidents have inevitably expanded their untrammeled control over policy. The man himself—his skills, energy, style, and goals—also makes a difference. A student of the presidency has compared Franklin Roosevelt and Dwight Eisenhower:

> . . . Roosevelt's methods were the product of his insights, his incentives, and his confidence. No President in this century has had a sharper sense of personal power, a sense of what it is and where it comes from; none has had more hunger for it, few have had more use for it, and only one or two could match his faith in his own competence to use it. Perception and desire and self-confidence, combined, produced their own reward. No modern President has been more nearly master in the White House.
> . . . With Eisenhower, seemingly, the case is quite opposite. . . . Through Eisenhower's first six years his power sense was blunt in almost the degree that F.D.R.'s was sharp. As late as 1958 he had not quite got over "shocked surprise" that orders did not carry themselves out. Apparently he could not quite absorb the notion that effective power had to be extracted out

of other men's self-interest; neither did he quite absorb the notion that nobody else's interest could be wholly like his own. And he seems to have been unaware of all his natural advantages in turning different interests toward his own.[22]

A president who is reluctant to develop the potential power of the office, or does not know how to, is obviously likely to be less influential than one who both wants and knows how to increase and retain presidential authority.

Variations in the Strength of Other Actors

Obviously the president's power depends on the extent to which other actors are in a position to exercise control over him or the matters he deals with. To put the point in a way that will now be familiar to the reader: the more that authority on a given matter is partitioned among other individuals, offices, and institutions outside his control, the less the president's power will be. In general, the president is most severely limited when his constitutional authority is clearly restricted; when he operates in an area where he has no unique legitimacy; when no emergency is thought to exist; where public opinion is well defined, highly structured, and not responsive to the president; and where well-organized groups outside the Executive Branch regularly participate in the kind of decision at hand. Conversely, the president's own control over a decision is greatest where his constitutional authority is broad and ill defined; he has a special legitimacy; an emergency is thought to exist; public opinion is weak, unstructured, and highly responsive to the president; and where few if any well-organized groups outside the Executive Branch regularly participate. Decisions vary in the extent to which these factors are present. However, domestic policies often fall most clearly into the first category, while foreign and military policies sometimes fall into the second.

Domestic policies. On most questions of domestic policy and sometimes on foreign policy, the president is hedged in by the Congress, the Supreme Court, his own officials, his party leaders, public opinion, the national communications media, and the prospect of coming elections, both presidential and congressional. Observers who look at the presidency from a distance can easily underestimate how much these factors limit the president's range of action. For decades, the Congress rejected presidential proposals on civil rights and medical care. Within three months after President Truman ordered the government to seize the steel industry during the Korean war, the Supreme Court held his action unconstitutional, and the steel mills had to be returned at once to private

---

22. Neustadt, *Presidential Power*, pp. 161, 163–164.

hands. To pick another example from the experience of a strong executive with a penchant for decisive action, Truman dallied month after month before relieving General MacArthur of his command in Korea for failure to execute orders. For not only was MacArthur a distinguished general with a following in Congress and the country, but also, as Truman said later, MacArthur "was a commander in the field. You pick your man, you've got to back him up."[23] A president may have to discard or modify a policy because of negative responses from farmers, doctors, an ethnic group, a region, union leaders, an industry . . . for the publics that comprise 'public opinion' have sanctions: congressional and presidential elections.

In fact, in recent decades most presidents have been severely mauled by Congress sooner or later. Even Franklin Roosevelt was stymied on domestic reform from 1938 onward by a congressional coalition of Republicans and Southern Democrats. Neither Harry Truman nor John F. Kennedy was able to get much legislation past the Congress. Richard Nixon suffered the unprecedented humiliation of having two of his candidates for the Supreme Court turned down by the Senate and some of his key legislative programs defeated, emasculated, or modified.

Thus election to the office of the presidency by no means carries with it the authority to carry out the policies which the successful candidate promised to execute during his campaign. Even if the president has a stronger claim to being a spokesman for a national majority than anyone else in the United States, the system of partitioned power means that his claim is not ordinarily backed up with the political resources to make it good.

Foreign affairs. Questions of foreign policy are sometimes rather like matters of domestic policy. Thus most presidential requests for foreign aid have been cut by the Congress, often severely, despite the best efforts of the White House to retain the full amounts requested. It is true, nonetheless, that certain kinds of foreign policy issues have come closest to the situation of wide presidential discretion just described. Roosevelt's conduct of the Second World War, Truman's decision to enter Korea, Kennedy's decisions on the Bay of Pigs and the Cuban missile crisis, Johnson's escalation and Nixon's deescalation of the war in Vietnam, and Nixon's attempted rapprochement with China were all cases where a president was able to exercise enormous discretionary power.

The constitutional provisions making the president commander-in-chief and leader on foreign policy proved to be a veritable cornucopia of unchallengable legal authority. In addition, from Lincoln's time onward, the presidency accumulated a special legitimacy on these matters:

---

23. *Ibid.,* p. 146. The incident is described and analyzed in considerable detail in the Neustadt book.

people expected the president to take the lead. Moreover, whenever a widespread sense of emergency existed, potential opposition was hesitant and easily squelched by suggestions that it was unpatriotic or incompetent to act in these domains; public opinion was unstructured and malleable; the country was thought to be in danger or at least in need of a decisive military response, hence all loyal citizens were expected to rally behind the president; in crisis the people must trust their leaders, and so on. Finally, in these circumstances, well-organized groups capable of giving advice and participating in decisions were almost exclusively located in the Defense Department, the State Department, and the White House itself. When it was caught in a seeming emergency, the Senate Foreign Relations Committee would be inclined to back away. The plethora of organized interest groups that would have leaped into action at the first sign of movement on such issues as taxation, labor relations, agricultural subsidies, tariffs and quotas, and many other domestic subjects simply did not exist. Thus the early opponents of the war in Vietnam confronted just such a situation. The political processes that usually operate in domestic affairs to provide a well-organized and articulate minority with some leverage on policy somewhere in the Executive Branch, Congress, or the Court were simply not operating in decisions on Vietnam. Lacking well-established organizations with ready access to Congress and the executive, often short on the political skills necessary to develop political access and a permanent organization, cut off from the leadership of both major parties, unable to persuade the courts to intervene, for some years opponents of the war, though more numerous than, say, farmers, had far less influence on policy than farm lobbies. Their inability to use conventional means effectively is undoubtedly one reason why they so often relied on the technique of mass demonstrations.

Appraisal. Is the president, then, too powerful—or not powerful enough? On domestic matters, the American president is not more independent of popular, constitutional, or legislative controls than the chief executives of many other polyarchies. Today, Theodore Roosevelt might have to modify his observation that "there inheres in the Presidency more power than in any other office in any great republic or constitutional monarchy of our times."[24] The president is more at the mercy of Congress than, for example, the British prime minister is at the mercy of Parliament. If the president is, or at least can be, more powerful than the premier of the Third and Fourth Republics of France, his discretion is more limited than was that of President de Gaulle in the Fifth Republic.

A more relevant criterion, however, is whether the presidency has accumulated such massive resources of power that a skillful president

---

24. Quoted in John Blum, *The Republican Roosevelt* (New York: Atheneum, 1963), p. 107.

can, on important issues, act counter to the preferences of a congressional majority or majority opinion in the country; or, worse, can systematically manipulate congressional and public opinion in order to achieve his purposes. That the president sometimes chooses policies that do not have the support of congressional majorities is undeniable. But for the most part he must do so negatively, as Jackson did, by means of the veto. It is exceedingly difficult, perhaps impossible, for him to persist in positive policies that a majority in both houses of Congress oppose, for the Congress has too many ways of getting revenge on the president: investigating committees, denial of funds, rejection of appointments, and the ultimate threat, impeachment. Moreover, a president who defies Congress cannot succeed in his defiance unless he and his policy have more support in the influential publics of the nation than the congressmen he opposes. A president who persists in opposing *both* the Congress *and* a large fraction of articulate opinion is headed for certain defeat, one way or another.

Because American politics is more a matter of articulate and influential minorities than of cohesive majorities, it is by no means easy to tell at any given moment whether the president or the Congress has the greater public support in a conflict. In pressing a controversial policy, a president always assumes the risk of miscalculating congressional or public opinion. Can he warp public or congressional opinion to his own desires? That the president has enormous resources for influencing opinion is obvious: his prestige, the constant attention focused on him by all the media of communications, his unequalled access to information. By holding a press conference, as Franklin Roosevelt demonstrated, the president can, in effect, write an editorial on behalf of his policies in every newspaper in the country, even those hostile to him. Yet his prestige is a fragile thing, as Gallup polls have shown over the last several decades.[25] Perhaps no better record of how limited his ability is to manipulate public opinion at will can be found than the testimony of these polls (Figure 11.1). His slightest mistakes are ruthlessly exploited— usually exaggerated—by the opposition; the least breath of scandal is turned against him; and if he claims the benefits of good times when they occur during his administration, he is also a handy target for resentment when the economy declines or things go badly in international politics (which sooner or later, they do). As for Congress, the limits of the president's capacity for bending that stubborn body to his desires

---

25. In "Presidential Popularity from Truman to Johnson" *(American Political Science Review,* 64 [March, 1970], 18–34), John E. Mueller analyzed the responses to the question used in Figure 11.1. He found that on the average the four presidents began with a popularity rating at 69%; irrespective of international crises, economic events, and war their popularity rating declined 6% a year on the average. He also found, however, that these averages concealed wide variations; thus Eisenhower's popularity did not decline at all, while Truman's and Johnson's plummeted.

Figure 11.1
Presidential Popularity

"Do you approve of the way President ———— is handling his job as president?"
(By four-month periods: Jan.-April; May-Aug.; Sept.-Dec.)

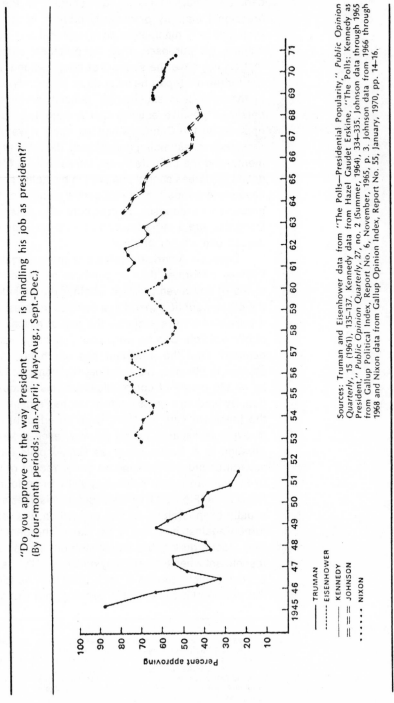

Sources: Truman and Eisenhower data from "The Polls—Presidential Popularity," *Public Opinion Quarterly*, 15 (1961), 135-137. Kennedy data from Hazel Gaudet Erskine, "The Polls: Kennedy as President," *Public Opinion Quarterly*, 27, no. 2 (Summer, 1964), 334-335. Johnson data through 1965 from Gallup Political Index, Report No. 6, November, 1965, p. 3. Johnson data from 1966 through 1968 and Nixon data from Gallup Opinion Index, Report No. 55, January, 1970, pp. 14-16.

are demonstrated by the frequency with which Congress rejects his legislative proposals.

Yet if the presidency is in many ways an office of circumscribed power, cases in which a president has been able to act with little control beyond his own advisers and his own conscience, particularly on foreign military crises, have created a profound sense of concern among some observers, both inside and outside the Congress. In the early 1970s this concern was reflected in congressional efforts to reassert control on such crucial matters as the use of troops abroad. In 1971, a liberal Republican senator from New York and a conservative Democratic senator from Mississippi both introduced bills to limit the president's power to commit the nation to war without the consent of Congress. "The decision to make war is too big a decision for one mind to make and too awesome a responsibility for one man to bear," Senator Stennis of Mississippi told the Senate in introducing his bill. "There must be a collective judgment given and a collective responsibility shared."[26]

The question remains, then, whether the combination of the design, half by accident, of the Founders plus the growth in the presidency over nearly two centuries have not left us with an office simultaneously too demanding and too powerful. In a polyarchy that aspires toward democracy, should any single citizen, no matter what his office, be as powerful as the president of the United States?

A modern description of the British monarchy in the early eighteenth century seems uncomfortably close to fitting the American presidency in the twentieth:

> Despite the numerous limitations placed upon the royal power since 1660, the king remained the dominant figure in political life. The Constitution endowed the monarch, as chief executive, with control of Government patronage and national policy, a share in one or both of which is ever the goal of the aspiring politician. He who would secure place, honour, pension, or other favor must go to Court. He who would influence the great decisions of state must first convince his Majesty. It should be said, however, that in neither of these areas was royal power absolute. . . . Though the Constitution made no distinction between royal policy and national policy, the king could not carry out decisions strenuously disapproved by a parliamentary majority and devoid of the necessary financial support. On the other hand, to obtain a favour or to implement a design opposed by the monarch was extremely difficult. Nothing but heavy pressure from external circumstances could ordinarily force the king to act against his will. If not absolute, therefore, royal control of policy and patronage was at once so extensive in its scope, so pervasive in its influence, and so concentrated in the king's person that politics inevitably revolved about the throne.[27]

---

26. *The New York Times,* May 12, 1971, p. 14.

27. Archibald S. Foord, *His Majesty's Opposition 1714–1830* (Oxford: Oxford University Press, 1964), pp. 16–17.

The twentieth century has seen the emergence of powerful leaders in polyarchies and non-polyarchies alike: Roosevelt, Churchill, Nehru, Adenauer, de Gaulle; Mussolini, Stalin, Hitler, Tito, Castro, Mao Tse-Tung. This phenomenon has been interpreted as the reemergence of the Prince, the rebirth in a new guise of monarchy, the age of Caesars.

In an age of Caesars, should the presidency be scaled down to more nearly human proportions? Can it be? How, and at what price?

Like most students of the presidency, most Americans seem to agree that the office has served the republic well. From its first beginnings, it has been in perpetual evolution; there is little room for doubt that this great political office will continue to evolve. In what ways? Though we can now see the office of the president far more clearly than the men could who tried to design it in 1787, like them, we cannot foresee clearly the shape that office will take in the future. But we can be sure that the future character of the American polyarchy will depend heavily on the way the presidency evolves.

SUMMARY 1. Presidents have filled out the loose design of the office prescribed in the Constitution, and in doing so have enlarged the presidency by defining a number of roles the president can and indeed is expected to play.

2. These include his responsibilities and powers as head of state, party leader, spokesman for national majorities, national leader in times of crisis, chief of foreign affairs, policy initiator, and administrative head.

3. Among the problems of the presidency for which no clear solutions have so far emerged are:

☐ The *burden* of the office, which may well have become too great for any man to discharge satisfactorily.
☐ The *power* of the office. On the one hand the president's power tends to be highly circumscribed on domestic matters, where power is extensively partitioned. On certain foreign-military decisions, on the other hand, his power is often of vast scope.

Congress as Representative: The Design

If the president has become the main source of drive, energy, and leadership in the American political system, what functions does the Congress perform?

The design of the Congress presented the Convention not only with some of its easiest problems but also with a few of its thorniest ones. That there must be a legislative body was a matter beyond debate. That it must consist of two houses; that one of these must represent 'the people'; that the national legislature must have power to make national law; that this body would be the chief if not, in fact, the exclusive source of national law, other than the Constitution itself; that it would serve as a check on the president—these propositions were not seriously contested.

So far, then, as the intentions of the Convention are clear, the minimum functions of the Congress were three: to make national laws, to represent 'the people,' and to check and control the power of the chief executive. These functions were obviously interrelated. Given the political ideas prevalent in the United States at that time, and in the Convention, the only legitimate source of new laws, other than amendments to the Constitution, would be the legislature. Most of the delegates doubtless took it for granted that policy-making would consist almost entirely of law-making, that proposals for new laws would originate in the legislature, which would examine these proposals, act on them and, if it so decided, give them the necessary stamp of legality. To make policy was to make law; to make law was to legislate; and only a legislature could legislate. Q.E.D.

Essentially what gave legitimacy to a legislature in the law-making process was its representative character. The legislature was to represent, to stand for, to serve on behalf of the citizens of the United States.

That the Congress should (and would) also serve as a check on the chief executive followed from the general principle of partitioning power by pitting one part of government against another: "by so contriving the interior structure of the government as that its several constituent parts may, by their mutual relations, be the means of keeping each other in their proper places," as the authors of *The Federalist* were to put it.[1]

While the delegates no doubt took this checking role of the Congress for granted, they said surprisingly little about it at the Convention. In the light of later developments, this is a curious omission—probably accounted for in two ways. In the first place, the delegates saw the legislature as the most dynamic and most dangerous branch; hence they were preoccupied—one might almost say obsessed—with the problem of building adequate restraints on that body. When they spoke of the relations between chief executive and Congress, their concern was invariably with the role of executive as a check on the Congress, not the other way around.

In the second place, as we saw in Chapter 10, throughout most of the Convention it appeared that the president was going to be elected by the Congress. This in itself, it was assumed, would provide a powerful check by legislature on executive; hence the delegates may have assumed that further discussion of the adequacy of Congress's power to check the president was unnecessary. Indeed, the problem, in their eyes, was quite the opposite; if Congress elected the president, would this not give the legislature too much control over the executive, and, conversely, the executive too little independence of the legislature? In the end, as we know, they solved this problem by creating an executive elected independently of the Congress.

DISAGREEMENTS Yet if the delegates to the Constitutional Convention were evidently in substantial agreement that the national legislature they proposed to create would, at a minimum, make national laws, represent the people of the United States, and help control the chief executive, they did not agree on other matters; certain questions that were controversial in 1787 and uneasily decided at the Convention remain controversial today. Nor could the delegates to the Convention accurately foresee the shape of future problems as the United States developed into a great nation and then a world power.

Of the questions left unsettled by the Convention, two are particularly important.

1. Hamilton et al., *The Federalist* No. 51, p. 336.

□ First, even if it be assumed that Congress is to 'represent the people' in some sense, should it represent each citizen equally, or should some minorities or 'interests' be given extra protection by means of extra weight in the national legislature?

□ Second, if the Congress is to make laws and to check the executive, how far should its control over policy and appointments extend?

I propose to explore the first of these questions in this chapter, and the second in the next.

MAJORITIES IN THE HOUSE, MINORITIES IN THE SENATE

Like everyone else who has ever seriously examined the problems of 'representing the people,' the men at the Convention were confronted by some exceedingly difficult questions. If their compromises helped to shape the American political tradition, their conflicting viewpoints persist within that tradition down to the present day.

The House: Spokesman for Majorities

The House of Representatives, as Sherman of Connecticut suggested it be named, presented only modest difficulties. Although there was scattered opposition to the idea that one house of Congress was to be elected by the people, that proposal passed early and easily and was never subsequently contested. Yet it seems to have been widely assumed at the Convention that the House of Representatives would be the driving force in the system; that the people's representatives would be turbulent and insistent; that they would represent majorities and would be indifferent to the rights of minorities; that the people would be the winds driving the ship of state and their representatives would be the sails, swelling with every gust. Gouverneur Morris evidently reflected the dominant view when he remarked that "the first branch, originating from the people, will ever be subject to *precipitancy, changeability,* and *excess.*"[2]

Given their agreement on the need to partition power, not least the power of a majority and its representatives, it followed that the "popular branch" (like every other branch) must be hedged in by constraints: by the Constitution itself, the president, the courts, the states, and, not least, the other house of Congress.

The Senate: Bastion of Minorities

It was in the composition of the other house that the Convention faced one of its most difficult problems, to which it gave a compromise solution that a majority of the delegates probably opposed in principle

---

2. *Documents,* p. 838. The quotation is from the notes of Yates; Madison recorded substantially the same words, p. 319.

but had to accept out of expediency. The problem had two sides, one intellectual and the other political. Although the second has been much emphasized, the first has been almost ignored. Yet it goes to the heart of a problem still debated in the United States.

The intellectual problem turns on this question: Is it possible to protect minorities by giving them a larger share of representatives in a legislature than they would be entitled to simply by their numbers, without at the same time creating a potential injustice to other minorities or to majorities? The Convention wrestled with this problem, as Americans have ever since; but it cannot be said that the Founders came up with an intellectually defensible solution.

Morris's solution. Gouverneur Morris, as might be expected, saw the question as a straightforward one of protecting the rich minority from the 'people' and vice versa. What qualities, he asked, are necessary in the second branch of the Congress if it is to check the excesses of the people's representatives:

> . . . *Abilities* and *virtue,* are equally necessary in both branches. Something more then is now wanted. 1. the checking branch must have a personal interest in checking the other branch, one interest must be opposed to another interest. Vices as they exist, must be turned agst each other. 2. It must have great personal property, it must have the aristocratic spirit; it must love to lord it thro' pride. . . . 3. It should be independent. . . . To make it independent, it should be for life. . . . By thus combining & setting apart, the aristocratic interest, the popular interest will be combined agst it. There will be a mutual check and mutual security. 4. An independence for life, involves the necessary permanency. . . .[3]

In this blunt view of the ineradicable conflict of social classes, "the rich" versus "the rest," "the aristocratic interest" versus "the popular interest," Morris may have overstated his case, but he undoubtedly reflected a common view.

Madison's solution. In a masterly analysis marked by his customary moderation, Madison espoused a not dissimilar point of view; but he arrived at a different solution. One of Madison's most impressive utterances, it is worth reproducing in full:

> In order to judge of the form to be given to this institution, it will be proper to take a view of the ends to be served by it. These were first to protect the people agst their rulers: secondly to protect the people agst the transient impressions into which they themselves might be led. A people deliberating in a temperate moment, and with the experience of other nations before them, on the plan of Govt most likely to secure their happiness, would first be aware, that those chargd with the public happiness, might betray their trust. An obvious precaution agst this danger wd be to divide the trust be-

---

3. *Ibid.,* pp. 319–320.

tween different bodies of men, who might watch & check each other. In this they w^d be governed by the same prudence which has prevailed in organizing the subordinate departments of Gov^t, where all business liable to abuses is made to pass thro' separate hands, the one being a check on the other. It w^d next occur to such a people, that they themselves were liable to temporary errors, thro' want of information as to their true interest, and that men chosen for a short term, & employed but a small portion of that in public affairs, might err from the same cause. This reflection w^d naturally suggest that the Gov^t be so constituted, as that one of its branches might have an opp^y [opportunity] of acquiring a competent knowledge of the public interests. Another reflection equally becoming a people on such an occasion, w^d be that they themselves, as well as a numerous body of Representatives, were liable to err also, from fickleness and passion. A necessary fence ag^st this danger would be to select a portion of enlightened citizens, whose limited number, and firmness might seasonably interpose ag^st impetuous councils. It ought finally to occur to a people deliberating on a Gov^t for themselves, that as different interests necessarily result from the liberty meant to be secured, the major interest might under sudden impulses be tempted to commit injustice on the minority. In all civilized Countries the people fall into different classes hav^g a real or supposed difference of interests. There will be creditors & debtors, farmers, merch^ts & manufacturers. There will be particularly the distinction of rich & poor. It was true as had been observ^d [by Mr. Pinkney] we had not among us those hereditary distinctions, of rank which were a great source of the contests in the ancient Gov^ts as well as the modern States of Europe, nor those extremes of wealth or poverty which characterize the latter. We cannot however be regarded even at this time, as one homogeneous mass, in which every thing that affects a part will affect in the same manner the whole. In framing a system which we wish to last for ages, we sh^d not lose sight of the changes which ages will produce. An increase of population will of necessity increase the proportion of those who will labour under all the hardships of life, & secretly sigh for a more equal distribution of its blessings. These may in time outnumber those who are placed above the feelings of indigence. According to the equal laws of suffrage, the power will slide into the hands of the former. No agrarian attempts have yet been made in this Country, but symptoms, of a leveling spirit, as we have understood, have sufficiently appeared in a certain quarters to give notice of the future danger. How is this danger to be guarded ag^st on republican principles? How is the danger in all cases of interested coalitions to oppress the minority to be guarded ag^st?[4]

Madison posed the problem clearly. The popular branch might act out of impulse, ignorance, or interest "to commit injustice on the minority." The second branch must therefore be so constituted as to "aid on such emergencies, the preponderance of justice by throwing its weight into that scale."[5]

But how was the second branch to be made up? Here was the nub of the difficulty. If the second branch were elected by the people (as Wilson, the most persistent advocate of a democratic republic, proposed),

4. *Ibid.*, pp. 279–281.
5. *Ibid.*, p. 281.

then it would represent the same interests as the other house and would hardly serve as a check on it. Gerry of Massachusetts, worried by the fact that farmers vastly outnumbered businessmen, observed: "To draw both branches from the people will leave no security to the latter [commercial] interest; the people being chiefly composed of the landed interest, and erroneously supposing, that the other interests are adverse to it."[6] What interests were the senators supposed to represent? Why should *these* particular interests be given special weight? And how were senators to be chosen to represent these interests? Although the first two questions were logically prior, debate turned almost entirely on the last question. Yet it is the first two that were—and are—most troublesome.

WHICH MINORITIES? Should a legislature represent interests or individuals? It cannot do both. For if interests are to be given equal representation, then individuals must be denied equal representation. There is no way out of this dilemma. And why should some interests be given more power than others? It might be argued that unless a certain interest were given extra numbers in the legislature, it would be unjustly treated by a legislative majority. This was the essence of Morris's and Madison's argument. Yet, in this solution to the problem of majority 'tyranny,' there are two exceedingly serious difficulties that neither Morris nor Madison dealt with.

First, since almost any minority might be unjustly treated by a majority, it would seem to follow that *every* minority should be over-represented—doctors, lawyers, college professors, businessmen, trade unionists, cotton farmers, wheat farmers, tobacco farmers, Catholics, Jews, Negroes, 'Wasps' (White Anglo-Saxon Protestants). We quickly arrive at an absurdity. Morris and Madison were rescued from absurdity because of the simplicity of prevailing conceptions of the interests of the country in 1787. Charles Cotesworth Pinckney suggested that "the people of the U.S. may be divided into three classes—*professional men . . .; commercial men . . .; the landed interest. . . .*"[7] This simple scheme was reasonable in 1787; it would be unacceptable today.

Second, if an interest is given special weight, what is to prevent it from using its added power unjustly toward the majority? If a minority has enough representation to prevent a majority from acting unjustly toward it, it will also have enough representation to prevent a majority from acting justly. Are we to suppose that minorities invariably act justly, and majorities never? Neither Morris nor Madison made such an un-

---

6. *Ibid.*, p. 170.
7. *Ibid.*, pp. 271–272.

tenable assumption. If, as Morris said, the rich always have and always will "strive to establish their dominion and enslave the rest," what would happen if the rich were given enough power to veto the actions of a majority that wanted to enact, say, a progressive income tax? Would the rich not use their power in naked self-interest to prevent themselves from being taxed more heavily than others? Or suppose that the rich are mistreating their employees: is a legislative majority to be prevented from passing laws regulating employer-employee relations, simply because the rich are opposed?

Estates of the Realm?

In conceiving of the representation of interests in different houses, men like Morris were reverting to a medieval conception of a parliament that represented the estates of the realm. In Britain there was the House of Lords for church and aristocracy, the House of Commons for the commoners—though in actual practise in 1787 only a tiny percentage of adult males could vote in elections to that House. Within two years, the king of France was to summon an anachronism that had not met since 1614, the Estates-General, which consisted of the First Estate, or lower clergy, the Second Estate or nobility, and the Third Estate or the 'people.' But the Third Estate lost no time in facilitating a revolution that forever ended the Estates-General in France. In Sweden, four estates—nobility, clergy, burghers, and peasants—had been represented in the Riksdag, or parliament, since the Middle Ages; under the impact of democratic ideas the four estates were finally to be abolished in 1866 and replaced by a bicameral legislature. In 1849, the ruler of Prussia would sway gently with the winds of revolution by providing universal suffrage— combined with a three-class system of voting under which a tiny minority consisting of the richest taxpayers elected one-third of the deputies in indirect elections, a second class of moderately well-to-do citizens elected another third, and the rest of the population, more than 80 percent of the taxpayers, chose the remaining third. ("It would be difficult to devise an electoral measure," it has been said, "more calculated to alienate the lower classes from the national political system."[8])

It is doubtful whether any members of the Convention, including Morris, entertained ideas of this kind. The Americans, after all, consisted almost entirely of small farmers plus a handful of merchants and artisans. There was no titled aristocracy, as in Britain, no clerical estate, as in France and Sweden. When one got right down to the nub of the matter, by European standards Americans were all commoners. Consequently, although the familiar distinction between the House of Lords and the

---

8. Stein Rokkan, "The Comparative Study of Political Participation," in *Essays on the Behavioral Study of Politics*, ed. Austin Ranney (Urbana: University of Illinois Press, 1962), p. 76.

House of Commons unquestionably influenced the thinking of the Convention about a second chamber, an American version of the House of Lords had to be . . . another House of Commons.

The concrete proposals presented to the Convention were, therefore, tame. Some delegates may have thought that property qualifications could be made higher for senators; but the point was not pressed, and in the end no property qualifications were set by the Convention for any public office. Some delegates may have envisioned special property qualifications for those who elected the senators, yet no such requirement was laid down. In the speech of Madison's quoted above, the only specific proposals he makes for insuring the kind of Senate he had in mind is, you will notice, that senators be elected for a long term—nine years—at a relatively advanced age. As it turned out, their term is for six years and the 'advanced' age is 30—six years younger than Madison himself when he made the speech.

What happened, then, to the idea of representing interests? Probably two things. First, however attractive the idea might have seemed abstractly, concrete proposals to overrepresent the rich—this was the only interest that anyone seemed to have in mind—were bound to end in palpable absurdities, fatal unpopularity, or both. In the America of 1787, the rich were not a traditional and legitimate aristocracy; they were never to become so. Even in England by 1787 it is doubtful whether the peerage could have gained by force or persuasion the special place in the British constitutional system it had inherited; instead it had only to hold onto the constitutional position in which it found itself. More than a century would elapse before the ancient power of the peerage over legislation would, for all practical purposes, finally be eliminated.

In the second place, the whole question of the composition of the Senate was abruptly changed from the problem of representing a special economic or class interest, as Morris and Madison had posed it, to the problem of representing a very different sort of interest: that of the smaller states.

States?

Madison and Morris, who fiercely opposed equal representation in the Senate for the smaller states and fought for representation according to population until it became clear that their solution might well wreck the whole scheme for a new Constitution, were, in a sense, hoist by their own petard. Having argued that the Senate should protect the minority interest against the majority interest, how were they to meet the arguments of delegates who contended that the smaller states, as an outnumbered minority, needed special protection from the more populous states? "Besides the Aristocratic and other interests, which ought to have the means of defending themselves," Johnson of Connecticut reasoned, "the States have their interests as such, and are equally entitled to like means."[9]

Wilson, the unswerving democrat (and happily for him, a delegate from a large state), encountered no difficulty in disposing of Johnson's argument on abstract democratic principles.

> . . . The gentleman from Connecticut in supposing that the preponderancy secured to the majority in the 1st branch had removed the objections to an equality of votes in the 2d branch for the security of the minority, narrowed the case extremely. Such an equality will enable the minority to controul in all cases whatsoever, the sentiments and interests of the majority. Seven States will controul six. . . . It would be in the power then of less than ⅓ to overrule ⅔ whenever a question should happen to divide the States in that manner. Can we forget for whom we are forming a Government? Is it for *men*, or for the imaginary beings called *States*?[10]

Madison found it all the more difficult to counter the small-state argument with a straightforward appeal to the principle of political equality among all citizens, as Wilson had done, because only a few days earlier, as we have just seen, he had asserted the desirability of using the Senate to give minorities special protection from majorities. Madison therefore combined an appeal to the majority principle with a pragmatic argument that there was in fact no small-state interest different from the interests of the large states.

> . . . It was urged [Madison said] continually that an equality of votes in the 2d branch was not only necessary to secure the small [states], but would be perfectly safe to the large ones whose majority in the 1st branch was an effectual bulwark. But notwithstanding this apparent defence, the majority of States might still injure the majority of people. 1. they could *obstruct* the wishes and interests of the majority. 2. they could *extort* measures repugnant to the wishes & interest of the Majority. 3. they could *impose* measures adverse thereto; as the 2d branch will probably exercise some great powers, in which the 1st will not participate. He admitted that every peculiar interest whether in any class of citizens, or any description of States, ought to be secured as far as possible. Whenever there is danger of attack there ought be given a constitutional power of defence. But he [Madison] contended that the States were divided into different interests not by their difference of size, but by other circumstances; the most material of which resulted partly from climate, but principally from the effects of their having or not having slaves. These two causes concurred in forming one great division of interests in the U. States. It did not lie between the large & small States: It lay between the Northern & Southern, and if any defensive power were necessary, it ought to be mutually given to these two interests.[11]

Madison's argument, he must have realized, could equally well be turned against the very position he himself had taken four days earlier. Perhaps it is for this reason that from this day forward it was Madison,

9. *Documents*, p. 297.
10. *Ibid.*, p. 307.
11. *Ibid.*, pp. 310–311.

the democratic-republican, and not the Madison fearful of majorities who invariably spoke on the troublesome question of representation in the Senate. From now on, Madison's position on representation in the Senate was usually indistinguishable from Wilson's.

In the end, as we know, the small states won. They did not win because they ever persuaded men like Madison and Morris, and least of all Wilson—the great architects of the Constitution—that their position was just. For these men never were converted. As so often happens in political affairs, the small states won simply because of their bargaining power. To Madison, Morris, and Wilson, better a Constitution that granted equal representation to states in the Senate than no Constitution at all. The bargain was struck. It has held ever since.

SUMMARY   1. In designing the Constitution, the Founders assumed that the House of Representatives, being popularly elected, would be a spokesman for popular majorities.

2. Given their commitment to partitioning power, they insisted that the House, like all the other institutions of government, must be hedged in by constraints, lest majorities become tyrannical.

3. The Senate, on the other hand, was to be a bastion for the protection of minorities.

4. Although there was general agreement that the Senate should represent different 'interests' from the House, there was vast disagreement over the application of this principle.

☐ Some delegates to the Convention, like Morris, thought that the Senate should protect the interests of the rich minority against the encroachments of popular majorities.

☐ Delegates like Morris were reverting to a medieval conception of a parliament that represented the 'estates' of the realm.

☐ Other delegates, including many from the smaller states, saw the Senate purely and simply as a bastion for the interests of the smaller states.

☐ A number of delegates, like Madison, reasoning from the principle of partitioning power, agreed that the Senate should represent interests different from the House but were at a loss to define what these interests ought to be.

5. Because of the threat by the delegates from the small states to reject a Constitution without equal state representation in the Senate, their demand was finally accepted. Though many delegates from larger states, like Madison and Morris, felt that equal representation of the states was bad in principle, they compromised simply in order to make the Constitution acceptable to all the states.

Congress as Representative: Performance

13

If the House was intended to represent the people and the Senate the states, to what extent has Congress fulfilled these expectations? Indeed, what, or whom, does Congress represent?

To answer these questions is no simple matter. It will help to distinguish between two aspects of representation. First, different citizens may be unequally represented because the boundaries of legislative constituencies—states in the case of senators, and congressional districts in the case of congressmen—operate so as to overrepresent some parts of the electorate and to underrepresent others. Second, as we saw in Chapter 5, different citizens may be unequally influential with respect to their representatives because they have different political incentives, skills, or resources: money, information, friendship, access, social standing, and the like.

THE SENATE: BASTION OF WHICH MINORITIES?

Small States?

Consider the first of these problems. In the Senate the people of the smaller states are of course overrepresented and the people of the larger states are underrepresented; that, after all, was precisely the point of the compromise. Yet the degree of over- and underrepresentation has increased since 1787. According to the various estimates used at the Convention, the largest state, Virginia, had a population some ten to fifteen times larger than the smallest state, Delaware. According to the Census of 1790, the free population of Virginia was eight times larger than that of Delaware, the total population twelve times. In 1960, the population of New York was almost seventy-five times that of Alaska; the population of California fifty-five times that of Nevada. As Table 13.1

Table 13.1
Advantage and
Disadvantage in the
Senate: 1965-70

State	State Electorate (000)	Percentages of Total Electorate	Cumulative Percentage	Index of Advantage[a]
1. Alaska	81	.12	.12	16.92
2. Wyoming	127*	.19	.31	10.79
3. Nevada	153	.22	.53	8.96
4. Vermont	157	.23	.76	8.73
5. Delaware	202*	.29	1.05	6.79
6. Hawaii	227	.33	1.38	6.04
7. North Dakota	239	.35	1.73	5.74
8. Montana	266*	.39	2.12	5.15
9. South Dakota	280	.41	2.53	4.90
10. New Hampshire	287	.42	2.95	4.78
11. Idaho	288	.42	3.37	4.76
12. New Mexico	300*	.44	3.81	4.57
13. Rhode Island	373*	.54	4.35	3.68
14. Maine	393*	.57	4.92	3.49
15. Utah	419	.61	5.53	3.27
16. Mississippi	450*	.66	6.19	3.05
17. Arizona	480	.70	6.89	2.86
18. Louisiana	519	.76	7.65	2.64
19. Nebraska	533*	.78	8.43	2.57
20. Arkansas	592	.86	9.29	2.32
21. South Carolina	653	.95	10.24	2.10
22. West Virginia	710*	1.04	11.28	1.93
23. Colorado	786	1.15	12.43	1.74
24. Oregon	814	1.19	13.62	1.68
25. Kansas	817	1.19	14.81	1.63
50 percent of the Senate				
26. Georgia	837	1.22	16.03	1.64
27. Oklahoma	909	1.33	17.36	1.51
28. Alabama	913	1.33	18.69	1.50
29. Kentucky	943	1.38	20.07	1.45

shows, in the period 1965–70, twenty-five states with 15 percent of the electorate furnished half the senators, while the eight largest states with more than half the electorate had only sixteen senators out of one hundred.

Yet Madison's judgment has been confirmed. The great conflicts have not been between large states and small states. Although there have been many lines of political cleavage in the United States, differences between large states and small states have surely been the least important of these. The tariff, slavery, civil rights, monetary and fiscal problems, taxation, regulation of business, welfare programs, foreign and military policies—none has produced conflicts between large states and small states. It would be difficult to demonstrate, therefore, that the small states have *needed* their extra influence in the Senate in order to protect themselves against the large states.

Table 13.1
(Continued)

State	State Electorate (000)	Percentages of Total Electorate	Cumulative Percentage	Index of Advantage
30. Maryland	1,134	1.65	21.72	1.21
31. Iowa	1,144	1.67	23.39	1.20
32. Tennessee	1,149*	1.68	25.07	1.19
33. Connecticut	1,207	1.76	26.83	1.14
34. Washington	1,236	1.80	28.63	1.11
35. Virginia	1,288	1.88	30.51	1.06
36. North Carolina	1,437	2.10	32.61	.95
37. Minnesota	1,571*	2.29	34.90	.87
38. Wisconsin	1,655	2.41	37.31	.83
39. Missouri	1,738	2.54	39.85	.79
40. Florida	2,024	2.95	42.80	.68
41. Indiana	2,053	3.00	45.80	.67
42. Massachusetts	2,230*	3.25	49.05	.61
50 percent of the electorate				
43. Texas	2,626*	3.83	52.88	.52
44. New Jersey	2,711*	3.96	56.84	.51
45. Michigan	3,093	4.51	61.35	.44
46. Ohio	3,743	5.46	66.81	.37
47. Illinois	4,450	6.49	73.30	.31
48. Pennsylvania	4,624	6.75	80.05	.30
49. New York	6,582	9.60	89.65	.21
50. California	7,102	10.36	100.01[b]	.19

Total Electorate: 68,545,000. Mean State Electorate: 1,370,900.

*1965.

[a]Index of advantage = $\dfrac{\text{mean state electorate}}{\text{actual state electorate}}$ = $\dfrac{1{,}370{,}900}{\text{actual state electorate}}$.

[b]Percentage is greater than 100 due to rounding.

Sources: U.S. Bureau of Census, *Statistical Abstract 1965*, Table 513, p. 377, Table 515, p. 379; *Statistical Abstract 1970*, Table 549, p. 364, Table 550, p. 365.

Other Minorities?

If the Senate has not had to protect the small states, has it, however, served to protect other minorities? If so, are these particular minorities entitled to special protection? Although the problem is a thorny one, the answer to the first question is probably yes; the answer to the second is, I believe, very much more debatable. Three preliminary observations are in order.[1]

In the first place, the argument for equal representation of states in the Senate frequently seems to rest upon a false psychological equation, in which small states are equated with small interests and small interests with small or defenseless persons. Our humanitarian desires to protect

1. The following discussion is adapted from Robert A. Dahl, *A Preface to Democratic Theory* (Chicago: University of Chicago Press, 1956), pp. 113–118.

relatively defenseless persons from aggression by more powerful individuals are thereby invoked on behalf of small states. But states consist of people; and it is the interests of people we are concerned with. What we need to know, therefore, is what sorts of people are benefited or handicapped by equal representation in the Senate.

I assume that we do not wish to endorse the principle that all small interest groups must have a veto on policy. For then we could never specify any situations short of unanimity in which a law-making majority should be permitted to act. And thus we would make impossible not merely the operation of the republican principle but government itself. The first to exercise their vetoes might be the gangsters, the murderers, the thieves—in short, the criminal population. The rest of us would not be far behind: capitalists, laborers, farmers, even college professors, the exploiters and the exploited, the social and the antisocial, the sweatshop operator, the labor racketeer, the income-tax evader, and a thousand other groups, would exercise their veto on public policy.

In the second place, we must also avoid the fallacy of assuming that if the Senate represents or overrepresents some minorities situated in certain geographical areas in the United States, it necessarily represents all minorities situated in those areas. This is clearly false. There are minorities within minorities. The dominant regional group may be represented in the Senate while the subordinate regional minority is excluded. Hence a Senate veto may merely preserve or extend the control of the dominant regional group over the subordinate minority. Blacks in the South and itinerant farm laborers of the West are clearly not the minorities who have benefited from equal representation in the Senate. Even in a situation of full political equality, a regional minority protected by equal representation of geographical units in a legislative body would be a majority in its own area; and the defeated minority in that region would be unprotected by equal representation. Indeed, if the minority in the region consisted of individuals with preferences like those of the majority in the whole electorate, equal representation of geographical areas would, paradoxically, divest this regional minority of protection in all cases where positive government action was required to prevent the regional majority from tyrannizing over it.

In the third place, equal representation of geographical units overrepresents some minorities concentrated in sparse areas but underrepresents those concentrated in heavily populated areas. Moreover, to the extent that a minority is not geographically concentrated, it receives no protection per se from equal state representation. In a society in which all minorities were distributed in equal proportions among the voters of every state, no minority would receive any protection per se from equal state representation. Why, then, this special tenderness toward minorities concentrated geographically in sparse areas?

In sum:

☐ The only minorities protected by equal state representation as such are geographical minorities concentrated in sparse areas.

☐ But some of the minorities in these areas are left unprotected; indeed, representatives of the dominant group may actually use their over-representation in the Senate to bar action intended to guard the unprotected.

☐ Minorities in heavily populated areas are underrepresented in a system of equal state representation.

☐ The conclusion seems inevitable that the benefits and disadvantages flowing from equal state representation in the Senate are allocated in an entirely arbitrary fashion and cannot be shown to follow from any general principle.

THE HOUSE: REPRESENTATIVES OF THE MAJORITY?

What then of the House? How has it represented the people or a majority of the people?

There is lurking in these innocent questions an implicit assumption that we know what it means for a congressman to 'represent the people.' The fact is, however, that the notion is shot through with problems. Should a representative seek to represent the people of his district, or the people of the United States? A majority only, or majorities and minorities? Opening up a classic debate, should he conceive of himself as a *trustee,* "a free agent [who] follows what he considers right or just—his convictions or principles, the dictates of his conscience," or a *delegate* of his constituents who seeks to discover and follow his constituents' views.[2] These are matters on which there has been enormous debate, and it would take us too far afield to explore the issues here.[3]

Yet it seems clear that if the principles of political equality and consent are to have any concrete meaning at all, voters should be able to select representatives who will reflect their views or values in legislative decisions. Certainly it would be incompatible with political equality and consent if the decisions of the legislature did not embody the basic preferences of a majority of the people but instead the conflicting preferences of some minority, whether that minority be the elected legislators themselves, other officials, or interest groups. In this day and age, even a representative who looks upon himself as a trustee for the best interests of his constituents, and not simply as their agent or

2. Heinz Eulau, John C. Wahlke, William Buchanan, and Leroy C. Ferguson, "The Role of Representative: Some Empirical Observations on the Theory of Edmund Burke," *American Political Science Review,* 53 (September, 1959), 742–756, at pp. 749–750.

3. Cf. Hanna Fenichel Pitkin, *The Concept of Representation* (Los Angeles: University of California Press, 1967). See also Hanna Fenichel Pitkin, ed., *Representation* (New York: Atherton Press, 1969); and J. Roland Pennock and John W. Chapman, eds., *Representation (Nomos X)* (New York: Atherton Press, 1968).

delegate, would have to agree that his constituents ought to replace him in the next election if, after reflecting on his record, they were to conclude that he had not acted in accordance with their best interests. As we have already seen, the Founders themselves assumed pretty much without argument that the House would reflect the preferences of a majority of the people.

Standards of Performance

Starting from this simple assumption, what standards can we use to judge the performance of the House of Representatives? Many people, including some of the justices of the Supreme Court, evidently believe that the principles of political equality and consent would best be met if the House of Representatives met the following requirements:

1. *One man, one vote:* The country must be divided into districts of approximately equal population (or voters).
2. *Single member districts with plurality elections:* Each district must elect one and only one representative. The candidate who gains the most votes (in American parlance, a plurality) should win the seat.
3. *Popular control:* When a representative votes on legislative matters, thanks to elections his vote should pretty generally, and certainly over the long run, correspond with the views of a majority of the people (or voters) in his district.
4. *Legislative majority rule:* The House should make its decisions by majority vote of its members.

It may come as a blow to one who adheres to these standards to discover that the House of Representatives has not regularly conformed with these principles; what is more, even if it did, it would not necessarily insure political equality, majority rule, and minority representation.

ONE MAN, ONE VOTE The Constitution, you may recall, does not require that House members be elected by districts; it leaves "the Times, Places and Manner of holding Elections for . . . Representatives" to the state legislatures (Article I, Section 4). In practise the states have been divided by the state legislatures into a number of districts equal, normally, to the number of representatives. Moreover, the same system exists for state legislatures themselves: the state legislators are also elected in districts. Now the obvious consequence of this arrangement is that with changes in population in the states, the heavy hand of history may produce growing disparity between the number of citizens in one district and another. This is what happened to the House of Representatives.

Originally, as we have seen, most of the population of the United States lived in rural areas. As the urban dwellers increased and finally outnumbered the rural population, the number of representatives they were granted in the state legislature failed to increase at the same rate. The explanation is simple: since reapportionment was up to the state legislators, since any reapportionment could only reduce the proportion of legislators elected by the rural population, and since the existing state legislatures were already controlled or strongly influenced by representatives drawn from rural districts, quite naturally the rural representatives who dominated the state legislatures were unwilling to pass bills providing for the reduction of their own power through reapportionment. Hence the House of Representatives came to overrepresent the rural and small-town areas at the expense first of the cities and later of the suburbs. What this overrepresentation of the rural and small-town areas meant in practise was that the House somewhat overrepresented what might loosely be called 'conservative' attitudes.

Paradoxically, while population changes were making the House less responsive to cities and suburban areas, the same changes were making the Senate more so. For few states lacked one or more big cities and extensive suburban areas; in every state, the rural and small-town population shrank. By 1950, 80 percent of the people in the Northeast lived in urban areas; in the West 70 percent; in the North Central region, 64 percent; and in the least urbanized region, the South, just under half.[4] Consequently, while a great many senators had to be sensitive to the concerns of their urban voters, a substantial number of members of the House could safely ignore the cities and the suburbs.[5]

On the whole, then, far from being a turbulent forum for the people, "ever subject to precipitancy, changeability, and excess," the House had become a slightly more conservative institution than the Senate or the presidency. Its members were more inclined to share the views of farmers and small-town folk than those of the working classes in the cities or the white-collar workers and executives in the suburbs; more likely to think nostalgically of a United States that had disappeared some generations ago than to press vigorously for solutions to problems of the urban America that now existed.

On a number of occasions, citizens in various states appealed to the Supreme Court to remedy the inequalities in representation in state legislatures and in the House of Representatives. But, until 1962, the Court steadily refused to intervene, on the ground that inequitable representation was not a judicial matter but was a "political question" that could only be remedied by the appropriate political bodies.[6] Because

4. M. Gendell and H. L. Zetterberg, eds., *A Sociological Almanac for the United States* (New York: Bedminster Press, 1961), Table 86, p. 83.

5. See Lewis A. Froman, Jr., *Congressmen and their Constituencies* (Chicago: Rand McNally, 1963), "Why the Senate Is More Liberal than the House," ch. 6.

6. See, for example, *Colegrove* v. *Green*, 328 U.S. 549 (1946).

Table 13.2
Votes and Seats in a
Hypothetical Legislature

Districts		Votes for:				Seats won by:	
		Liberty		Equality			
N	%	N	%	N		Liberty	Equality
40	90	360,000	10	40,000		40	0
60	40	240,000	60	360,000		0	60
Totals 100	60	600,000	40	400,000		40	60

the legislative majorities that controlled these bodies would only decrease their own power by reapportionment, naturally they refused to approve of laws or constitutional amendments that would have remedied the situation. Consequently the position of the Court meant, in effect, that nothing could be done. Beginning in 1962, however, the Court reversed its traditional position in a series of historic decisions that laid down the requirement of "one man, one vote" not only for both houses of all state legislatures but for the United States House of Representatives itself.[7] In the ensuing years, reapportionment by state legislatures and courts brought the House ever closer to districts of equal population.

SINGLE-MEMBER
DISTRICTS WITH
PLURALITY
ELECTIONS

Will apportioning the House into districts with equal populations—the principle of one man, one vote—insure political equality and majority rule? Not necessarily. For even if every representative were to act as a spokesman for his constituents' views (a problem we shall examine in a moment), *single-member districts with plurality elections neither insure majority rule nor minority representation.*

An extreme example will readily show why such a system cannot insure majority rule. For the sake of simplicity, let us assume that a legislature has one hundred representatives elected from a voting population of one million, divided into one hundred equal districts, each with ten thousand voters. Suppose that 60 percent of the voters cast their ballot for candidates of the party of Liberty and 40 percent for candidates of the party of Equality. Imagine further that the partisans of Liberty are heavily concentrated in forty districts, while the partisans of Equality are somewhat more dispersed, as in Table 13.2. The partisans of Liberty, though a decisive majority of voters, would win only a minority of seats, while the partisans of Equality, though only a minority of voters, would win a decisive majority of seats.

Yet if single-member districts with plurality elections do not insure majority rule, neither do they guarantee minority representation. Suppose that instead of being concentrated, the partisans of Liberty were

7. The leading decisions were *Baker* v. *Carr*, 369 U.S. 186 (1962), *Wesberry* v. *Sanders*, 376 U.S. 1 (1946), and *Reynolds* v. *Sims*, 377 U.S. 533 (1964). For a further discussion, see Robert A. Goldwin, ed., *Representation and Misrepresentation* (Chicago: Rand McNally, 1968).

evenly dispersed over all one hundred districts. Since 60 percent of the voters in every district would vote for the party of Liberty, it would win 100 percent of the seats. You will notice that a party with a bare 51 percent of the voters could win 100 percent of the seats and thereby deny any representation to 49 percent of the voters! The distortion grows even worse when there are more than two parties. Suppose three parties split the vote 34 percent–33 percent–33 percent. Then the party with 34 percent of the vote *could* win every seat—even though two-thirds of the voters had cast their ballots for another candidate, and might prefer either of the losers to the winner. As the number of parties increases, so of course does the potential of this system for absurdity.

Because the single-member district with plurality elections cannot insure either majority rule or minority representation, a number of polyarchies (including such sturdy polyarchies as Switzerland, the Netherlands, and all of the Scandinavian countries) have rejected this solution and have instead adopted systems of proportional representation (PR). PR schemes are designed to insure a close correspondence between the percentage of votes cast for the candidates of a given party and the percentage of seats the party wins. Many Americans oppose PR because of fears that PR would produce a multiplicity of parties—as, indeed, it probably would. We shall return to this point in later chapters. For most Americans, however, the single-member district is probably little more than an article of faith. Even the eminent justices of the Supreme Court failed to note that with single-member districts and plurality elections, merely to establish districts of equal size does not really guarantee "one man, one vote." For as our examples have shown, voters who are in the majority can receive a disproportionately larger payoff in seats than voters who are in the minority. It is arguable, then, that the principle of one man, one vote logically requires the introduction of PR. Incidentally, it is worth noting that nothing in the Constitution definitely prescribes single-member districts nor prohibits states from choosing representatives under a PR system.

POPULAR CONTROL   Achieving satisfactory electoral arrangements may prove to be far easier than insuring that representatives reflect the views of constituents. For this is less a problem of mechanics than of information and incentives.

Three Conditions

Suppose for the moment that electoral arrangements provided satisfactorily for one man, one vote and distributed seats to majorities and minorities in ways we regard as fair. What further conditions would be required to insure that a representative's vote on legislative issues corresponds pretty closely with the views of a majority of his constituents?

Figure 13.1
Paths to Popular Control

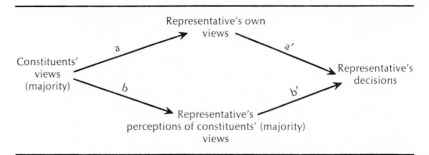

To simplify the matter, let us push to one side the special (and serious) problem created by nonvoting, and assume that most constituents do vote. Then the following conditions would appear to offer a strong guarantee of popular control over elected representatives:

1. *Constituent awareness.* Constituents are aware of the positions that candidates take on issues. Thus when incumbents run for reelection, their constituents are aware of their past voting records.
2. *Appropriate choice.* Armed with this knowledge, constituents vote in favor of the candidate whose policies are closest to their own.
3. *Corresponding policy decisions.* When he acts on matters before the House, the representative adopts positions that correspond with the views of a majority of his constituents because:
   a. He seeks to act according to their views (a delegate) *and* he is aware of how a majority of his constituents stand; or
   b. He seeks to act according to his own views (a trustee) *but* as a result of condition 2 his views coincide with those of a majority of his constituents.
These two paths are shown in Figure 13.1.

It would be unreasonable to expect that these conditions would be fully met in a representative system in a large country. Yet a path-breaking study of voters and representatives during 1958–60 resulted in disturbing evidence that these conditions are very far indeed from being achieved in the United States.[8] Because this study has not yet been replicated, its findings should be regarded as somewhat tentative. Yet they fit too well with other surveys to be dismissed as wildly aberrant.

---

8. Donald E. Stokes and Warren E. Miller, with the facilities of the Survey Research Center, University of Michigan, surveyed voters in 116 randomly selected congressional districts and interviewed the incumbent congressmen and major party candidates for the House from the same districts. Their findings have been published in Angus Campbell, Philip E. Converse, Warren E. Miller, and Donald E. Stokes, *Elections and the Political Order* (New York: Wiley, 1966), chs. 11 and 16; and in an article by Warren E. Miller, "Majority Rule and the Representative System of Government," in *Mass Politics,* eds. Erik Allart and Stein Rokkan (New York: Free Press, 1970), ch. 10.

Some Disturbing Evidence

Constituent awareness. Only a small minority of constituents seem to be aware of the positions that candidates for the House of Representatives take on issues. Here are some findings:

☐ Of the people who lived in districts where the House seat was contested in 1958, 59 percent—well over half—said that they had neither read nor heard anything about either candidate for Congress, and less than one in five felt that they knew something about both candidates.

☐ Of people who went to the polls 46 percent conceded that they did so without having read or heard anything about either man.

☐ The incumbent candidate is by far the better known. In districts where the incumbent congressman was opposed for reelection in 1958, 39 percent of the respondents knew something about him. Only about 20 percent said they knew anything at all about his opponent.

☐ Even voters who say they know something about a candidate appear to know almost nothing of his policies or his party's programs. The popular image of the congressman is almost barren of policy content. References to current legislative issues comprised not more than a thirtieth part of what the constituents had to say about their congressmen.

☐ The information of constituents aware of their congressman consisted mainly of diffuse value judgments: he is a good man, he is experienced, he knows the problems, he has done a good job, and the like. Beyond this the congressman's image consisted of a mixed bag of impressions, some of them wildly improbable, about ethnicity, the attractiveness of family, specific services to the district, and other facts in the candidate's background.[9]

Appropriate choice. Given the fact that most voters lack the requisite information, ordinarily they do not base their vote on a judgment of the candidates' policies. Instead, they vote predominantly on the basis of party loyalty:

☐ In 1958 only one vote in twenty was cast by persons without any sort of party loyalty. And among those who did identify themselves with a

---

9. All these propositions are direct quotations or paraphrases from Campbell et al., *Elections and the Political Order*, pp. 204–207. However, a 1970 Gallup Survey adds further confirmation. The relevant questions and percentages were: "Do you happen to know the name of the present representative in Congress from your district?" Yes, 53 percent; No, 47 percent. "Do you know how your representative voted on any major bills this year?" Yes, 21 percent; No, 75 percent; Don't know, 4 percent. "Is your representative a Democrat or a Republican?" Don't know, 38 percent. "Has your representative done anything for the district that you definitely know about?" Yes, 19 percent; No, 76 percent; Don't know, 5 percent. "Has your representative done any favors for you?" Yes, 4 percent; No, 96 percent. "How much thought have you given to the coming November elections . . . quite a lot or only a little?" Quite a lot, 25 percent; Some, 18 percent; Little, 42 percent; None, 15 percent (Gallup Opinion Index No. 64, October, 1970, pp. 9–14).

party, only one in ten voted against their party. As a result, something like 84 percent of the vote that year was cast by constituents voting their usual party line.

☐ Traditional party voting is seldom connected with current legislative issues. In saying what they liked and disliked about the parties, only about 15 percent of the comments of party loyalists dealt with current issues of public policy.

☐ Moreover, only about half the voters actually knew which party had controlled the Congress during the two years prior to the election.[10]

Corresponding policy decisions. The extent to which the positions adopted by representatives correspond with the views of their constituents varies a good deal from one issue-area to another. The correspondence is moderately high in some key issue-areas, negligible in others. It was found that:

☐ The way a representative voted was influenced both by his own views (*a'* in Figure 13.1) and by his perceptions of the opinions of his district (*b'* in Figure 13.1). Indeed, together these two factors strongly influenced his voting in all three issue-areas.

☐ Representatives felt that their chances of reelection depended quite substantially on their personal record and standing.

☐ The correspondence between the views of constituents and the way representatives voted was quite high on civil rights, lower on social-welfare measures, and nonexistent or even negative on foreign policy.[11]

Sources of Variation in Constituent Control

Why this variation? The answer lies in the variation in the influence bearing on a congressman on different matters and at different times.

Going back for a moment to Figure 13.1, we can readily see how each of the links from constituent attitudes to the congressman's vote on roll calls may be weak or broken by the impact of other forces.

Constituent influences. From the evidence we have just been examining, it is apparent that links *a* and *b* are often weak and sometimes virtually nonexistent. Consider the link at *a,* for example. Given the relatively low salience of issues and policies in the mind of the average voter when he votes for his congressman, it is hardly surprising that he often casts his ballot for a candidate whose views happen to be quite different from his own. It turned out, in fact, that of the three issue-areas examined in the

---

10. Campbell et al., *Elections and the Political Order,* pp. 197–199.

11. *Ibid.,* pp. 206, 362–366; and Miller, "Majority Rule and the Representative System," pp. 300–301.

study mentioned previously, only on civil rights did the representative's own attitude correlate strongly with his constituents' attitudes. And much of this correlation is accounted for by Southern congressmen who, like their constituents, sharply opposed legislative proposals on civil rights.

All the factors that would weaken the link at *a* also weaken it at *b*. It might be hard even for a pollster with a sophisticated survey to sort out majority attitudes on a great many policy questions. The representative, of course, is no pollster, and his 'surveys' are usually unsystematic and prone to error.

In the real world, communication between constituents and members of Congress is a highly uncertain matter. It is bound to be, in a large country, as one can easily see by performing a simple mental experiment: If every adult in an average congressional district tried to gain the attention of his representative for half an hour, and if the congressman were to devote ten hours a day the year round to nothing but communicating with his constituents, it would take a quarter of a century for him to hear all of them!

The fact is, of course, that most people do not communicate with their congressmen at all. In a typical year, probably something under 15 percent of the population ever write or talk to a congressman or any other public official in order to give their opinions on a public issue. The minority of citizens who do try to influence Congress by no means always represent majority opinion. It has been found again and again that certain factors are associated with higher levels of political activity of any kind, and these would apply to efforts to influence congressmen.

There is still another element of great importance. People who happen to be aroused about an issue because their goals, values, prestige, esteem, income, ethnic loyalties, or other interests are involved, are, it is obvious, much more likely to influence a congressman than people who are not aroused. Moreover, because of uncertainties in communication, their activity may make their numbers and resources seem greater than they are. Bauer, Pool, and Dexter found, for example, that businessmen who favored tariff protection were more likely to write their congressmen in 1954–5 than those who favored tariff reductions; thus, although public sentiment favored a liberal trade policy by about three to one, to congressmen who surveyed their mail it might have looked as if the public actually favored protectionist policies by two to one.[12]

---

12. Bauer, Pool, and Dexter, *American Business and Public Policy,* p. 211. See also Lewis A. Dexter, "The Representative and His District," ch. 8, in *The Sociology and Politics of Congress* (Chicago: Rand McNally, 1970). This is a revised version of an article originally appearing in *Human Organization,* 16 (Spring, 1957). Part 2 of *Sociology and Politics of Congress* discusses the issue of what congressmen attend to at considerably greater length. From the converse standpoint, the issues involved are discussed in greater depth in Lewis A. Dexter, *How Organizations Are Represented in Washington* (Indianapolis: Bobbs-Merrill, 1969), especially "When the Job Is Chiefly Lobbying," ch. 4; and "Helping and Seeking Help on Capitol Hill," ch. 5; pp. 55–101.

Figure 13.2
Paradigm for Explication
of Roll Call Behavior

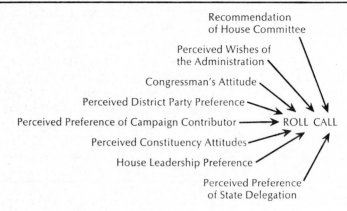

Recommendation
of House Committee

Perceived Wishes of
the Administration

Congressman's Attitude

Perceived District Party Preference

Perceived Preference of Campaign Contributor ⟶ ROLL CALL

Perceived Constituency Attitudes

House Leadership Preference

Perceived Preference
of State Delegation

Source: Allart and Rokkan, *Mass Politics*, p. 292.

Given all these difficulties in knowing what a majority of his constituents wants, how does a congressman arrive at his judgments about their views? One of the most perceptive observers of Congress, Lewis A. Dexter, suggests:

> A congressman's conception of his district confirms itself, to a considerable extent, and may constitute a sort of self-fulfilling prophecy.
> A congressman hears most often from those who agree with him.
> Some men automatically interpret what they hear to support their own viewpoint.
> In more general terms, what congressmen hear and how they interpret what they hear depends on who they are.
> For any particular congressman, his interpretation results from his being the particular kind of person he is and is reputed to be.
> A congressman's reputation among those who might want to influence him determines in large measure what actually is said to him.
> Some communications tend to be unclear in their meaning. A good deal of so-called lobbying by constituents tends to be nothing more than a social visit and a general discussion.
> What the congressman listens to is partly accidental.
> 'Pressure' is how you see it. What you call pressure, or what you feel to be pressure, depends on how thick your skin is.
> Opportunism is also where you see it. Few congressmen attribute their friends' decisions or their own to opportunism.[13]

Other influences. But, of course, the attitudes of constituents are by no means the only influences to which the congressman responds. He is, in fact, the object of a number of different efforts to influence his behavior, including the way he votes on roll calls. The main sources of

13. These statements are verbatim quotations from Dexter, "The Representative and His District," pp. 151–175.

direct influence are indicated in Figure 13.2. Thus just as the president's power varies with the strength of other factors, so does that of the congressman. With some crucial modifications, we may say about the congressman what was said about the president in Chapter 11: In general, a representative is most severely limited when the constitutional authority of Congress is clearly restricted; when he operates in an area where he has no unique legitimacy; where an emergency requiring executive action is thought to exist; where public opinion is well defined, highly structured, and not responsive to the congressman himself; and where well-organized groups outside his own committees regularly participate in the kind of decision at hand. Conversely, he is most free to act independently when the constitutional authority of Congress is broad; the Congress has special legitimacy to act; no emergency is thought to exist; public opinion is weak, unstructured, and highly responsive to the congressman himself; and where few if any well-organized groups outside his own committees regularly participate.

Each of these factors varies a good deal. Thus on foreign policy, typically the attitudes of constituents are extremely general, unstructured, and relatively responsive (particularly in emergencies) to the president, and a "number of Congressmen are disposed to follow the administration's advice, whatever they or their districts think."[14] Consequently there is often little or no relation on foreign policy issues between the attitudes (if any) of a majority of constituents and the position a congressman takes on these matters—even though he may confidently believe himself to be expressing the attitudes of his constituents. At the other end of the spectrum, on such questions as civil rights and racial integration, public opinion is likely to be much more articulate, definite, visible, organized, angry, and in Southern and border states before blacks had any significant voting strength, unified. In this case the representative becomes almost exclusively an agent of his district; when he does not, his constituents will, for once, be aware of his record, and are more than likely to vote against him. An example is provided by the defeat of Congressman Brooks Hays in Arkansas's Fifth District in 1958:

> Although the perception of Congressman Hays as too moderate on civil rights resulted more from his service as intermediary between the White House and Governor Faubus in the Little Rock school crisis than from his record in the House, the victory of Dale Alford as a write-in candidate was a striking reminder of what can happen to a Congressman who gives his foes a powerful issue to use against him. . . . Not a single voter in our sample of Arkansas's Fifth District was unaware of either candidate. What is more, these interviews show that Hays was regarded both by his supporters and his opponents as more moderate than Alford on civil rights and that this perception brought his defeat. In some measure, what happened in Little

---

14. Campbell et al., *Elections and the Political Order,* p. 362.

Rock in 1958 can happen anywhere, and our Congressmen ought not to be entirely disbelieved in what they say about their impact at the polls. Indeed, they may be under genuine pressure from the voters even while they are the forgotten men of national elections.[15]

SUMMARY Congress has not altogether fulfilled the expectations of the Founders that the Senate would protect the interests of minorities, particularly the small states, while the House would reflect the desires of popular majorities.

1. In the Senate, by and large, the major political cleavages have not been along the axis of small versus large states. As to other minorities, it appears that

□ The only minorities protected by equal state representation as such are geographical minorities concentrated in sparse areas.
□ Some minorities in these areas are unprotected and vulnerable.
□ Minorities in heavily populated areas are underrepresented.
□ The benefits and disadvantages to various minorities from equal state representation in the Senate seem to be allocated arbitrarily and do not appear to follow any general principle.

2. In the House:

□ Only in recent years has enforcement by the Supreme Court of the principle of one man, one vote led to districts of approximately equal population.
□ Yet the method of choosing representatives from single-member districts by means of plurality elections insures neither majority rule nor minority representation.
□ Popular control over the House, it appears from recent if somewhat tentative evidence, is further handicapped because:
  1. Most constituents are unaware of the positions candidates for the House take on issues.
  2. Partly as a result, most voters do not base their vote on a judgment of the candidates' policies.
  3. As a result of the first two factors and others, the extent to which the positions on issues taken by congressmen correspond with their constituents' views varies a good deal from one issue-area to another. One study showed relatively high correspondence on civil rights and virtually none on foreign affairs.

---

15. *Ibid.*, pp. 369–370.

Congress as Policy-Maker: Performance

14

In the ways their governments arrive at national policies, polyarchies vary over a much greater range than is commonly supposed. No other polyarchy makes its policies by processes quite like those typically used in the United States. A visitor from Britain or Sweden who was familiar with government policy-making only in his own country would very likely be confused and puzzled by American policy-making. He might be aghast as well.

The Congress contributes substantially to the distinctiveness of policy-making in the United States. In no other polyarchy does the national legislature have quite the same functions and power in policy determination as the Congress. To say that the Congress is different is not, of course, to say that it is better or worse than other legislative bodies, judged by democratic standards or other criteria.

Taken together, three features tend to distinguish the role of Congress in policy-making from the role of parliaments in most other polyarchies:

☐ *Shared power and cooperation:* On a great many decisions the president and each house of Congress have very considerable influence, yet ordinarily none of the three has enough influence to prevail completely against the determined opposition of the others. Hence their cooperation is required.

☐ *Antagonism and conflict:* Yet there is ordinarily a certain amount of antagonism and conflict between the president and the Congress and between House and Senate.

☐ *No decisive procedure:* Unlike many other polyarchies, there is no established procedure for putting an end to these conflicts and bringing about a state of harmony. No single process, such as a national election, is truly *decisive* in granting any actor, party, or coalition the authority needed to carry out its policies.

SHARED POWER
AND COOPERATION

The president and each of the houses of Congress have substantial resources for bringing influence to bear on making national policies. As we saw in Chapter 11, on some types of important decisions, the president has, at times, all but escaped the control of Congress. Yet over the whole domain of policy such unlimited presidential discretion is comparatively rare. Indeed, it may prove to be a phase in the oscillation in the balance of presidential and congressional influence on policy-making that has always been an aspect of their relationship. Some of these oscillations are short run, from one term or president to the next. Some are long run. At the extreme phases of these long-run oscillations, the president or Congress may be dominant. Yet these extreme phases seem incapable of persisting, for both president and Congress have too many resources that are rooted in the Constitution and in other general features of the American system. These resources may lie dormant in the extreme phases, but they do not vanish.

Historical Oscillations

Thus the influence of Congress reached its historical apex in the three decades after the Civil War; indeed, during these years, Congress exercised very nearly a complete monopoly over the initiation and determination of national policy. For some time Congress also enjoyed virtually complete control even over presidential appointments. The control of the president over policy and appointments had begun to recede immediately after Lincoln's death. The "Whig" view, as it has been called, of the ascendancy of Congress over the president was pushed to its outermost limits by the radical Republicans who dominated the House of Representatives under the leadership of Thaddeus Stevens.[1] In order to tie the hands of the president, in 1867 the Congress passed (over Johnson's veto) a Tenure of Office Act that was designed to prevent the president from removing officials (including Cabinet officers) without the consent of the Senate. Johnson, who rightly believed that the act was unconstitutional, chose to defy Congress and dismiss his secretary of war, Stanton, who was openly disloyal to him. The House then voted 126 to 47 to impeach the president. As everyone knows, Johnson escaped conviction in the Senate by only one vote. Had he been convicted, it is conceivable that the United States would have changed, de facto, to a parliamentary system under which the president would be

1. See Fawn M. Brodie, *Thaddeus Stevens, Scourge of the South* (New York: Norton, 1959), pp. 324 ff.

dependent on the continuing 'confidence' of the Congress, lacking which he would be impeached.

Peak of congressional influence. Although Johnson escaped conviction, the Congress nonetheless became the center of energy in the system. Under President Grant, control over both policies and appointments fell exclusively into the hands of Congress; the president became little more than a tarnished figurehead. ". . . The predominant and controlling force, the centre and source of all motive and of all regulative power," observed a young historian and political scientist named Woodrow Wilson in 1885, "is Congress."[2]

Congress's monopoly of control was exercised chiefly through its innumerable committees; de facto control was lodged with the committee chairmen, each lord of his own domain, and with leaders elected in the party caucus, most notably the Speaker of the House, who toward the end of the century became a personage as important as the president —and a good deal more powerful with respect to legislation.

President after president yielded control over policy without a murmur. The Whig view was gospel to the presidents themselves. This was the age of industrial growth, new fortunes, the worship of business success, and a widespread faith in the virtues of an uncontrolled economy, particularly in the Republican party, which controlled the White House throughout most of this period. The ascendant political forces of the day had no broad program of legislation or reform to enact; vigorous government was a danger; a weak president controlled by a Congress concerned more with patronage than with broad legislative programs provided a political system perfectly adapted to the purposes of business, so long as corruption did not interfere with profits or alienate the growing middle classes.[3]

Resurgence of the presidency. The resurgence of the presidency from the nadir reached under Grant was gradual. It may seem unbelievable today, but the greatest battles between president and Congress during this period resulted from the attempts of Presidents Hayes, Garfield, and Cleveland to regain from the Senate control over their own Cabinet appointments, an effort in which each succeeded only after considerable travail. But none of these men had the slightest intention of asserting control over policy, which they took for granted was entirely in the domain of the Congress.[4] It was only around the turn of the century, with

2. Woodrow Wilson, *Congressional Government: A Study in American Politics* (New York: Meridian Books, 1956), p. 31.

3. See E. E. Schattschneider, "United States: The Functional Approach to Party Government," in *Modern Political Parties,* ed. S. Neumann (Chicago: University of Chicago Press, 1956), pp. 194–218, especially at p. 197.

4. The principal battles over appointments are described in Binkley, *President and Congress,* ch. 7, pp. 145–167.

McKinley and Theodore Roosevelt, that greater control over policy came to be lodged in the White House.

Thus the power of Congress over policy and appointments has declined since its apex in the period after the Civil War. In the twentieth century not only has the president broken the monopoly of Congress over policy—and, of course, over appointments—but, as we have seen, he has also largely taken command over the initiation of new policies.

Yet the Congress is now a far more active institution, far better equipped to deal with complex matters of public policy, far more deeply involved in an incredible range of important issues than it ever was or could be in the nineteenth century. What has happened is this: in the post–Civil War period, during a time when the doctrine of complete laissez faire marched triumphant and the foreign policy of the United States limited the country to a role of neutrality and isolation, there was, in plain fact, very little policy for either president or Congress to initiate and to enact. But, in the twentieth century, government regulation and control, welfare programs, foreign affairs, military policy, and the taxation and spending measures required for all these purposes have produced a veritable "policy explosion." If Congress were to do no more than to consider the principal measures submitted to it by the chief executive, it would have plenty to do; yet the Congress does considerably more than this.

In this sense, then, the power of Congress has grown: the decisions Congress makes by modifying, passing, or rejecting measures affect all of us, and the whole world, to an incomparably greater extent today than in the nineteenth century. If the Congress had not met after 1868, and had left behind a dutiful caretaker president to enforce existing laws, neither the United States nor the world would have been much different several decades later from what, in fact, they were. But the United States of the 1970s could not possibly exist legally on the statutes of the 1920s.

In sum, in the post–Civil War period, Congress enjoyed a monopoly control over policies mostly of trivial importance; even if its influence in some key decisions has been small, as we saw in Chapter 11, on the whole it is true that today Congress shares with the president control over policies of profound consequence.

Congress as Policy-Maker Today

Input and output. In recent decades the input and output of laws requiring congressional action has become staggering. In the First Congress, one hundred forty-four measures were introduced. Throughout the first twenty-five years of the nineteenth century, the number of measures introduced climbed steadily from one Congress to the next. Nor did the upward trend stop after the initial phase. The number of measures introduced reached its highest point with the Sixty-first Congress (1909–11) when over forty-four thousand measures were introduced. Many of these were 'private bills': claims for property damage or personal injury by government agents; matters of immigration, citizenship, or deportation of specific individuals; correction of individual military and naval records; private land bills, and the like. Changes in congressional rules (involving, among other things, delegation of many such decisions to executive officials) have reduced the number of private bills. In the second quarter of the twentieth century the number of private measures introduced in each Congress varied from a low point of something over eight thousand in the middle of the Second World War to a high point of nearly twenty-five thousand during the Seventy-first Congress (1929–31).

The output of public measures has not kept pace with this enormous input. The First Congress passed a total of one hundred eight public bills. The output of the Congress gradually increased until about 1930, when it seems to have stabilized at a number varying between six hundred and one thousand public measures passed in each Congress.[5]

Congress remains, both formally and actually, a key organ in making laws. In many other democracies the parliament has become a rubber stamp for the cabinet, or at least a body with a dutiful majority that can be relied on to pass without resistance the measures submitted to it by the cabinet. By comparison, the American Congress is far too independent of the president and the American parties, far too heterogeneous, to make this possible here except in rare circumstances. It is true that when Franklin Roosevelt took office in the bleakest days of the Great Depression, he found a Congress eager to do his bidding. "The first months of the New Deal," the leading historian of that period has written, "were to an astonishing degree an adventure in unanimity."[6] Yet the honeymoon, the famous Hundred Days, did not last even through the crisis of the Depression. After 1933, Congress gradually recovered self-confidence; and in 1937 Northern Republicans and Southern Democrats forged an alliance that all but brought the period of New Deal reform to an end. Again, from 1963 to 1965, President Johnson matched Roosevelt's 1933–7 record for new legislation. Thanks in part to Johnson's exceptional skills with Congress and in part to the crushing Democratic majorities resulting from the 1964 elections (the largest since 1938 in the House and since 1942 in the Senate), one major bill after another passed Congress. But by 1966 Congress was again displaying a more independent spirit.

If the Congress continues, then, to be a formidable participant in

5. These figures will be found in *Historical Statistics*, pp. 689–690.

6. Arthur M. Schlesinger, Jr., *The Coming of the New Deal* (Cambridge: Houghton Mifflin, 1959), p. 423.

making laws, certain developments have nonetheless greatly qualified its role.

Initiative. First, as we saw in Chapter 11, the initiative in legislation has increasingly shifted in this century to the executive. The Congress no longer expects to originate measures but to pass, veto, or modify laws proposed by the chief executive. It is the president, not the Congress, who determines the content and substance of the legislation with which Congress deals. The president is now the motor in the system; the Congress applies the brakes. The president gives what forward movement there is to the system; his is the force of thrust and innovation. The Congress is the force of inertia—a force, it should be said, that means not only restraint but also stability in policies.

Variations. Second, as we have also seen, the relative importance of president and Congress in policy-making is not and probably cannot be static. It varies with the circumstances and with the kinds of policies at stake. Although the Congress, despite its reputation to the contrary, sometimes acts with exceptional dispatch, legislatures have never proved as suitable as executives for handling emergency actions. Like all legislatures, Congress is most handicapped in times of crisis and in dealing with military and foreign affairs. On questions where time and secrecy are not of the essence, Congress is much stronger—on legislation having to do with domestic affairs or with aspects of foreign affairs not removed from purview of Congress by the need for speed or circumspection: policies with respect to agriculture, labor, business, taxation, immigration, appropriations, and the like. Finally, on all questions having to do with the distribution of benefits or deprivations, Congress tends to play an important part; even during the Second World War, when it was a matter of deciding how the burdens of war were to be distributed among different groups of Americans, Congress played a preeminent role.[7]

Presidential decisions. In the third place, it must always be kept in mind that laws, these days, are only one part of policy. Many of the most important decisions, particularly in foreign and military affairs, do not require legislation, at least not directly. Sometimes, too, even where legislation is required, the chief executive has, for all practical purposes, already committed the Congress and the country; in these cases Congress may modify but it cannot easily reverse the basic commitment that has been entered into. Thus Congress could play only a passive role in our entry into the Korean war, the increasing U.S. presence in Vietnam from 1956 onward, suspension of nuclear testing by the executive, etc.

---

7. See Roland Young, *Congressional Politics in the Second World War* (New York: Columbia University Press, 1956).

Other forms of influence. Fourth, Congress participates in policy-making in many ways other than by making laws. Its informal participation, usually by consultation between president and congressional leaders, is traditional and important. Many actions technically within presidential discretion, frequently including actions on foreign and military affairs, are taken by the president only after he consults with congressional leaders to find out whether he will have adequate support for the decision he proposes to make. If he does not, he may back down. Thus, in 1954, when the fall of the French fortress of Dienbienphu in Indo-China was imminent, a defeat which the French foresaw would mean their collapse in Southeast Asia, President Eisenhower, Secretary of State Dulles, and Admiral Radford, then chairman of the Joint Chiefs of Staff, advocated aiding the French with an air strike by Navy and Air Force planes. In a secret meeting, under questioning from congressional leaders, including Majority Leader of the Senate Lyndon Johnson, it became apparent that congressional leaders were reluctant to support the action unless the administration could find allies abroad, particularly Britain. But Britain, too, was reluctant; and in the end the plan was abandoned. Even in this case, in the view of one observer, the president could probably have won congressional support "provided he had asked for it forcefully and explained the facts and their relation to the national interest of the United States." But he did not, and his soundings of congressional opinion evidently did prevent immediate intervention in support of the French.[8] Sometimes the Congress tries to tie the president's hands publicly by passing a resolution, as in the series of resolutions from 1951 to 1961 in which one or both houses declared, in most cases unanimously, their opposition to admitting Communist China to the U.N. Sometimes, on the other hand, when it suits his purposes, the president openly asks for an expression of congressional approval, as when President Lyndon Johnson obtained a joint resolution indicating congressional support for actions during a crisis in the Gulf of Tonkin in August, 1964. To the discomfiture of some congressmen, the president later used this resolution as evidence of congressional authorization for his policy of bombing North Vietnam, increasing the number of American troops, and escalating American participation in other ways.

Congressional committees also share with the president a substantial measure of influence over the administrative agencies. Indeed, probably no national legislature in any other polyarchy has greater influence over bureaucracy, and most have far less. Committees acquire and maintain this influence because they control appropriations and legislation wanted by the agencies. Committee influence over admin-

---

8. See Chalmers M. Roberts, "The Day We Didn't Go to War," *The Reporter*, September 14, 1954, 31–35, reprinted in *Legislative Politics USA*, ed. T. J. Lowie (Boston: Little, Brown, 1962), pp. 240–248. The quotation is at p. 248.

istration is exercised chiefly by means of hearings, both public and off-the-record, and by investigations. Like the president, a congressional committee can often influence policies informally without actually spelling out their demands in a law. This is accomplished by day-to-day contacts between committee staff and people in the executive agencies, on-site visits, inspection tours, informal briefings, and the like. It is important to keep in mind, too, that while presidents, cabinet members, heads of departments, and even bureau chiefs come and go, many ranking members on congressional committees remain in Congress serving on their committees a very long time, during which they acquire a great deal of knowledge and often a proprietary interest in the agencies that fall within the jurisdiction of their committee.

Finally, Congress participates in policy-making in an important indirect way, by serving as a source of information to the public—and sometimes to the Executive Branch. Congressional debates and discussions, particularly on the floor of the Senate, and the hearings conducted by congressional committees produce a steady flow of reports and news about existing and proposed policies. A committee hearing in which witnesses are heard over weeks, months, and even years is often a vital instrument in calling public attention to an issue and winning support for or against some proposal. Although it is impossible to assess the exact weight such hearings have had, it would be a mistake to underestimate their importance by looking only for effects on *general* public opinion; for often what committee hearings do is to change, solidify, or mobilize the opinions of *specific* publics whose influence is critical to a particular piece of legislation—cotton farmers, the leaders of the AFL-CIO, an ethnic group, bankers, the elderly.

ANTAGONISM   **Causes**
AND CONFLICT   Yet if president and Congress must ordinarily share in the process of making decisions, they do not ordinarily do so harmoniously.

Different interests. Aside from jealousies and antagonisms that have their origins in personalities and institutional loyalties, conflict also stems from the fact that the president, the Senate, and the House each reflects, and in a sense represents, a different congeries of interests. An individual or organization with good access to a powerful committee chairman in the Senate, for example, may have little access to the chairman of the equivalent committee in the House, and perhaps none at all to the White House or influential agencies in the Executive Branch.

Each also has to keep a different set of constituents in mind. Even if elected politicians often misperceive the views of their constituents, and (as we saw in the last chapter) congressmen often do; they give thought to the actions they think will win or lose favor among their constituents. On a hasty view of the matter one might suppose that since the president, the Senate, and the House are all chosen by the same American electorate it must follow that each has pretty much the same general set of constituents in mind. Yet this is not the case.

Different electorates. To begin with, it is not strictly true to say that their electorates are identical. Voting turnout in congressional elections in off years is ordinarily about 25 percent smaller than the electorate in presidential elections. Moreover, the off-year electorate is not just a smaller cross section of the electorate in presidential years, for in off-years elections there is a much larger decline in voting by independents than by partisan voters who loyally support one of the two major parties and rarely vote for the other. The off-year electorate is therefore more partisan, more bound to one of the two parties, than the presidential electorate. In addition, of course, changes in mood, temper, and issues may occur in the two-year interval between presidential and midterm elections. The net effect, often, is to produce majorities in House or Senate at odds with one another or with the President on key issues. Although the prospect of conflict is most evident when midterm elections give the opposition party a majority in one or both houses, conflict is normal even when the president and a majority of members of each house are of the same party. We shall explore these shifts in the electorate in more detail in Chapter 19, but the important point to keep in mind here is that midterm elections enhance the possibility of conflict among the president and the two houses of Congress.

Different constituencies. An even more important source of conflict, perhaps, is the fact that even in presidential years the national electorate is carved up into different constituencies for the president, senators, and congressmen. These differences influence their perceptions and calculations as to the key groups that need to be appeased in one way or another. Their calculations of the needs, interests, attitudes, pressures, and future responses of their particular constituents—calculations clouded with a good deal of uncertainty and misinformation—almost inevitably lead to different conclusions when made by a majority of 436 representatives, a majority of 100 senators, or the president. These differences in judging what their constituents want or oppose contribute to the conflict.

NO PROCEDURE   What most sharply distinguishes policy-making in the United States from
IS DECISIVE   the process existing in most other polyarchies is the absence of any
                      established procedure for eliminating conflicts among the president and

the two houses. In some (though by no means all) polyarchies a particular process is *decisive* with respect to policy-making. An institution or process is decisive if, by winning a victory, a party or coalition will have all the authority it needs to carry out its policies during a limited term of office. In some polyarchies, elections are relatively decisive. In some, the *formation of the cabinet* is pretty decisive. In others, there is no decisive procedure; the United States is one of these.

Contrasts
Britain. By contrast with the United States, in Britain periodic elections for seats in the House of Commons are relatively decisive. By winning a majority of seats, a party is in a position to select the prime minister. The prime minister in turn chooses his cabinet. Because British parties are highly unified the prime minister and his cabinet, being the de facto leaders of the victorious party, can confidently assume that their majority in the House of Commons will support the party's basic policies. In the highly unlikely event that an important proposal by the cabinet was rejected by the House, the cabinet would resign and new elections would be held. In practise, however, this almost never happens because party discipline is strong enough to insure a majority of votes for all key policies proposed by the cabinet. The opposition party, knowing that it cannot defeat the cabinet on any major issue, concentrates on winning public opinion to its programs and candidates so that it can win a future parliamentary majority. Parliament itself is not, then, a site for genuine encounters so much as it is a forum from which to influence the next election. Parliamentary debate is not intended to influence Parliament as much as the public—and hence future elections. Negotiations by the opposition to enter the cabinet would, on the whole, be futile, and everyone knows it.

Other polyarchies. In some polyarchies where elections are a good deal less decisive than in Britain, the formation of the cabinet is relatively decisive. The Scandinavian countries serve as examples. There, when a party or several parties with a majority of seats in the parliament enter into a coalition and constitute a cabinet, the policies they have agreed on stand a very good chance of being enacted. Because the parties in the coalition usually have a majority of the parliament, and because their members are unified and disciplined in their voting and particularly reluctant to upset the apple cart by voting against the coalition program and thus bringing about the downfall of the cabinet, the cabinet can generally count on getting a majority of votes for its policies.

The United States
In some polyarchies, however, neither elections nor cabinet forma-

tion are really very decisive. In fact, no single process may be truly decisive. This is the case in the United States. A president who has just won a majority of popular and electoral votes after campaigning in behalf of his platform may be quite unable to persuade Congress to enact the policies he proposes. Nor is there likely to be a disciplined majority in Congress capable of carrying through its own program. Even when voters elect a president and majorities in both houses all from the same party, the elections are likely to be far more indecisive than in Britain. Well-informed political commentators, for example, will speculate as to just how much of the president's program or the party's platform will actually be adopted by Congress. For in the United States policy-making typically involves a vast amount of negotiation and compromise, and, even so, great risk that proposals advanced by the president or congressional leaders will be significantly modified or even defeated outright. Thus there is no established procedure for eliminating the conflicts among the president and the houses of Congress. In parliamentary systems where the cabinet must have the confidence of a majority of the parliament (or the lower house), conflict between cabinet and parliament would ordinarily be resolved by the resignation of the cabinet. Either a new cabinet would be formed or new elections would be called. But of course no such mechanisms exist in the United States.

The Founders' commitment to partitioning power, as we saw, prevented them from devising a system in which the executive would be wholly dependent on the Congress, much less on the lower house. Nor were they able to see as clearly as we can today that the British parliamentary system was moving away from the separation of powers that had been described and praised by Montesquieu, the great French political theorist whose work was a veritable bible for many of the Founders.

Would a Parliamentary System Be Better?

It is intriguing to speculate how the American polyarchy would function under a parliamentary system, or with arrangements that would permit the calling of elections in case of continuing deadlock. These have been seriously proposed at various times. Despite their complaints, however, Americans have been unwilling to entertain seriously the notion that the Constitution needs altering in any fundamental way. Aside from the uncritical assumption of many ordinary citizens that American constitutional arrangements are the best in the world, scholars are aware of how difficult it is to predict what will happen when institutions that operate well in one country are transplanted to another. The parliamentary system seems to operate most vigorously in relatively homogeneous countries with unified parties and a national structure that is unitary rather than federal, as in Britain or the Scandinavian countries. Where these conditions are lacking, the parliamentary system often produces weak and ineffectual coalition governments or elaborate systems for handling conflict that are not demonstrably superior to the interminable negotiation, bargaining, and compromise that characterize the American polyarchy. Nonetheless, Americans might improve their policy-making processes if they were a good deal more experimental about their political and constitutional arrangements than they have been since 1787.

SUMMARY Taken together, three features tend to make the role of Congress in policy-making rather different from that of national legislative bodies in most other polyarchies:

1. Because Congress and the president share power over policy-making, they must cooperate. Although there are short-run and long-run oscillations in the relative influence of the one or the other, both possess independent resources of power.

2. There is ordinarily a certain amount of antagonism and conflict between the president and Congress or between the House and the Senate.

3. Unlike many other polyarchies, there is no established procedure for putting an end to these conflicts and bringing about a state of harmony, as in some parliamentary systems where either elections or cabinet formation tend to be decisive. Proposals for introducing some such arrangements in the United States have never made much headway, partly because of the exceptional, if often unthinking, deference most Americans display toward their Constitution, and partly because the consequences are hard to predict.

The Supreme Court and Judicial Review: Design and Development

According to the Greek version of democratic theory, the sovereign people ought to rule directly through their assembly. According to the theory of representative democracy developed in the late eighteenth century, the people could properly rule indirectly through an elected assembly. With the appearance of the popularly elected chief executive, symbolized in the United States by Andrew Jackson, democratic ideals adjusted to the notion that the people might rule jointly through an elected legislature and an elected executive. Since democratic theory has been stretched to accord legitimacy to these institutional developments in the American polyarchy, can it also be stretched to give legitimacy to the United States Supreme Court?

The problem is this: the Supreme Court is not an elected body; it is, indeed, intentionally insulated from electoral politics. Yet it has the authority, which Americans call *judicial review,* to strike down legislation enacted by elected representatives, whether a federal law approved by the Congress and the president, a state law approved by a state legislature and governor, or a municipal ordinance approved by, let us say, city council and mayor. Is not judicial review a distinctly undemocratic element in the American polyarchy? If so, should it be permitted to exist?

The problem would not arise if Americans had self-consciously chosen to construct an aristocratic republic or meritocracy. For an aristocratic republic might very well have given a Supreme Court the power to nullify laws passed by the representatives of the people. A Supreme Court so armed could shield aristocratic power from popular attack. But because Americans created a polyarchy where democratic principles of political equality and consent are the main grounds of legitimacy for political institutions, the extraordinary position of the Supreme Court in the American political system has ever been a source of controversy.

There are three general grounds on which one might base a claim to the legitimacy of judicial review: that judicial review is implied by the Constitution, which is itself accepted as legitimate; that it rests on a long-standing tradition that for all practical purposes incorporates judicial review into the constitutional system; and that it is implied by the principles of democratic government.

Because the tradition itself gains acceptability from a line of reasoning intended to prove that judicial review is implied by the Constitution, the first two grounds tend to be fused into one; let me call this fusion of the two claims the traditional constitutionality of judicial review. The third ground for judicial review, deriving from democratic theory, is, as we shall see, unquestionably the weakest.

THE UNCERTAIN DESIGN OF THE FOUNDERS

The traditional constitutionality of judicial review must start with the intentions of the men who framed the Constitution, for, if they had never intended judicial review, it would be unreasonable (in the absence of an amendment) to argue that it is implied by the terms of the Constitution! Unfortunately, what the Founding Fathers intended the Supreme Court to be is a highly debated question; even more unfortunately for the clarity of this debate, judging from the records of the Convention, the delegates scarcely discussed the functions of the proposed Court. The discussion most relevant to the question of judicial review was stimulated by a highly controversial provision (ultimately rejected) in the Virginia plan. That provision and the brief but sharp skirmishes it produced are interesting for what they reveal about the intentions, or lack of them, of the Founding Fathers.

The Virginia Plan

The proposal in question—it was the eighth in the series of resolutions that historians have called the Virginia plan, introduced on May 29 by Randolph of Virginia—provided for a Council of Revision to consist of the president "and a convenient number of the National Judiciary." This Council was to have a veto on laws passed by Congress or by a state legislature. Although the proposal did not say so explicitly, discussion among the delegates reveals their clear understanding that the Council's veto was to be used much as the president has come to use his veto: to block 'bad' laws, even though these might not be unconstitutional. Under Randolph's proposal, the Congress could overcome the Council's veto simply by passing the measure a second time. As to state laws, the plan evidently intended to provide that a state legislature could overcome the veto by passing a measure a second time with a larger than ordinary majority in each house of the state legislature; the exact number or proportion was left blank in Randolph's proposal.

Like the Constitution itself, the Virginia plan said not one word about the power of judicial review as we know it: i.e., the power to decide on the constitutionality of laws. Many delegates distinguished sharply between the power of the courts to declare acts of Congress or the state legislatures *unconstitutional,* and the proposed Council of Revision which was for the purpose of inhibiting 'bad' but not necessarily unconstitutional legislation. A delegate might, then, have taken one of four positions.

1. Against both. At least two delegates were against granting the federal judiciary the power to declare laws *unconstitutional* (i.e., judicial review), and against giving it any voice on *policy* questions (i.e., the Council of Revision). One was John Mercer of Maryland. As a State Federalist, Mercer probably anticipated the dangers to state power from a federal court when he remarked that he "disapproved of the Doctrine that the Judges as expositors of the Constitution should have authority to declare a law void. He thought laws ought to be well and cautiously made, and then to be uncontroulable."[1] Mercer—who arrived at the Convention late, left within two weeks in protest against the trend toward National Federalism, refused to sign the finished document, and fought against its ratification—can hardly be regarded as a representative figure of the Convention. Yet he was supported by one of the important men at the Convention, John Dickinson, who confessed that he

> . . . was strongly impressed with the remark of Mr. Mercer as to the power of the Judges to set aside the law. He thought no such power ought to exist. He was at the same time at a loss what expedient to substitute.[2]

Some of the other delegates who opposed the Council of Revision may also have been against judicial review; but their remarks are too ambiguous to allow a firm conclusion.[3]

2. For both. At the other extreme, some of the most influential members of the Convention were in favor of giving the judiciary not only the power to declare laws unconstitutional but also a veto over *policy* questions by means of the Council of Revision. Representatives of this view included two of the strongest advocates of a democratic republic, Wilson and Mason, and one of the most outspoken supporters of an aristocratic republic, Gouverneur Morris. Madison, too, spoke with great

---

1. *Documents,* p. 548.
2. *Ibid.,* p. 549.
3. E.g., Gorham, Strong, Rutledge; see *ibid.,* pp. 423–429.

force in behalf of the Council; and while he did not say so explicitly, his arguments do imply that the judiciary would have the power to decide on the constitutionality of laws. These men argued that decisions on constitutionality would not go far enough: for 'bad' laws might nonetheless be perfectly constitutional. For example, Wilson, who stubbornly upheld the virtues of the proposed Council of Revision after it was twice voted down, contended:

> . . . It had been said that the Judges, as expositors of the Laws would have an opportunity of defending their constitutional rights. There was weight in this observation; but this power of the Judges did not go far enough. Laws may be unjust, may be unwise, may be dangerous, may be destructive; and yet may not be so unconstitutional as to justify the Judges in refusing to give them effect. Let them have a share in the Revisionary power, and they will have an opportunity of taking notice of these characters of a law, and of counteracting, by the weight of their opinions the improper views of the Legislature.[4]

Mason, Madison, and Gouverneur Morris argued along similar lines.[5] Morris was explicit as to some of the "bad laws" he wanted checked: "Emissions of paper money, largesses to the people—a remission of debts and similar measures. . . ."[6]

3. Only policy. Some delegates could have been *against* judicial review and *for* the Council. Although this alternative seems rather illogical, a case could undoubtedly be made for it, and it is conceivable that a few delegates silently supported it. Yet since no one advocated this position, openly or by indirection, it is reasonable to conclude that none of the delegates adhered to it.

4. Only constitutionality. Finally, some delegates who believed that the judiciary would have the power to declare laws *unconstitutional* opposed giving the courts the power to veto laws simply on the ground that they were bad laws. These delegates argued that while it was appropriate for judges to decide on the *constitutionality* of laws, they were unsuitable for deciding on the *wisdom* of laws. Although a number of delegates expressed distrust of the courts as policy-makers—more seemed to agree on this than any other point—only two of these explicitly favored judicial review of constitutionality. One of these was the State Federalist, Luther Martin. The other was the National Federalist, Gerry of Massachusetts, who doubted

> . . . whether the Judiciary ought to form a part of it [the Council], as they will have a sufficient check agst encroachments on their own department

---

4. *Ibid.,* p. 422–423.
5. *Ibid.,* pp. 426–428.
6. *Ibid.,* p. 425.

by their exposition of the laws, which involved a power of deciding on their Constitutionality. In some States the Judges had actually set aside laws as being agst the Constitution. This was done too with general approbation. It was quite foreign from the nature of ye office to make them judges of the policy of public measures.[7]

Despite the eloquent support given to the idea of a Council of Revision by Wilson, Madison, and Morris, the proposal was decisively rejected. When it was first taken up on June 4, Gerry's substitute motion to give the veto power to the president without the participation of the judges was passed by a vote of eight states to two.[8] Undaunted, two days later, Wilson (Madison seconding his motion) tried again. They gained the support of only three states—Connecticut, New York, and Virginia —and were opposed by eight. Most delegates must have thought the matter firmly settled, but Wilson and Madison evidently felt too strongly to let the idea drop. On July 21, they once more introduced a motion for the Council of Revision. Although they were voted down again, they may have felt that the opposition was softening, for despite the fact the motion received favorable votes only from the same three states as before, two states, Pennsylvania and Georgia, were divided, leaving only four states in opposition. (New Jersey was recorded as "not present.")[9] Heartened, perhaps, by signs that the opposition was weakening, Madison and Wilson tried once more on August 15; but this time the delegates gave them short shrift and voted their motion down 8–3, virtually without debate.[10]

The Founders' Intentions

What conclusions as to the intentions of the Founding Fathers can we draw from these debates?

First, the record of the debates leaves their intentions unclear. Probably a great many delegates did not have very precise intentions with respect to the powers of the judiciary.

Second, it is a reasonable inference that a majority of the delegates accepted the notion that the federal courts would rule on the constitutionality of state and federal laws involved in cases before them. Some additional though by no means conclusive evidence is provided by the bold and unambiguous stand announced in *The Federalist* No. 78— written, ironically, by Hamilton, who had taken no part in the debates on the judiciary:

---

7. *Ibid.*, p. 147.
8. *Ibid.*, p. 152.
9. *Ibid.*, p. 429.
10. Of the states originally favoring the proposal, only Virginia remained, Connecticut and New York having deserted to the opposition; however, Virginia was joined this time by Delaware and Maryland (*Documents*, p. 548).

. . . By a limited Constitution, I understand one which contains certain specified exceptions to the legislative authority; such, for instance, as that it shall pass no bills of attainder, no *ex-post-facto* laws, and the like. Limitations of this kind can be preserved in practice no other way than through the medium of courts of justice, whose duty it must be to declare all acts contrary to the manifest tenor of the Constitution void. Without this, all the reservations of particular rights or privileges would amount to nothing.[11]

Third, it is also a reasonable inference that a majority of delegates rejected the notion that judges should participate in policy-making. It was for exactly this reason, it appears, that the Council of Revision was turned down three times. Ever since the Convention defenders of judicial review have generally assumed that judicial review is legitimate only on questions of constitutionality and illegitimate on questions of policy. This is the explicit position of the Supreme Court itself.

JOHN MARSHALL'S BOLD DESIGN

In the light of these observations, it is difficult to sustain the view that when Chief Justice John Marshall enunciated the doctrine of judicial review in the famous case of *Marbury* v. *Madison*[12] on February 24, 1803, he usurped powers that the Founding Fathers had intended to deny to the federal judiciary. Marshall's argument, in fact, adhered closely to the reasoning of Hamilton in *The Federalist* No. 78, which was in line, as we have seen, with what one can reasonably infer to have been the dominant view at the Convention.

Marshall's argument was succinct and persuasive:

1. The Constitution is the supreme law of the land, binding on all branches of the government—legislature, executive, the judiciary.
2. The Constitution deliberately establishes a government with limited powers.
3. Consequently "an act of the legislature, repugnant to the constitution, is void." If this were not true, then the government would be unlimited; and the Constitution would be an absurdity.
4. "It is emphatically the province and duty of the judicial department to say what the law is."
5. "So if a law be in opposition to the constitution . . . the court must determine which of these conflicting rules governs the case. This is of the very essence of judicial duty."
6. "If, then, the courts are to regard the constitution, and the constitution is superior to any ordinary act of the legislature, the constitution

---

11. Hamilton et al., *The Federalist*, p. 505.

12. 1 Cranch 1937 (1803). Reams have been filled about this famous case and concerning judicial review. A detailed history of the case itself has been written by a Supreme Court justice Mr. Justice Harold Burton, "The Cornerstone of Constitutional Law: The Extraordinary Case of Marbury v. Madison," *American Bar Association Journal*, 36 (October, 1950), 805–883.

and not such ordinary act, must govern the case to which they both apply."

7. Hence if a law is repugnant to the Constitution, when that law comes before a court, the judges are duty bound to declare that law void in order to uphold the supremacy of the Constitution.[13]

Marshall's opinion has the majestic finality of Euclid. It has been quoted and paraphrased thousands of times in defense of judicial review, by judges, lawyers, historians, political scientists, and others. Since Marshall's time, the Supreme Court has used the power of judicial review on more than four-score occasions to strike down federal legislation. It has used the power many more times—no one has ever calculated how many—to hold state laws unconstitutional. The Court's actions have invariably been met with protest. Yet more often than not, critics protest a particular decision but not the general principle of judicial review. And the bitterest critics of the Court in one decade are often the Court's boldest defenders in the next.

Thus the principle of judicial review is firmly anchored simultaneously in tradition and a highly compelling rational-legal appeal to the supremacy of the Constitution.

There remains, nonetheless, the nagging question of democracy.

JUDICIAL REVIEW AND DEMOCRATIC PRINCIPLES

Does the power of judicial review entail a nondemocratic, an aristocratic, even an oligarchic principle of government? The defenders and critics of judicial review have wrestled with this question ever since *Marbury v. Madison*. Jefferson may have had *Marbury v. Madison* in mind when in his old age he wrote to a friend that "the judiciary in the United States is the subtle corps of sappers and miners constantly working underground to undermine the foundations of our confederated republic. . . . A judiciary independent of a king or executive alone is a good thing; but independence of the will of the nation is a solecism, at least in a republican government."[14]

A Dialogue

The controversy can perhaps be summarized best in an imaginary dialogue between a critic and an advocate of judicial review:

Critic: I am quite willing to concede that a tradition of constitutionality may convey a measure of legitimacy to judicial review. I contend, nonetheless, that judicial review is definitely an undemocratic

13. *Marbury v. Madison,* 1 Cranch 1937 (1803).

14. Letter to Thomas Ritchie, December 25, 1820, in Paul Leicester Ford, ed., *The Writings of Thomas Jefferson* (New York: G. P. Putnam's Sons, 1899), pp. 170–171, quoted in John R. Schmidhauser, ed., *Constitutional Law in the Political Process* (Chicago: Rand McNally, 1963), pp. 145–146.

element in the American polyarchy. After all, most of the people in eighteenth-century Britain no doubt regarded their constitutional system —kings, lords, and all—as legitimate. Yet you would not argue, I'm sure, that eighteenth-century Britain was a democracy. Aristocracies, monarchies, even dictatorships, I suppose, might acquire legitimacy in the eyes of the people they rule; yet they would not be democratic. In different times and places, all sorts of political institutions have acquired a certain degree of legitimacy; yet I would not want many of these institutions in this country, nor, I imagine, would you. I wonder if judicial review hasn't generated a conflict between two different principles of legitimacy accepted by Americans—a conflict between our traditions of constitutionality and our supposed commitment to democracy. Our commitment to democracy logically requires us to uphold the principles of political equality and consent. Yet it is patently absurd to say that the Supreme Court reinforces these principles when it strikes down laws supported by a majority of the people's representatives in Congress and by the one nationally elected official we have, the president. What I say, then, is this: judicial review may be good or it may be bad, but it is obviously not democratic.

Advocate: I disagree. As Hamilton and Marshall said, ours is a *limited* government; our democratic ideal is definitely not majority-rule democracy but a *limited* democracy with partitioned power. Judicial review is a key element in the partitioning of power. I don't contend, as Marshall did, that judicial review is inherent in a written constitution; I know as well as you do that a number of other polyarchies that were not in existence when Marshall wrote his famous opinion now have written constitutions, and yet do not give their courts the power of judicial review. I would contend, however, that the *limited* character of our government is an absolutely essential characteristic. Stripped of its constitutional limitations, ours would be a totally different system. Moreover, we Americans continue to believe strongly in limited government. And judicial review helps to preserve limited government by protecting the Constitution from violations by state governments, by the federal government, or by particular parts of the federal government, such as the Congress. This is why Americans overwhelmingly believe in judicial review. Do you contend that democracy requires *unlimited* government?

Critic: You misunderstand me. I know full well that we possess a written Constitution. I realize that someone has to interpret the meaning of what is written in that Constitution. I can see that in the course of events cases come to the courts which depend on what the Constitution means. So, in deciding the cases before them, the courts must interpret the Constitution. Let me remind you, however, that the United States is not the only country in the world with a written constitution. In fact, most polyarchies have a written constitution. Yet many of them do not have judicial review—and I think it fair to say that not one has a supreme court as powerful as ours.

Advocate: I do not quite see how we could function without judicial review.

Critic: What are you afraid of—the American people? But if the American people wanted unlimited government, do you really think that a few men on our Supreme Court could prevent it? Why, the voters would elect a president and a Congress who would impeach and convict the justices one day and appoint new ones the next! Limited government exists in this country not because the Supreme Court wants it but because, as you said yourself, we Americans want it. And limited government will cease the day Americans cease to want it, no matter what nine men on a court may say or do. So long as the bulk of the American people want limited government, they will elect representatives to Congress and the presidency who adhere to this commitment. If Americans should stop wanting limited government, they will elect revolutionaries committed to unlimited government, and our Constitution will be as dead as the Articles of Confederation. So here is my answer: The best protection for limited government in a polyarchy, in fact the only protection, consists of the people and their elected representatives. What I am saying is this: Polyarchy depends on the self-restraint of the people. If they don't exercise self-restraint, you won't have a polyarchy and no court can keep it for them. If they do exercise self-restraint, then you don't need to have judicial review.

Advocate: What you say is all very well in the abstract. But remember, ours is also a federal system. Suppose a state government violates the Constitution—for example, by depriving some of its citizens of their right to assemble or to speak freely? A majority of the voters in the United States might oppose the state action, but even if they knew about it—which they probably would not—what could they do?

Critic: I admit that federalism complicates matters. Most federal polyarchies, I notice, do have some form of judicial review; in this respect Canada, Australia, and, more recently, India have all rejected the British pattern. Another federal polyarchy, West Germany, also has judicial review. I am quite willing to endorse the principle, on purely democratic grounds, that national majorities should prevail over state majorities. Even so, I do not see why you couldn't adopt the Swiss pattern; the federal judiciary could review the constitutionality of state laws but not of federal laws.

Advocate: If you need judicial review in order to keep the states from invading the powers of the federal government, doesn't the logic of your argument cut the other way, too? What if the federal government invades the powers of the states?

Critic: That might once have been a forceful argument. But is it not true that today the federal government can constitutionally regulate almost anything through its powers over taxation and interstate commerce? If the federal government does not regulate everything, that is only because the president and Congress do not want to do so. Again, you see, restraints depend on the people and their elected representatives, not on the courts.

Advocate: You ignore the possibility that a demagogic president or a large congressional majority, or both together, might pass laws that would deprive some particular minority of important constitutional rights.

Critic: Don't we have periodic elections? If we Americans really believed in these rights, we would vote out such a Congress at the next election. If we did not, I do not see how the Supreme Court could maintain our rights, at least in the long run.

Advocate: In the long run, no. But do we have to forget about the short run? A majority of voters, or a majority of their representatives, might act under the transitory pressures of impulse, passion, hysteria, crisis. Politicians might not be steadily antilibertarian; yet they might be temporarily so. In such cases the Court could void laws passed during short-run aberrations.

Critic: Isn't this the heart of the matter? You assume that a majority of Americans and their elected representatives cannot always be trusted to act within the spirit of limited government. You believe that when they are misguided, the Supreme Court can maintain the essential conditions of a libertarian polyarchy by nullifying federal laws contrary to a Constitution designed for limited government. I admit that your argument is persuasive. But it raises two problems. First, will the Supreme Court really stand up against a majority in order to protect some embattled minority that is threatened by a federal law, or will it not be moved by much the same passions and prejudices as the majority of people and their representatives? Second, even assuming now that the Court does stand against majorities, will it uphold general and abstract principles of right or justice, or will it instead strike down laws it disapproves on grounds of *policy*? Judges are human. As Jefferson said in 1820: "Our judges are as honest as other men, and not more so. They have, with others, the same passions for party, for power, and the privilege of their corps."[15] Even when judges are not swayed by the same passions and prejudices as a majority, they may be moved by the passions and prejudices of a particular minority. If they use judicial review and the claim of 'constitutionality' simply to impose their own views about good and bad laws, have they not contrived to evolve into exactly the kind of body that your Constitutional Convention thought it was preventing?

Advocate: Well, we both seem to agree on one thing anyway:

---

15. Letter to Jarvis in 1820, quoted in *Thomas Jefferson on Democracy*, p. 64.

Americans seem to want judicial review. But if, as you say, they can sweep it aside when they do not want it, how in the world can you argue that there is anything undemocratic about judicial review?

Theory and Experience

Our imaginary dialogue has suggested several observations.

To begin with, from the perspective of democratic principles, it is *federal* legislation, not state or municipal law, that sets the greatest challenge to the legitimacy of judicial review. It is reasonable to argue, at any rate, that in order to make their rule effective, the people of the *United States* might properly establish a supreme court with authority to negate state and municipal laws contrary to the national laws and Constitution. Orthodox majority-rule democracy would surely make it legitimate for the people of a country to insure that the preferences of *national* majorities prevailed over those of minorities, even if these minorities happened to be a majority of a state or a locality. Because federal legislation creates the problem, we concentrate mainly on it here.

Democratic theory unclear. However, our dialogue also suggests that democratic theory provides no absolutely decisive argument as to the legitimacy of judicial review of federal legislation, laws passed by Congress and ordinarily not only signed but actively sponsored by the president. In the American polyarchy, judicial review seems to furnish a nice paradox:

☐ Because a nonelected body exercises final authority to nullify legislation enacted by the elected representatives of the people, judicial review seems to run flatly counter to the principles of consent and political equality.
☐ Yet if a preponderant proportion of Americans adhere to the ideal of limited—not majority-rule—democracy and support the Court's authority as an element in a system of partitioned power, to abolish judicial review would appear to make the overall design of the system less, not more, responsive to the preferences of the citizen body.

Comparative experience. Nonetheless, if theory provides no crystal clear answers, experience shows that judicial review is not inherent in polyarchy. Judicial review does not exist in most polyarchies. Probably in none is the authority of the highest court as broad as that exercised by the Supreme Court of the United States.

It follows, therefore, that adequate protection for the basic rights and institutional guarantees of polyarchies does not *necessarily* require the existence of judicial review. In fact, some countries with extraordinarily high levels of security for the rights of individuals and groups, such as Britain and the Scandinavian countries, have not granted their judiciary the power to nullify acts of their parliaments.

Two Alternative Possibilities

The extent to which the exercise of judicial review supports or conflicts with democratic principles would depend significantly on the *particular purposes* for which it was used. We can imagine two extreme possibilities:

☐ *The Court as a Privileged Interest Group.* Judicial review might simply permit members of the Supreme Court and groups whose views they happen to reflect to impose on the country their own preferences, biases, views, and ideological commitments in ways that had nothing to do with, or even ran flatly counter to, democratic goals such as political equality and consent.

☐ *The Court as Protector of the National Polyarchy.* The exercise of judicial review might help to reinforce the principles of political equality and consent and thereby strengthen polyarchy. Thus the Judicial Branch would insure that legislatures, executives, administrators, and lower courts adhered to the principle of political equality in their decisions, decision-making processes, modes of representation, etc.; and they might support the principle of consent by guaranteeing that basic political rights of minorities would not be overridden through actions by law-making majorities, administrators, or lower courts.

A people committed to democratic ideals would surely reject the first kind of performance. Yet they might support the second in order to make sure that if they were to lapse momentarily from what they regarded as their deepest principles, the judiciary would nonetheless insure that these principles were upheld.

SUMMARY 1. Because judicial review does not appear to be implied in the principles of consent and political equality, its existence in the American polyarchy has always been a source of controversy and unresolved problems.

2. The legitimacy of judicial review in the American polyarchy rests heavily on tradition. Yet at the Constitutional Convention itself, the Founders appear to have been uncertain in their views as to the authority of the Supreme Court. It seems reasonable to conclude from their debates that a majority rejected the idea that judges should participate in *policy-making* but accepted the notion that federal courts would rule on the *constitutionality* of state and federal laws in cases brought before them.

3. It was Chief Justice John Marshall who in *Marbury v. Madison*

definitely established the existence and the rationale for judicial review. That decisive precedent and Marshall's arguments have come to form the heart of the traditional belief in the legitimacy of judicial review.

4. Yet the traditional arguments do not answer the question whether the power of judicial review is consistent with the principles of political equality and consent—whether, in short, judicial review is a distinctly undemocratic element in the American polyarchy.

5. An exploration of this question reveals that the answer must depend to some extent on the actual performance of the Court—whether it has used its power to protect or advance particular views and interests, or to uphold the principles of political equality and consent.

The Supreme Court and Judicial Review: Performance

16

How then has the Supreme Court actually used its extraordinary authority?

THE RECORD An examination of the cases in which the Supreme Court has held *federal* legislation unconstitutional leads to a number of observations.

The Uncertain Line Between Policy and Constitutionality

To begin with, the boundary between decisions about *policy* and decisions about *constitutionality* has proved a difficult one for the Court to discover and abide by. Since the Court's claim to legitimacy rests on the validity of this distinction, it is always at pains to insist that its decisions are made purely on constitutional grounds and have nothing to do with the views the justices may hold on matters of public policy. The record, however, suggests otherwise. In an earlier day it was perhaps easier to believe that the Constitution is so clear and certain rights are so natural and self-evident that their fundamental validity is as much a matter of definite knowledge, at least to all reasonable creatures, as the color of a ripe cherry. But today we know that the line between abstract right and policy is extremely hard to draw. A court can and does make policy decisions by going outside established 'legal' criteria found in precedent, statute, and Constitution. In this respect the Supreme Court occupies a most peculiar position, for it is an essential characteristic of the institution that from time to time its members decide cases where constitutional criteria are not adequate in any realistic sense to the task. The distinguished legal scholar and member of the Court, the late Mr. Justice Frankfurter, once described the business of the Supreme Court in these words:

> It is essentially accurate to say that the Court's preoccupation today is with the application of rather fundamental aspirations and what Judge Learned Hand calls "moods," embodied in provisions like the due process clauses, which were designed not to be precise and positive directions for rules of action. The judicial process in applying them involves a judgment . . . that is, on the views of the direct representatives of the people in meeting the needs of society, on the views of Presidents and Governors, and by their construction of the will of legislatures the Court breathes life, feeble or strong, into the inert pages of the Constitution and the statute books.[1]

Very often, then, the cases before the Court involve alternatives about which there is severe disagreement in the society, as in the case of segregation or economic regulation; the very setting of the case is, then, 'political.' Moreover, these are usually cases where competent students of constitutional law, including the learned justices of the Supreme Court themselves, disagree; where the words of the Constitution are general, vague, ambiguous, or not clearly applicable; where precedent may be found on both sides; and where experts differ in predicting the consequences of the various alternatives or the degree of probability that the possible consequences will actually ensue.

If the Court were assumed to be a 'political' institution, no particular problems would arise, for it would be taken for granted that the members of the Court would resolve questions of fact and value by introducing assumptions derived from their own predispositions or those of influential clienteles and constituents. However, since much of the legitimacy of the Court's decisions rests upon the belief that it is not a political institution but exclusively a legal one, to accept the Court as a political institution would solve one set of problems at the price of creating another. Nonetheless, if it is true that the nature of the cases arriving before the Court is sometimes of the kind I have described, then the Court cannot act strictly as a legal institution. It must, that is to say, choose among controversial alternatives of public policy by appealing to at least some criteria of acceptability on questions of fact and value that cannot be found in or deduced from precedent, statute, and Constitution.

Court versus Congress and President:
Minor Victories

A second conclusion to emerge from the record is that the Court rarely wins its battles with the president and Congress on matters of

---

1.   Justice Felix Frankfurter, "The Supreme Court in the Mirror of Justices," *University of Pennsylvania Law Review,* 105 (April, 1957) 781–796, at p. 793.

major policy, particularly if successive presidents and Congresses continue to support the policy the Court has called unconstitutional. The Court wins skirmishes; in a long war it may win a battle; it does not win continuing wars with Congress. On this point the evidence is overwhelming:

Court versus past Congresses. More than half the decisions in holding federal acts unconstitutional were decided by the Supreme Court more than four years after the legislation was enacted. Thus the Court frequently does not confront *current* legislative majorities so much as past majorities.

Court versus current Congresses. Where the Court confronts the major policies of a current president and Congress, it nearly always loses. In about two-thirds of the cases involving major policies of current lawmaking majorities, the Court's decision has, in effect, been reversed by congressional action—often simply by rewriting the law. Dramatic evidence is provided by twelve decisions in which a Supreme Court controlled by a conservative majority declared various aspects of FDR's New Deal unconstitutional. Of these, four involved trivial or minor policies. One involved a major New Deal policy contrivance, the NRA; it seems fair to say, however, that President Roosevelt and his advisers were relieved by the Court's decision of a policy that they had come to find increasingly embarrassing. In view of the tenacity with which FDR held to his major program, there can hardly be any doubt that, had he wanted to pursue the policy objective involved in the NRA codes, as he did for example with the labor provisions, he would not have been stopped by the Court's special theory of the Constitution. As to the seven other cases, whatever some of the eminent justices might have thought during their fleeting moments of glory, they did not succeed in interposing a barrier to the achievement of the objectives of the legislation; and in a few years most of the constitutional dogma on which they rested their opposition to the New Deal had been unceremoniously swept under the rug.

Court versus Congress and President: Major Delays

Nonetheless, although the Court loses most of its battles against a persistent president and Congress, the fact is that on some matters it has delayed policies for more than a decade and even more than a generation. What is more, if the views that finally prevailed on the Court are correct, then its lengthy obstruction had no proper constitutional basis. For example:

Workmen's compensation. A congressional act requiring employers to compensate longshoremen and harbor workers injured on the job was invalidated by the Supreme Court in 1920. In 1922, Congress passed a new law which was, in its turn, knocked down by the Court in 1924. In 1927 Congress passed a third law, which was finally upheld in 1932. Thus the Court delayed workmen's compensation for twelve years.

Child labor. Two child labor cases represent the most effective battle ever waged by the Court against legislative policy-makers. The original legislation outlawing child labor, based on the commerce clause, was passed in 1916 as part of Wilson's New Freedom. Like Franklin Roosevelt later, Wilson was somewhat unlucky in his Supreme Court appointments; he made only three appointments during his eight years, and one of these was wasted, from a policy point of view, on Mr. Justice McReynolds. Had McReynolds voted 'right,' the subsequent struggle over the problem of child labor need not have occurred, for the decision in 1918 was by a Court divided five to four, McReynolds voting with the majority. Congress moved at once to circumvent the decision by means of tax power, but in 1922 the Court blocked that approach. In 1924, Congress returned to the engagement with a constitutional amendment that was rapidly endorsed by a number of state legislatures before it began to meet so much resistance in the states remaining that the enterprise miscarried. In 1938, under a second reformist president, new legislation was passed twenty-two years after the first; thus a Court with a New Deal majority finally accepted child labor legislation in 1941, and thereby brought to an end a battle that had lasted a full quarter-century.

Bastion of Minority Rights?

It might be thought, nonetheless, that the Court has had a splendid record in protecting the fundamental rights of otherwise defenseless minorities against encroachment by the president and Congress. In this view of the Court's role we would expect to find a considerable number of important cases in which the justices have declared laws passed by Congress or orders of the president unconstitutional on the ground that they impaired the rights of citizens granted by the first ten amendments (the Bill of Rights). In fact, however, on this score the record of the Supreme Court over its *whole* history is remarkably unimpressive. For it is only recently that the Court has done much to protect minority rights—or at any rate the rights of otherwise weak or defenseless minorities:

1. There have been only two cases, both in the 1960s, in which the Court has ever held a provision of federal law unconstitutional as

contrary to the fundamental liberties of religion, speech, press, and assembly guaranteed by the First Amendment. Both cases involved federal legislation directed toward alleged Communists.[2]

2. In about ten cases, the Court has held congressional acts unconstitutional because they violated other provisions of the Bill of Rights, chiefly Amendments Four to Seven, and the Fourteenth Amendment. With the exception of several recent cases, an inspection of the issues in all the earlier cases indicates that the lawmakers and the Court were not very far apart. Moreover, the issues were mainly of such a minor sort that it is doubtful whether the fundamental conditions of liberty in this country were altered by more than a hair's breadth as a result. In several recent decisions, however, the Court has denied validity to congressional acts limiting the freedom of unpopular political minorities, particularly Communists.[3]

3. Over against these decisions we must put the fifteen or so cases in which the Court used the protections of the Fifth, Thirteenth, Fourteenth, and Fifteenth Amendments to preserve the rights and liberties of a relatively privileged group at the expense of the rights and liberties of a submerged group: chiefly slaveholders at the expense of slaves,[4] white people at the expense of nonwhites,[5] and property holders at the expense of wage earners and other groups. These cases, unlike some of the relatively innocuous ones previously discussed, all involved liberties of genuinely fundamental importance, where an opposite policy would have meant thoroughly basic shifts in the distribution of rights, liberties, and opportunities in the United States—where, moreover, the policies sustained by the Court's action have since been repudiated in every civilized nation of the Western world, including our own.

---

2. In 1965 in *Lamont* v. *Postmaster General* and *Fixa* v. *Heilberg* the Supreme Court struck down a provision of a comprehensive postal law passed in 1962 which required that "Communist political propaganda" must be withheld by the Post Office unless the addressee requested delivery. The Court held that the requirement infringed on the addressee's freedom of speech. In 1967 in *U.S.* v. *Robel* the Court in a 6-2 ruling held unconstitutional a provision of the Subversive Activities Control Act of 1950 that barred members of Communist action organizations from employment in defense facilities. Speaking for the Court, Chief Justice Earl Warren said that the provision was "an unconstitutional abridgment of the right of association protected by the First Amendment." He also noted, however, that nothing in the holding would "deny Congress the power under narrowly drawn legislation to keep from sensitive positions in defense facilities those who would use their positions to disrupt the nation's production facilities."

3. Thus in 1965, in *Albertson* v. *Subversive Activities Control Board*, a unanimous Court held that members of the Communist party of the United States could not be required to register as such with the Justice Department under provisions of the Subversive Activities Control Act. The requirement was held to violate the members' right against self-incrimination protected by the Fifth Amendment. In 1967, the Circuit Court of Appeals for the District of Columbia held unconstitutional on the same grounds a provision of the Act requiring party officers to register. The Justice Department did not appeal the ruling and thus its sixteen-year effort to enforce these provisions ended in total failure.

4. *Dred Scott* v. *Sandford,* 19 How. (U.S.) 393 (1857).

5. *United States* v. *Reese,* 92 U.S. 214 (1876); *United States* v. *Harris,* 106 U.S. 629 (1883); *United States* v. *Stanley* (Civil Rights Cases), 109 U.S. 3 (1883); *Baldwin* v. *Franks,* 120 U.S. 678 (1887); *James* v. *Bowman* 190, U.S. 127 (1903); *Hodges* v. *United States,* 203 U.S. 1 (1906); *Butts* v. *Merchants & Miners Transportation Co.,* 230 U.S. 126 (1913).

Protector of National Polyarchy Against State and Local Attacks

As our dialogue in the last chapter suggested, the problem of judicial review from a democratic perspective arises in its most acute form with respect to *federal* legislation, not state and local actions. In the domain of state and local actions the record of the Court, although uneven over its whole history, in this century has been increasingly closer to the model suggested in the last chapter of protector of the national polyarchy. In innumerable cases it has declared unconstitutional state or local laws, practises, and actions held to infringe on fundamental rights guaranteed by the Constitution;[6] it has markedly enlarged the scope of those rights;[7] since the failure of a last-ditch conservative Court to halt the New Deal, the Court has provided a constitutional foundation for the vast new national powers employed by all subsequent administrations in behalf of their programs; and, as we saw in Chapter 13, the Court has imposed the principle of one man, one vote on unwilling legislative bodies.

THE COURT AS A POLITICAL INSTITUTION

How can we explain the behavior of the Court over the long run? Why does it have such a spotty record as protector of the national polyarchy? Why has it moved more sharply in this direction in recent years, particularly against incursions by state and local governments? A large part of the answer lies in the fact that the Supreme Court is inescapably a participant in the larger political process of the American polyarchy.

Part of the Dominant Coalition

National politics in the United States, as in other stable polyarchies, is dominated by relatively cohesive alliances that endure for long periods of time. One recalls the Jeffersonian alliance, the Jacksonian, the extraordinarily long-lived Republican dominance of the post–Civil War years, and the New Deal alliance shaped by Franklin Roosevelt. Each is marked by a break with past policies, a period of intense struggle, followed by consolidation, and finally decay and disintegration of the alliance.

Except for short-lived transitional periods when the old alliance is disintegrating and the new one is struggling to take control of political institutions, the Supreme Court is inevitably a part of the dominant

---

6. For example, in *Julian Bond* v. *James "Sloppy" Floyd* (1966) a unanimous Court held that Julian Bond's exclusion from the Georgia House because of his statements against the war in Vietnam violated the First Amendment. In *Bachellar* v. *State of Maryland* a unanimous Court held that where it was impossible to determine whether convictions for disorderly conduct in blocking a public sidewalk resulted from the unpopular views of the defendants (they were arrested during a demonstration against the war in Vietnam), the convictions violated the First Amendment and must be reversed.

7. For example, in *Goldberg* v. *Kelly* (1970) by a vote of 5–3 the Court held that a welfare recipient was denied due process under the Fourteenth Amendment because his public assistance payments were terminated with no opportunity for him to have a hearing. In *Pickering* v. *Board of Education* (1968) the Court unanimously held that a public school teacher may not be dismissed for criticizing the school board unless the criticism is knowingly or recklessly false.

national alliance. It becomes so for an exceedingly simple reason: the eminent justices of the United States Supreme Court are mortal. They grow old. Sooner or later they retire or die. As they leave the Court new justices acceptable to the current coalition take their place.

Over the whole history of the Court, one new justice has been appointed on the average of every twenty-three months. Thus a president can expect to appoint two new justices during one term of office; and if this were not enough to tip the balance on a normally divided Court, he would be almost certain to succeed in two terms. For example, Hoover made three appointments; Roosevelt, nine; Truman, four; Eisenhower, five; Kennedy in his brief tenure, two. Presidents are not famous for appointing justices hostile to their own views on public policy; nor could they expect to secure confirmation of a man whose stance on key questions was flagrantly at odds with that of the dominant majority in the Senate. When Nixon violated this assumption in 1970 by his attempt to appoint first Clement Haynsworth and then George Carswell, he was twice defeated. Typically, justices are men who, prior to appointment, have engaged in public life and have committed themselves publicly on the great questions of the day. As the late Mr. Justice Frankfurter pointed out, a surprisingly large proportion of the justices, particularly of the great justices who have left their stamp upon the decisions of the Court, have had little or no prior judicial experience. Nor have the justices—certainly not the great justices—been timid men with a passion for anonymity. Indeed, it is not too much to say that if justices were appointed primarily for their 'judicial' qualities without regard to their basic attitudes on fundamental questions of public policy, the Court could not play the influential role in the American political system that it does in reality.

It is reasonable to conclude, then, that the policy views dominant on the Court will never be out of line for very long with the policy views dominant among the law-making majorities of the United States. And it would be most unrealistic to suppose that the Court would, for more than a few years at most, stand against any major alternatives sought by a law-making majority. The judicial agonies of the New Deal will, of course, come quickly to mind; but President Franklin D. Roosevelt's difficulties with the Court were truly exceptional. Generalizing over the whole history of the Court, one can say that the chances are about two out of five that a president will make one appointment to the Court in less than a year, two out of three that he will make one within two years, and three out of four that he will make one within three years. President Roosevelt had unusually bad luck: he had to wait four years for his first appointment; the odds against this long interval are about five to one. With average luck, his battle with the Court would never have occurred; even as it was, although his 'court-packing' proposal did formally fail, by the end of his second term in 1940 Roosevelt had appointed five new justices and he gained three more the following year.

As an element in the leadership of the dominant alliance, the Court tends to support the major policies of the alliance. Acting solely by itself with no support from the president and Congress, the Court is almost powerless to affect the course of national policy.

The Supreme Court is not, however, simply an *agent* of the alliance. It is an essential part of the political leadership and possesses some bases of power of its own, the most important of which is the unique legitimacy attributed to its interpretations of the Constitution. This legitimacy the Court jeopardizes if it flagrantly opposes the major policies of the dominant alliance; such a course of action, as we have seen, is one in which the Court will not normally be tempted to engage.

It follows that within the somewhat narrow limits set by the basic policy goals of the dominant alliance, the Court *can* sometimes make national policy. Its discretion, then, is not unlike that of a powerful committee chairman in Congress who cannot, generally speaking, nullify the basic policies substantially agreed on by the rest of the dominant leadership, but who can, within these limits, often determine important questions of timing, effectiveness, and subordinate policy. Thus the Court is least effective against a current law-making majority—and evidently least inclined to act. It is most effective when it sets the bounds of policy for officials, agencies, state governments, or even regions, a task that has come to occupy a very large part of the Court's business.[8]

The main objective of presidential leadership is to build a stable and dominant aggregation of minorities with a high probability of winning the presidency and one or both houses of Congress. Ordinarily the main contribution of the Court is to confer legitimacy on the fundamental policies of the successful coalition.

But if this were the only function of the Supreme Court, would it have acquired the standing it has among Americans? In fact, at its best —and the Court is not always at its best—it does more than merely confer legitimacy on the dominant national coalition. For one thing, by the way it interprets and modifies national laws, perhaps but not necessarily by holding them unconstitutional, the Supreme Court sometimes serves as a guide and even a pioneer in arriving at different standards of fair play and individual right than have resulted, or are likely to result, from the interplay of the other political forces. Thus in recent years, as we have seen, the Court has modified by interpretation

8. "Constitutional law and cases with constitutional undertones are of course still very important, with almost one-fourth of the cases in which written opinions were filed (in recent years) involving such questions. Review of administrative action . . . constitutes the largest category of the Court's work, comprising one-third of the total cases decided on the merits. The remaining . . . categories of litigation . . . all involve largely public law questions" (Frankfurter, "The Supreme Court in the Mirror of Justices," p. 793).

or declared unconstitutional provisions of federal law restricting the rights of unpopular and even widely detested minorities—military deserters, Communists, and alleged bootleggers, for example. The judges, after all, inherit an ancient tradition and an acknowledged role in setting higher standards of justice and right than the majority of citizens or their representatives might otherwise demand. If the standards of justice propounded by the Court are to prevail, for reasons we have already examined they cannot be too remote from general standards of fairness and individual right among Americans; but, though some citizens may protest, most Americans are too attached to the Court to want it stripped of its power.

There are times, too, when the other political forces are too divided to arrive at decisions on certain key questions. At very great risk, the Court can intervene in such cases; and sometimes it may even succeed in establishing policy where the president and Congress are unable to do so. Probably in such cases it can succeed only if its action conforms to a widespread set of explicit or implicit norms held by the political leadership: norms which are not strong enough or are not distributed in such a way as to insure the existence of an effective law-making majority but are nonetheless sufficiently powerful to prevent any successful attack on the legitimacy and power of the Court. This is probably the explanation for the relatively successful work of the Court in enlarging the freedom of Negroes to vote during the past three decades, in its famous school integration decisions, and the reapportionment cases.

Legitimizers

Yet the Court does even more than this. Considered as a political system, polyarchy is a set of basic procedures for arriving at decisions. The operation of these procedures presupposes the existence of certain rights, obligations, liberties, and restraints; in short, certain patterns of behavior. The existence of these patterns of behavior in turn presupposes widespread agreement (particularly among the politically active and influential segments of the population) on the validity and propriety of the behavior. Although its record is by no means lacking in serious blemishes, at its best the Court operates to confer legitimacy, not simply on the particular and parochial policies of the dominant political alliance, but upon the basic patterns of behavior required for the operation of a polyarchy.

Yet in order to *confer* legitimacy, the Court must itself *possess* legitimacy. To the extent that the legitimacy of every political institution in the American polyarchy depends finally on its consistency with democratic principle, the legitimacy of judicial review and the Court's exercise of that power must stem from the presumption that the Court is ultimately subject to popular control. The more the Court exercises self-restraint and the less it challenges the policies of law-making majorities, the less the need or the impulse to subject it to popular controls. The more active the Court is in contesting the policies of law-making majorities, the more visible becomes the slender basis of its legitimacy by democratic standards, and the greater the efforts will be to bring the Court's policies into conformity with those enacted by law-making majorities.

If the persistent temper of a dominant coalition is to use the Court as a privileged interest group or a protector of privileged interest groups, as in the period after the Civil War, no Court can long persist as protector of the national polyarchy. By yielding—and aging, retirement, and death make yielding ineluctable—the Court may gain the confidence and respect of the coalition's leaders in the White House and Congress. Yet it will lose the confidence and respect of those who search for its legitimacy in democratic principles. And at the next swing of the political pendulum, the Court may well find that it has impaired its own legitimacy.

Where the dominant coalition is prepared to allow or even encourage the Court to act as defender of the national polyarchy, the Court will gain in such legitimacy as it may draw from democratic principles. Yet in such periods, as in the others, the Court will rarely find it necessary to nullify any major policies of the dominant political coalition. Even as defender of the national polyarchy, then, its victories against the president and Congress are likely to be rare and transitory. Thus in this role—and it is hard to find grounds for legitimacy in any other—it will serve mainly as an arbiter in the federal system, protecting the fundamental requisites of polyarchy against incursions by minorities in states and localities. Although it has not always played this role well, and at times not even at all, it has probably performed better in recent decades than throughout most of its previous history.

In the end, however, we must not lose sight of the fact that the Court's power of judicial review over *national* legislation is, at best, an exceedingly weak guarantee of polyarchy in the United States. At its worst, the Court's power of judicial review has no claim to legitimacy according to democratic criteria.

SUMMARY   An examination of the performance of the Supreme Court in the actual cases in which it has declared federal laws unconstitutional indicates that:

1. The line between decisions about the wisdom of policy and decisions about constitutionality has been a difficult one for the Court to discover and abide by.

2. The Court has rarely succeeded in using judicial review to prevent the president and Congress from gaining any major policies on which they agree.

3. However, in some instances the Court has delayed reforms for a decade or more. These include such matters as workmen's compensation and the abolition of child labor, which the Court finally accepted as constitutionally valid.

4. Until recently, the Court has not made a significant contribution as protector of the rights of otherwise weak or defenseless minorities against incursions by the federal government.

5. However, through judicial review the Court has made an important contribution, particularly in recent decades, as protector of the national polyarchy against encroachment by state and local governments.

These aspects of the Court's performance are largely to be explained as follows:

1. Because members of the Court inevitably age, they retire or die and are replaced by new appointees.

2. In making appointments, the president and Senate pay attention not only to the constitutional views of the candidate but also to the implications of his views or record for matters of public policy.

3. Thus if a coalition persists for some time in controlling the presidency and Congress, it is certain to gain a majority of members of the Court who are sympathetic with the general policy views and goals of the dominant coalition.

4. The extent to which the Court is, at the one extreme, a privileged interest group or, at the other, a defender of the national polyarchy depends, then, largely on the mood, temper, and outlook of the dominant forces in the presidency and the Congress.

5. For this reason, the Court's power of judicial review over national legislation appears to be a rather weak guarantee of polyarchy.

The Other Eighty Thousand Governments

17

Although the national government is only one of many governments that Americans support, it is the largest, most inclusive, and most powerful of all the governments within the United States. The national government receives from most Americans a greater share of their loyalty, obedience, affection, and taxes than any other government. It is without much question the dominant government in the American polyarchy.

The national government is one out of more than eighty thousand governments of all kinds existing within the boundaries of the United States. Of these, more than a fourth are school districts, although the number of these has declined precipitously since the 1930s. Even if we ignore school and special districts and consider only general territorial governments, the states, counties, municipalities, townships, and towns have numbered altogether close to thirty-eight thousand for the last thirty or forty years (Table 17.1).

These territorial governments below the national level are of bewildering variety and complexity. The governments of the fifty states constitute a vast field in themselves. The thousands of towns and cities create a political tapestry even more complex. It has been estimated, to take one example, that the metropolitan area around New York City alone includes 1,467 "distinct political entities."[1] A monumental study entitled *Governing New York City*[2] (as befits the largest city in the country) amounts to over eight hundred pages.

What contributions do territorial governments below the national level make to the American polyarchy? If one tries to imagine how the

---

1. Robert C. Wood, *1400 Governments* (Garden City: Doubleday Anchor, 1964).

2. Wallace Sayre and Herbert Kaufman, *Governing New York City* (New York: Russell Sage Foundation, 1960).

Table 17.1
Number and Type of
Government Units in the
United States, Selected
Years, 1942-67

Unit of Government	Number				Change 1942–1967
	1942	1957	1962	1967	
U. S. Government	1	1	1	1	0
States	48	48	50	50	+2
Counties	3,050	3,047	3,043	3,049	−1
Municipalities	16,220	17,183	17,997	18,048	+1,828
Towns and Townships	18,919	17,198	17,144	17,105	−1,814
School Districts	108,579	50,446	34,678	21,782	−86,797
Special Districts	8,299	14,405	18,323	21,264	+12,965
Total	155,116	102,328	91,236	81,299	−73,817

American political system might operate without them, four possible contributions suggest themselves:

1. By reducing the workload of the national government, they make polyarchy at the national level more manageable.
2. By permitting diversity and the denationalizing of conflict, they sometimes reduce conflicts at the national level and thus make polyarchy at the national level more viable.
3. By providing numerous more or less independent or autonomous centers of power throughout the system, they further partition power.
4. By facilitating self-government at local levels, they greatly expand the opportunities for learning and practising the ways of polyarchal government in the United States.

MAKING NATIONAL POLYARCHY MORE MANAGEABLE

The imagination boggles at the attempt to conceive of the United States as a polyarchy operating at the national level by means of elected leaders and competitive political parties and locally through a centralized bureaucracy, federally appointed and controlled, that would administer tasks now carried on by thirty-eight thousand territorial governments. After all, most self-governing nations are no larger than our larger states.

Alternatives
Complete centralization. How would a completely centralized system actually function in the United States? On the one hand, the system might be centralized not only in law but *in fact* was well. In this case, would not the weight of the chief executive and the insensitivity of the national bureaucracy to local variation crush local diversity? What is more, the burdens on national policy-makers—the president, the Congress, the courts, the administrative agencies—would be frightful; to

superimpose these new tasks on their present duties (which, we have seen, are already enormous) would surely create a work load well beyond their capacities to handle.

De facto decentralization. National policy-makers might meet such an impossible work load by either neglecting their duties or delegating decisions to other officials. To the extent that national officials delegated decisions to other officials who were closer to the local scene, the system might become centralized in law but decentralized in fact. National uniformity would doubtless be too rigid and oppressive to remain tolerable for long. National officials would develop strong but informal local ties. Local pressures would be felt. The wise administrator would learn to adapt his policies to local circumstances. Sooner or later, American citizens might conclude that law should conform more closely to fact. In short: If local governments did not exist, they would quickly be invented.

De facto centralization. It might be objected, however, that there is a third alternative, and that this alternative has actually come to pass in the United States: a system decentralized in constitutional and legal form but centralized in fact. It is often said that the rapidly increasing role of the national government has deprived local territorial governments of their older functions; 'the demise of local government' is as common a theme in the United States as 'the rise of the executive' and 'the decline of Congress.'

The Expansion of Local Governments

Because the degree of centralization or decentralization of an organization has so far proved all but impossible to measure, one cannot meet the argument directly by producing satisfactory evidence on the amount of change in centralization in the political system of the United States over the past half century. But a fairly large number of different indicators do reveal that the role of local governments in American life has actually *expanded* in this century. Evidently what has happened is that all our territorial governments—national, state, and local—have increased their functions; whether it be national, state, or local, every government carries out more tasks today than it did a few generations ago.

For example, the expenditures, revenues, and functions of the state and local governments have steadily grown in recent decades. True, since the high period of the New Deal in 1936, federal expenditures have risen faster than those of the state and local governments. But the lion's share of federal outlays has been consumed by national defense, international relations, space programs, veterans' services, and interest on the public debt. If we eliminate these items, we discover that the difference virtually disappears: in the quarter century from 1938 to 1967 the expenditures of the federal government increased a little more than eightfold, the expenditures of state and local governments a little less than eightfold (Figure 17.1). 'Obsolete' state and local governments spend far more than the federal government for education, highways, health and hospitals, public welfare, and housing and community development (Figure 17.2). Revenues from strictly state and local sources— that is, excluding all federal grants, which amounted to 7 percent of the total in 1938 and 14 percent in 1963—were ten times greater in 1967 than in 1938 (Figure 17.3). Of about thirteen million civilians employed by government in 1969, about one in four were federal employees, more than one in five were state employees, and a bit less than half were employed by local governments (Figure 17.4).

Far from having lost functions, then, the local governments have been gaining new ones. There is no record that state and local governments spent any funds at all for housing development until 1938, when they spent 3 million dollars. In 1963 they spent 446 million dollars. The state and local governments are a major factor in the national economy. In 1967 their expenditures for civil functions were equivalent to 12 percent of the gross national product, compared with 5.5 percent for the federal government (Table 17.2).

There are then no valid grounds for doubting that both in fact and in law the local territorial governments of the United States assume a huge burden, which in their absence would have to be discharged, somehow, by federal officials. It seems reasonable to conclude that in a country as vast and as complex as the United States, local governments are necessary simply (if for no other reason) in order to achieve a level of efficiency in government high enough to make polyarchy at the national level tolerable. Without the local governments, governmental institutions at the national level would probably go under from the sheer weight of their burdens.

The Criterion of Efficiency

One might nonetheless wonder whether local governments in the United States operate above some minimum level of tolerability. They may provide enough efficiency to keep the system stumbling along. But are they anything like as efficient as they should be?

Unfortunately, dear though it be to advocates of governmental reform, the criterion of efficiency does not take one very far. For if efficiency is measured by the ratio of valued 'inputs' to valued 'outputs,' then to one who believes strongly in the values of democracy, the efficiency of state and local governments must be measured in large part by comparing their costs, using the term in a very broad sense

Figure 17.1
Federal, State, and Local
Expenditures, 1938-67

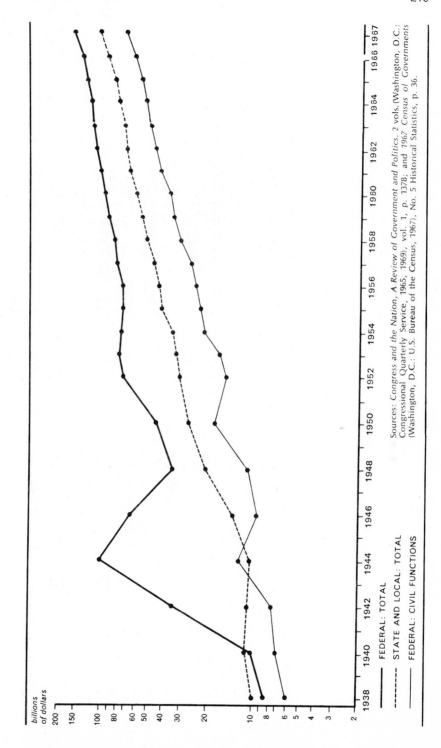

billions
of dollars

FEDERAL: TOTAL

STATE AND LOCAL: TOTAL

FEDERAL: CIVIL FUNCTIONS

Sources: *Congress and the Nation, A Review of Government and Politics,* 2 vols. (Washington, D.C.: Congressional Quarterly Service, 1965, 1969), vol. 1, p. 1378; and *1967 Census of Governments* (Washington, D.C.: U.S. Bureau of the Census, 1967), No. 5 *Historical Statistics,* p. 36.

Figure 17.2
General Expenditure by
Level of Government and
Function (other than for
national defense and
international relations),
1968-9

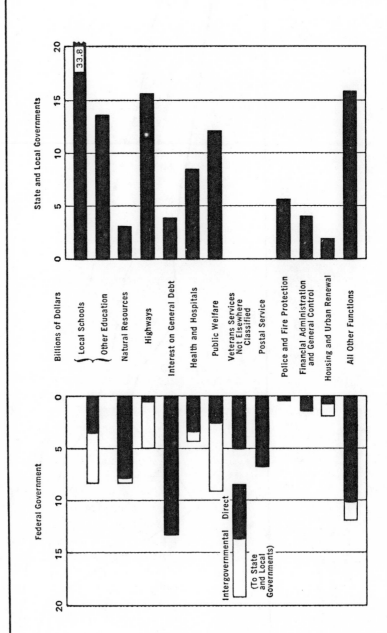

Billions of Dollars

Local Schools
Other Education
Natural Resources
Highways
Interest on General Debt
Health and Hospitals
Public Welfare
Veterans Services Not Elsewhere Classified
Postal Service
Police and Fire Protection
Financial Administration and General Control
Housing and Urban Renewal
All Other Functions

State and Local Governments

Federal Government

Intergovernmental Direct (To State and Local Governments)

Source: U.S. Department of Commerce Chart Book, Governmental Finances and Employment (Washington, D.C.: U.S. Bureau of the Census, 1970), p. 3.

Figure 17.3
Federal, State, and
Local Revenues, 1938-67

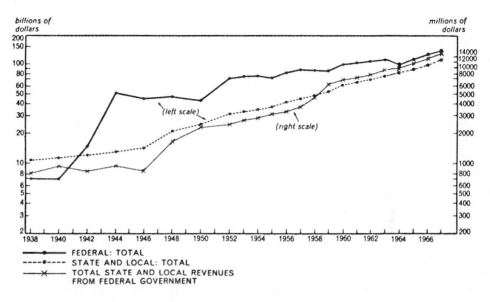

FEDERAL: TOTAL
STATE AND LOCAL: TOTAL
TOTAL STATE AND LOCAL REVENUES
FROM FEDERAL GOVERNMENT

Sources: *Congress and the Nation*, vol. 1, p. 1378; and *1967 Census of Governments*, No. 5 Historical Statistics, pp. 33, 39.

indeed, against their contributions by democratic criteria of performance. We remain then pretty much in the place from which we started. If efficiency is measured by the ratio between actual output and a theoretically maximum output, how are we to decide what is a theoretical maximum?

It seems perfectly reasonable to ask how well state and local governments perform the various tasks assigned to them by law. Are they efficient administrative units in the narrow sense that they economize, cut costs, act with expertness and dispatch? The question seems reasonable, but it is nonetheless almost impossible to answer. One must first ask a counter question: With what are we to compare them? If we compared state and local governments with some theoretical ideal, it would be easy to show that like every other human institution they fall very far short of ideal achievement. But we know this much in advance. We can scarcely compare state and local governments with private firms, because neither the inputs nor the outputs of state and local governments are sufficiently like those of private enterprise to make comparisons valid. How can we compare the relative efficiency of the New York police in controlling crime and traffic with the efficiency of General Motors in

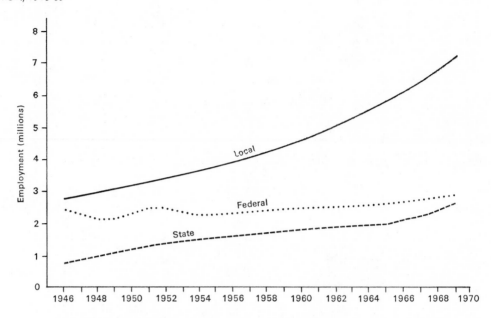

Figure 17.4
Trends in Government
Employment, 1946-69

Sources: *Congress and the Nation,* vol. 1, p. 1393; *1967 Census of Governments,* No. 5 Historical Statistics, p. 60; 1968 and 1969 figures from *Statistical Abstract 1970.*

producing and marketing automobiles? There seems to be little possibility of a useful or even a meaningful comparison; even those intrepid spirits who would contend that General Motors is the more efficient of the two organizations would not propose, I imagine, to turn the police force of New York City over to General Motors.[3]

Can we compare the administrative efficiency of state and local governments with that of federal agencies? Here again we run into formidable problems because of the differences in outputs—the services performed. In any case, an adverse comparison would be highly misleading if it led one to conclude that the federal government would perform local functions more 'efficiently,' in the restricted sense, than the local governments themselves.[4] For we need to know what would happen to

3. Two economists, Frank Levy and Edwin M. Truman, have pointed out the pitfalls in comparing an organization producing economic goods with one producing government goods in their "Toward a Rational Theory of Decentralization: Another View," *American Political Science Review,* 65 (March, 1971), 172–179.

4. From this point forward the term *local governments* means state and local, except where the context clearly implies the more restricted meaning of a city, town, county, etc. There is no generally accepted word to cover both state and local; local, therefore, will have to do the work of two.

Table 17.2
General Expenditure for
Civil Functions by All
Levels of Government as
Percentage of Gross
National Product,
Selected Years, 1902-67

Year	GNP (billions of dollars)	Expenditure as Percentage of GNP		
		Federal	State-Local	Total
1902	$ 21.6	1.1	4.7	5.8
1927	96.3	1.5	7.5	9.0
1938	85.2	5.9	10.3	16.2
1948	259.4	3.4	6.8	10.2
1963	583.9	4.0	11.1	15.1
1967	793.5	5.5	11.8	17.3

Sources: Figures for 1902–63, James A. Maxwell, *Financing State and Local Governments* (Washington: The Brookings Institution, 1965), Appendix Table A-3, p. 243; for 1967, *1967 Census of Governments*, No. 5 Historical Statistics, pp. 36–40. Intergovernmental payments are charged to the level of government making final disbursement.

the present level of efficiency of federal agencies if the federal government were to take on all the additional tasks now performed at local levels.

Perhaps the only way out of this dilemma is to compare similar local units with one another. Yet, given the enormous variety of local governments, even this is a much more formidable enterprise than it might seem.

Conclusions. Thus, despite its glossy appeal, the criterion of efficiency does not take one very far. For appraising governments, 'efficiency' is a concept either too slippery to be meaningful or too precise to be applicable. However, three observations may nevertheless be permissible. First, American state and local governments have generally lagged behind the federal government in introducing reforms thought to contribute to administrative efficiency: in the development of a neutral and expert civil service, an executive budget, a single chief executive with substantial hierarchical control over administrative agencies, an adequate specialized staff for the chief executive, and so on. Corruption seems to occur more frequently, and on a bigger scale, in local units than in the federal government. Pay scales are lower, both at the start and at the end of one's career.

Second, there are enormous variations among the different units of local government. By almost any objective test, the best local government would be as efficient as any found in the federal government; the worst are appalling. Between the best and the worst, there is a whole universe of types. No one can ever judge the quality of local government in the United States by his experience with one or two units.

Third, whatever weight one may give to the democratic contributions of local governments (we shall proceed to that matter at once), it is obvious that the American polyarchy would be a very different system without local governments that enjoy a great measure of autonomy.

**REDUCING
CONFLICTS BY
DIVERSITY AND
DENATIONALIZATION**

If one cannot speak with much confidence about the efficiency of local governments as administrative units, one can say more about their efficiency as instruments of polyarchy. To begin with, how does the existence of thirty-eight thousand local territorial governments affect the course and severity of political conflicts?

The contributions of local government are, I think, two. Local governments make it possible for different groups of citizens to arrive at different solutions to problems. And they reduce the strain on the national political system by keeping many questions out of the national arena.

The Possibility of Diverse Solutions

It is a great and inescapable defect in any system of rule by majorities that on all questions in which the policy of a minority conflicts with the policy preferred by a majority, neither can prevail without frustrating the desires of the other. In this respect the hypothetical universe of majority-rule democracy is rather different from the hypothetical universe of a free market; the hypothetical citizen is not equivalent to the hypothetical consumer. In a model 'free' market it does not matter that in my role as consumer I prefer buying books to phonograph records, while you prefer records to books. Within broad legal limits, we may both spend our incomes as we please, and the market will respond. In the market, differences among individuals in tastes and values need not lead to conflict among them.

Why not, then, substitute the market for the government? The most important reason is that there are a great many matters which the mechanisms of the marketplace are ill equipped to handle—including the sovereign question as to what should and what should not be left to the market. If I as a citizen wish to raise taxes and spend more money in order to construct new schools, and if you prefer lower taxes and no new schools, we cannot both get what we want. We cannot, that is, if we are in exactly the same political system. But if you and the people who think like you are in one political system, while I and other like-minded people are in another, we can perhaps both have what we want. In this way we could both be free to go our own different ways; both our governments might enjoy the full consent of all its citizens. Here is the kernel of truth in Rousseau's belief that small autonomous democracies consisting of like-minded citizens offer the greatest promise of freedom and self-government.

Denationalizing Conflict

Their local governments permit Americans to take or to keep many questions out of the great arena of national politics, and therefore out of a strictly either/or kind of conflict; they make it possible for Americans to deal with many problems in different ways, ways presumably more in harmony with local tastes and values than any national solution could possibly be. To this extent, the presence of a vast network of local governments with a good deal of autonomy has probably reduced by a considerable margin the severity of conflict that a wholly national system would run into. By *denationalizing* many conflicts, local governments can reduce the strain on national political institutions. The importance of denationalizing conflicts can hardly be overestimated, particularly in a large country like the United States where there is great diversity in resources and local problems.

Limits. Yet the experience of the United States with the question of the role of black people in American life also suggests some limits on the process of denationalizing conflicts.[5] For some sixty years after the Constitutional Convention, national conflict over slavery was reduced by denationalizing the conflict. All the famous compromises of the pre-Civil War period were agreements to denationalize the question of slavery. Within little more than a decade after the end of the Civil War, the issue of the place of the freed Negro was denationalized: for another sixty years or more national conflict on this issue was avoided. When the question of the place of Negroes in American life became nationalized, as it did in the 1850s and again a century later in the 1940s, that question turned into one of the most explosive issues in American politics. In the first case, nationalizing the conflict led directly to civil war; in the second, to violence and federal troops, to Little Rock, Freedom Riders, murders in Mississippi, demonstrations, Selma, and passage of Civil Rights Acts in 1957, 1960, 1964, and 1965.

Local injustice. This experience reveals some of the limits to the process of denationalizing conflicts. It is quite one thing to denationalize a dispute by allowing various groups of like-minded people to follow their own desires; but it is quite another to take a dispute out of the national arena in order to hand it over to local despots, as we Americans did in the case of blacks for all except a few decades in our national history.

The case of blacks is, admittedly, an extreme one, and it is worth keeping that fact in mind. It is an extreme case partly because as both slave and freeman, the Negro lacked allies, at least in substantial numbers, outside the South. Members of a minority who feel oppressed in their localities would ordinarily search for allies in the national political arena, and they would count on their allies to keep the dispute alive in the Congress and in presidential elections—in short, to prevent the conflict from becoming fully denationalized. Today, Southern blacks have no lack of allies outside the South—nor, for that matter, in the

---

5. Compare with Chapter 24.

South itself; consequently it would be impossible to denationalize that conflict today.

Unwillingness. In some disputes, then, the parties simply will not allow the issue to be cast out of national politics. This is a second limit to the process of denationalizing conflicts. The more interwoven the fabric of society, the less likely it is that different localities will be permitted to go their different ways—at least if these ways are very different from one another. The Kansas-Nebraska Act of 1854 was intended by Senator Douglas to put an end to the rising conflict over whether slavery was to be legal in new states carved out of the Western territories; he hoped to denationalize the dispute by letting the settlers in each new state decide the matter for themselves. Yet his bill was no sooner law than the political forces of the North and West began to realign themselves. For, while it had once been possible to denationalize the issue of slavery in the Old South, it proved impossible to denationalize the question of slavery in the territories (cf. Chapter 24).

With these reservations in mind, it is nonetheless true that the existence of local governments with a considerable measure of autonomy does permit extensive variations among communities in the way they carry on their activities. There are differences in the variety and range of functions. But perhaps more common are differences in levels of expenditure, in emphasis, in administrative and political styles, in the sorts of people who hold office, and in their attitudes. Educational facilities, public health, unemployment compensation, hospital care, city planning, community redevelopment, and dozens of other activities vary enormously in quality and quantity from state to state and even from locality to locality. The differences are mainly a function of the resources available; but not entirely. For example, in 1961, state expenditures for public schools were in rough proportion to state income per capita in twenty-seven states, but markedly high in relation to income in eleven states, and markedly low in ten states.[6] Or, to take another example from the field of education, in New England private schools, colleges, and universities have played a much more significant part than they do in the Middle West, where resources have been poured almost exclusively into public education.

American local governments have, then, permitted an important measure of local variety and heterogeneity. In so doing, doubtless they have reduced the strain on national institutions. People are able to work out many of their problems in their states and localities, finding solutions which would lead to interminable debate and conflict if they were imposed uniformly throughout the United States. Even though the most

---

6. Herbert Jacob and Kenneth N. Vines, eds., *Politics in the United States, A Comparative Analysis* (Boston: Little, Brown, 1965), p. 354, Table 1.

pressing questions of the day cannot be denationalized, the existence of local autonomy helps to free the national arena for precisely these 'national' issues.

PARTITIONING
POWER

Tocqueville's Question

Alexis de Tocqueville was deeply concerned with discovering the answer to the question: How, if at all, can liberty and democracy be maintained in a society of equals? Tocqueville was both fascinated and repelled by the Janus faces of equality. An increasing equality was, he thought, not only inevitable in America and Europe, it was also a necessary condition for democracy. At the same time, Tocqueville, like Aristotle, believed that extensive political, economic, and social equalities created a natural political environment for the tyrant. Thus he formulated a dilemma for democrats: a necessary condition for democracy is also a condition that facilitates despotism. The whole of the two-volume *Democracy in America* can be read as an exploration of the circumstances in which tyranny might be avoided and liberal democracy preserved in a society of equals.

His fear. The problem, as Tocqueville saw it, was this: In a society of equals, there are no intermediate institutions or classes with enough power to prevent the rise of a despot. Having eliminated aristocracy, a society of equals needs institutions to perform the political function that Tocqueville attributed, perhaps overgenerously, to a well-established aristocracy—some force to stand in the way of the aspiring despot. In a nation of equals, no individual is strong enough to stop the despot; and citizens are incapable of acting as a body except through leaders. Even should citizens want to oppose the despot (Tocqueville thought that they probably would not), in the absence of an intermediate stratum of leaders they would be impotent. It was a haunting and evocative picture that Tocqueville painted of that peculiar tyranny in which democracy might one day culminate, the tyranny of an equal people united under a popular leader, the special tyranny that was appropriate to democracy because it would thrive on the very equality so indispensable to democracy.

> I think, then, that the species of oppression by which democratic nations are menaced is unlike anything that ever before existed in the world; our contemporaries will find no prototype of it in their memories. I seek in vain for an expression that will accurately convey the whole of the idea I have formed of it; the old words *despotism* and *tyranny* are inappropriate: the thing itself is new, and since I cannot name, I must attempt to define it.
>
> I seek to trace the novel features under which despotism may appear in the world. The first thing that strikes the observation is an innumerable

multitude of men, all equal and alike, incessantly endeavoring to procure the petty and paltry pleasures with which they glut their lives. Each of them, living apart, is as a stranger to the fate of all the rest; his children and his private friends constitute to him the whole of mankind. As for the rest of his fellow citizens, he is close to them, but does not see them; he touches them, but does not feel them; he exists only in himself and for himself alone; and if his kindred still remain to him, he may be said at any rate to have lost his country.

Above this race of men stands an immense and tutelary power, which takes upon itself alone to secure their gratifications and to watch over their fate. That power is absolute, minute, regular, provident, and mild. It would be like the authority of a parent if, like that authority, its object was to prepare men for manhood; but it seeks, on the contrary, to keep them in perpetual childhood: it is well content that the people should rejoice, provided they think of nothing but rejoicing. For their happiness such a government willingly labors, but it chooses to be the sole agent and the only arbiter of that happiness; it provides for their security, foresees and supplies their necessities, facilitates their pleasures, manages their principal concerns, directs their industry, regulates the descent of property, and subdivides their inheritances: what remains, but to spare them all the care of thinking and all the trouble of living?

Thus it every day renders the exercise of the free agency of man less useful and less frequent; it circumscribes the will within a narrower range and gradually robs a man of all these uses of himself. The principle of equality has prepared men for these things; it has predisposed men to endure them and often to look on them as benefits.

After having thus successively taken each member of the community in its powerful grasp and fashioned him at will, the supreme power then extends its arm over the whole community. It covers the surface of society with a network of small complicated rules, minute and uniform, through which the most original minds and the most energetic characters cannot penetrate, to rise above the crowd. The will of man is not shattered, but softened, bent, and guided; men are seldom forced by it to act, but they are constantly restrained from acting. Such a power does not destroy, but it prevents existence; it does not tyrannize, but it compresses, enervates, extinguishes, and stupifies a people, till each nation is reduced to nothing better than a flock of timid and industrious animals, of which the government is the shepherd.[7]

His hope. In spite of his melancholic vision of the possible fate of democratic societies, Tocqueville was hopeful about the United States—precisely because Americans had not destroyed the intermediate institutions, the democratic alternatives to aristocracy. Indeed, Americans had not only conserved and strengthened certain old institutions, they had even created some new ones. In the power, autonomy, and self-consciousness of the legal profession, in the freedom of the press, in a variety of private associations, political and nonpolitical, Americans had, he thought, developed their substitutes for the political functions of an aristocracy as an offset to tyranny. Constitutional arrangements them-

7. Tocqueville, *Democracy in America*, vol. 2, pp. 336–337.

Table 17.3
United States Presidents,
1900-68: Previous
Elective Offices

	State Legislature	Governor	U.S. Congress House	Senate	Vice-President
McKinley		*	*		
T. Roosevelt	*	*			
Taft					
Wilson		*			
Harding	*			*	
Coolidge	*	*			*
Hoover					
F. D. Roosevelt	*	*			
Truman				*	*
Eisenhower					
Kennedy			*	*	
Johnson			*	*	*
Nixon			*	*	*

selves had added even more barriers to halt the eager tyrant. Among these constitutionally created barriers were, naturally, the federal system and the tradition of local self-government.

How Local Governments Help

Looking back from our present perspective, what can we say to Tocqueville's judgment? Do state and local governments help to tame our political leaders?

Socialization. The first and most obvious contribution of local representative institutions is to provide a training ground in which political leaders learn the political arts required in a polyarchy. In the terminology of contemporary political science, local institutions carry on the functions of political socialization and recruitment. The enormous number and variety of governments in the United States, many of them with elective offices and many involved in some way with party or factional politics, provide a vast political school that turns out a sizeable stratum of subleaders with at least modest political skills. Many of the national political leaders are drawn from this pool of those trained in local and state politics; it is this pool, too, that often furnishes the local leaders in moments of emergency—when, for example, a possible unjust local regulation threatens to become a reality and citizens feel the need to act.[8]

Thus, of the thirteen men elected president in this century, all except three—Taft, Hoover, and Eisenhower—had previously held elective

8. For example, see William K. Muir, Jr., *Defending "The Hill" Against Metal Houses,* ICP case series, no. 26 (University, Ala.: University of Alabama Press, 1955); and Robert A. Dahl, *Who Governs? Democracy and Power in an American City* (New Haven: Yale University Press, 1961), pp. 192 ff.

Table 17.4
Previous Offices Held by
United States Senators,
1959-71

	Percent of Senators who had held following offices
State legislator	32%
United States representative	30
Law enforcement	24
State governor	17
Local office	14
Administrative offices, governmental	13
Statewide elective office	12
Congressional staff	3

Sources: *Congressional Directory*, *Who's Who in American Politics*. Total number of senators included, 152. This excludes the judiciary because of the difficulty in determining whether the office is elective or appointive.

political office. Of the ten with experience in an elective office, six had held office as governor or member of the state legislature (Table 17.3). A large proportion of congressional leaders have also held a state office of some kind, usually an elective office. Just as being senator or governor is the best public position from which to win the presidency, so, too, the Senate itself recruits a large share of its membership from the House and from state or local offices (Table 17.4).

Most state governors first learn their craft in state and local politics. Out of almost one thousand governors elected in the United States from 1870 to 1950, slightly over half had previously been in the state legislature, a fifth had held local elective office, and nearly a fifth had held some statewide elective office.[9]

A base for opposition. The state and local governments also help to provide a secure base to which opposition may retire when it has suffered defeat elsewhere, in order to sally forth and challenge its opponents at the next election. If the two major parties are highly competitive at the national level, perhaps the weaker competition and even the numerous local party monopolies are the price to be paid. In the thirty-six year period from McKinley's election in 1896 to Franklin Roosevelt's election in 1932, the Democratic party enjoyed only eight years in the White House; it had a majority in the Senate during only six years. Yet, thanks to their secure fortress in the South and their bastions in northern cities like New York, Boston, and Chicago, they remained a formidable party at every election and were able to organize

9. Joseph A. Schlesinger, *How They Became Governor* (East Lansing: Governmental Research Bureau, 1957), p. 11. See also his *Ambition and Politics: Political Careers in the United States* (Chicago: Rand McNally, 1966).

the national campaign in 1932 that brought Roosevelt into office for the first of his four terms. The Republicans recovered from the devastation of Roosevelt's famous landslide in 1936 because their state and local party strongholds were never completely overrun. By 1938 they were, in coalition with Southern Democrats, powerful enough to bring further New Deal reforms to a halt. Within individual states the situation is often much the same: the party or faction that controls the state house encounters its toughest opposition in the big cities.

Partitioning power. Finally, the state and local governments have helped to partition power. In the United States, as we have seen, basic constitutional arrangements partition the power of national officials. The state and local governments have undoubtedly contributed to the extreme partitioning of power characteristic of the American polyarchy. State and local governments have provided a number of centers of power whose autonomy is strongly protected by constitutional and political traditions. A governor of a state or the mayor of a large city may not be the political equal of a president (at least not often), but he is most assuredly not a subordinate. In dealing with a governor or a mayor, a president rarely if ever commands; he negotiates; he may even plead. Here, then is a part of the intermediate stratum of leadership that Tocqueville looked to as a barrier to tyranny.

The state and local governments have contributed something further to the partitioning of power. They have increased the options available to citizens. Citizens who find one group of leaders unsympathetic to their wishes can often turn to another group that influences a different level or sector of government. Thus a group that finds its needs ignored at the local level may turn to the state or to the federal government; the system also works the other way round. In its earlier years, for example, the American labor movement, often blocked in its efforts to win national legislation, turned to state governments to lead the way in the regulation of the working day, workmen's compensation, employment of women and children, and unemployment compensation. In recent decades, it has more often concentrated its efforts for positive gains on the national government, where it is assured of more sympathetic attention than in many of the states. At the state level, the labor movement has grown more concerned with occasional negative actions—such as blocking laws limiting the right to strike.

FACILITATING SELF-GOVERNMENT: THE DARKER SIDE How much do the state and local governments help to democratize the American polyarchy by enlarging the area of self-government? In particular, to what extent do local elections help citizens to participate in local decisions and to elect leaders responsive to their wishes?

As with the criterion of efficiency, the problem posed by these questions is to find a suitable yardstick with which we can compare local governments.

There can be no question that, like the national government, local governments fall very far short of ideal democracy. But perhaps a more useful comparison is with the national government, since both sets of governments exist within the same general political culture and society. In two respects, local politics in the United States seems to operate at lower levels of performance than national politics.

Less Party Competition

In the first place, party competition is weaker at local levels than at the national level. The frequency of two-party competition, in fact, is roughly correlated with the size of the political unit: it declines from the national arena to statewide contests for U.S. senator, governor, and other statewide elective offices, and declines again from statewide elections to contests in smaller units—congressional districts, cities, and towns. Though we do not have the data one would need to confirm the hunch, there is every reason to suppose that two-party competition is rarest of all in the smallest units: wards, councilmanic districts, state legislative districts, and the like. To overstate the point: effective contests for office and votes in a larger area do not result from effective electoral contests between the parties in the smaller areas; they are produced by parties that are highly unequal in strength in the smaller units. The smaller the area, evidently, the more difficult it is for the opposition to challenge the incumbents by presenting a rival slate at elections.

The principle that the smaller the area the less the chances of two-party competition is quite evident from the data. Nationally, the Democratic and Republican parties are highly competitive. The presidency is contested vigorously in great nationwide campaigns; the outcome is always to some extent in doubt; over the years the presidency shifts back and forth from one party to the other. The Congress, too, is the site of considerable party competition. Neither party can take for granted that it will control either the presidency or the Congress after the next election.

In many states, though by no means all, party competition is a good deal weaker than it is in the national arena. For example, between 1914 and 1954, in six states of the Old South the Republicans did not win a single election for governor, United States senator, or presidential electors. During the same period, the Democrats won no elections in the northern state of Vermont. In five more southern states and one northern state (Maine), the second party did not win more than one election out of every ten. In another nine states, the second party won fewer than one election out of four.[10]

Using elections for governor and for the members of each house of the legislature from 1946 to 1963, Austin Ranney classified the party systems of the fifty states by averaging

> four basic figures: (1) the average per cent of the popular vote won by Democratic gubernatorial candidates; (2) the average per cent of the seats in the state senate held by the Democrats; (3) the average per cent of the seats in the state house of representatives held by the Democrats; and (4) the per cent of all terms for governor, senate, and house in which the Democrats had control.

In 1965 his classification of the fifty states was as follows:

> One-party Democratic (.90 or higher): 8 states.
> Modified one-party Democratic (.70 to .8999): 9 states.
> Two party (.30 to .6999): 25 states.
> Modified one-party Republican (.10 to .2999): 8 states.
> One-party Republican (less than .10): no states.[11]

Not only is competition greater in the national arena than in statewide contests; it is also greater in statewide elections than in smaller units. Similarly, elections for U.S. senator are more closely contested than elections for the House of Representatives. Figure 17.5 shows this dramatically. In the twelve most populous states, in less than 9 percent of the contests for House seats in 1970 the Republican and Democratic candidates split the vote in the 45–55 percent range. In senatorial elections from 1966 to 1970, 48 percent of the contests fell into this highly competitive range.

In the towns, cities, counties, and state legislative districts, party competition is probably even weaker. Unfortunately, we lack good data with which to test this conjecture. But we do know that in a very high proportion of American cities elections are required by law to be nonpartisan: the name of a political party cannot appear on the ballot. Everywhere except the Middle Atlantic states, most cities over twenty-five thousand require nonpartisan elections for local offices (Table 17.5). Even in cities where elections are formally and actually contested by both parties, the second party is often weak and rarely if ever wins the mayor's office or a majority of councilmen.

All this does not mean, of course, that in these states and cities there is no active competition for public office. There is. Where the

---

10. The data are from Austin Ranney and Willmoore Kendall, *Democracy and the American Party System* (New York: Harcourt, 1956), Tables 2, 3, and 4, pp. 162–164. In 1956 Ranney and Kendall classified twenty-six states as two-party systems, ten as one-party states, and twelve as modified one-party states. Another classification will be found in Joseph A. Schlesinger, "A Two-Dimensional Scheme for Classifying the States According to Degree of Inter-Party Competition," *American Political Science Review,* 49 (December, 1955), 1120–1128.

11. Austin Ranney, "Parties in State Politics," in Jacob and Vines, *Politics in the United States,* pp. 64–65.

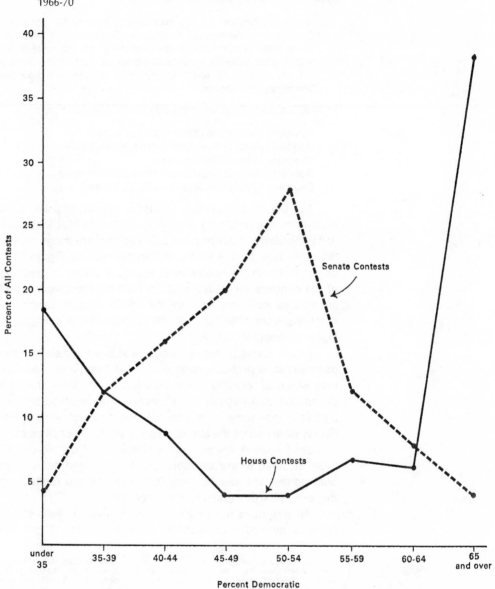

Figure 17.5
Party Competition in the
Twelve Most Populous
States: House Candidates,
1970; Senate Candidates,
1966-70

Percent of All Contests

Senate Contests

House Contests

under 35   35-39   40-44   45-49   50-54   55-59   60-64   65 and over

Percent Democratic

States include California, Florida, Illinois, Indiana, Massachusetts, Michigan, New Jersey, New York, North Carolina, Ohio, Pennsylvania, and Texas.

Table 17.5
United States Regions
Ranked by Proportion of
Nonpartisan Cities, 1970

Region	Number of Cities 25,000 and Over	Percentage Nonpartisan
West	143	91.4
Plains	59	88.4
Border	42	78.5
Mountain	31	77.5
Great Lakes	187	68.5
South	152	63.1
New England	85	56.5
Middle Atlantic	134	13.4

Source: 1970 Census Tracts, Preliminary Estimates, and *Municipal Yearbook, 1968.*

Regions are defined: *West:* Alaska, California, Hawaii, Oregon, Washington; *Plains:* Colorado, Iowa, Kansas, Nebraska, North Dakota, Oklahoma, South Dakota, Wyoming; *Border:* Kentucky, Missouri, Tennessee, West Virginia; *Mountain:* Arizona, Idaho, Montana, Nevada, New Mexico, Utah; *Great Lakes:* Illinois, Indiana, Michigan, Minnesota, Ohio, Wisconsin; *South:* Alabama, Arkansas, Florida, Georgia, Louisiana, Mississippi, North Carolina, South Carolina, Texas, Virginia; *New England:* Connecticut, Maine, Massachusetts, New Hampshire, Rhode Island, Vermont; *Middle Atlantic:* Delaware, Maryland, New Jersey, New York, Pennsylvania.

second party is weak, competition often takes place *within* the dominant party. Yet even when intra-party conflict is sharp, it must necessarily occur not between highly organized parties but between individuals or loose factions. To be sure, in some one-party states, as in Louisiana over an extended period, two rival factions within the same party may perform many of the functions of political parties.[12] In general, however, the absence of sharp competition for office by organized political parties seems to accentuate the significance of personal qualities and to diminish emphasis on policies.[13]

Less Participation

If local governments fall somewhat short of the national government in the extent to which two or more organized parties compete vigorously to win elections and gain control over the policy-making machinery of government, they also seem to evoke less participation by citizens than the national government. In this respect, the local governments have disappointed the hopes of democratic ideologues like Jefferson who believed that the true centers of American democracy would be the local governments, which would attend to the problems of daily life of most interest and importance to the citizen, and, lying within easy reach, would be his most responsive and responsible instruments of self-government.

---

12. Allan P. Sindler, "Bifactional Rivalry as an Alternative to Two-Party Competition in Louisiana," *American Political Science Review,* 49 (September, 1955), 641–662; and *Huey Long's Louisiana* (Baltimore: Johns Hopkins Press, 1956).

13. Sindler, "Bifactional Rivalry"; see also the classic statement in V. O. Key, Jr., *Southern Politics* (New York: Knopf, 1949). A good statement of the findings may be found in Greenstein, *American Party System,* pp. 66–70.

Table 17.6
Percentage of Population
of Voting Age Who Vote
in City and
National Elections

Presidential election, 1960[a]	63.8%
House of Representatives, 1960[a]	59.4
Elections for city officials, 1961-2[b]	46.5
Concurrent with state or national elections	43.5
Not concurrent	31.2

Sources: a. *Congress and the Nation*, vol. 2, p. 438; and b. Robert A. Alford and Eugene C. Lee, "Voting Turn-out in American Cities," *American Political Science Review*, 62 (September, 1968), 796–813; Table 1, p. 803. The data are for 80% of the cities above 25,000 population in 1960.

In elections. So far as one can judge from available data, citizens are less active in state and local elections than in national elections. Although the evidence is by no means all one-sided, one fact is clear: presidential elections attract a larger number of voters (and probably much more attention) than most elections to state and local offices. From a half to two-thirds as many citizens turn out for city elections as for national elections (Table 17.6). However, since all contests, including those for the House and Senate in midterm elections, fare badly in comparison with the presidential contest, participation in state[14] and local elections is not too much lower than in off-year congressional elections, as in 1962.

The myth of a golden age. It is sometimes thought that participation in local governments was much higher in the good old days; that lower participation is entirely a modern phenomenon, resulting from the increased importance of national affairs. But such scattered evidence as we have does not seem to sustain this belief in a golden age of local democracy. For example, data on voting in New Haven, Connecticut, from 1820 to recent times show conclusively that the proportion of citizens who have voted in elections for mayor has always been less than those who have voted in presidential contests (Figure 17.6).

It is difficult to say how common this pattern was in the nineteenth century. Turnout in state and national elections in the first half of the nineteenth century showed considerable variation from state to state. In Connecticut, turnout was invariably higher for national than for state elections; yet in the neighboring New England states, gubernatorial elections produced the higher turnout. New York and New Jersey were like Connecticut; in Virginia, as elsewhere in the Old South, turnout was higher in state elections than in national elections.[15]

---

14. Lester W. Milbrath, "Political Participation in the States," in Jacob and Vines, *Politics in the United States*, states that "turnout in state elections is closely comparable to turnout in Representative elections. If the state or Representative election occurs in a non-Presidential year, the turnout is likely to be significantly lower" (p. 37).

15. Cf. Richard P. McCormick, *The Second American Party System, Party Formation in the Jacksonian Era* (Chapel Hill: University of North Carolina Press, 1966), pp. 99, 123, 133, 186, 248, and *passim*.

Figure 17.6
New Haven, Connecticut:
Percentage of Citizens
21 Years Old and Over
Voting in Presidential and
Mayoralty Elections,
1860-1950

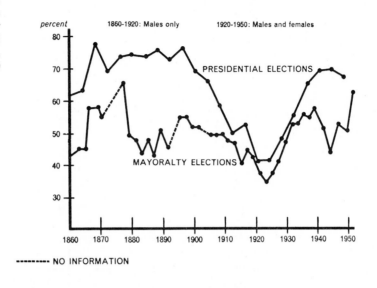

Source: Dahl, *Who Governs?* p. 277.

Thus the evidence points to several conclusions, mainly negative. It is not true, as an enthusiastic follower of Rousseau or Jefferson might hold, that the smaller a political unit is, the more its citizens will participate in political affairs. To the extent that voting is a fair measure of participation, the Rousseau-Jefferson hypothesis is definitely not true today. Although there was probably greater variation in patterns of electoral participation in the first part of the nineteenth century than there is today, the Rousseau-Jefferson hypothesis was not confirmed by experience even then. Nor is it true that participation in state and local elections has fallen off as these units have grown in size and as the role of the national government has expanded.

In short, local territorial governments in the United States are not, and evidently never have been, distinctive sites for high levels of civic participation.

FACILITATING SELF-GOVERNMENT: THE BRIGHTER SIDE

There is no blinking the fact that by democratic criteria local governments—like the national polyarchy—are highly defective. Yet, to right the balance, one needs to consider what polyarchy would be like in the United States if representative governments did not exist in the states and localities. While one might argue persuasively that the best alterna-

Level of Governmental Affairs	Rank of How Closely Followed				Total[a]	N
	First	Second	Third	Fourth		
International	20%	16%	22%	42%	100%	983
National	32	31	26	10	99	983
State	17	33	27	22	99	983
Local	30	20	25	25	100	983
Total[a]	99%	100%	100%	99%		
N	983	983	983	983		

[a] Total percentages do not equal 100% due to rounding.
Source: Jennings and Zeigler, "The Salience of American State Politics," p. 525.

tive to what we have now is more self-goverment, it would be hard to make a good case that, from a democratic point of view, we would be better off with less.

It may be worth asking, then, how the local governments in the United States compare with the national government as institutions of self-government. Are they markedly worse? Although a precise answer is impossible, the evidence does support three propositions:

First, citizens seem to be about as concerned with local affairs as with national and international affairs.

Second, except by comparison with voting in presidential elections, citizens participate as much in local as in national politics, if not more.

Third, they probably have greater confidence in their capacity to act effectively at local levels.

Concern

The degree of interest expressed by Americans in state and local affairs compares favorably with their level of interest in national affairs. Some excellent evidence on this point is furnished by an analysis of data from surveys made during the elections of 1966 and 1968.[16] After weeding out 17 percent of the respondents who indicated that they paid hardly any attention at all to government and public affairs, the 1966 survey (Table 17.7) found that:

□ About as many people give their attention to local affairs as to national affairs. Thirty percent say they follow local affairs more closely than national or international affairs, compared with 32 percent who follow national affairs more closely, and 20 percent for international affairs.
□ State affairs rank fourth (17 percent), just behind international affairs.

---

16. M. Kent Jennings and Harmon Zeigler, "The Salience of American State Politics," *American Political Science Review*, 64 (June, 1970), 523–535. Incidentally, the findings correct a view I had advanced earlier that "the average American is bound to be much less concerned about the affairs of his state than of his city or country" in Robert A. Dahl, "The City in the Future of Democracy," *American Political Science Review*, 61 (December, 1967), 968.

Table 17.8
Estimated Degree of
Impact of National and
Local Governments on
Daily Life

	National Government	Local Government
Great effect	41%	35%
Some effect	44	53
No effect	11	10
Other, don't know, etc.	4	2
	100%	100%
Total number of cases	970	970

Source: Almond and Verba, *The Civic Culture*, pp. 80–81.

Table 17.9
"On the whole, do the
activities of the national
(local) government tend to
improve conditions in this
area, or would we be better
off without them?"

	National Government	Local Government
Yes, tend to improve	74%	69%
Sometimes improve, sometimes not	18	23
Better off without them	3	4
Other, don't know, etc.	5	4
	100%	100%
Total number of cases	970	970

Source: Gabriel A. Almond and Sidney Verba survey, unpublished data.

However, 50 percent rank state affairs either first or second. In the 1968 survey 37 percent said they paid a great deal of attention to state politics, and another 51 percent said they gave it some attention.
□ Evidently some citizens tend to give special attention to state and local affairs, others to national and international affairs. Both groups are about the same size.

Concern for local politics should hardly be surprising, since many of the problems that people regard as urgent and important require some action by local governments: education, crime, poverty, welfare, public health, racial discrimination, housing, parking, streets and highways, to name a few. A national survey conducted in the 1950s contained a finding that probably still holds good: the percentage of Americans who felt that the local government had some effect or great effect on their day-to-day lives was actually a shade larger than the percentage who felt this way about the national government. As one might expect, more people thought the national government had *great* effect; but more also thought that local government had *some* effect (Table 17.8). Similarly the percentage who felt that on the whole the activities of local government "tend to improve conditions in this area" was quite high, though a trifle short of the percentage who felt the same way about the activities of national government (Table 17.9).

Participation

The relatively lower turnout in local elections than in presidential elections does not prove that Americans are less active in local affairs. For one thing, the presidential contest is unique. Even if voters were as involved in local affairs as in national affairs, as the evidence suggests they are, the lower frequency of sharp two-party competition would probably reduce the turnout at elections, partly because the contest itself would be less exciting, partly because the parties would work less vigorously to get out the vote. Moreover, voting is only one form of participation; some of the other ways of participating in politics are more easily carried on at the local than at the national level: getting in touch with one's councilman about a torn-up street is a good deal easier than getting in touch with one's congressman or senator or the president about the war in Vietnam.

Even if local governments fall far short of potential and ideal, they do provide channels through which citizens may express their views on local matters when they have an urge to do so. In the 1959 survey in New Haven, mentioned earlier, a sample of registered voters was asked: "Have you ever contacted any local public officials or politicians to let them know what you were interested in?" More than one out of every four registered voters said they had. Sixteen percent said they had had some contact with political or governmental officials in New Haven in the past year. In fact, 8 percent said they had been in touch with the mayor at some time and 11 percent with some other city official. Admittedly, these are not the high percentages one might hope for in a polyarchy, but to the extent that local channels do exist and are used by citizens, the domain of self-government is enlarged.

Citizen Effectiveness

Evidence does suggest that Americans look on their local governments as more accessible, more manageable, more responsive. In an exhaustive study of the political attitudes of fifteen lower middle-class citizens in an Eastern city, Robert Lane found:

> . . . The fact is that these men were pretty discouraged by the idea of *doing* something about any big problems. . . .
> Eastport's common men find themselves politically impotent on most important specific issues, do not petition or write letters with any frequency, are dubious of the wisdom of the electorate on these issues, see elections as only partially successful instruments for imparting instructions to candidates, find themselves often confused by the complexity of public affairs, and tend to think of elected officials as better judges of policy than they themselves are.[17]

Yet far from being alienated, most of these fifteen men felt that they were politically important. How, Lane asks,

---

17. Lane, *Political Ideology*, pp. 164–165.

Table 17.10 The Sense of Understanding of Issues	National and International	Local Issues
Very well	7%	21%
Moderately well	38	44
Not so well	37	23
Not at all	14	10
Depends, other, don't know, etc.	4	2
	100%	100%
Total number of cases	970	970

Source: Almond and Verba survey, unpublished data.

. . . do they come to have this sense of political importance? One reason is that many of them have political connections and for local matters they *have* influence, can get close to somebody who may pretend to more authority than he has but who conveys to his circle of acquaintances the sense that they are in communication with important people when they speak to him.[18]

There are also other reasons, of course; but this sense of accessibility and responsiveness may be an important one. The national survey taken in the 1950s, mentioned a moment ago, tends to confirm the hunch that the closeness, accessibility, and comprehensibility of local government enhance the confidence of citizens that they can *do something* about local affairs. Almost two out of three respondents agreed and only a third disagreed with the statement that "politics and government are so complicated that the average man cannot really understand what is going on." Yet the number who said that they understood "local issues in this town or part of the country" very well was three times as large as the number who said they understood "the important national and international issues facing the country" very well. In fact, over half the respondents said that they did not understand national and international issues at all or not so well, compared with only a third who felt this way about local issues (Table 17.10).

Nor is it only a matter of being able to grasp local issues better; citizens also seem to think that they can act more effectively at the local level. To be sure, not many ever do act at either local or national levels. In fact, seven out of ten respondents in this survey said they had never tried to influence a local decision, while eight out of ten said they had never tried to influence the Congress. Yet many were confident that, if the need arose, they would act and might even be successful. What did they think they could do, they were asked, if a law or regulation which they considered "very unjust or harmful" were being considered by the local government or by Congress? The number who said that it was

18. *Ibid.*, p. 165.

	Local Regulation	National Law
Very likely or moderately likely	28%	11%
Somewhat unlikely	15	18
Not at all likely, impossible	25	36
Likely only if others joined in	25	24
Other, don't know	6	9
	100%	100%
Total number of cases	970	970

Source: Almond and Verba survey, unpublished data.

very likely or moderately likely that they would do something about the law or regulation was slightly larger in the case of a local law (49 percent) than for a national law (42 percent). The number who said that it was not at all likely that they would do something about an unjust law or regulation was a little less for local laws (27 percent) than for national laws (33 percent). The percentages who expected that they could be successful in their efforts were somewhat higher in the case of the local law (Table 17.11).

SUMMARY The eighty thousand governments in the United States below the level of the national government, particularly the fifty states and the thirty-eight thousand local territorial governments, contribute to the operation of the American polyarchy in four ways:

1. They make polyarchy more manageable at the national level by reducing the work load of the national government.

2. They reduce conflicts at the national level and thus help to make polyarchy at the national level more viable because:

☐ They allow for the possibility of diverse solutions to problems and thus mitigate the coercive possibilities of uniformity imposed by national majorities.

☐ They permit some potential conflicts to be taken out of the arena of national politics to be handled at local levels. However, the process of denationalizing conflicts is subject to two defects: it may permit injustices, as in the case of Southern blacks; and for this or other reasons, the parties to the conflict may not allow an issue to be removed from national politics.

3. They create numerous more or less independent and autonomous centers of power. As a result:

☐ They provide a training ground for political leaders to acquire the arts of governing in a polyarchy.

□ They help provide oppositions with a base when they are defeated elsewhere.

□ They help to partition power.

4. They help to enlarge the domain of self-government by increasing the opportunities available for citizen participation in controlling governments. Although in comparison with the national government, the achievements of local governments are mixed, the findings nonetheless indicate that they play an important role:

□ In comparison with the national government, at local levels there is less party competition, and less participation in elections.

□ However, evidence indicates that citizens are as much concerned with local as with national and international affairs.

□ The easier accessibility of local governments makes it easier for citizens to get in touch with officials.

□ Citizens feel they can grasp local issues better and can be more effective in dealing with them.

Political Parties:
The Unforeseen Element

18

In recasting classical ideas about direct democracy into forms suitable for a representative system, nothing was more self-evident than the need for an elected legislature. The belief that an elected chief executive might also contribute an important element of 'democratic' representation, as we saw, came later; in this country that view has been pretty widely accepted from the Jacksonian period onward. Fitting the Supreme Court into a 'democratic' framework, as we saw in Chapters 16 and 17, has been infinitely more difficult; perhaps Americans are more ready to interpret judicial review as a 'democratic' device than a scrupulous attention to theory and practise would permit.

Yet the legitimacy of these major political institutions of American polyarchy, all prescribed in outline by the Constitution, appears to be considerably stronger than that of another institution which, though central to the operation of polyarchy, was unanticipated by the Founders and is nowhere mentioned in the Constitution: the system of political parties. Political parties have been among the most visible and important elements in the American polyarchy for a century and three-quarters, yet many Americans continue to doubt their legitimacy. Whereas two out of three Americans believe that elections are highly important in making the government responsive to the people, only four out of ten concede as much for political parties (Table 18.1). Nearly seven out of ten persons in a 1966 Wisconsin survey agreed with the proposition that "More often than not, the political parties create conflict where none really exists" (Table 18.2). Even more revealing: over 40 percent believed that party conflict is more harmful than helpful and the country would be better off without it.

In contrast to these popular views of parties, most contemporary

Make the government	(Percent)	
pay attention:	Elections[a]	Parties[b]
A good deal	65%	40
Some	25	39
Not much	6	13
Don't know	4	7
Total %	100%	99%
N =	(1450)	(1450)

[a] "How much do you feel that having elections makes the government pay attention to what the people think?"

[b] "How much do you feel that political parties help to make the government pay attention to what the people think?"

Source: Jack Dennis, "Support for the Institution of Elections by the Mass Public," *American Political Science Review*, 64 (September, 1970), p. 831, Table 7. The survey data were obtained from the 1964 Election Study by the University of Michigan Survey Research Center.

Items	Percent							
	Strongly Agree	Agree	Agree-Disagree	Disagree	Strongly Disagree	Don't Know	Not Ascertained	Total Percent[a]
"More often than not, the political parties create conflicts where none really exists."	9%	60	11	13	—*	6	1	100%
"It would be better if, in all elections, no party labels were put on the ballot."	4	30	8	50	6	3	—*	101%
"The parties do more to confuse the issues than to provide a clear choice on them."	6	48	23	18	1	3	1	100%
"Our system of government would work a lot more efficiently if we could get rid of conflicts between the parties altogether."	8	35	11	33	8	3	2	100%
"The conflicts and controversies between the parties hurt our country more than they help it."	4	37	17	36	3	3	1	101%

[a] Some rows do not add to 100% due to errors of rounding. N = 607.

* Less than 1%.

Source: *Ibid.*, Table 6.

democratic theorists insist that party competition and conflict are cardinal processes for enhancing popular control in a large system. Given the institutional guarantees of polyarchy, parties are inevitable; from a democratic perspective, they are also thought to be desirable.

Why was it, then, that the Founders failed to perceive the importance of parties? How did political parties come about? What contributions *do* they make? Why is it that democratic theorists believe parties are desirable, whereas so many citizens doubt their legitimacy?

THE FOUNDERS' LACK OF FORESIGHT

Nothing—not the uncertainty, nor the lack of foresight, nor the dread—about parties should be surprising. For, as late as the time of the Constitutional Convention, although political parties existed in embryo, they were very far from being developed anywhere in the world into mature organizations as we know them today. As for factions, were not their evils well known? "In examining the history of nations, we discover examples of the pernicious tendency of faction," a New York jurist wrote in 1794. To prove his point he conjured up "the mortal conflict which existed between the houses of York and Lancaster," the disputes in France between Catholics and Huguenots, the fall of Athens and the decline of the Roman Republic.[1]

He had a point. Even as late as the end of the eighteenth century, it took extraordinary vision not to see political parties as destructive.

Factions: The Bane of Republics[2]

Of the three great milestones in the development of democratic institutions—the right to participate in governmental decisions by casting a vote, a system of representation, and the right of an organized opposition to appeal for votes against the government in elections and in parliament—the last is, in a highly developed form, so wholly modern that there are people now living who were born before it had appeared in most of Western Europe.

Throughout recorded history, it seems, stable institutions providing legal, orderly, peaceful modes of political opposition have been rare. If peaceful antagonism between factions is uncommon, peaceful competition among organized, permanent political parties is an even more exotic historical phenomenon. Legal party opposition is, in fact, a recent unplanned invention that has been confined for the most part to a handful of countries. Even more recent are organized political parties that compete peacefully in elections for the votes of the great bulk of the adult population able to exercise the franchise under nearly universal suffrage. Universal suffrage and enduring mass parties are, with few exceptions,

1. William Wyche, "Party Spirit," in *The Making of the American Party System 1789 to 1809*, ed. Noble E. Cunningham, Jr. (Englewood Cliffs: Prentice-Hall, 1965), p. 13.

2. The first part of this section is adapted from the preface to Robert A. Dahl, *Political Oppositions in Western Democracies* (New Haven: Yale University Press, 1966).

products of the twentieth century; a hundred years ago they did not exist outside the United States.

Because some conflict of views seems to be unavoidable in human affairs, political societies have always had to deal somehow with the fact of opposition. Nevertheless, that there might legitimately exist an organized group within the political system to oppose, criticize, and if possible oust the leading officials of government was until recently an unfamiliar and generally unacceptable notion. When the men at the American Constitutional Convention of 1787 expressed their fear of "factions" as the bane of republics, they spoke the traditional view.

Previous experience. The most long-lived republic in history, the aristocratic republic of Venice, explicitly forbade the formation of enduring political organizations. Venice, like Rome before it, sought to provide in her constitution sufficient checks and balances among officials to prevent arbitrary decisions and to insure a large measure of consensus for the laws; thus organized opposition was seen as unnecessary and a danger to the stability of the republic. Not all the premodern democracies and republics went quite so far as Venice. Factions, coalitions, and alliances of one kind or another existed in and outside of the popular assemblies of Athens, and in the late Roman republic political alliances sought votes both for candidates and for laws in various popular assemblies. But evidently these groups were never highly organized, had no permanent structure, and even lacked definite names. Moreover, factions typically settled their differences sooner or later, as they had come to do during the last century of the Roman republic, by bloodshed.

The system of managing the major political conflicts of a society by allowing one or more opposition parties to compete with the governing parties for votes in elections and in parliament is not only modern, then; surely it is also one of the greatest and most unexpected social discoveries that man has ever stumbled onto. Up until two centuries ago, no one had accurately foreseen it. In Britain during the eighteenth century, rival groups had formed in Parliament, to which the names Whig and Tory were often applied. But

> . . . Whig and Tories did not constitute political parties as they came to be in the late nineteenth and twentieth centuries. Those labels were often adopted by, or foisted upon, men who had little in common and few or no real ties. In 1714 and for many years thereafter, the basic political unit was the group or connexion, often called a party, formed under the leadership of a successful politician.[3]

In the parliament of Sweden during what came to be known as the Era

---

3. Foord, *His Majesty's Opposition,* p. 20. See also Sir Ivor Jennings, *Party Politics,* vol. II: *The Growth of Parties* (Cambridge: The University Press, 1961), pp. 24 ff.; Sir Lewis Namier, ed., *The Structure of Politics at the Accession of George III* (New York: St. Martin's Press, 1961), "The Electoral Structure of England," ch. 2.

of Liberty from 1718 to 1772, parliamentary factions "strongly reminiscent of the parallel groupings of Whigs and Tories in eighteenth century Britain" also developed.[4]

But these factional groups in Britain and Sweden were a long way from modern parties. There is little reason to suppose that in the late eighteenth century American political leaders knew anything about the Swedish system. As for Britain, the significance of the Whig and Tory factions in Parliament was quite unclear at the time, even in Britain; it was only much later that, looking backward, one could perceive in them the barest beginnings of a party system that has continued to develop and to change down to the present day.

Older usage of party. The word *party* itself did not have quite the same meaning to men like Washington, Madison, and Jefferson that it has today. Political party has come to signify an institution, a durable, organized force that outlasts the particular individuals who adhere to it at any moment. But when American political leaders used the term in the late eighteenth century—as they did more and more frequently from the Constitutional Convention onward—they seem to have had in mind a *current of political opinion*, rather than an organized institution. Terms like *party, faction, interest, sect, division,* or *group* were used more or less interchangeably.[5]

Initial hostility to parties. Men at the Constitutional Convention and in public life during the first two decades were often confused as to the nature of party. No one, I imagine, thought that political conflict could be avoided entirely. But some important leaders seem to have believed that *persistent* cleavages of opinion could be avoided; perhaps men would come fresh to each question, ready to examine it with an open mind unclouded by attachments to any lasting faction or party. Leaders who held this view attacked "the spirit of party" for its baneful effects, as Washington did in his Farewell Address. When parties began to be organized, these men predicted terrible results: "Party spirit is the demon which engendered the factions that have destroyed most free governments," thundered the distinguished Senator Hillhouse of Connecticut in a Senate speech in 1808. "Regular, organized parties only, extending from the northern to the southern extremity of the United States, and

---

4. Dankwart A. Rustow, *The Politics of Compromise* (Princeton: Princeton University Press, 1955), pp. 11–12.

5. See for example Madison's "A Candid State of Parties" published in the Philadelphia *National Gazette* in 1792, reprinted in Cunningham, *Making of the American Party System*. Speaking of the time of the Revolution, Madison says that "those who espoused the cause of independence and those who adhered to the British claims, formed the parties of the first period." A moment later, he begins to speak of divisions: "The Federal Constitution . . . gave birth to the second and most interesting division of the people . . those who embraced the constitution . . . those who opposed the constitution. . . . This tate of parties was terminated . . . in 1788" (pp. 10–11).

from the Atlantic to the utmost western limits, threaten to shake this Union to its centre."⁶ One difficulty with this view was that it was often—though not always—espoused by Federalists, who, so it appeared, did not object to the existence of their own party but only to that of their opponents, the opposition that Jefferson and Madison had the temerity to organize into a party.

It was in response to views like these that Federalist leaders sought to curb the nascent party of opposition; and it takes no great exercise of the imagination to conceive that the issue of a democratic versus an aristocratic republic hung in the balance during the years from 1794 to 1800. In 1794, President Washington himself took the occasion of the Whisky Insurrection in western Pennsylvania to attack the Democratic Societies "as centers of sedition and resistance to government and re-quested the Senate and House to follow his lead. The Senate complied, but in the House Madison argued eloquently that it was unconstitutional for Congress to censure the clubs. Their members were simply exercising their right of free speech."⁷ As Madison put it in a letter to Monroe, "The game was to connect the Democratic Societies with the odium of the insurrection, to connect the Republicans in Cong[ress] with those societies, to put the P[resident] ostensibly at the head of the other party, in opposition to both."⁸

The Alien and Sedition Acts passed by the Federalists in 1798 were animated by a similar hostility to criticism by opposition, and enforce-ment was a partisan matter. The Sedition Act in particular was used to bludgeon the opposition; twenty-five persons were prosecuted under the act, and ten of them, all Republican editors and printers, were convicted.⁹

As it turned out—fortunately for the future of the American polyarchy —the actions of the Federalists did nothing to prevent and much to inflame the spirit of party they found so odious; consequently they, along with the leading Republicans, must be counted among the true, if un-witting, architects of modern parties. It was because of the views of Federalists—and because it was the Republicans, after all, who were being jailed for opposition—that Jefferson and Madison were so deeply alarmed by the Alien and Sedition Acts, which they saw as not only unconstitutional but also a despotic threat to republican government. They registered the strength of their objection by the Kentucky Resolu-tion (drafted by Jefferson) and the Virginia Resolution (drafted by Madi-son) which denounced the Acts as unconstitutional and proposed as "the rightful remedy" a method that seventy years later, employed by other

---

6. Cunningham, *Making of the American Party System*, p. 25.
7. Page Smith, *John Adams,* 2 vols. (Garden City: Doubleday, 1962), vol. 2, p. 865.
8. Quoted in Noble E. Cunningham, Jr., *The Jeffersonian Republicans, The Formation of Party Organization 1789–1801* (Chapel Hill: University of North Carolina Press, 1957), p. 66.
9. Morris, *Encyclopedia of American History*, p. 129.

hands and in other circumstances, was to set off the final round of events that culminated in secession and civil war. That remedy was for the states to "nullify" the allegedly unconstitutional acts of the national government.

Growing acceptance. Fortunately, the time of the Federalists was running out; the tide of republicanism was running in. When that tide swept Jefferson into office in the election of 1800, he pardoned the Republican editors and printers still in prison; the detestable Sedition Acts expired the day before he took the oath of office; he allowed the Alien Act to expire the following year. Thus the doctrine that political parties were constitutionally protected, an uncertain and even contested doctrine during the last decade of the old century, came to rest on firmer ground during the first decade of the new.

Unlike many of their Federalist opponents, Jefferson and Madison held that opposing and persistent cleavages of opinion—parties in this sense—were inevitable in a free republic, even if, in some circumstances, their clashing ambitions might endanger the existence of the republic. In 1813, after four years away from Washington and the White House, Jefferson wrote his old friend John Adams that

> men have differed in opinion, and been divided into parties by these opinions from the first origin of society; and in all governments where they have been permitted freely to think and to speak. The same political parties which now agitate the U.S. have existed thro' all time. . . . To me then it appears that . . . these will continue thro' all future time: that every one takes his side in favor of the many, or of the few, according to his constitution, and the circumstances in which he is placed.[10]

EARLY DEVELOPMENT OF PARTIES

Are Parties Inevitable in Polyarchies?

The fact that rival parties now exist in every polyarchy and not in a single dictatorship hints at the possibility that parties may be inevitable in any organization that accepts democratic principles. If by *party* we mean organized, institutionalized parties, to leap to this conclusion would be going too far; small democratic organizations in which consensus is high sometimes get on without organized parties. But rival parties operating at the national level do seem inescapable with the main institutional guarantees of polyarchy, whether that nation be as small as Iceland or as huge as the United States.

To begin with, the kinds of liberties and institutional guarantees that define polyarchy—freedom of speech, press, and assembly, for example—make parties possible; or to put it in a slightly different way, it would be next to impossible both to prohibit all political parties and

10. Cunningham, *Making of the American Party System,* pp. 19–20.

to allow full freedom of speech, press, and assembly. Stern and prolonged application of the Sedition Act might have curbed parties, but
only by curbing freedom of speech, press, and peaceful assembly.

The possibility of parties does not, however, mean that they are
inevitable. What carves the actual out of the possible is in this case the
ceaseless striving of political leaders for victory: their incessant efforts
to win elections and marshall legislative majorities in support of particular persons, policies, or programs. The instrument invented in the
United States between 1789 and about 1809 for winning elections and
marshaling legislative majorities was the political party. If necessity is
the mother of invention, then given the goals of ambitious men and the
existing stock of knowledge, techniques, and institutions, the political
party was as certain to be invented as the cotton gin, the steam engine,
and interchangeable machine parts.

So whatever the intentions of the Founding Fathers may have been,
their Constitution, if it were kept to, made political parties not only
possible but inevitable. With the Bill of Rights the Constitution made
parties *possible;* with the institutions of representation and election
designed in Articles I and II, it made parties *inevitable.*

Birth of Parties

We can see the parties struggling to be born in the early springtime
of the new republic. In this country as elsewhere, parties were not
spontaneous growths: they were created by the interaction of leaders
and responsive followers. To be sure, in 1793 there was across the
country a sudden and seemingly spontaneous flowering of popular
associations that called themselves Democratic or Republican societies.
These associations were uniformly on the side of what were coming to
be called Republicans in distinction to Federalists. Yet as a historian has
observed "they were partisans of the Republican interest, but they were
not a party." For they did not nominate candidates, manage election
campaigns, or seek to control legislatures.[11] They also lacked another
characteristic of parties—durability. Within three years most of these
societies had vanished.

It was not in these associations that the germ of party first appeared
but, as in Britain and Sweden, in the national legislature. For, whatever
Washington might have hoped, we can observe men like Hamilton,
Madison, and Jefferson struggling to invent the political party.[12] The first

---

11. Cunningham, *Jeffersonian Republicans, Formation of Party Organization,* p. 64.

12. See *ibid.,* and also Cunningham, *Jeffersonian Republicans in Power,* and *Making of the
American Party System;* Charles, *Origins of the American Party System;* William N. Chambers,
Political Parties in a New Nation, The American Experience 1776–1809 (New York: Oxford University Press, 1963); Manning J. Dauer, *The Adams Federalists* (Baltimore: Johns Hopkins Press,
1953).

Congress left few traces of party voting.[13] But Hamilton's economic program stimulated an opposition, led by Jefferson and Madison, that was to consolidate itself more and more fully in the succeeding Congresses. Probably nothing did more to foster this consolidation than the opposition in Congress to Jay's Treaty in 1795. The Republicans, as the congressional followers of Madison and Jefferson had begun to call themselves, held a caucus, the first in congressional history, to determine whether they would vote for the appropriations required to put the treaty into effect.[14] Under the stimulus of leadership, organization, and antagonism, both Federalists and Republicans became increasingly cohesive. When Jefferson became president, he had little difficulty in converting both the Republican party and the party caucus into efficient instruments for marshaling the votes of the Republican majorities in the Congress.

Institutional Development

The institutions that have been used ever since to mobilize party support in Congress were well developed by the end of Jefferson's two terms in office: the caucus of the party faithful to determine the party line; the election of a partisan rather than a neutral Speaker of the House by the majority party; the development of recognized party leaders; close collaboration between the president and his party leaders in the Congress; and the judicious use of patronage by the president to solidify support.

Meanwhile, need had fostered additional party institutions. There was, above all, the problem of nominations. It was as obvious to Hamilton, Madison, Jefferson, and their peers as it is to us that unless they could marshal their forces in behalf of a single candidate, the opponents might win.[15] In 1796, both parties used an informal (and secret) congressional party caucus to gain agreement on the presidential candidate; thereafter, the device was regularly and openly used until 1824, when it fell into decay. (The present system of a national nominating convention began in 1831 with the new Anti-Masonic party, and in 1832 with the Jacksonian Democrats.)

Yet, unlike the factions and germinal parties in the eighteenth-

---

13. Cunningham, *Jeffersonian Republicans, Formation of Party Organization,* p. 7.
14. *Ibid.,* p. 82.
15. In the case of the presidency the problem was further complicated because as the Constitution then stood party leaders had to insure that their candidate for the vice-presidency received fewer votes than their presidential candidate. As one might imagine this provided splendid opportunities for intrigue, as in 1796 when Hamilton conspired to secure *more* votes for the Federalist vice-presidential candidate, Pinckney, than for the presidential candidate, Adams. In the end the maneuver failed, but Jefferson, the presidential candidate of the Republicans, received the second largest number of electoral votes after Adams, and thus became vice-president under Adams. In 1800, the Republicans failed to arrange properly for votes to be thrown away; as a result the Republican candidates for president and vice-president, Jefferson and Burr, ended in a tie. That was broken by Congress only after a lengthy crisis. The Constitutional defect, which by now was apparent to all, was eliminated in 1804 by the Twelfth Amendment.

century parliaments of Britain and Sweden, incipient parties in the United States confronted still other needs, and it was these needs that added to the structure of the parliamentary, or legislative, party, additional elements that made it recognizably modern—modern in the sense that the Model-T Ford, primitive though it may appear alongside one of the chrome-plated monsters of the present day, nonetheless symbolizes the beginning of a radically new era in transportation. These needs were created because the United States was already a republic with broadly based suffrage, voters who had to be mobilized, won, persuaded, held firm. Thus there was an obvious need for party organization not only in the Congress but throughout the country, in every state and in every locality: to make nominations for numberless public offices from U.S. senator to dog catcher, to skirmish in a variety of elected legislative bodies, to carry on the never-ending series of electoral campaigns, to mobilize voters. To intelligent and ambitious men who not only clearly perceived but enthusiastically embraced the institutions of a democratic republic—as many old Federalists were unable or unwilling to do— these needs were palpable, the means perhaps less obvious but by no means obscure to the eager and discerning eye. And so by the end of Jefferson's two terms in office, the major parts of the modern machinery of the American party system had been invented.

Some of the instructions issued in 1805 to party workers by Alexander Wolcott, the Connecticut "State-manager" (as he signed himself) of the Republican party, would still be appropriate today:

> . . . I ask you . . . to appoint in each town of your county, an active, influential, republican manager. . . .
> The duties of a TOWN-MANAGER will be,
> 1st. To appoint a district manager in each district or section of his town, obtaining from each an assurance that he will faithfully do his duty.
> 2d. To copy from the list of his town the names of all male inhabitants, who are taxed.
> 3d. To call together his district managers, and with their assistance to ascertain,
> 1st. The whole number of males, who are taxed [i.e., eligible to become voters],
> 2d. How many of the whole number are freemen [i.e., voters],
> 3d. How many of the freemen [voters] are decided republicans.
> 4th. How many — — — decided federalists.
> 5th. How many — — — doubtful.
> 6th. How many republicans who are not freemen, but who may be qualified [to vote] at the next proxies.

Wolcott went on with further instructions that would cheer the heart of any party leader today.[16]

Where the Republicans moved with amazing speed to construct the

___

16. The document is in Cunningham, *Making of the American Party System*, pp. 115–118.

required machinery, the Federalists held back; their organization never came close to matching that of their opponents. Their lingering predilection for an aristocratic republic seems to have blinded them to their true place in a more democratic republic, clouded their understanding of their real prospects, and thus perhaps contributed to their neglect of party machinery. In any case, this neglect was probably one cause of their decline.[17]

As Federalism began to disappear and the Republicans commanded ever wider support, the machinery of party was allowed to decay. But it never was totally lost, nor was the memory of it. There was no need to invent the political party a second time. During Jackson's presidency, party machinery was quickly rebuilt. And it has endured ever since.

SUMMARY 1. Modern democratic theory assigns a central role to conflict and competition among rival political parties. Yet the centrality of parties was not foreseen by the Founders and even today many Americans question the legitimacy of party conflict.

2. The Founders' lack of provision for political parties might be explained by

☐ Their fear of the destructive effects of faction.
☐ The absence of organized political parties in earlier republics and their primitive development in eighteenth-century Britain.

3. Whatever their specific intentions, however, the Founders made political parties both *possible* and *inevitable.* The Bill of Rights guaranteed the legality of parties, and thus insured their possibility. The need to win elections and marshal legislative majorities made parties inevitable.

4. After an initial period of Federalist hostility to parties and organized opposition culminating in the Alien and Sedition Acts in 1798, the victory of the Republican party, organized and led by Jefferson and Madison, secured the acceptability of political parties in the American polyarchy.

5. In order to gain the votes in Congress and among the electorate needed for its policies, the Republican party began to develop most of the features that have characterized political parties in the American polarchy ever since.

---

17. Shaw Livermore, Jr., *The Twilight of Federalism, The Disintegration of the Federalist Party* 1815–1830 (Princeton: Princeton University Press, 1962), pp. 8–9, 29–30.

Eight Characteristics of
The American Party System

The party systems of modern polyarchies are of great variety and complexity. Because the party system of each country is a particular combination of characteristics, every country can make a passable claim to the uniqueness of its party system. Among the polyarchies of the present day, multi-party systems are the most numerous; yet even they differ greatly. Only a few countries have followed the British two-party model; Britain herself does not always adhere to it, for sometimes a third party plays a critical role in British politics. The American version of the two-party model has not yet been precisely copied in any other polyarchy.

Although one of the two contemporary parties did not emerge until the 1850s, the American party system took pretty much its present shape before the end of Jackson's presidency. What makes that party system distinctive is its combination of eight characteristics.

A TWO-PARTY SYSTEM
The first and most obvious characteristic of the American party system is the fact that national elective offices—the presidency and the Congress—are monopolized by two parties. In no other large polyarchy (and only a few smaller ones) do third parties have so slight a representation in national politics as in the United States. Since 1860 every presidential election has been won by either a Democrat or a Republican; in only four presidential elections during that period has a third party ever carried a single state. In American politics, rapid growth in third-party votes is a sure sign of a deviant state of affairs, as in 1860 when the opposition to Lincoln was divided among three candidates, in 1892 when the Populist party was the vehicle of widespread discontent among farmers and urban workers, in 1912 when Theodore Roosevelt split the

Table 19.1
Third Party Seats Won
in Elections to Congress,
1862-1970

Seats	Elections	
	House	Senate
None	21	27
One	7	15
2-5	21	11
6-10	9	1
11-15	4	1
16-20	2	0
More than 20	0	0
Total elections	51	51

Source: *Congress and the Nation*. vol. 2, p. 26.

Republican party, in 1948 when the States' Rights party fought another losing skirmish in the long battle for white supremacy, or in 1968 when widespread unrest and discontent with Democratic and Republican leadership helped George Wallace to capture over 13 percent of the presidential vote. Since 1862, one of the two parties has always had a clear majority of seats in the House; in the Senate, independents or third-party members have prevented a clear majority during a total of ten years. The number of seats held by third-party members is almost always extremely low (Table 19.1).

Why Only Two Major Parties?

A moment ago, I offered some reasons why more than one party is likely to exist in a polyarchy. But, if the most frequent pattern is for polyarchies to have more than two important parties, why are there only two major parties in the United States?

Patterns of consensus and cleavage. Part of the explanation is to be found in the patterns of consensus and cleavage that ordinarily (though not always, as we shall see) characterize American political life. In earlier chapters we saw how a considerable measure of ideological convergence developed in the United States. As a result, comparatively few Americans disagree sharply on many essential matters that in other polyarchies help to create large followings for separate parties—separate Catholic parties in Italy and the Netherlands, for example, or separate Protestant parties in the Netherlands, or farmers' parties in the Scandinavian countries, or separate working-class parties throughout Europe. In addition, the normal pattern of crosscutting cleavages, which we shall examine in Chapter 22, facilitates the existence of two fairly comprehensive catchall parties that manage to find a place for practically every active interest.

Electoral mechanics. In the second place, electoral mechanics have an impact. It hardly seems open to question that the introduction of any of the common systems of proportional representation for the election of representatives to Congress would encourage splits in the major parties and serious competition from additional parties. Systems of proportional representation under which a party's share of seats in the legislative body is approximately equal to its share of votes in the country are used in most European polyarchies and contribute to (even if they do not completely explain) the existence of three or more sizeable parties.

In the United States, congressmen and senators, like M.P.'s in Britain, are elected in districts (or states) under the principle of winner-take-all. Notice how the two systems—proportional representation (PR) and winner-take-all—bear on the calculations of voters and politicians. Under PR, voters and politicians can be sure that the proportion of seats won by a party will be very nearly the same as the party's nationwide share of votes. Consequently, under PR, voters know that they will not throw away their vote by voting for a minority party; and leaders of minority parties do not have much of an incentive to consolidate with other parties in order to win elections. Under the winner-take-all system, on the other hand, the share of seats a party wins ordinarily varies a good deal from its share of votes. It is easy to see why: if the voters for all the parties were spread evenly throughout the country, the largest party would win *all* the seats. Fortunately, party support is, in fact, unevenly distributed around the country; a second party can therefore win victories in districts or regions where its votes are heavily concentrated. But the general effect—let us call it the snowballing effect—is to reward the winning party with a larger share of seats than votes, and to penalize the second party by awarding it a share of seats smaller than its share of votes.

These tendencies are clearly revealed in a 1971 study by Tufte and Ashenfelter.[1] In Figure 19.1 the percentage of the total popular votes received by Democratic candidates for the House in all elections from 1900 to 1970 is plotted against the percentage of total House seats won by Democrats. The dotted line shows what the relationship would be if the percentage of seats won by a party was equal to the percentage of total votes gained by that party; 40 percent of the votes would give a party 40 percent of the seats, and so on. The actual line fitted to the results of the congressional elections since 1900 departs drastically from the line of equality. Thus when Democrats poll less than about 45 percent of the popular vote they tend to lose a disproportionate share of the seats; at 40 percent of the popular votes, for example, they tend

1. Edward R. Tufte and Orley C. Ashenfelter, "The Relationship between Seats and Votes in Two-Party Systems," forthcoming.

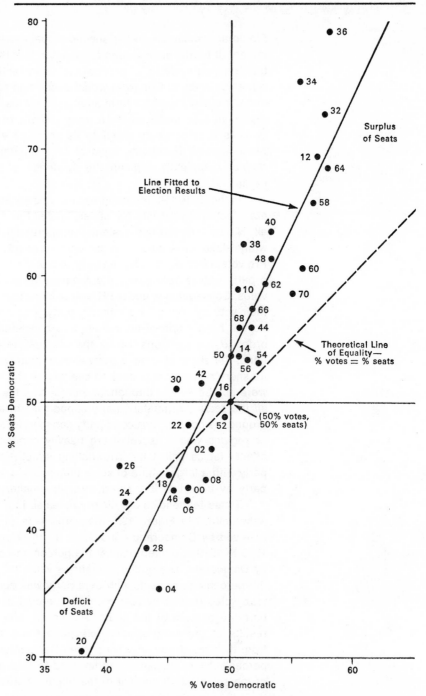

Figure 19.1
Relation between Seats
and Votes, U. S. House
of Representatives,
1900-70

Source: Tufte and Ashenfelter, "Relationship Between Seats and Votes."
Notes: The date of each election is shown beside the dot. The equation of the fitted line is:
% Seats Democratic = 2.09% Votes Democratic − 50.66. r^2 = 0.87. Standard error of slope = 0.14.

to win about 33 percent of the seats. On the other hand, when Democrats exceed about 45 percent of the popular vote, they profit disproportionately in seats; for example with 55 percent of the popular vote, they tend to win about two-thirds of the seats.

You will notice in Figure 19.1 that the Republicans have been disproportionately underrepresented whenever they have received a minority of popular votes—which, as it happens, has been most of the time since 1930. As the majority party, on the other hand, the Democrats have been disproportionately overrepresented in the House. Both effects—under- and overrepresentation—are more exaggerated the greater the percentage of the popular vote won by the Democrats. In fact, apportionment and Democratic dominance in the South seem to have provided the Democrats with a systematic advantage; throughout most of this century they have been in a position to win 50 percent of the seats with less than 50 percent of the votes.

For a third party, the effects of the winner-take-all system are devastating. Although a small percentage of Americans vote for third-party candidates in nearly every election, they often gain no seats at all and never win anything like a proportionate number (Figure 19.2). In the election of 1920, for example, the third-party candidates for the House won 1.4 million votes, or 5.6 percent of the total, and acquired exactly one seat out of 435, or slightly more than one-fifth of one percent!

The same principle operates in Senate elections. So, too, in presidential elections; because all the electoral votes of a state go to the presidential candidate with the largest share of popular votes in that state, the snowballing effect in presidential elections is even more visible. Because the presidency is the most strategic post in the entire political system, and because it is completely indivisible, in a presidential contest the winner does indeed take all and leaves no crumbs to the loser. Consider what happens, then, in an election like that of 1912 when Taft and Theodore Roosevelt split the Republicans asunder. Taft won 23 percent of the popular votes but only 1.5 percent of the electoral votes; Theodore Roosevelt won 27 percent of the popular votes and only 16.5 percent of the electoral votes; while the victor, Woodrow Wilson, gained 82 percent of the electoral votes by winning forty out of forty-eight states —yet he had only 42 percent, less than a majority, of the popular votes. To a politician, the instructions contained in this kind of election are unambiguous: If you want to win a presidential election, don't split your party; don't back a third party; concentrate instead on building up the largest possible coalition of interests, no matter how heterogeneous, in support of the candidate of one of the two major parties.

Party loyalties. A third reason why two parties, not three or more, monopolize national politics is the force of habit and tradition. The two

Figure 19.2
Third Parties: Votes and
Seats, U. S. House of
Representatives, 1920-68

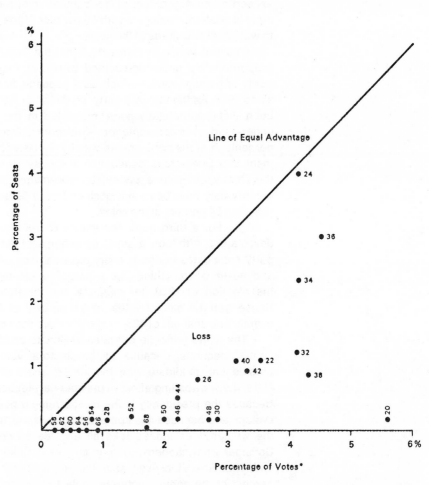

* Reporting of third-party votes is subject to considerable error. Different sources frequently disagree on totals.

Sources: 1920 to 1956: *Historical Statistics*; 1956 to 1962: *Congressional District Data Book* (Washington, D.C.: Government Printing Office, 1963); 1964 to 1968: *Statistical Abstract 1970*.

parties have been dominant for a century; the invariable fate of third parties is to be overwhelmingly defeated and often to disappear after one election. Many people acquire their basic political orientations and loyalties early, when they are still strongly under the influence of parents and family. This is true also of attitudes toward the parties; hence party loyalties tend to be transmitted from parents to children. The mere fact then that the Republican and Democratic parties monopolize votes during one generation makes it very much easier for them to monopolize votes during the next generation. To break out of a minority position on the other hand, a third party must overcome the enormous inertia of habit.

VARIABILITY OF EFFECTIVE COMPETITION The second characteristic of the American system is that the degree of effective competition between the two parties varies greatly throughout the country and, in general, declines with the size of the unit. As we saw in Chapter 17, many towns and cities lack effective two-party competition either because party support is overwhelmingly one-sided or because the functions of parties have been curtailed by nonpartisan elections— or both. Party competition is likely to be closer at the state level, as we saw; yet only about half the states can be regarded as having two-party systems. At the national level, however, the parties compete on a more even basis. To be sure, during long periods, one of the two parties may win the presidency much more often than the other: the Republicans from 1896 to 1932, the Democrats from 1932 to 1952. But measured by the proportion of congressional seats and votes in presidential and congressional elections, neither party manages to hold a big lead for very long.

The degree of party competition also changes over time (Figure 19.3). A two-party system virtually vanished as the Federalists died out. During and after Jackson's presidency, a new two-party system emerged. In fact, under this "second American party system," as one writer has called it, "the two new parties were balanced and competitive in every region. For a very brief period—between 1840 and 1852—the nation, for the only time in its history, had two parties that were both truly national in scope."[2] The disintegration of the Whigs, the rise of the Republicans as a strictly non-Southern party, which it has remained until recently, the creation of the one-party South—all led to a decline in two-party competition. Since about 1946, however, there has been rising competition between the two parties, with the Democrats increasing in strength in upper New England and the Midwest, and the Republicans growing throughout the South.

DIFFUSION AND DECENTRALIZATION OF CONTROL Third, control over nominations and the policies of the parties is diffused; in many cases control is decentralized to state and local organizations. This is not to say that the parties are democratically controlled, for they are not; but neither is control as tightly centralized in the hands

2. McCormick, *The Second American Party System*, p. 14.

Figure 19.3
Presidential Elections,
1864-1968: Percentage of
Total Popular Votes Cast
for Democratic, Republican,
and Third-Party
Presidential Candidates

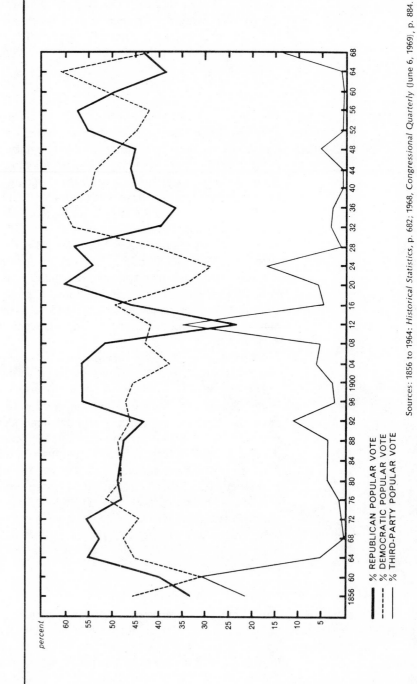

% REPUBLICAN POPULAR VOTE
% DEMOCRATIC POPULAR VOTE
% THIRD-PARTY POPULAR VOTE

Sources: 1856 to 1964: Historical Statistics, p. 682; 1968, Congressional Quarterly (June 6, 1969), p. 884.

of a single set of leaders as in many parties in other polyarchies.

Even in the presidential nominating convention, one of the few methods by which American national parties act collectively, control is generally diffuse. Except for the party of a president at the end of his first term—when it is about as certain as anything can be in American politics that the president will completely dominate the convention that nominates him—control over a convention is usually spread so thin and the outcome so uncertain that millions of Americans, including the best informed ones in the midst of the convention, continue to speculate about the outcome of the winning ballot. Senatorial nominations are decentralized to state organizations; nominations of congressmen to state and district organizations. Control over nominations of state and local officials is, of course, highly decentralized. And within states and localities, control is still further diffused by the direct primary.

Much the same diffusion and decentralization applies to policies; the incumbent president can largely determine presidential policy, and that, as we have seen, is a good deal; but control over the policies and votes of his party colleagues in Congress is comparatively modest—and in the states and localities negligible.

Causes

Why is control over party nominations and policies much more diffused and decentralized in the United States than in some of the important parties in other democracies?

Federalism. The most potent factor is probably the sheer force of federalism. Federalism insures that the states and localities are in a great many respects autonomous, independent of direct control by national officials. Strong state and local political organizations can be built without federal patronage or largesse and can survive electoral defeat at the national level; the innumerable nominations for state and local office, the never-ending cycle of state and local elections make it very much easier for the men on the spot to exert control than for national officials to do so. In addition, most of the laws controlling nominations, elections, party organization, and party finance, all highly strategic matters for party leaders, are passed and enforced by state governments.

Urban machines. Another factor of considerable historical importance is the weight that urban machines have had within the two parties, particularly the Democratic party.

Attitudes. Then, too, traditional American political attitudes, as we have seen, seem to endorse diffusion and decentralization of power in all of our political institutions; it should not be too surprising if these attitudes carry over into the political parties. Among Americans, centralized parties seem to lack the legitimacy that they have in countries like Britain and Sweden, with ancient and strong traditions of hierarchy and centralization.

Institutionalism. Finally, the past weighs heavily on the future simply because diffusion and decentralization of party control are thoroughly institutionalized. A party leader who sought to centralize control over nominations and policy would be throwing out a clear-cut challenge to thousands of party leaders whose power would thereby be diminished. Since men rarely yield power cheerfully, any national leader who sought to gain more control over his party would stir up fierce opposition from state and local leaders in the entrenched strongholds of party power throughout the length and breadth of the country. Diffused as it is, the individual power of these local leaders is not great on the national scene; united, they would be an awesome force. Knowing in advance that the most likely outcome would be their own disastrous defeat, national leaders never lay down the challenge.

LOW COHESION   Fourth, much the same factors that operate to prevent centralization of control in the parties also inhibit the development of parties that are highly united in support of particular policies. The most visible evidence of unity in a party is the extent to which members of a party vote the same way when they are confronted by bills and other measures in a legislature. If all the members of a party in a legislature always voted the same way, a party would of course display complete unity. In a two-party system, if each of the parties were perfectly unified, then on every legislative question over which the parties disagreed all the members of one party would vote one way while all the members of the other party would vote against them. Because total party unity is unusual, some studies of party cohesion define a 'party vote' in a two-party system as one in which 90 percent of the one party votes for and 90 percent of the other against a question. Comparative studies using this measure show that while British and American parties may have been about equally low in cohesion in the nineteenth century,[3] in this century British parties display far greater unity in voting in the House of Commons than do our parties in the Congress (specifically the House).

High cohesion in the national legislature is not uncommon among the larger parties in many other polyarchies. To this extent the relatively low cohesiveness displayed by American parties is something of an

3. A. Lawrence Lowell, "The Influence of Party upon Legislation in England and America," *Annual Report of the American Historical Association for 1901*, 2 vols. (Washington, 1902), vol. 1, pp. 321–544.

anomaly, and—despite the beliefs of many Americans—not inherent in a 'democratic' political system.

A word of caution is needed, however. Party unity is very far from being a negligible factor in the Congress. None of the other lines of cleavage in Congress—metropolitan-rural, North-South, liberal-conservative—seem to predict as well as party the way members will divide over a number of different issues and sessions. Thus the author of one statistical study of the question concluded that

> quantitative analysis of roll call votes shows, contrary to majority opinion, that significant differences exist between our major parties. While it is true that American discipline falls short of that achieved in some European democracies, and is less effective than party discipline in the McKinley era in the United States, evidence of great party influence can still be found. Party pressure seems to be more effective than any other pressure on Congressional voting, and is discernible on nearly nine-tenths of the roll calls examined.[4]

And in some state legislatures—Connecticut, for example—the parties are about as cohesive as in any European parliament.[5]

IDEOLOGICAL SIMILARITY AND ISSUE CONFLICT

Fifth, although the parties frequently differ on specific issues, they are not markedly different in ideology. This does not mean, as is sometimes said, that American parties advocate no ideology at all. They do. But unlike parties in many European countries, both Republicans and Democrats in the United States advocate much the same ideology. Both parties express a commitment to democracy, to the Constitution, and to the key social and economic institutions of American life: privately owned business firms, universal free public education, separation of church and state, religious toleration, and the like. To a European accustomed to the sound and fury of clashing ideologies, American party battles seem tame and uninteresting.

Differences in Rhetoric

In this case likeness is not identity, however. To a Buddhist the differences between Baptists and Episcopalians might seem negligible—but they are not so negligible to Baptists and Episcopalians. Although Republicans and Democrats profess to worship the same gods and endorse the same commandments, the rhetoric employed by the leaders of the two parties tends to announce different emphasis. These differences in emphasis vary over time. To generalize from recent decades, one might say that where Democratic rhetoric emphasizes the equality

---

4. Julius Turner, *Party and Constituency: Pressure on Congress* (Baltimore: Johns Hopkins Press, 1951), p. 23.

5. Cf. Duane Lockard, *New England State Politics* (Princeton: Princeton University Press, 1959), p. 279.

of Americans in dignity, respect, and rights, Republican rhetoric emphasizes their liberties and differences in capacities; where Democratic rhetoric extolls the accomplishments of the federal government, Republican rhetoric extolls the benefits of action through state and local governments; where Democratic rhetoric emphasizes the virtues and possibilities of public action through government, Republican rhetoric emphasizes the virtues of business enterprise; where 'regulation of business' is often portrayed as desirable in Democratic rhetoric it is more often portrayed as evil in Republican rhetoric; where Democratic rhetoric declaims the needs and aspirations of the less well off—the poor, the underprivileged, the culturally deprived, the aged—Republican rhetoric declaims the needs and aspirations of the solid and successful strata. (Both, of course, unendingly praise the virtues of the average man, the middle class, the middle-of-the-road, the taxpayer, the American way.)

Similarities in Ideology

Despite differences like these in nuance and emphasis, the ideological commitments of leaders in both parties are usually so much alike that opponents find it tempting to distinguish themselves ideologically from one another by gross exaggerations, caricatures, and downright falsehoods typical of many American campaigns. Because it provided a firmer basis than usual for ideological distinctions, the 1964 presidential campaign was something of a deviant case. The Republican candidate, Senator Goldwater, unashamedly professed an extremely 'conservative' ideology that was intended to be, and was, at odds with the 'liberal' or 'liberal-conservative' ideology that most Republican and Democratic spokesmen had espoused for several decades. Even so the senator's 'conservatism' was scarcely distinguishable from the prevailing ideology of both parties in the nineteenth century; and 'conservatives' found it difficult to formulate a coherent expression of abstract ideology that did not simply restate platitudes long since incorporated into the rhetoric of both parties.

Differences in Policies

The most marked difference between the parties is not in their ideologies but in their programs and policies. The differences are often much greater than a mere examination of rhetoric would lead one to expect—greater sometimes, in fact, than the difference between European parties that substitute rhetoric for concrete programs. It is very far from being the case that the parties adopt identical platforms at their national conventions. And although American parties are not as cohesive as parties often are in other countries, on many issues Democrats and Republicans divide quite sharply. The content of party conflict changes from one historical period to the next; but in every generation there are persistently divisive issues that distinguish Democrats and Republicans. Thus, in a study of the four sessions of 1921, 1931, 1937, and 1944, it was found that Democrats and Republicans in the House disagreed markedly on measures pertaining to tariff; patronage; government (as opposed to private) action on electric power, crop insurance, and other matters; the size of the federal bureaucracy; public works; social, welfare, and labor matters; and farm policy.[6]

When the president lines up on one side and the leaders of the opposition party on the other, the chances are particularly good that a high proportion of Democrats will vote one way and Republicans another. From 1961 to 1968, for example, the Democrats in the House and Senate gave much more support to the measures of the Democratic administration than did the Republicans. After the election of a Republican president in 1968, naturally Republicans in House and Senate gave the president more support than the Democrats (Figure 19.4).

Causes

The explanation for this combination of ideological similarity and conflict over issues goes to the very heart of the American political system. An overwhelming proportion of American voters do not sharply divide on norms that in other countries generate followings for ideologically divergent parties. A party that preaches anti-democratic doctrines, revolutionary aims, hostility to the Constitution or constitutional processes, religious, racial, or ethnic conflict, the repression or favoring of a particular religion, or nationalization of the means of production at best appeals to a small part of the electorate. The two major parties do not diverge very much ideologically; and the major parties direct their appeal to the great bulk of the electorate. For reasons we have already explored, the effect of the election machinery is to reduce even further the prospect of success for an ideologically divergent party. Hence, paradoxically, party conflict in campaigns, elections, and policy-making constantly reinforces the prevailing ideology and weakens the impact of political movements with rival ideologies. A similarity of ideological perspectives among most Americans has insured the success of ideologically similar parties; and the domination of American politics by ideologically similar parties has in turn reinforced the similarity of ideological perspectives among the American people.

Yet, because these ideological perspectives are not identical but vary in strength, emphasis, and to some extent even in content, they allow

6. The difference between the percentage of Democrats and the percentage of Republicans who voted for a given measure on a roll call was on the average more than 50 percent. On tariff measures, the average difference was almost 80 percent (Turner, *Party and Constituency*, pp. 36–38).

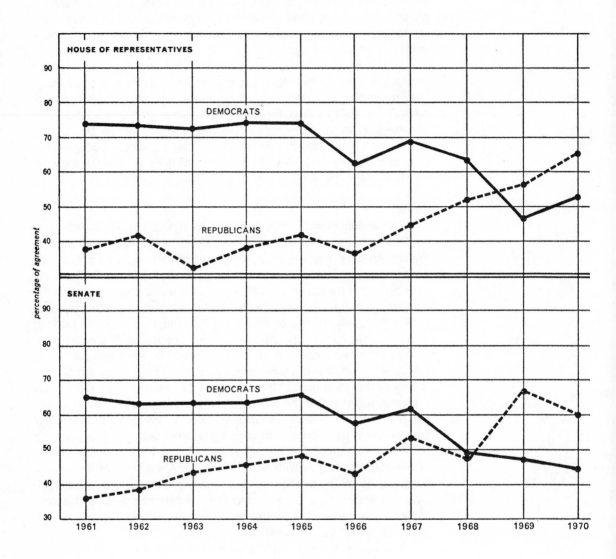

Figure 19.4
Presidential Support
Scores, 1961-70

Source: Presidential Support Scores from The Congressional Quarterly Service. Number of roll calls used to determine presidential support scores were: for House: 1961, 65; 1962, 60; 1963, 71; 1964, 52; 1965, 112; 1966, 103; 1967, 127; 1968, 103; 1969, 47; 1970, 65. For Senate: 1961, 124; 1962, 125; 1963, 115; 1964, 97; 1965, 162; 1966, 125; 1967, 165; 1968, 164; 1969, 72; 1970, 91.

for considerable—at times extensive—divergence on matters of policy. The strategy of the parties, then, is to seek support among voters not only by proclaiming their own ideological purity and the horrendous deviation of the other party from ideological orthodoxy, but also by advocating policies they expect to appeal to voters. But, it might be asked, if both parties want to win the largest number of votes, why don't they both advocate the same policies? Often, of course, they do. But there are several important reasons why they do not. For one thing, like other people politicians also lack perfect information about voters' attitudes; in the absence of perfect information there is considerable uncertainty as to what strategy will have the greatest appeal and will maximize votes in the coming election. Like other people, politicians fill in areas of ignorance by making guesses. And, like other people, the hunches of politicians are shaped by their own experiences, prejudices, wishes, and fantasies; by the views of people on whom they depend for information and advice; by their conceptions of what their most loyal and deserving supporters actually want; and even by their views as to what is 'best for the country.'

DIFFERENCES IN PARTY FOLLOWINGS

The sixth characteristic of American parties has a double aspect: (1) With few exceptions, each of the parties draws votes in significant numbers from every stratum of the population; but (2) many strata consistently vote more heavily for one party than the other. In general, then, neither party has a monopoly of the votes within any category of Americans. Yet the hard core of undeviating supporters for each party is located in different strata. Nothing is static, of course, including the composition of party followings. But the hard core of each party is particularly slow to change.

Figure 19.5 displays some of the important differences in the way people in different groups voted in presidential elections in the 1950s and 1960s. The groups most favorable to the Republicans were people of higher incomes and social status, with college educations and professional and managerial occupations, people in medium-sized towns and cities, and Protestants. Groups most favorable to the Democrats were people of lower incomes and social status, with grade-school and high-school education, working in skilled or unskilled manual occupations, trade-union members and their families, residents of metropolitan areas, Catholics, and Negroes.

The followings, the policies, and the ideological emphases of each party usually reinforce one another. Democrats use rhetoric and advocate policies designed to appeal to their followers in working-class occupations and the big cities; Republicans use rhetoric and advocate policies designed to appeal to their followers in the business community and

Figure 19.5
The American Electorate,
1948-68: Percentage of
the Two-Party Vote Won
by Democratic Presidential
Candidates in Various
Categories of Voters

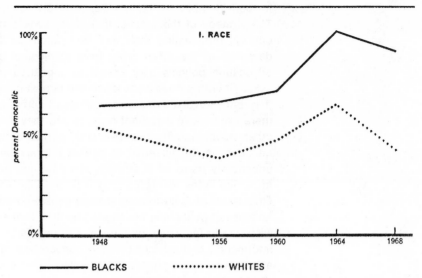

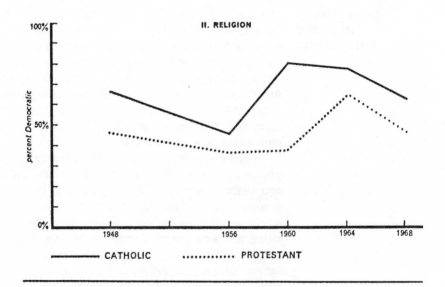

small towns. When the Democrats place more emphasis on equality and
the virtues of the underprivileged, and Republicans on opportunity and
the virtues of the more privileged, they are appealing to their respective
hard cores of loyal followers. Yet neither party wishes to ignore potential
votes in other social strata; hence each party designs its rhetoric and its

Figure 19.5
(Continued)

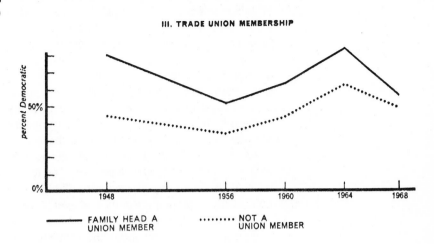

III. TRADE UNION MEMBERSHIP

——— FAMILY HEAD A   ········· NOT A
      UNION MEMBER   UNION MEMBER

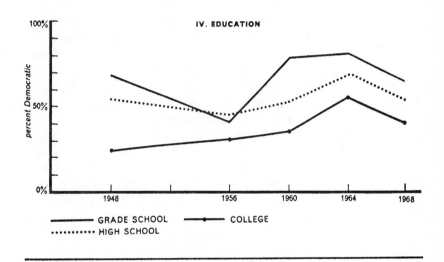

IV. EDUCATION

——— GRADE SCHOOL   —●— COLLEGE
········· HIGH SCHOOL

program not only to retain the loyalty and enthusiasm of its hard core of zealous adherents but at the same time to win over less-committed voters in all the major categories of the population.

DURABILITY   The seventh characteristic of American parties is their extraordinary durability. The life of the Democratic party can be traced as far back as President Jackson in 1830 with no historical cavils; and a good claim can be made that the present party is the direct institutional descendant of Jefferson's party. The Republican party has contested every national election since 1856. The two parties have thus dominated national politics for a century. No other party system in the world is so old.[7]

Why have American parties endured so long? First, by assiduously seeking to advance and protect the interests of the social groups from which they draw their most dependable support, the parties retain a hard core of loyal followers even in greatest adversity. These social groups endure; their loyalty helps the parties to endure. For the Democrats, the two low points in this century were the presidential elections of 1920, when they received 34 percent of the popular votes, and 1924, when their share plummeted to 29 percent. The low points for the Republicans were 1936 (36.5 percent) and 1964 (38.5 percent). Thanks to their hard core of loyalists, neither party has ever come close to being wiped out.

Second, with an extraordinary number of people, party loyalties are acquired early in life, under the influence of family and friends, and thereafter remain unaltered except under the impact of a major trauma like the Great Depression. Third, the parties have been skillful enough to adjust their programs and even their rhetoric to changing times and popular attitudes, though ever since the 1930s the Republicans have found it difficult to adapt to the transformations brought on by the Depression and the New Deal. Combined with all of these factors, the electoral system and the ideological cohesion of the great bulk of the electorate have, as we saw earlier, made it exceptionally difficult—in fact, impossible so far—for a third party to win over enough voters to displace either of the two major parties.

Yet despite the extraordinary durability of the two major parties and the historic inability of third parties to make much headway in the American polyarchy, the turbulence that marked American political life from the mid-1960s onward was accompanied by a measure of disenchantment with both the parties (Figure 19.6).

This was reflected not only in the unexpected degree of support for the insurgency of Senator McCarthy in the 1968 presidential primaries and at the Democratic nominating convention but also in the extent of the defection of voters from the regular party candidates to George Wallace.[8] As the decade ended, some students of American politics had begun to entertain serious doubts that the two parties so long dominant in American political life would remain so much longer.[9]

---

7. In Britain, the Conservatives trace their lineage back to the late eighteenth-century Tories led by the younger Pitt; the Liberals to the Whigs led by Charles James Fox; but Labour dates back only to 1905.

8. Compare Seymour Martin Lipset and Earl Raab, "The Wallace Whitelash," *Trans-action,* 7 (December, 1969), 23–25.

9. Walter Dean Burnham, "The End of American Party Politics," *Trans-action,* 7 (December, 1969), 12–22; and Frederick G. Dutton, *Changing Sources of Power: American Politics in the 1970s* (New York: McGraw-Hill, 1971).

Figure 19.6
The Decline of Party
Loyalty, 1956-66

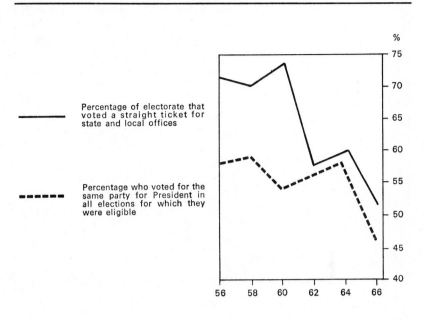

Percentage of electorate that
voted a straight ticket for
state and local offices

Percentage who voted for the
same party for President in
all elections for which they
were eligible

Source: Burnham, ''End of American Party Politics,'' p. 13.

**VARIABILITY IN
PARTY SUPPORT**

Whether the recent difficulties of the parties in maintaining their support
are the beginning of a long-run decline or will turn out to be a short-run
change is hard to predict because of one other characteristic of American parties, probably the most obvious and in some ways the most important: the extent to which each of the parties is effective in winning
loyalty and support does vary markedly over time. The history of American
parties shows how rapidly the electoral fortunes of a party may change.
No politician is likely to forget this lesson. As a consequence the typical
party politician works zealously to discover what voters want. When he
knows or thinks he knows what voters want, he tries to shape the political
strategies of his party in order to win their votes on election day.

Two types of elections. In a loose way, American national elections—
or, more precisely, a brief series of several elections—can be classified into two broad categories: maintaining elections and realigning
elections.[10]

_____
10. The following discussion draws on V. O. Key, Jr., ''A Theory of Critical Elections,''
Journal of Politics, 17 (February, 1955), 3–18; Campbell et al., *The American Voter,* pp. 531 ff.;
Angus Campbell, ''Voters and Elections: Past and Present,'' *Journal of Politics,* 26 (November,
1964), 745–757; Angus Campbell, ''Surge and Decline: A Study of Electoral Change,'' ''A Classification of the Presidential Elections,'' and Campbell et al., ''Stability and Change in 1960: A
Reinstating Election,'' ch. 5, pp. 78–95, all in Campbell et al., *Elections and the Political Order.*

Maintaining elections are normal; realigning elections are abnormal. Maintaining elections seem to occur during periods of moderate conflict; realigning elections are more likely during periods of severe conflict. The most important realigning elections in American history were probably these: 1796–1800, 1856–1860, 1892–1896, and 1932–1936.

Maintaining Elections

In maintaining elections, preexisting party loyalties predominate. The great bulk of the electorate consists of people who identify themselves with one of the two major parties. Between elections and during the campaigns their party loyalties are not severely strained. They perceive no serious conflict between their habitual loyalty to a party, and the candidates, policies, programs, and actions of that party. Their loyalty and the absence of highly divisive issues within the party tend in fact to soften or eliminate their perceptions of differences between themselves and their party.

Maintaining elections, then, are stabilizing elections. They reflect and even reinforce party loyalties and perpetuate preexisting voting patterns in the electorate with only small changes. In a series of maintaining elections, the parties may be quite evenly matched or one party may have a significant advantage. In the first situation, a small change in the electorate may reduce the previous majority to a minority. All the national elections from 1874 to 1894 were maintaining elections, but the elections were remarkably close. In 1880, the Republican presidential candidate (Garfield) won with a plurality less than 40,000 votes; in 1884, the Democrat (Cleveland) won with a plurality less than 30,000 votes. In eight out of the ten congressional elections, the Democrats gained a majority in the House; in only two elections did they gain a majority in the Senate.

Where one party acquires a significant advantage, as the Republicans did from 1896 to 1932, the other party loses more or less regularly. Until there is a major realignment in voters' loyalties, the minority party is likely to win the presidency only if there is a split in the majority party as in 1912 when Wilson won the presidency with 42 percent of the popular vote, or if they have the good fortune to nominate a candidate of extraordinary popularity, like General Eisenhower in 1952 and 1956, who manages to win votes for *himself* even though he cannot win voters for his *party*.

Changes: long run versus short run. As these examples suggest, even during a long series of maintaining elections, political attitudes and loyalties are never completely frozen. Even maintaining elections may reflect changes of four kinds:

☐ Slow, *long-run shifts* may occur throughout practically the *entire electorate,* as in the period 1896–1928 when there seems to have been a long-run shift toward the Republicans throughout the North, or from 1936 to 1964 when a massive glacial shift toward the Democrats took place.

☐ Superimposed on the slow, secular shifts in the electorate as a whole, *long-run changes* also take place within *specific groups* at much slower or faster rates; for example from 1936 to 1964, the proportion of Negroes voting Democratic increased much more rapidly than among any other group.

☐ *Short-run fluctuations* usually occur from presidential to midterm congressional elections; typically there is a drop-off in the percentage of the vote cast for candidates of the president's party.

☐ *Short-run surges* may also occur in presidential elections, as in 1952 and 1956 when, despite the long-run increase in the percentage of voters who identified themselves with the Democrats, General Eisenhower nonetheless won enormous personal victories.

Explanation of short-run changes. The best explanation for these last two short-run changes has been furnished by Angus Campbell.[11] His explanation rests upon four characteristics of elections:

1. The size of the turnout in national elections depends on a combination of intrinsic political interest and the impact of short-term political forces. People with a high level of intrinsic interest vote in most or all national elections; people with little intrinsic interest vote only when additionally stimulated by impelling short-term forces. The weaker the total impact of the short-term forces, the smaller will be the total turnout.

2. The smaller the turnout in a national election, the greater the proportion of the vote which is contributed by people of established party loyalties and the more closely the partisan division of the vote will approach the basic underlying division of standing commitments to the two parties, what Lord Bryce referred to years ago as the "normal voting strength."

3. The larger the turnout, the greater the proportion of the vote which is made up of marginal voters, people who have relatively weak party identification, relatively little intrinsic political interest, and relatively little political information.

4. If the sum of the short-term forces is approximately balanced in its partisan impact, the total vote will not vary from the vote division to be expected from the underlying "normal party strength." If the sum of the short-term forces favors one candidate-party alternative over the other it will swing the vote division toward that alternative, with the greatest movement occurring among the marginal voters. The greater the total impact of the short-term forces, the greater will be the potential deflection from the "normal party strength."[12]

---

11. Campbell, "Voters and Elections."
12. *Ibid.,* p. 748.

In presidential elections, turnout is invariably higher than in mid-term elections. This helps to explain both the midterm decline of the party in power and the occasional surge of votes toward one presidential candidate during periods of moderate conflict, when the shift clearly cannot be attributed to the destabilizing effects of severe conflict. Angus Campbell suggests

> . . . that the familiar off-year loss does not depend on an inevitable cooling of the public ardor for the President's party, although this undoubtedly occurs in particular years. It depends rather on a pattern of circulation of votes which is characteristic of presidential and off-year elections. In the relatively stimulating circumstances of a presidential election the turnout is high. As we have just noted, the regular voters whose intrinsic political interest is high enough to take them to the polls even under less stimulating conditions are joined by marginal voters who are less concerned with politics but may be activated if the stakes seem high. Ordinarily one of the two candidates standing for the presidency will be benefited by the political circumstances of the moment more clearly than the other, either because of embarrassments of the party in power, the personal qualities of the candidates, domestic or international conditions, or for other reasons. The advantaged candidate will draw to him the votes of a majority of the marginal voters, who have relatively little party attachment and are responsive to such short-term influences. He will also profit from some defections by regular voters from the opposition party who are sufficiently tempted to break away from their usual party vote at least temporarily. In moving toward the advantaged candidate both the regular and the marginal voters, especially the latter, tend to support both the candidate and his party ticket. In the off-year election which follows, two movements occur. The regular voters who moved across party lines to support a presidential candidate they preferred are likely to move back to their usual party vote when that candidate is no longer on the ticket. The marginal voters who had given the winning candidate a majority of their votes in the presidential election do not vote in the election which follows. Both of these movements hurt the party of the candidate who benefited from the votes of the two groups in the presidential election. The loss of congressional seats is the result.[13]

Thus a series of maintaining elections can be likened to a rather stable sand dune on the edge of the ocean in the absence of great storms. Occasional winds change the shape of the dune somewhat. A steady wind from one direction may gradually displace the center of the entire dune to the left or to the right. Not all parts of the dune change at the same rate. Nonetheless, its shape and position remain substantially unchanged from one year to the next.

Realigning Elections

A series of realigning elections is better symbolized by a sand dune subject to the pressure of a storm. Disorganized by the storm, its

---

13. *Ibid.*, pp. 750–751.

structure momentarily destroyed, it undergoes violent changes in form and position. After the storm, one who had long regarded it with affection might find it impossible to recognize the old dune.

In a series of realigning elections, then, the party loyalities of a great mass of voters are first torn loose and then reattached either to a new party or to the opposite party. After a series of realigning elections has run its course, party alignments are decisively different. The balance of support may be tilted significantly away from one party toward another. A party may even be destroyed. Severe political conflicts precede and accompany realigning elections. In times of severe conflict, the issues of politics are too visible to enable many voters to remain loyal to a party that holds a position in the conflict markedly different from their own.

Examples. The elections of 1796–1800 were realigning elections—though if we consider that the parties were still in their infancy, perhaps a more appropriate term would be *aligning* elections. In any case, conflicts disrupted the coalition that had made the Constitution, weakened the Federalists, and crystallized so much support for the Democratic-Republicans that after their victory in 1800 they were never defeated by the Federalists.

The elections of 1856–1860 were realigning elections. The Whigs disintegrated in the North. Northern Whigs, Free Soilers, and even many northern and border-state Democrats turned toward the Republican party. While Reconstruction temporarily created Republican governments in the South, as quickly as it was permitted to do so the South became the Solid South; and it remained so until the 1950s and 1960s.

The national elections from 1892 to 1896 were realigning elections. From 1876 to 1892, the Democrats and Republicans had been running neck-and-neck in presidential races. In four of these elections, the Democratic candidate had outpolled the Republican in popular votes; in the fifth (1880), the Republican, Garfield, had won with a margin of less than 10,000 votes over his Democratic rival—a difference of less than one-half of one percent of the total popular vote! In the late 1880s, agrarian discontent fanned into flame the most important third-party movement since the rise of the Republicans: the People's party. In 1896, Populists and Democrats jointly endorsed William Jennings Bryan as their candidate for president. But the Republicans, led by William McKinley, turned back the agrarian challenge. For the first time since 1872, the Republican candidate won a majority of popular votes. The Middle West, where the Democrats had developed strength, became a Republican stronghold. No Democratic candidate again won a majority of popular votes until Franklin Roosevelt's election of 1932; and except in 1912 and 1916, Democratic candidates lost by huge margins. From 1900 to 1932, the Democrats polled fewer votes than the Republicans in all congressional elections save three; not once did they win a majority of all popular votes.

The presidential elections from 1932 to 1936 were also realigning elections, for they marked a shift away from the Republican party toward the Democrats that continued for the next three decades. In the nine presidential elections from 1932 to 1964, the Republicans won only twice —with General Eisenhower in 1952 and 1956. In that thirty-four year period, Republicans had majorities in the House of Representatives for only four years. The extent to which deeper underlying tides were running against the Republican party was strikingly visible in the midst of its greatest triumph, the 'surge' election of 1956 in which General Eisenhower was swept into office by a crushing majority; for the second time since the election of 1876, the party that won the presidency did not win a majority of seats in the House.

For the past quarter century, the Gallup poll has been asking its samples: "In politics, as of today, do you consider yourself a Republican, Democrat, or Independent?" The responses reveal a steady shift away from the Republicans to the Democrats from 1940 to 1964. From 1964 onward, support for the Democrats, though still monumentally larger than that for Republicans, declined to about the levels of 1940–5 (Table 19.2).

SUMMARY The following combination of characteristics distinguishes the American party system from that in other polyarchies:

1. National elective offices—the presidency and the Congress— have been overwhelmingly monopolized by only two parties. Factors that tend to limit competing parties to two in the American polyarchy are:

☐ The normal pattern of moderately high consensus and crosscutting cleavages.
☐ The impact of a winner-take-all electoral system.
☐ The persistence of party loyalties.

2. The degree of effective competition between the two majorities varies greatly over time and throughout the country and, in general, declines with the size of the unit.

3. Control over nominations and policies is diffused. In many cases control is decentralized to state and local organizations. The principal causes of diffused and decentralized control are federalism, urban machines, American beliefs about partitioning power, and institutionalization.

4. Comparatively speaking, American parties are much less united in their support of particular policies than parties in many other polyarchies.

Table 19.2
"In politics as of today,
do you consider yourself
a Republican, Democrat,
or Independent?"

	Democrat	Republican	Independent
1940	42%	38%	20%
1950	45	33	22
1960	47	30	23
1964	53	25	22
1966 (June)	48	26	26
1968 (July)	46	27	27
1970	45	29	26

Sources: Figures for 1940-64, American Institute of Public Opinion, July 5, 1964; for 1966-70, Gallup Opinion Indices for months shown.

5. Moreover, although the parties frequently differ on specific issues, they are much less different in ideology than parties in most polyarchies.

6. With few exceptions each party draws votes in significant numbers from every stratum of the population. Many strata, however, consistently vote more heavily for one party than the other.

7. The two major parties have been of exceptional durability. They are, in fact, among some of the oldest political institutions existing anywhere. Recently, nonetheless, some observers have been raising doubts as to their continued survival.

8. The extent to which each party has been effective in winning loyalty and support has varied a great deal over time. Even during periods that leave the bare advantage with one of the parties, there are significant short-run fluctuations. In addition, from time to time major realignments take place when party loyalties are massively disrupted and large numbers of voters shift from one party to the other, thus shifting the longer-run balance of advantage to different coalitions of forces. Some observers believe that a period of realignment began in the late 1960s and may result in substantial, though as yet unforeseeable, alterations in the traditional two-party system.

The Performance of
Political Parties:
Contributions to Polyarchy

In the light of long experience, not only in the United States but in all other polyarchies, there is no longer much ground for doubting that political parties make substantial contributions to the operation of a polyarchy—at any rate to a polyarchy in a large country. To most democrats who reflect on the problem, the positive contributions of parties far outweigh their negative aspects. But in many polyarchies, not the least in the United States, the negative aspects stimulate a lively interest in the possibility of reforming the parties or the party system.

The principal contributions of parties, it might be suggested, are three:

☐ They facilitate popular control over elected officials.
☐ They help voters to make more rational choices.
☐ They help in the peaceful management of conflicts.

Yet each of these propositions must be qualified. To explore adequately the contributions and defects of parties, even American parties, would require a volume in itself. The essays, monographs, and full-scale books that appraise political parties and advance or criticize proposals for reform would form a sizeable library.

A brief discussion can nonetheless open up some of the major questions.

PARTIES AND POPULAR CONTROL One of the strongest claims made for political parties is that they assist the electorate in gaining some degree of control over elected officials and, thus, over the decisions of government.

Contributions

Aggregating individual preferences. For one thing, they carry on much of the organizing that makes a large-scale system of elections, representation, and legislation workable. The ambitions that induce party politicians to carry on these organizing tasks may repel democratic purists who would prefer motives closer to those invoked in the noble rhetoric with which men good and bad usually cloak their deepest purposes. Yet, whatever one may think of the motives of party politicians, these men (and women) perform some functions that are essential if polyarchy is not to dwindle into flatulent ineffectuality: nominations, for example. In the absence of concerted effort, an election in which a candidate satisfactory to a majority *might* have emerged victorious may be won instead by a candidate who is satisfactory only to a minority. Surely it is no virtue if a majority of like-minded voters are presented with three satisfactory candidates to run against a fourth candidate they agree is worse; for if they distribute their votes over the three they like, the fourth may win even though he be the most objectionable. Once like-minded voters see that it is worthwhile to organize themselves around a single candidate they have already acquiesced in the beginnings of a party.

Organizing opposition. The organization furnished by party is particularly necessary if an opposition is to exist. The dominant forces have somewhat less need of party organization; a president might, for example, operate with a sort of nonparty coalition. This is no doubt why party machinery fell into decay when opposition temporarily became merely an exercise in futility during the long death agonies of the Federalists and before the reappearance of new cleavages around which an opposition could form. When there was no opposition, there were no effective parties. One could also put it the other way round. When there is no party, there is not likely to be an effective opposition. To displace the incumbents, who have the resources of government at hand, an opposition needs to organize, focus its forces, keep up the pressure, draw in every possible ally—all of which spells party. It is, thus, no accident that in Europe it was usually the Labour or Socialist opposition parties that first developed modern party organization—during the lengthy period they dwelt in opposition before assuming office.

Preventing one-party dominance. Then, too, the sheer efficiency of party organization for winning political victories means that a single party, unchecked by another, would be a danger in a republic. One party needs to be counterbalanced by another. Let there either be no parties, or at least two parties, but never only one party, the citizens of a republic might well resolve. For if there is only one party, those among us who disagree with it will surely be outweighed, even though we be more numerous than our opponents. Since we cannot prevent at least one party from forming, lest by doing so we destroy our republican liberties, let there always be two parties or more. In this way we shall insure another kind of separation of powers and create additional checks and balances to sustain our liberties.

Pooling the resources of the many. A fourth way in which parties assist popular control is to enable the many to pool their resources to offset the advantages of the few. This is doubtless one reason why Federalists looked upon parties with less enthusiasm than did Republicans. The chief resources of the many are their numbers and their votes; unorganized and leaderless they are no match for smaller numbers with wealth, skills, information, and informal organizational networks. Even when parties are internally oligarchic, as they generally are, a party competing for the votes of the otherwise unorganized many gives them more power than they would have if there were no parties at all.

Tendencies toward Internal Oligarchy

Despite these contributions, parties have been subjected to a barrage of criticism on the ground that they are internally undemocratic and are ruled by oligarchies.[1] The charge is in considerable measure true. That the nominations and policies of political parties tend to be controlled by leaders, rather than the rank and file of members or registered supporters, seems undeniable. There is, as we saw, more decentralization and diffusion of control in the two American parties than in many European parties; even so, both the Democratic and Republican parties would be more accurately described as coalitions of oligarchies than as democratic organizations.

Nominations: from caucus to convention. Given the democratic ideology prevailing among Americans, it was to be expected that efforts would be made to 'democratize' control over nominations in American parties; these efforts have diffused power, but they have not by any means turned the parties into 'democratic' systems. As we saw, presidential candidates were first nominated by the Federalist and Republican caucuses in Congress. While the caucus continued to be used for several decades for presidential and vice-presidential nominations, an alternative system began to develop for nominating candidates to other offices, national,

1. Among the most famous and most influential criticisms of this kind were those of Moisei Ostrogorski, *Democracy and the Organization of Political Parties*, edited and abridged by S. M. Lipset, 2 vols. (Garden City: Anchor Books, 1964), first published in 1902; and Michels, *Political Parties*, in 1915. For an appraisal of Ostrogorski, see Austin Ranney, *The Doctrine of Responsible Party Government* (Urbana: University of Illinois Press, 1962). For a critique of Michels, see John D. May, "Democracy, Organization, Michels," *American Political Science Review, 59* (June, 1965), 417–429.

state, and local. This was the nominating *convention,* which, being a representative system, seemed more appropriate than the caucus to the spirit of democracy. The caucus fell into even worse repute because it sometimes dramatized for all to see the fact that nominations were made by unrepresentative cliques. One such episode, in 1824, killed the congressional caucus as a device for nominating presidential candidates. Of two hundred sixteen Republicans in Congress who were invited to attend the nominating caucus that year, only sixty-six attended. This small minority proceeded to nominate for president of the United States a minor league politician, W. H. Crawford. In the election Crawford ran well behind Andrew Jackson, who led the other candidates in popular and electoral votes, and also behind John Quincy Adams, who trailed Jackson but ultimately won the presidency when the House of Representatives had to decide the election. The convention made its first appearance for a presidential nomination in September, 1831, when the brief-lived Anti-Masonic party nominated candidates for president and vice-president at a convention in Baltimore. Henry Clay's National Republicans (soon to become the Whigs) followed suit in December, also in Baltimore. Jackson's followers, the Democratic Republicans, met in the same city in May, 1832, to nominate Jackson and Van Buren.[2] Ever since then, the national convention has been used for nominating presidential and vice-presidential candidates.

Although national nominating conventions are representative in form, probably no one who knows how they work would argue that they are very democratic. At most, the convention is a contest among coalitions of state and local party leaders. Because representative techniques seemed to have failed, advocates of democratic control over nominations turned to direct democracy: party members or supporters would themselves choose the candidate of their party. This was the direct primary.

Direct primary. Toward the end of the last century the convention began to be displaced by the direct primary, which is now almost universally employed for party nominations to executive offices other than the presidency and the vice-presidency. Yet even the direct primary has not democratized the parties—in part, of course, simply because most people do not participate in crucial day-to-day decisions or, for that matter, even in the primaries. In examining fifteen non-Southern states over the period 1932–52, the late V. O. Key discovered that "in three out of four primaries . . . the total Democratic primary vote plus the total Republican primary vote did not exceed 35% of the number of citizens 21 years of age or over. . . . At the extreme of high participation

---

2. These events are described in Ostrogorski, *Democracy and the Organization of Political Parties,* vol. 2, *The United States,* pp. 17–39.

in only one out of twelve primaries did more than 50% of the potential vote turn up at the polls."[3]

Internal Oligarchy and External Polyarchy

Running a party, like operating any other complex institution, is a full-time business; and as in other institutions, power tends to accrue to those who make it a full-time business. Consequently, neither American political parties nor those of any other country are likely to be very democratic in their internal operations. But how much does internal party democracy really matter? Political parties are sometimes likened to business firms competing for customers—the customers being in this case the voters. And just as business firms are driven by competition to satisfy consumers, even if they are *internally* not governed by consumers in the way that a consumers' cooperative is, so, it is sometimes argued, competitive parties will fulfill all of the essential functions of democratic control listed earlier, even though each party is internally controlled by its leaders.[4]

Seen from this perspective, the most important question is not who runs the parties but to whom are the parties responsive? To the leaders themselves, to the rank-and-file registered party member, or to the voters? If the main function of competing parties is to insure that the views of voters are translated into government policies, then it is less important that parties be internally democratic than that they be responsive to the views of the voters.

In actual practise, American parties seem to respond to all three forces: to the party leaders, to the rank-and-file, and to the voters. What happens if a party responds more to its leaders than to the voters? The answer seems obvious: It will probably be defeated in elections—if the other party is closer to the views of the electorate.

There is some interesting evidence bearing on this point. In 1957–8, three social scientists surveyed about half the delegates and alternates to preceding presidential nominating conventions and compared the views of these party 'leaders' with a national survey of voters. The results revealed that on five major categories of issues—public ownership of resources, government regulation of the economy, equality and welfare, taxes, and foreign policy—the differences in views were as follows:

☐ The greatest difference in views was between Democratic and Republican leaders.
☐ Almost equally great was the difference between Republican leaders and Democratic followers.

3. V. O. Key, Jr., *American State Politics: An Introduction* (New York: Knopf, 1956), p. 134.
4. An interesting and important theoretical analysis bearing on this subject will be found in Anthony Downs, *An Economic Theory of Democracy* (New York: Harper & Brothers, 1957).

- ☐ Democratic followers and Republican followers showed the slightest —and indeed often negligible—differences in their views.
- ☐ There were relatively small differences in views between Democratic leaders and Democratic followers.
- ☐ But—the most startling finding—the differences between Republican leaders and Republican followers were almost as great as the difference between Republican leaders and Democratic followers.
- ☐ And there was actually a greater difference between Republican leaders and Republican followers than between Democratic leaders and Republican followers![5]

What these findings strongly suggest, then, is that by the late 1950s the Republican leaders big and small around the country, the activists who exercise dominant influence over nominations and policy, no longer represented their Republican followers, nor—and this is even more important—did they represent the great bulk of the voters, Republicans or Democrats.

During this period, as we have seen, voters continued their steady shift in allegiance toward the Democratic party. Then, in 1964, the most ideologically conservative activists in the Republican party, whose views probably represented only a minority among Republican voters and an even smaller minority in the electorate as a whole, seized control of the nominating convention from the Republican 'establishment,' nominated Senator Goldwater, and suffered one of the three or four worst defeats in the entire history of the party.[6]

The lesson seems fairly clear: When the policies of party leaders get too far out of line with those desired by the voters, support for the party will erode, and the party is likely to get beaten in elections.

In sum: The main contribution that parties make to popular control is not to be found in their internal operations but in their external effects—in competing for votes, organizing elections and legislatures, strengthening the opposition, providing offsetting checks to one another, and helping the many to overcome the otherwise superior resources of the few.

**PARTIES AND
RATIONALITY**   Of what value is popular control, however, if voters are simply duped by party leaders or mindlessly vote for their parties without weighing

5. Herbert McClosky, Paul J. Hoffman, and Rosemary O'Hara, "Issue Conflict and Consensus among Party Leaders and Followers," *American Political Science Review*, 54 (June, 1960), 406–427, Table 1, p. 410, and *passim*.

6. For an analysis, see P. E. Converse, A. R. Clausen, and W. E. Miller, "Electoral Myth and Reality: The 1964 Election," *American Political Science Review*, 59 (June, 1965), 321–336. The percentages of the total popular vote received by the Republican presidential candidate in their four great defeats were: 1964, Senator Goldwater, 38.5; 1936, Alfred M. Landon, 36.5; 1912, William H. Taft, 23.2; and 1856, John C. Fremont, 33.1. In 1912 Theodore Roosevelt, the Progressive candidate, received 34.9 percent of the votes, many of them from Republicans; Woodrow Wilson, the Democratic candidate, received only 41.9 percent of the votes.

the candidates and the issues? It might be argued that even if parties do help the electorate gain some degree of control over elected officials, the control of the voters is in large measure spurious because it is irrational. Do parties reduce the irrationality of politics—or do they actually increase it?

It would be absurd to attribute to political parties all the forms of irrational and nonrational behavior that have ever been commonplace in human affairs and that exist in political systems of all sorts. The relevant question is whether parties change the amount and kinds of 'irrational' behavior from what would exist in the absence of parties.

Unhappily, the question is all but unanswerable. 'Levels' or 'amounts' of irrationality are terms that at best have only metaphorical meaning. No one has been able to measure changes in 'the amount of rationality' in political systems. The most extreme cases of collective irrationality in modern times have occurred in dictatorships, I believe, where whole populations have fallen under the absolute domination of paranoid leaders like Stalin and Hitler. By comparison, stable polyarchies appear to be models of rational action. The question is, then, whether poly-archies would be more—or less—rational without competing parties.

One could theorize endlessly in response to this question without arriving at a conclusive answer. Let me therefore confine my conjectur-ing—for this it must be—to two aspects that everyone would agree do characterize political parties: (1) Parties present to voters a very small number of alternatives out of the total number theoretically available. This effect is particularly strong in a two-party system with single-member districts; for at elections the voter is usually confronted with only two rival candidates. (2) Each party develops a core of followers whose loyalty is fortified by nonrational factors like sentiment, pride, jealousy, combativeness, gamesmanship, and habit.

Reducing Alternatives

Consider the first point. A voter presented with two rival candidates, might prefer neither of them so much as a third possible candidate who failed to win a nomination by either party. Similarly, on some matter of policy a voter may like the policy proposed by both parties less than some other alternative neither party is willing to advance. Reasoning along these lines, one might conclude that multi-party systems would offer voters a more rational choice than two-party systems. Yet, if four parties are better than two, are eight parties better than four? And sixteen parties better than eight? Or, for that matter, why not a separate candidate for every point of view held by any citizen in the country? But suppose the voter were confronted with a choice among twenty parties and twenty candidates. Might he not then reason as follows: These are too many alternatives; I cannot possibly appraise them all.

Anyway, what do I gain if the man I vote for wins? If there are twenty parties in the parliament, my representative and all the others will have to make many compromises by the time they reach the final decision. How do I know what compromises they will make? Would it not be much better if most of the compromises had been made already, so that I could then choose between two possible coalitions, knowing roughly the direction in which each would go if it won a majority of seats . . . ?

Evidence does, in fact, suggest that the need to choose among a large number of parties is, for all except a small minority of voters, highly confusing and may lead, as in France, to seriously discrediting the whole party system.[7]

Such reasoning might cause a voter to oscillate between two poles. At one pole, accepting the need for eliminating alternatives in order to arrive at a decision, he would enjoy the advantage of being confronted at elections by only two major alternatives. At the other pole, accepting the need to have his favorite alternative presented to him in order to have full freedom of choice, he would enjoy the advantage of being confronted at elections by a wide array of alternatives. Carried to an extreme, the first would result in a plebiscite, like several under the French Fifth Republic, where the only choices were to vote yes or no to a simple proposition. In this case, the voter might feel badly cheated and powerless because the choices were too narrow. The second solution, carried to the other extreme, would result in an array of choices so great that no voter could possibly estimate the effect of his vote on the ultimate outcome of the election and parliamentary bargaining. In this case, he might feel badly cheated and powerless because the choices were far too many.

The fact remains, then, that whenever a diversity of viewpoints and desired alternatives exists among the citizens of a polyarchy, the citizens must, sooner or later, by one process or another, reject all but one alternative (even if the final choice is, in effect, the null alternative of inaction). There is no escaping this process; it is the essence of 'rationality'; the only question is where and how it takes place. Much of the process of winnowing out alternatives could take place *before* an election, or *in* the election itself, or in negotiations *after* the election. All party systems do some winnowing *before* an election, making the *election* itself more decisive by reducing the alternatives, thus leaving less winnowing to be done *after* the election by bargaining and negotiation among members of different parties. The contrast is most marked between the British two-party system and a multi-party system like that of Italy, or France under the Third and Fourth Republics. The American party system, like the

---

7. Philip Converse and Georges Dupeux, "Politicization of the Electorate in France and the United States," in Campbell et al., *Elections and the Political Order,* ch. 14, especially pp. 277–278.

multi-party systems of the Scandinavian countries or the Netherlands stands somewhat in between.

The notion, then, that parties increase irrationality in making choices by reducing the alternatives is based upon too simple a picture of the processes by which collective political decisions can be made, for all such processes necessarily involve a drastic reduction in the alternatives. Although the question is obviously exceedingly complex, it seems much more reasonable to conclude (as most students of party do) that on the whole the parties play a beneficial role in this process.

Consequences of Party Loyalty

Consider now the second aspect of parties, the fact that they develop a core of followers loyal to the point of blind, nonrational support. The more the parties succeed in their efforts, it might be said, the more the weight of reason in politics is bound to decline. Parties may be the backbone of polyarchy, but all bone and no brain makes for a dull system. Does party loyalty insure the rationality of voters?

There are four markedly divergent answers.

Ostrogorski's solution: spontaneous combination. The first and oldest, traceable to Rousseau, was the dominant theme of one of the earliest systematic analyses of British and American parties, that by Moisei Ostrogorski in 1902.[8] "Ostrogorski's conception of democracy," a modern critic has said, "was essentially atomistic. He thought of a democratic society as one in which isolated individuals engage in the rational discussion of public affairs, freely combining with other individuals on the basis of identity of views on particular issues."[9] To Ostrogorski all permanent parties are bad. Party loyalty turns into a kind of religious dogma:

> . . . To prevent the great mass of adherents on whom rests the power of the party from escaping it, their minds and their wills must be inveigled by every kind of device [Ostrogorski wrote]. . . . They unite their contingents in superstitious respect for pure forms, in a fetish-like worship of the "party," inculcate a loyalty to its name and style, and thus establish a moral mortmain over men's minds. . . . They stereotype opinion in creeds which enforce on it a rigid discipline, they conceal the divergences of views that arise by composite programmes in which the most varied problems are jumbled together, which promise everything to everybody.[10]

Ostrogorski's solution was simple. It consisted

> in discarding the use of *permanent* parties . . . and in restoring and reserving to party its essential character of a combination of citizens *formed specially for a particular political issue.* . . . [A] party holding its members, once they

---

8. Ostrogorski, *Democracy and the Organization of Political Parties.*
9. Ranney, *The Doctrine of Responsible Party Government,* p. 115.
10. Ostrogorski, *Democracy and the Organization of Political Parties,* vol. 2, p. 354.

have joined it, in a viselike grasp would give place to combinations forming and reforming spontaneously, according to the changing problems of life and the play of opinions brought about thereby. Citizens who part company on one question would join forces in another.[11]

Second view: the rational independent. Although in the United States, as we shall see, the parties approximate the condition described in the last sentence more closely than Ostrogorski could have known, in this country as in every other polyarchy his specific solution has been decisively rejected in favor of permanent parties. A second view, seemingly more in keeping with reality, became much more widely accepted than Ostrogorski's. This is the view that while the great bulk of the voters are party loyalists who act not so much in pursuit of rational aims as from nonrational loyalties, a considerable body of independents stands outside the two parties. It is the votes of these independents, the argument runs, that essentially determine elections. And independents, it is said, are relatively rational and reflective: it is they who give genuine consideration to the candidates and programs of the two parties and then make their choices. Consequently, so long as the number of these thoughtful independents is sufficiently large and the number of loyalists on each side is less than a majority, the independents determine the outcome. Hence party competition places the decisive voice in elections exactly where it belongs, with the more thoughtful, judicious, and reflective citizens committed to neither party. Unlike Ostrogorski's appraisal, this view is on the whole favorable to the role of parties: they are useful, at any rate, as long as they do not gain so many partisans that they no longer need to contest for the votes of the independents.

The irrational voter. Alas for this optimistic view, it was based almost exclusively on data available within easy reach of the armchair. Beginning with the presidential election of 1940, social scientists used the new techniques of opinion surveys in a series of studies that have revolutionized our knowledge about American voters.[12] From these studies, based upon lengthy and carefully analyzed interviews with a scientifically selected sample of the electorate, a new picture emerged—based for the first time, it seemed, on hard fact. In this new group portrait, the

---

11. *Ibid.*, p. 356 (emphasis added).

12. The principal studies for the following elections are: 1940: Paul F. Lazarsfeld, Bernard Berelson, and Hazel Gaudet, *The People's Choice*, 2nd. ed. (New York: Columbia University Press, 1948). 1944: Sheldon J. Korchin, "Psychological Variables in the Behavior of Voters," Doctoral dissertation, Harvard University, 1946. 1948: Bernard R. Berelson, Paul F. Lazarsfeld, and William N. McPhee, *Voting* (Chicago: University of Chicago Press, 1954). 1952: Angus Campbell, Gerald Gurin, and Warren E. Miller, with the assistance of Sylvia Eberhart and Robert O. Mc-Williams, *The Voter Decides* (Chicago: Row-Peterson, 1954). 1954: Angus Campbell and Homer C. Cooper, *Group Differences in Attitudes and Votes, A Study of the 1954 Congressional Elections* (Ann Arbor: University of Michigan Press, 1956). 1956: Campbell et al., *The American Voter.* 1960: Campbell et al., *Elections and The Political Order;* Ithiel de Sola Pool, Robert P. Abelson, and Samuel P. Popkin, *Candidates, Issues and Strategies, A Computer Simulation of the 1960 Presidential Election* (Cambridge, M.I.T. Press, 1964).

face of the rational voter is all but invisible. For social scientists have learned what was plausible enough all along: people who are most interested and most informed about politics are also likely to be the most partisan, and the least partisan voters are likely to be uninterested and uninformed about issues, personalities, and other aspects of a campaign. Unfortunately for the older portrayal of the independent as the ideal voter, it now became clear that the less partisan or more 'independent' of party loyalties a voter is, the less likely he is to be interested in politics, to be informed about candidates and issues, to go to the polls, or, if he does, to make up his mind judiciously after carefully reflecting on the alternatives. The portrait of the voter painted by these studies is, then, rather gloomy. On the one hand, it appears, most voters are party loyalists who vote less out of an intelligent concern for policy than from sheer loyalty, habit, and inertia. On the other hand, the reflective independent, once honored for his contribution, scarcely exists in real life. A voter who is not interested enough in politics to be partisan is unlikely to be interested enough to have an intelligent judgment on the election.

In the light of the evidence from these recent studies, campaigns and elections began to seem rather meaningless. The overwhelming number of interested voters, these surveys revealed, make up their minds even before the campaign starts. In fact, the more interested a voter is the more likely he is to make up his mind even before the candidates are nominated! To be sure, some voters are open-minded. Those who have 'open' minds during the campaign and do not decide how they will vote until the polling day draws near are very likely to have minds so open, it seems, as to be downright vacant. An election, looked at in the bleakest light shed by the data, seemed to be little more than sound and fury, signifying nothing . . . a tale told by an idiot.

The sometimes rational voter. Combined with a measure of healthy iconoclasm endemic among social scientists, the hard facts of election studies helped to give wide credence to this perspective among social scientists engaged in studying elections. Yet there is some reason for thinking that, as is often the case, a plausible view had been pushed too far. In a book which he was unable to complete before his death, the late and highly distinguished political scientist V. O. Key had moved to a counterattack with an array of evidence drawn from opinion surveys covering every presidential election from 1936 to 1960.[13] According to Key's evidence, even if not many voters change their minds as a result of a campaign, many more decide from *one presidential election to the*

13. V. O. Key, Jr., with the assistance of Milton C. Cummings, Jr., *The Responsible Electorate, Rationality in Presidential Voting 1936–1940* (Cambridge: Harvard University Press, 1966).

next to shift their vote from the presidential candidate of one party to that of the other party. The proportion of voters who shift between one presidential election and the next probably fluctuates somewhere in the neighborhood of 15–20 percent. If we add to these 'shifters' the new voters (i.e., who have not voted in a previous election), then the rest, the 'standpatters' who do not change from one election to the next are in the neighborhood of 60–70 percent of the electorate. More important, Key also found a moderately close connection between one's views on policy and one's chances of shifting or standing pat. Far from being will-less partisans, the standpatters tend to be voters whose views are closer to those of the party they support than to the other party. The shifters tend to be people who, by shifting, give support to the party that is closer to their views than the party they had supported in the preceding elections. The portrait that emerges from Key's analysis is, on the whole, a benign one: ". . . voters are not fools. To be sure, many individual voters act in odd ways indeed; yet in the large the electorate behaves about as rationally and responsibly as we should expect, given the clarity of the alternatives presented to it and the character of the information available to it."[14]

On Key's showing, then, the American voter appeared to cast his vote with a reasonably intelligent judgment as to which party is more likely to pursue the kinds of policies he prefers. Key's analysis was, however, severely limited by the nature of his data and his conclusions were not fully accepted by some political scientists.[15] Yet some subsequent research has tended to corroborate Key's view that on matters they feel are important to them, a substantial number of voters discriminate competently between parties and presidential candidates.[16] Voters are par-

---

14. *Ibid.*, p. 7.

15. In their analysis of the 1968 election Philip E. Converse, Warren E. Miller, Jerrold G. Rusk, and Arthur G. Wolfe affirm the value of Key's contribution, point out some of the deficiencies in his methodology, and conclude that Key's view is partly but not wholly corroborated by the 1968 election. Wallace voters were clearly issue-oriented: "The pattern of correlations between issue positions and the vote for these 'changers' would support Key's thesis of a 'rational' and 'responsible' electorate even more impressively than most of the data he found for earlier elections." However, for voters who supported Nixon and Humphrey, "it is *party* that towers over all other predictors, and the central 1968 issues tend to give rather diminutive relationships. . . . It seems clear from the 1968 data that one of the cardinal limiting conditions is the 'drag' or inertia represented by habitual party loyalties: as soon as features of the situation limit or neutralize the relevance of such a factor, issue evaluations play a more vital role" ("Continuity and Change in American Politics: Parties and Issues in the 1968 Election," *American Political Science Review,* 63 [December, 1969], 1083–1105).

16. Thus David E. Repass concluded from an analysis of the issues in the 1960 and 1964 elections, as the public saw them, that "by and large the voting public has at least a few substantive issues in mind at the time of an election, and the voters seem to be acting more responsibly than had previously been thought. . . . We have shown that the public is in large measure concerned about specific issues, and that these cognitions have considerable impact on electoral choice" ("Issue Salience and Party Choice," *American Political Science Review,* 65 [June, 1971], 389–400). From the analysis of responses of a random sample of registered voters in Hawaii in the 1968 presidential campaign, Michael J. Shapiro concludes that "for our sample and with respect to our referent population of voters, voting choices are rational" ("Rational Political Man: A Synthesis of Economic and Social-Psychological Perspectives," *American Political Science Review,* 63 [December, 1969], 1106–19). Less direct but relevant evidence is also contained in William H. Riker and William James Zavoina, "Rational Behavior in Politics: Evidence from a Three Person Game," *American Political Science Review,* 64 (March, 1970), 48–60.

ticularly sensitive to objective changes in economic conditions. One study of presidential popularity from Truman to Johnson as reflected in Gallup polls found that "an economy in slump harms a President's popularity, but an economy which is improving does not seem to help his rating."[17] And from a study of fluctuations in voting for candidates for the House of Representatives from 1896 to 1964, Kramer concludes:

> One basic finding to emerge . . . is that election outcomes are in substantial part responsive to objective changes occurring under the incumbent party; they are not "irrational," or random, or solely the product of past loyalties and habits, or of campaign rhetoric and merchandising. In this respect, our findings support those of Key, based on quite different data.
>
> Economic fluctuations, in particular, are important influences on congressional elections, with economic upturn helping the congressional candidates of the incumbent party, and economic decline benefiting the opposition. In quantitative terms, a 10 per cent decrease in per capita real income would cost the incumbent administration 4 or 5 per cent of the congressional vote, other things being equal. . . . This would translate into a loss of around 40 House seats—a respectable shift.[18]

PARTIES AND CONFLICT

What of the possible third contribution of American parties, the contribution they make to the peaceful management of political conflicts? Do they not actually intensify conflict—as many Americans believe—and, at times, endanger the prospect for a peaceful settlement of disputes?

The answer to these questions is somewhat obscure. As we shall see in the next part of this book, the extent to which party competition softens or inflames conflicts doubtless depends on the prevailing pattern of cleavages. Because patterns of cleavage and conflict form a large and complex topic that bears heavily on the operation of the American polyarchy, we turn our attention to these matters in the next part of this book.

SUMMARY

The possible contributions of political parties to polyarchy are generally thought to be three:

1. Political parties facilitate popular control over governmental leaders by:

☐ Aggregating individual preferences.
☐ Organizing oppositions.
☐ Preventing one-party dominance.

---

17. John E. Mueller, "Presidential Popularity from Truman to Johnson," *American Political Science Review*, 64 (March, 1970), 18–34.

18. Gerald H. Kramer, "Short-term Fluctuations in U.S. Voting Behavior, 1896–1964," *American Political Science Review*, 65 (March, 1971), 131–143. The quotation is from pp. 140–141. It should be added that the article is mathematically too difficult to be recommended to the ordinary reader.

☐ Pooling the resources of the many to offset the advantages of the few.

Internally, however, political parties show strong tendencies toward oligarchy. Attempts to democratize the process of nominations, at first by replacing the caucus with the convention and later by replacing or supplementing conventions with direct primaries, have not fully offset the tendency to internal oligarchy.

Nonetheless, internal party democracy probably has less effect on the responsiveness of government in a polyarchy than the extent to which the parties are competitive with one another.

2. Parties may facilitate more rational choices among voters. The extent to which parties enhance rationality is, however, confused by two different tendencies:

☐ On the one hand, by aggregating individual preferences, political parties help to reduce the number of alternatives confronting those who participate in decisions, including the voters. In reducing alternatives, the parties contribute to an inescapable requirement of rational action.

☐ On the other hand, parties become objects of irrational loyalties, affections, and hostilities that often appear to cloud the judgment of the voter when he is confronted by alternative candidates or issues.

Because of the effects of seemingly blind partisan loyalties, the effect of parties on voter rationality is a subject of dispute.

☐ Ostrogorski contended that parties interfere with rational choice and should be replaced by "combinations forming and reforming spontaneously." However, no polyarchy operates with free-forming organizations rather than parties.

☐ For many years it was popular to hold that even if party loyalists behave irrationally, elections are ordinarily decided by relatively rational independent or nonpartisan voters. However, systematic surveys conducted over several decades have shown that voters without partisan attachments are, on the whole, more poorly informed and more prone to irrational political judgments than partisan voters.

☐ These findings led to a third view, common among social scientists who had immersed themselves in the depressing findings of surveys, that voting is not a very rational act. In this view, most voters are partisans who vote from loyalty, habit, and inertia; while the voter who lacks partisan loyalties is likely to be indifferent and poorly informed.

☐ More recently, however, evidence has been adduced to suggest that substantial numbers of voters are at least moderately rational in their voting decisions. It has been found that voters tend to support the congressional candidates of the incumbent party when the economy is rising, and turn to the candidates of the opposing party during periods of economic decline.

3. Political parties may help in the peaceful management of conflicts. However, the extent to which the parties diminish or exacerbate conflicts very likely depends on the prevailing pattern of cleavages, which will be examined in the next section.

Conflict And Conciliation In The American Polyarchy

Conflict and Conciliation

21

Not so very long ago polyarchy was viewed almost everywhere as a radical, even revolutionary, system of government. A political system in which the national government is chosen by means of free elections in which most adult male citizens are entitled to vote and where political parties are actively competing for votes—this kind of system is a twentieth-century achievement. In most of the polyarchies of the present day—Britain and Sweden, for examples—manhood suffrage was significantly restricted until the time of the First World War. (Women were excluded from voting in national elections in the United States, as nearly everywhere else, until 1919; in Switzerland, that paragon of stable democracy, women had no right of suffrage under the federal constitution until 1971, though some cantons had granted it.) During most or all of the nineteenth century, many countries that are now polyarchies were oligarchies in which power was constitutionally lodged in the hands of a few—for example, Germany, Italy, Austria, and, until the advent of the Third Republic in 1874, France.

In the period between the world wars, as polyarchies were endangered by new revolutionary movements—Communism, Fascism, Nazism—the view that polyarchy is a radical or revolutionary system began to wane. While revolutionary dictatorship came to be widely looked upon—and in many polyarchies feared—as the wave of the future, advocates of democratic values went over to the defensive. In the quarter century after the onset of the Great Depression in 1929–30, the very survival of polyarchies was desperately challenged by the newer forms of revolutionary dictatorship in a series of contests where the outcome was highly uncertain. After the end of the Second World War, the contest extended to the developing parts of the world. There, where democratic political habits and traditions are lacking and human misery is greatest, revolutionary dictatorships frequently blend nationalism, Marxism, and opportunism with much of the rhetoric and some of the ultimate aims of democracy, but few of the practises of polyarchy.

As the polyarchies assumed the posture of defense, their intellectuals frequently displayed a mood of pessimism and even a kind of desperate masochistic satisfaction in announcing the obsolescence of polyarchy. Perhaps because totalitarian change was so great a danger, political theorists, sociologists, and many others began to place heavier stress on the conditions necessary for a stable polyarchy. Perhaps because internal conflict had grown so menacing, they also focused on *consensus*. Thus stability and consensus each became a sort of fetish, particularly among American political scientists and social theorists. By contrast, conflict and change were perceived not so much as offering the possibility of a better future (as democratic ideologues a century earlier would have said), but as menacing the foundations of polyarchy and its substantial, if still incomplete, attainment of democratic goals.

Quite possibly this intellectual mood reached a peak in the 1950s and has since been waning. However that may be, what is astonishing in retrospect is how much conflict many polyarchies have managed to absorb in the twentieth century, and how much change they have sponsored. In Britain, Sweden, Denmark, Belgium, and the Netherlands, to name a few cases, the extension of the suffrage and the democratization of political life were themselves profound yet ultimately peaceful changes. In almost every polyarchy, including the United States, twentieth-century leaders have carried through extensive—one might almost say revolutionary—programs of social reconstruction in order to mitigate the inequalities, the insecurities, and the injustices that industrialization and urbanization perpetuated, intensified, generated, or rendered more obviously unnecessary and capable of being eliminated. The heartening fact is that countries that already had achieved or were well advanced on the road to polyarchy before the First World War have nearly everywhere won and kept the loyalty of their people to democratic principles and the institutional practises of polyarchy: for example, Switzerland, Britain, Norway, Sweden, Denmark, Iceland, Finland, Holland, Belgium, Canada, Australia, New Zealand—and, of course, the United States. In these countries, the working classes—once a source of internal danger because they were excluded from political life—have been integrated peacefully into the political system; in most of these countries, socialist and labor parties, drawing their strength mainly from skilled and unskilled workers, have participated extensively in government. Nor, in these countries, have the older elite groups, the aristocratic strata or the middle classes, been seriously alienated by democratization. In short, in these countries, extensive social and political changes have not prevented, but have even encouraged, conciliation among different social groups and the pacification of many ancient internal hostilities.

The United States, too, has undergone changes that half a century ago no one foresaw: the expansion of welfare measures and government intervention in the economy; the almost overnight assumption by the United States of its role as a major, *the* major, world power; and since the early 1950s steps toward the ultimate political, economic, and social liberation of blacks.

To look upon polyarchies as incapable of significant change is, then, to misread the evidence of this century. In fact, perhaps only in the relatively small number of countries where polyarchy is quite firmly rooted can *extensive change* be reconciled with *extensive consent.* For there is a great deal of evidence to show that more profound changes can be made in the attitudes of people when they *participate* in changes (as they must if their consent is needed) than when they are *coerced.* Coercive change is more likely to produce speedy and outwardly dramatic yet superficial changes in attitudes. With participation, changes may seem to be taking place more slowly because consent is not won instantly, yet changes with consent are likely to be deeper and more long-lasting.[1]

Nonetheless, it would be a false gloss on reality to say that change is easy in polyarchies, or to contend that change and stability pose no problems. For change almost always entails conflict between conservative social forces who gain or believe they gain from preserving the existing state of affairs or the direction in which things are moving, and their challengers whose aspirations require changes in the status quo or in the general direction of historical movement.

It is the set of problems involved in change and conflict, in stability and consensus that I now propose to explore. Before focusing explicitly on the American polyarchy, however, it will help if we first try to sort out some of the key problems and possibilities.

CHANGE: INCREMENTAL, COMPREHENSIVE, REVOLUTIONARY

One of the commonest characteristics of literary utopias is that nothing ever changes. Yet it is a central fact of life that no living system is ever static. What is true of living organisms is also true of systems consisting of live human beings—economic systems, social systems, political systems.

Since change is ubiquitous, it is possible to examine it from a thousand different perspectives and to classify it in a thousand different ways. Let us focus our attention on *political* change and the *sources* or causes of political change.

---

1. Sidney Verba, *Small Groups and Political Behavior* (Princeton: Princeton University Press, 1961), "The Participation Hypothesis: Application of a Small Group Finding," ch. 9; "The Participation Hypothesis: The Generality of a Small Group Finding," ch. 10.

Two Key Aspects of Political Change

Political change may be distinguished as to location and magnitude.

Location. As to location, change may take place in:

1. The operating *structure* of government, as when a polyarchy replaces an oligarchy, a dictatorship replaces a polyarchy, a presidential system replaces a parliamentary system, or direct election of senators replaces election by state legislatures.
2. The *policies* adopted and enforced by the government, as when Congress passed civil rights acts in 1964 and 1965, or Medicare in 1965.
3. The *relative influence* of different strata and groups on the policies and decisions of government, as after the election of 1800 when small farmers and southern planters clearly gained greater influence while New England commercial interests lost.
4. The social, ethnic, religious, psychological, or other significant *characteristics of political leaders,* as when blacks gained public office in the South during Reconstruction, and again following the Civil Rights Acts of 1964 and 1965. (In what follows I propose to ignore this last kind of political change, important as it is, and concentrate on the others.)

Magnitude. Political change may be small or great with respect to each of these locations or dimensions. For the sake of simplicity, however, let me reduce change to three magnitudes.[2]

1. Incremental, or marginal, when
   a. The operating structure is unaltered, except perhaps in matters of detail.
   b. Changes in policies are gradual and incremental rather than sweeping innovations or reversals of established policies. And,
   c. These changes result from negotiating and bargaining among spokesmen for groups whose relative influence remains more or less stable or subject only to gradual changes.
2. Comprehensive, when
   a. The operating structure is unaltered, except in matters of detail.
   b. Sweeping innovations or decisive reversals of established policies occur. And,
   c. These policy changes result from significant shifts in the relative influence of different groups.
3. Revolutionary, when comprehensive change in policies and relative

---

2. The reader who enjoys playing with typologies — a somewhat barren enterprise to which social scientists are strongly addicted — may wish to construct for himself the eight possible combinations of 'small' versus 'large' changes in structures, policies, and group influence.

influence (2b and 2c) is also combined with profound alterations in the operating structure of government. Broadly used in this way, the term applies only to the location and magnitude of change and implies nothing as to the means by which changes are brought about. In the broad usage, then, revolutionary change may be peaceful or violent.[3]

Political Change in the United States

Incremental change. Incremental change is the normal pattern in American political life. Although incremental change often seems depressingly slow and is rejected by revolutionaries as inadequate, a few examples will show how much can be achieved by means of a series of small but steady changes. Anything that grows at the rate of 3 percent a year will double in size about every twenty-three years; at 5 percent a year it will double in fourteen years. The United States achieved its extraordinarily high gross national product by growing at a rate of about 3⅔ percent a year from the 1840s onwards. The population increased from 17 million in 1840 to more than 200 million in 1970 by growing at an average rate of about 2 percent a year. Gross national product per capita during this period grew at the rate of about 1⅔ percent a year; personal consumption at about 1¾ percent a year. The world population explosion that has caused so much concern in recent years is produced by annual increments of only 2 to 4 percent. The highest rate of growth in per capita gross national product in the 1950s in any industrial country, Communist or non-Communist, was less than 7 percent. The average annual increase in the population of cities over 20 thousand in the United States from 1920 to 1950 was less than one-fifth of one percent. Sixty-two percent of the American population of voting age cast votes in the presidential election of 1964; if the percentage of the population voting were to grow by only 3 percent a year, more than 95 percent of the potential electorate would vote in the election of 1980. If output per man-hour in the United States increases by 5 percent annually, in fifty years each worker would produce eleven times as much as he does now.[4]

Incremental change, then, can be a powerful means for transforming a society—and has been so in the United States. However, comprehensive changes also occur at times; in fact, comprehensive changes

---

3. A stricter usage emphasizes the attempt to bring about revolutionary changes by 'revolutionary' means; i.e., overthrowing the existing government by force. When we examine alternative strategies for bringing about changes in the conduct of the government in Chapter 26, the term will be used in this narrower sense.

4. The data on which the calculations in the paragraph are based were drawn from the following sources: Bruce M. Russett, ed., *World Handbook of Political and Social Indicators* (New Haven: Yale University Press, 1964), Tables 1, 7, 10, 45; Hearings Before the Joint Economic Committee, Congress of the United States, April 7–10, 1959, Part 2, Table 1, p. 271; Abram Bergson and Simon Kuznets, *Economic Trends in the Soviet Union* (Cambridge: Harvard University Press, 1963), Tables VIII.2, VIII.3, and VIII.4, pp. 337–340; *Congress and the Nation*, vol. 1, p. 1532; Louis J. Walinsky, "Keynes Isn't Enough," *The New Republic*, 154 (April 16, 1966), 14–16.

are, as we shall see in later chapters, associated with some of the most dramatic events in American political history.

Revolutionary change. What of revolutionary political changes? The war between the American colonies and Britain is properly called a revolution, for it resulted in a profound change in the structure of government, in the relative influence of Americans and British officials, and in the policies pursued by the government. Making and adopting the Constitution might also be regarded as revolutionary in the sense employed here, even though that revolution, unlike the preceding one, was free of violence. For the Constitution clearly represented a decisive change in governmental structure; the policies of the new government, particularly Hamilton's economic policies, were sweeping innovations; and (the point is more debatable) the new government was associated, even if briefly, with a significant increase in the influence of men of commerce and finance. The Hartford Convention in 1814 and the South Carolina legislature in 1832 (of which more in Chapter 23) might be said to have *sought* revolutionary change, unsuccessfully. The Civil War was one part revolution, one part the failure of a revolution. The Secessionists failed to revolutionize the structure of government by seceding and establishing an independent confederacy. Yet if the North defeated the South's revolution, Lincoln and the Republicans represented a decisive shift of influence away from southern planters to free farmers, commerce, industry, and northern labor; and the legislation and constitutional amendments enacted during and after the Civil War constituted sweeping, indeed revolutionary, shifts in long-established policies. The challenge of the Confederacy was, however, the last large-scale appeal to a revolutionary change of regime that has been made in American politics; since that time, proposals for revolutionary change have been the exclusive monopoly of tiny political movements.

SOURCES OF POLITICAL CHANGE

Why do political changes come about? What generates the forces that lead to political changes?

To seek satisfactory answers to these questions would take us far beyond the confines of this book and into a domain where knowledge is rather speculative. Processes of change are obviously of critical importance to understanding the past, acting in the present, and shaping the future; they have been much studied, yet they are not at all well understood.

Changes in Technology

It is possible to distinguish some of the important factors that trigger political changes. One is changes in technique or technology. A new technique, instrument, or machine is introduced. Because it outperforms the old, practical men acting from practical motives replace the old with the new. As the new technique spreads, it alters opportunities, advantages, handicaps, relations among people, groups, regions. There are changes in access to resources of power, changes in perspectives, ideas, ideologies, changes in demands, changes in patterns of conflict and agreement. And so political change occurs.

The introduction of gunpowder into Europe ended the military superiority of the mailed and mounted knight; it heralded the day of the musket and foot soldier. And so it helped to bring feudalism to an end. The mariner's compass vastly expanded the possibilities of navigation; it facilitated the discovery of the New World and the creation of overseas empires; it was to one of these that Englishmen fled and created a new social, economic, and political order. Eli Whitney's invention of the cotton gin, as every American schoolchild is taught, made cotton a highly profitable crop; the profitability of cotton stimulated the spread of slavery and the domination of the South by a planter class. Thus, in the endless, complex, and little-understood chain of causes of which Whitney's invention is an early link, there is also the Civil War, the Ku Klux Klan, the "separate but equal" doctrine, its overthrow by the Supreme Court decision of 1954, and the Civil Rights Acts of 1964 and 1965.

Changes in Social and Economic Institutions

Changes in social and economic institutions may also precipitate political changes. Institutional changes may of course be triggered by technological changes; the relationships are extraordinarily complex. The modern, privately owned, limited-liability business corporation was an institutional change that swept away most other forms of business in the nineteenth century. The competitive price system and the free market were institutional innovations of the late eighteenth and early nineteenth century. They responded to, but they also generated, technological changes; they created a new business class, a new middle class, a new urban proletariat, and a new set of problems, conflicts, and political changes that have not come to an end. In England, the same dense network of causes, one historian has argued, connects an innovation in 1795 by well-meaning justices of the peace trying to cope with rural unemployment and poverty to the triumph of the ideas of Adam Smith, the scrapping of all governmental controls over the price of labor, land, goods, and capital, and thence, in reaction and self-defense, to English socialism and the welfare state.[5] Why did the United States become a land of small free farmers in the nineteenth century, while Brazil did not? Both had a great supply of land. But the Englishmen who settled

---

5. Karl Polanyi, *The Great Transformation* (New York: Rinehart & Co., 1944).

America did not bring feudal institutions here, whereas the Portuguese and Spanish in Latin America did.

Changes in Ideas and Beliefs

There are, in the third place, ideas and beliefs. Simple mechanistic interpretations of history treat ideas in the minds of men as mere reflections of technology and institutions. Ideas are not, certainly, completely autonomous; but neither are technology and institutions. The relationships are too complex to try to sort out here. Yet ideas, beliefs, perspectives, and ideologies do change, and it is obvious that these changes often precipitate political changes. As Tocqueville pointed out in his introduction to *Democracy in America,* equality had long been spreading throughout Europe before the Americans founded their republic. Equality was spreading—ineluctably, so it seemed to him—as an idea and as a fact. If a growing equality in the actual conditions of life helps to sustain the idea of equality, may not the idea of equality help to sustain the fact of equality? Or, to take a more specific example, arguments over the virtues and vices of balanced budgets—an issue over which a number of Americans have displayed considerable passion—are above all a question of ideas and beliefs, indeed of abstract theories and models (even if often exceedingly primitive ones) of the relations between budgetary deficts and surpluses and such matters as full employment and foreign trade. Differences in ideas about these matters have steadily led to conflict between academic economists and conservative bankers.

Interaction of Change

Ideas, institutions, and techniques are intertwined in ways too complex to unravel. During Andrew Jackson's great conflicts over the Bank of the United States, why did none of the protagonists give serious consideration to a solution that would probably be one of the first to occur to a presidential adviser or a member of Congress today: a government regulatory commission to keep the Bank in check? In large part, it seems, because the regulatory commission as an institution had really not yet been invented and its possibilities were not yet understood. The perceptions, ideas, ideology, if you will, that have developed with the growth of the regulatory state of the twentieth century were for all practical purposes not present in 1830. Jackson did not reject the idea of a regulatory commission in the sense that a critic of regulation might reject it today; nor could he have adopted the idea of a regulatory commission. For he simply did not perceive the idea as we do today, nor did anyone else in his time.

Thus perspectives change, social and economic institutions change, technology changes. And these changes trigger political changes. But government and politics are not necessarily mere by-products of changes. Government policy may trigger changes in ideas, in social and economic institutions, in technology. The policies and practises of the New Deal surely helped to change the perspectives of Americans about the proper role of government. It was government action that created a new institution in the Tennessee Valley Authority. It was government action that produced the institutions of modern Social Security (action in this country was long antedated by the innovation in Europe). And it was government action that led directly to the most awesome technological innovation in history, the unleashing of nuclear power.

THE DEPTH OF CHANGE AND CONFLICT

When one reads about some great revolution, one is inclined to suppose that sooner or later everyone in the society was, surely, drawn into the orbit of the revolution. Yet it might be far more realistic to assume—as some theorists have—that rapid historical changes and political conflicts of all kinds, even great revolutions, directly involve only the tiniest and most visible minorities, the activists and elites, in spheres political, social, economic, cultural, religious. Probably the truth lies somewhere between these extreme views. Unfortunately it is impossible to specify precisely where the truth does lie, for our knowledge is severely limited.

The unhappy fact is that until the late 1930s, when systematic opinion surveys first began to be used, no means existed for measuring the spread of views and opinions in a population. As a result, we may never recapture the data needed for estimating in any except a very crude way how views were distributed in the past; we cannot therefore know much about detailed or rapid changes in views. We cannot go back to the eve of the Civil War and conduct a survey of the opinions of a properly selected sample of Americans and follow it up with one in 1865 to see what changes had occurred. Hence historical generalizations about the way opinions were distributed among Americans (or any other population) before about 1936 must be treated with great caution. Yet we cannot hope to understand past changes and conflicts without making some assumptions as to attitudes in the general population—among voters, for example.

It is useful, I think, to take as a central hypothesis that certain general characteristics of political life which have been found to hold since the 1930s were also true of American citizens before the 1930s. There are, certainly, no plausible grounds for thinking otherwise, and there is a good deal of indirect evidence in support of the hypothesis.

What is striking from modern evidence is how many Americans there are to whom political life is totally foreign. A substantial proportion of American adults—probably not less than one out of four nor more than one out of two—are for all practical purposes apolitical. Politics is so remote from their lives as to lack much meaning: they rarely vote or otherwise participate in politics, and their views on political matters are uninformed and shallow. These people constitute what might be called the apolitical strata. They seem to constitute a significant proportion of every citizen body in all historical periods. And there is not much doubt that in the United States the apolitical strata have always constituted a sizeable group.

It is highly reasonable to suppose, then, that during all periods of American history the 'burning issues of the day,' the 'great debates,' the 'fierce conflicts' of politics have scarcely engaged the attention of the apolitical strata at all; perhaps a quarter to a half of the adults have always been so wholly involved in the events of their daily lives—worries over jobs, income, health, family, and friends—that they have barely followed what later generations regard as great historical events. Ordinary voters who do at least bother to vote are no doubt more engaged. But it is the minority of politically active citizens who are highly active politically—and most of all the tiny minority of leaders—who have always been most fully engaged in political conflicts. No matter how important historians might regard it today, to most Americans in 1854, the passage of the Kansas-Nebraska Act was doubtless very much less interesting and important than the marriage of a daughter, a son moving west, a death in the family, the baby's croup, the bad harvest, the local scandal.

But of course when the leaders and the politically active citizens fail to resolve their differences, as they did in 1860, the cost in lives is levied on the whole people.

CONFLICT: MODERATE AND SEVERE Utopias are not only marked by the absence of change, they are also unflawed by conflict. Most utopias are pervaded by the deathly stillness of the graveyard. Yet in every political system there is perpetual and unceasing conflict.

In a polyarchy, conflict is particularly visible because it is permitted; it is not all driven underground; it is protected, even institutionalized.

Now it is true that conflict can be dangerous to a political system. And citizens take a certain gamble when they opt for a polyarchy. For the citizens of a polyarchy may react to severe political conflict in ways that endanger or destroy the survival of their political system: by violence, suppressing one's opponents, civil war, secession, disloyalty, even by widespread demoralization, apathy, and indifference.

Yet to say that severe political conflict is undesirable is not to say that all political conflict is undesirable. So long as men have different views and the liberty to express their views, conflicts will exist. To condemn all political conflict as evil is to condemn diversity and liberty as evils. If you believe that some diversity is inevitable, and that liberty is desirable, then you must hold, logically, that political conflict is not only inevitable but desirable.

This is therefore the dilemma: In a polyarchy moderate political conflict is both inevitable and desirable. Yet severe political conflict is undesirable, for it endangers any political system, and not least a polyarchy. A polyarchy can escape from this dilemma only if conflict is somehow kept within bounds. But how is this possible? How can conflict, like atomic energy, be tamed and put to peaceful purposes?

Indicators of Severe Conflict

It is not easy to say precisely what one means by the severity or intensity of a conflict, but the essential criterion appears to be this: Within a particular political system the more that the people on each side see the other side as enemies to be destroyed by whatever measures may be necessary, the more severe a conflict is. Evidence that a conflict is increasing in severity would therefore be an increasing harshness of language in which one's opponents were portrayed as implacable enemies to be annihilated; an increasing stress on or actual employment of violence against opponents; or an increasing use of means to victory that previously were regarded as impermissible, illegitimate, perhaps even illegal or unconstitutional.

Factors Affecting the Severity of Conflict

What circumstances, then, are likely to lend moderation to a dispute or, conversely, to inflame it into a conflict of great severity?

The stakes. To begin with the most obvious point, how severe a conflict is depends on how much is at stake. The more at stake, the harder a question is to settle.

Mutual benefits or zero-sum game. But how severe a conflict is also depends on whether the people engaged in the dispute can discover mutually beneficial solutions. The ideal outcome, naturally, would be one in which all the contestants were not only better off than before but better off than under any alternative solution. To be sure, if solutions of this kind were common, conflict would rarely occur. Nonetheless, there is a clear difference between a dispute in which no contestants can come out ahead except by making others worse off ("If you win, I lose," or what mathematicians call a "zero-sum game"); and a dispute in which there is a solution under which no one will be worse off than before, and some may even be better off. If two people are faced with a deal in which every dollar A gains will make B worse off than he is now, neither of them has much incentive to negotiate. If the best solution for

Figure 21.1
Agreement Piles Up
Heavily on One Side:
The J Curve

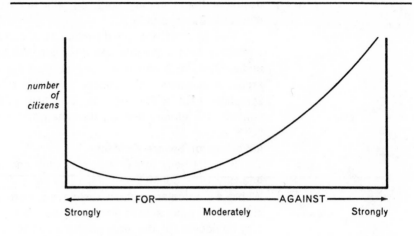

both is identical—if each stands to gain most by one solution—then negotiation is hardly necessary. If, on the other hand, A's best solution is different from B's, but there appear to be compromise solutions under which one or both might be better off than they are now and neither worse off, both have every reason to negotiate in order to arrive at a mutually acceptable decision.

The worst possible conflict, then, is one involving very high stakes and no solutions other than the mutually incompatible kind, "If you win, I lose." Consequently, conflicts involving two mutually incompatible ways of life among different citizens are bound to place an exceedingly serious strain on a polyarchy. Here the term *way of life* means the rights, privileges, and human relationships a group most highly prizes—their families and friends, economic position, social standing, respect, religious beliefs, and political powers. Any group that sees its way of life at stake in a dispute will, obviously, be reluctant to compromise. If the whole society is divided and if no compromise is possible—if the conflict is over two competely incompatible ways of life—then any political system is likely to break down. There are no cases, I think, in which a polyarchy has managed to settle conflicts of this kind peacefully.

So far we have been concerned with the characteristics of the conflict itself. But the severity of a conflict also depends on the people who are engaged in it, particularly their numbers and their location in the political system.

Numbers. In a polyarchy, elections mean that sheer numbers are often important. Hence how severe a conflict is depends in part on how many citizens hold similar or moderate views and how many hold extreme

Figure 21.2
Disagreement is Moderate:
The Bell Curve

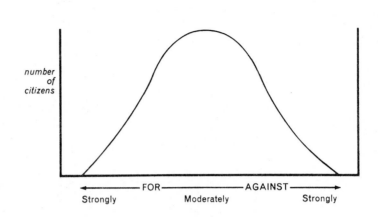

views. The greater the relative number of citizens who hold extreme (and opposing) views, the greater the danger that a conflict will be disruptive. Conversely, the greater the proportion of citizens who hold views that differ only slightly—that is, moderate views—the less the danger. In a stable polyarchy, the great bulk of citizens will, presumably, more or less agree on many questions. In some cases, the agreement would pile up so heavily on one side of an issue that the matter would cease to produce much controversy. A graph of such a distribution would assume the shape that statisticians, for obvious reasons, call a J curve[6] (Figure 21.1). A vast number of questions that might be of abstract interest to philosophers, moralists, theologians, or others who specialize in posing difficult and troublesome questions are, in any stable political system, irrelevant to politics because practically everyone is agreed and no one can stir up much of a controversy. If a controversy does arise because of the persistence of a tiny dissenting minority, in a polyarchy the chances are overwhelming that it will soon be settled in a way that corresponds with the view of the preponderant majority.

Sometimes people may disagree and yet hold moderate opinions. A distribution of this kind, which is sometimes called a bell-shaped or a double-J curve, is illustrated in Figure 21.2. When a conflict of views takes this shape, the chances are that it will be solved rather easily.

6. For theory and data bearing on the discussion in this section, see particularly Key, *Public Opinion and American Democracy,* ch. 2; and Dahl, *Political Oppositions in Western Democracies.* Discussions of relationships between the behavior of political parties and various distributions of political opinions may be found in Downs, *An Economic Interpretation of Democracy;* and Gerald Garvey "The Theory of Party Equilibrium," *American Political Science Review,* 60 (March, 1966), 29–38. A useful critique of some of the assumptions involved will be found in Donald E. Stokes "Spatial Models of Party Competition," in Campbell et al., *Elections and the Political Order,* ch. 9.

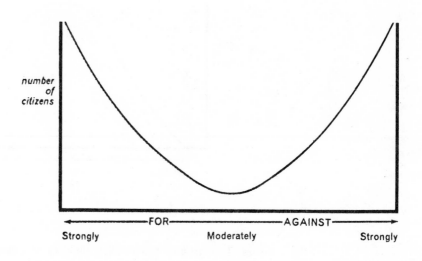

Figure 21.3
Disagreement is Severe
and Extreme: The U Curve

number of citizens

◄———————FOR———————————————AGAINST———————►

Strongly   Moderately   Strongly

Polyarchies with two major parties manage conflicts of this kind with special ease, because both parties tend to converge toward the center. Since an overwhelming number of voters are clustered at the center, and only a few at the extremes, the two major parties not only *may* ignore the extremes with impunity, they *must* do so if they want to win elections. The cost of making an appeal to voters with extreme attitudes is to lose the much more numerous support of the moderates near the center.

In cases of the first two kinds, where opinion is strongly one-sided or overwhelmingly moderate, the conflict is not likely to be severe. If the extremes predominate, however, conflicts of great severity are likely (Figure 21.3). Whenever extreme opinions grow at the expense of moderate opinions or one-sided agreement, obviously conflict becomes much more dangerous, for it is much harder to find a basis for mutually profitable compromises. Moreover, in these circumstances the political parties find it profitable to adapt their appeals to the views of citizens at the extremes. While extreme parties flourish, center parties grow weak. Sooner or later, one of the extreme parties or coalitions is likely to begin considering ways by which it may suppress or destroy the other, and violence is on the way.

Location. The severity of a conflict depends, however, not only on the sheer numbers of people who hold divergent views, but also on their

Figure 21.4
Moderation Among
Leaders, Extremism Among
Ordinary Citizens

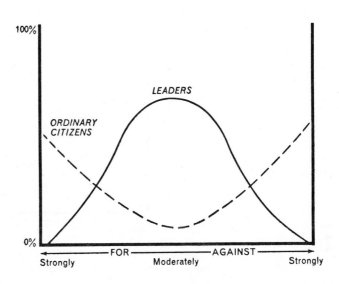

positions in the political system. *Officials and other political leaders* may be more moderate or more extreme in their views than ordinary citizens. Thus leaders may exaggerate or minimize the cleavages of opinion among the general population. The more they minimize cleavages, the less severe the political conflict; the more they emphasize and exaggerate differences of opinion, the more severe the conflict is likely to be. In Figure 21.4, leadership opinion is moderate, while rank-and-file opinion is sharply divided. In Figure 21.5, the situation is reversed; ordinary citizens are not as badly split as leaders. We would expect a situation like that suggested by Figure 21.5 to produce more severe political conflict and greater danger to a republic than the situation represented by Figure 21.4.

In a polyarchy, what could produce differences between the attitudes of ordinary citizens and the attitudes of political leaders? If political leaders were chosen at random from the general population, then significant differences would be most unlikely. But the selection of political leaders is, as we know, very far from a random process. Even in a polyarchy, some kinds of people are more likely to gain public office and power than others.

Citizens who are the most interested and active in politics are more likely to rise to the top than citizens who find politics uninteresting or otherwise unattractive. People who are interested and active in politics

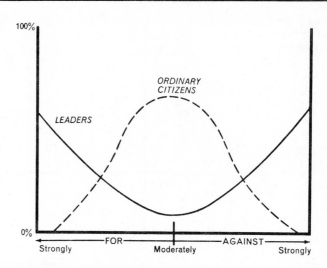

often differ in important respects from people who are less interested, less active, less effective, in short less influential. In the United States, for example, citizens who are most interested and active in politics and most confident that they can be effective tend also to have more education, higher incomes, and jobs of higher status. Because these conclusions are drawn from surveys made only since the 1930s, one cannot be certain that the differences of the last several decades existed earlier. But since much the same differences show up in other polyarchies, there is good reason to think that the social-psychological factors so evident now were also present in earlier years in the United States. In any case, if the more active, interested, and influential strata of citizens tend to differ from the rest of the population in education, income, and occupations, is it not likely that they will also differ in political views? Hence, instead of mirroring the political views of the rest of the population, leaders might be either more moderate or more antagonistic, and this may increase or decrease the severity of the conflict.

The way in which attitudes are distributed *geographically* is also relevant, particularly in countries where legislators are not chosen under some system of proportional representation. If a country is divided into election districts or states in which the office goes to the candidate with the most votes, and all other candidates with fewer votes are defeated, the intensity of a political conflict may depend on where different views are located in the country. An opposition minority that is concentrated in a particular region will find it easier to gain representation in the legislature than one that is dispersed more or less evenly throughout the nation. Moreover, even without extra representation because of the election system, a regional minority is in a relatively strong position to keep its views alive, to command conformity to its views within the region, to punish dissenters, and to portray their opponents as outsiders, aliens, foreigners.

Patterns of cleavage. The special effects of regionalism on conflict call attention to a broader observation—namely, that the severity of a conflict depends on the way in which one conflict is related to another. A society offers a number of different lines along which cleavages in a conflict can take place; differences in geography, ethnic identification, religion, and economic position, for example, all present potential lines of cleavage in conflicts. If all the cleavages occur along the same lines, if the same people hold opposing positions in one dispute after another, then the severity of conflicts is likely to increase. The man on the other side is not just an opponent; he soon becomes an enemy. But if (as Madison foresaw) the cleavages occur along different lines, if the same persons are sometimes opponents and sometimes allies, then conflicts are likely to be less severe. If you know that some of your present opponents were allies in the past and may be needed as allies again in the future, you have some reason to search for a solution to the dispute at hand that will satisfy both sides. The people on the other side may be your opponents today; but they are not your enemies, and tomorrow they may be your allies.

Political institutions. There is still one more factor to consider. Political institutions themselves may exacerbate conflicts, or make it easier to settle them. It is striking how in the hands of the English, the eighteenth-century Parliament became an institution for settling disputes that up until then—and in most other countries afterward—threatened the regime itself.[7] This development within Parliament does not wholly explain, of course, why Britain has not had a civil war since the seventeenth century; a fuller answer would require, among other things, an explanation of the path of parliamentary development itself. Nonetheless, the presence in Britain since the end of the seventeenth century of an institution that elaborated a set of conventions, devices, practises, and mechanisms for settling disputes has surely helped Britain to make changes and to negotiate internal conflicts peacefully for the past three hundred years.

It would take no great imagination to conceive of political institutions that would have the opposite effect, that would intensify rather than reduce conflict. Suppose, for example, that the American Consti-

7. Foord, *His Majesty's Opposition.*

tution automatically awarded the presidency and a majority on the Supreme Court to the party with the most numerous votes in an election, and awarded Congress to the party with the next largest number of votes. Conflict would then be built squarely into the constitutional system. (Because, as we have seen, the Founding Fathers deliberately sought to build conflict into the constitutional structure, the effects of their design on political conflicts in the United States will be discussed later.)

Although the extent to which political institutions intensify or soften conflicts is a highly complex matter, one might hope to distinguish political mechanisms according to whether they facilitate gaining *consent* through negotiation, or facilitate making *decisions* with or without much consent, or facilitate both *consent and decisions.*

A system that required extensive consent but made it difficult to reach a decision—for example, a system in which all decisions had to be made by unanimous vote—would so greatly prolong negotiations and impede decisions that the prospect of mounting a revolution in order to get something done might become increasingly attractive. On the other hand, in a system where it was easy for leaders to make decisions without seeking the consent of others, minor questions could be settled with dispatch. But when ordinary citizens seriously disagreed with one another or with their leaders in such a system, decisions could be imposed without their consent; to secure obedience many citizens would have to be coerced by the government. By embittering and alienating the citizens who were coerced, such a system might ripen disputes into resistance and revolution. Thus a system that could somehow facilitate both negotiation of consent and arriving at decisions might serve best to keep conflicts from becoming so severe as to generate a revolution.

CONFLICT: A PARADIGM Let me now draw together the threads of this discussion on conflict into a paradigm or model that will be helpful in understanding the next three chapters.

The intensity or severity of a political conflict in a polyarchy is indicated by the extent to which people on each side see the other as an enemy to be destroyed; evidence that political disagreements are becoming severe is an increase in threats or actual use of violence, suppression of opponents, civil war, secession, disloyalty, or a marked increase in demoralization, apathy, indifference, or alienation.

The intensity or severity of a political conflict depends on at least four sets of factors:

1. The way in which politically relevant attitudes are distributed among citizens and leaders.

a. The greater the number of citizens who hold extreme (and opposing)

Table 21.1
A Paradigm: Some Factors
that Moderate or Intensify
Political Conflicts

	Conflict is more likely to be	
	Moderate if:	Severe if:
1. The distribution of attitudes is	convergent	divergent
a. Attitudes of citizens are	convergent	divergent
b. Attitudes of political leaders and activists are	convergent	divergent
2. Lines of cleavage are	overlapping (crosscutting)	nonoverlapping (cumulative)
3. Threats to ways of life are	absent	present
a. Privileged groups feel	secure	seriously threatened
b. Aspiring groups feel	successful	frustrated
4. Political institutions provide		
a. Negotiations for consent but not decisions	no	yes
b. Decisions without consent	no	yes
c. Agreed processes for negotiating consent and arriving at decisions	yes	no

views, the more severe a conflict is likely to be. Conversely, the greater the number who hold moderate views, the less severe a conflict is likely to be.

b. The more extreme the views of political leaders and activists in comparison with the views of ordinary citizens, the more severe the conflict; conversely, the more moderate the views of leaders and activists in comparison with other citizens, the less severe the conflict is likely to be.

2. The patterns of cleavage. The more conflicts accumulate along the same lines of cleavage, the more severe they are likely to be; conversely, the more conflicts intersect along different lines of cleavage, the less severe they are.

3. How much is at stake.

a. The more at stake, the more severe a conflict is likely to be.

b. A conflict in which no contestant can possibly make himself better off except by making other contestants worse off is likely to be more severe than a conflict in which there is a possibility that no contestant need be worse off than before, and some may be better off.

c. Conflicts involving incompatible 'ways of life' are bound to be particularly severe.

4. The political institutions.

a. Political institutions and processes are likely to intensify conflicts if they require the groups involved to negotiate but do not provide any acceptable way by which leaders can terminate negotiations and arrive at a decision.

b. Political institutions and processes are likely to intensify conflicts if they make it possible for leaders to make decisions without engaging in negotiations to obtain the consent of the persons, groups, or parties involved.

c. Political institutions and processes are most likely to reduce the intensity of conflicts if they embody wide-spread agreement on procedures, *both* for negotiating in order to gain consent and for terminating the negotiations and arriving at a decision.

These propositions are summarized in Table 21.1.

Overlapping Cleavages— Low Polarization

22

Although Americans tend to agree on a great many questions, there are some over which they disagree. Over the course of American history, certain types of issues have recurred as subjects of conflict: the nature and extent of democratic processes, foreign policy, the role of the government in the regulation and control of the economy, the place of the Negro in American life.

Yet these issues do not ordinarily polarize Americans into two exclusive and antagonistic camps. Indeed, the pattern of disagreements in political attitudes and loyalties may itself actually inhibit polarization and encourage conciliation. In particular, two characteristics of the pattern of cleavages stimulate efforts toward conciliation and compromise and weaken pressures toward polarization.

First, differences in political attitudes, actions, and loyalties are not highly related to differences in region, social standing, occupation, and other socioeconomic characteristics. Of course there often is *some* relation; but it is usually rather weak. People in the same region, in the same status group, or in the same occupation do not tend to form distinct homogeneous political blocs. Consequently, *polarization of politics along social, economic, or regional lines is inhibited.*

Second, differences in political attitudes and loyalties are not highly interrelated among themselves. Two people who hold the same attitudes on one question frequently hold different attitudes on other questions. To overstate the point, every ally is sometimes an enemy and every enemy is sometimes an ally. Consequently, *polarization of politics along ideological lines is inhibited.*

REGIONAL DIFFERENCES Consider geography: American politics has often been described as a conflict between different sections or regions. And it is true, of course, that with respect to the place of the Afro-American in American life the cleavage between North and South has been persistent and sometimes bitter. As we shall see in the next chapter, from 1850 to about 1877 the bundle of issues associated with slavery and the Negro polarized American politics to an unprecedented degree.

With this single exception, however, regional conflicts have never polarized Americans into distinct camps. Like the other major sources of conflict in American politics, the importance of regional factors varies greatly from one issue to another; although powerful on any issue touching the role of blacks in American life, regional differences are only moderately important on other issues and even negligible on a great many questions. Moreover, regionalism in politics is probably declining. Finally, regional conflicts follow a pattern of overlapping cleavages, not polarization.

In Congress

Evidence for these propositions is readily available from the arena where regional conflicts might be expected to show up most clearly, in Congress.

Southern Democrats have displayed more unity in the way they vote in Congress than any other regional group. Yet even Southern regionalism is quite limited. The distinctiveness of Southern Democrats tends to be confined to a few issues, mainly those involving blacks.[1] From 1937 onward, it is true, a majority of Southern Democrats allied themselves on a number of occasions with a majority of Northern Republicans in voting against a majority of Northern Democrats. This conservative coalition was particularly noticeable during John F. Kennedy's presidency when it defeated a number of his legislative proposals. Yet even during this period, the coalition appeared on only 28 percent of the votes in the House and Senate in 1961, 14 percent in 1962, and 17 percent in 1963.[2]

Aside from Southern Democrats, it is difficult to find any persistent regional patterns in congressional voting. Among Republicans in Congress there is, in fact, no equivalent to Southern Democrats. One study of four sessions of Congress found that

> analysis of the party loyalty of Republicans from various sections reveals shifting alliances from session to session. In 1921 and 1931, West Central

1. See Raymond E. Wolfinger and Joan Heifetz, "Safe Seats, Seniority, and Power in Congress," *American Political Science Review*, 59 (June, 1965), 337–349; H. Douglas Price, "Are Southern Democrats Different?" in *Politics and Social Life: An Introduction to Political Behavior*, Nelson W. Polsby, R. A. Dentler, and Paul A. Smith (Boston: Houghton Mifflin, 1963), pp. 740–756; Turner, *Party and Constituency*, p. 130 fn. See also the conclusion of V. O. Key, Jr., on examining Senate roll calls for seven Senate sessions from 1933 through 1945: ". . . it is primarily on the race issue that the South presents a united front against the rest of the United States" (*Politics, Parties, and Pressure Groups*, 3rd. ed. [New York: Thomas Y. Crowell, 1952], p. 265); and also Key, *Southern Politics*, chs. 16 and 17.

2. *Congressional Quarterly Weekly Report* (April 17, 1964), p. 737.

	National	Region			
		East	Midwest	South	West
Favor	14%	19%	15%	8%	13%
Oppose	81	73	81	87	84
No opinion	5	8	4	5	3
	100%	100%	100%	100%	100%

Source: *Gallup Opinion Index* No. 58, April, 1970. The question asked was: "In general, do you favor or oppose the bussing of Negro and white school children from one school district to another?"

	National	Region			
		East	Midwest	South	West
Should	38%	45%	35%	29%	43%
Should not	62	55	65	71	57
	100%	100%	100%	100%	100%

Source: *Gallup Opinion Index* No. 65, November, 1970. The choice was: "Racial integration *should/should not* be speeded up."

and Border Republicans rebelled against majorities from other areas. In 1937 the West rebelled against the East. In 1944 Central states were in control of the party, and insurgency was strongest on the Pacific Coast, and to a lesser extent in the Northeast and Rockies.[3]

In the Population at Large

In the population at large, it is difficult nowadays to discover distinctive regional clusters of attitudes. Attitudes change, of course, and like other aspects of life, regional differences in attitudes are probably in decline. The South, long the most easily distinguishable region in the country, has in recent decades lost a good deal of distinctiveness in attitudes toward public policies. Even on sensitive racial questions differences between the South and other regions of the country have been diminishing—partly because the possibility of integration brings out similar attitudes in both North and South. In 1970, for example, majorities opposed to bussing school children were overwhelming in all regions and scarcely greater in the South than in the West and Midwest (Table 22.1). Although more Southern whites than Northern whites were opposed to speeding the pace of school integration, once again the proportion of Southern whites was not vastly higher than in the Midwest (Table 22.2). In actual fact, schools in the South were more integrated

3. Turner, *Party and Constituency*, p. 146.

Table 22.3		National	Region			
Attitudes Toward Four Different Problems			East	Midwest	South	West
Inflation[a]						
	Should	65%	62%	73%	61%	68%
	Should not	35	38	27	39	32
Campus Riots[b]						
	Should	79	74	87	76	83
	Should not	21	26	13	24	17
Poverty[c]						
	Should	61	64	61	59	59
	Should not	39	36	39	41	41
Crimes[d]						
	Should	91	93	92	88	90
	Should not	9	7	8	12	10

Source: Gallup Opinion Index No. 65, November, 1970. The choices were: (a) "The federal government should/should not take measures to keep wages (salaries) and prices at their present level"; (b) "Federal aid should/should not be denied colleges that do not expel students involved in campus riots"; (c) "Congress should/should not vote more money to improve the living conditions of poor people in the cities"; and (d) "Congress should/should not vote more money to help police and other law enforcement agencies to deal with crime."

by 1971 than in the rest of the country.[4] On other matters, the South is not, despite its reputation, significantly more 'conservative' on most questions than the rest of the country (Table 22.3)—and perhaps never has been.[5]

The Midwest was once thought to be the stronghold of isolationism. It may once have been. Yet opinion surveys over almost three decades have not revealed large differences between the opinions of Midwesterners and the rest of the country on international affairs.[6] A 1956 survey

4. In the eleven southern states of Alabama, Arkansas, Florida, Georgia, Louisiana, Mississippi, North Carolina, South Carolina, Tennessee, Texas, and Virginia, "the percentage of black pupils in majority-white schools — those with 50 or more per cent white children — rose from 18.4 per cent in the 1968–69 school year to 39.1 per cent in the 1970–71 school year. . . . For the nation as a whole the comparable figure rose from 23.4 per cent in 1968–69 to 33.1 per cent in the present school year.

"The percentage of black pupils attending all-black schools dropped from 68 per cent in the 1968–69 school year to 14.1 per cent in the 1970–71 school year. . . . Nationally the percentage of black pupils in fully segregated schools dropped from 39.1 per cent two years ago to 14 per cent today, marginally below the Southern figure. But the rate of decrease was far slower in the North than it was in the South" (New York Times, June 6, 1971, pp. 1, 37).

5. It is worth recalling that during the period of unrest from the 1870s to about 1896, the South seemed to be more 'radical' than the rest of the country. See Hannah G. Roach, "Sectionalism in Congress (1870 to 1890)," American Political Science Review, 19 (August, 1925), 500–526; and C. Vann Woodward, The Burden of Southern History (New York: Vintage Books, 1960), pp. 149 ff.

6. Since this statement runs contrary to a widespread impression you may wish to look at some surveys. During the two years preceding the entry of the United States into World War II, surveys showed that opinion in the East Central and West Central states was only slightly more 'isolationist' than in the other regions outside the South: the South was consistently less 'isolationist' and more 'interventionist.' Cf. the surveys reported in Cantril, Public Opinion 1935–1946, pp. 966–978. After America's entry into the war, opinion in favor of joining a world organization was as high in the Midwest as elsewhere, and may have been higher than in some other regions (Ibid., No. 7, p. 906; No. 35, p. 910).

Table 22.4
Region in Relation to
Distribution Along Scale
Measuring Attitudes
Toward American
Involvement in
Foreign Affairs

Internationalism	Midwest	Northeast	Far West	South
High	53%	59%	58%	56%
Medium	27	25	24	26
Low	20	16	18	18
	100%	100%	100%	100%
Number	372	469	177	398

Source: V. O. Key, *Public Opinion*, pp. 107, 562.

Table 22.5
Regional Distribution of
Foreign Policy Attitudes
in 1970

Issue	East	Midwest	South	West
Too much defense spending	56%	52%	37%	55%
Support U. N. peace force	67	60	65	62
Stronger U. N.	85	86	81	85
Admit Red China to U. N.	42	37	24	40
Deadline for withdrawal from Vietnam by January, 1972	61	69	56	56
Pro-Israel	48	37	42	50

Sources: April 15, 1971 Gallup Release, *Gallup Opinion Index* No. 58, April, 1970, and No. 65, November, 1970.

measuring attitudes "toward American involvement in foreign affairs" was very revealing (Table 22.4). Respondents were asked whether they agreed or disagreed with the following statements and the answers were distributed along an attitude measurement scale:

> "This country would be better off if we just stayed home and did not concern ourselves with problems in other parts of the world."
> "The United States should give economic help to the poor countries of the world even if they can't pay for it."
> "The United States should keep soldiers overseas where they can help countries that are against communism."
> "The United States should give help to foreign countries even if they are not as much against communism as we are."

Table 22.5 offers some evidence from surveys made in 1970 on a half dozen issues. The differences among regions on these issues were small.

The reputation of the Midwest as the center of isolationism may have been built upon the conduct of a number of militant isolationists in Congress from midwestern states. Yet a careful study of voting on foreign aid measures from 1939 to 1958 in the House of Representatives shows that

> Mid-western isolationism, to the extent that it did exist, was peculiar to the Republican party. G.O.P. Congressmen from the central regions were more isolationist than those from the East and Pacific coasts in each Congress. On the other side of the aisle, however, Democrats from the Mid-

west were consistently more internationalist than those from the Southern and Mountain states, particularly after the 77th Congress (1941–42).[7]

Factors Reducing Regional Cleavages

How then can we account for the fact that, if we exclude the question of the Afro-American, regional conflict is ordinarily moderate and does not split the country into persistently antagonistic divisions?

Absence of strong regional subcultures. In the first place, outside of the Old South, genuinely regional ways of life in sharp contradiction to one another have never developed in the United States. To be sure, there were and still are regional differences—in speech, in manners, in bearing, even to some extent in styles of life; and typically an American has some loyalties, of a sort, to his region. But (putting the South and the Afro-American to one side) these moderately differing regional cultures have never, as such, constituted much of a threat to one another, at least not in a politically relevant way. The fact that a man from Maine speaks in a fashion which someone from Oklahoma may find puzzling or amusing, or that a New Englander is more formal and less easygoing in his ways than a Westerner hardly constitutes the material for sharp and enduring political controversies. Regional differences in this sense have always been less the source of political conflicts than of superficial and usually good-natured rivalries, a standing opportunity for any speaker to flatter his audience by expounding the virtues of the region, and a justification for the belief, illusory but highly prized among Americans, that they are a people of incredible diversity.

Mobility. In the second place, Americans have never stayed long enough in one place to permit regional loyalties to gain the power they might have if people were more content with life in the old home town. That Americans are a restless people, a nation not only of immigrants but also of migrants, has become a national and international cliché; but it happens to be true. One American in four is now living in a state different from the one in which he was born. Of these migrant Americans, about half have moved from a state next to the present one, and the other half from some more distant state. About one person in seven was born in some other region. And what is true now, we learn from the census, has been true for at least a hundred years. The percentages for 1850 vary only slightly from those for 1950.[8] With an expanding frontier, Americans have always been on the move. In 1850, in the region consisting of Ohio, Indiana, Illinois, Michigan, and Wisconsin, one white resident out of

---

7. Leroy N. Rieselbach, "The Demography of the Congressional Vote on Foreign Aid, 1939–1958," *American Political Science Review*, 58 (September, 1964), 577–588, at pp. 582–3; see also Table IV, p. 582.

8. *Historical Statistics*, p. 41, Series C 1–14.

three had been born in some other region; further west in the seven states bounded by Minnesota and North Dakota on the north and by Missouri and Kansas on the south, more than one-half of the native white population had migrated from other regions; in Arkansas, Louisiana, Oklahoma, and Texas, slightly less than one-half were from outside that region. A century later, the frontier was the Pacific Coast, where more than half of the 1950 population had been born elsewhere—a quarter, in fact, in the Midwest; nearly half the people in the Mountain States came from a different region; even in the South Atlantic states about one white person in seven was not, by birth, a Southerner.[9]

Internal heterogeneity. Third, the various regions of the United States are internally very heterogeneous. So much so, in fact, that it is exceedingly difficult to decide how to draw regional boundaries: one must choose one set of states for one purpose, another set for a different purpose. The U.S. Census, the Federal Reserve Board, the Department of Agriculture, the student of electoral politics—all use rather different regions. Are there four regions in the United States—or fourteen?

New England and the South are, for historical reasons, the easiest to identify as distinct regions. Yet neither New England nor the South has ever been a political monolith. Both have been split internally along many different lines of cleavage. Socioeconomic conflicts have been as bitter among white Southerners as anywhere in the United States; indeed, it is not much of an exaggeration to say that the only question on which the white people of the South have ever been able to unite is on maintaining the subordination of the Negro—and even on this question there has generally been a dissenting minority. New England, unlike the South, has never had even this incentive to provide it with enduring political unity. As for other regions, they are even more heterogeneous politically.

Regional conflicts really socioeconomic. Fourth, what has passed for 'regional' conflict in the past has usually been no more than a special case of socioeconomic conflict. The 'regional' conflicts that occupy attention in history books generally occurred when the occupations or incomes of some people in one section of the country were thought to be threatened in some way by people in another section. Even slavery might be interpreted in this fashion. To some extent, the American economy has always been based upon regional specialization; different regions have somewhat different specialties.[10] Hence the economic needs, opportunities, and goals of some of the people in one region may

9. *Ibid.*, pp. 41, 43, Series C 15–24.
10. Cf. H. S. Perloff, E. J. Dunn, Jr., E. E. Lampard, and R. F. Muth, *Regions, Resources and Economic Growth* (Baltimore: Johns Hopkins Press, 1960).

come into conflict with those of another. When the country was predominantly agricultural, climate and soil influenced the kinds of crops produced; and the availability of markets was affected by location, transportation facilities, and tariffs. All of these factors created opportunities for conflict. But they were at base socioeconomic conflicts. If regional differences have rarely been great enough to polarize American society along regional lines, what then of socioeconomic differences?

SOCIOECONOMIC DIFFERENCES: OCCUPATIONS

Alas for simplicity, socioeconomic differences in the United States also tend to produce many intersecting lines of cleavage rather than one big dividing line, or even two or three of them.

The way in which a citizen makes his living, his occupation, his property, the source, amount, and security of his income, all these economic factors have been highly important in shaping the way different citizens appraise the stakes involved in political issues. Because Americans differ in their economic positions, and because differences in economic positions foster differing political views, political controversies can often—though by no means always—be traced to ways in which citizens differ from one another economically. Although economic explanations of American politics do not explain everything, they do explain a good deal.

Yet when we try to explain American politics by looking for economic factors, the resulting cleavages are more significant for their variety and complexity than for their simplicity. In fact, one soon makes three discoveries. First, socioeconomic differences do matter: there is usually some correlation, however weak it may be, between attitudes about politics and differences in social and economic positions. Second, however, you find that no matter how you classify Americans, whether in economic categories or any others, the groups invariably turn out to be politically heterogeneous; that is, on most questions any category of Americans is internally divided in its views in somewhat the same way the rest of the population is divided. Third, you also find that even when individuals or groups agree on one issue, they are likely to be split on another. This always seems to have been the case.

Before the Civil War when most Americans were farmers, differences in crops, markets, problems of transportation and competition, and effects of credit, mortgages, and the supply of currency all helped to produce political conflict. Conflicts over the tariff, national expenditures for canals and roads, banks, the control of the Mississippi—all can be partly explained by economic differences. Yet so far as one can now tell from rather inadequate data, the same economic groups were not always allied. Coalitions both in the electorate and in Congress were somewhat fluid. Even after the Civil War, as industrial capitalism began to displace agriculture in the American economy, the cleavage between business-men and urban proletariat did not come to dominate politics as it did in a number of European countries and as one might reasonably have expected it would in the United States.[11] Labor and socialist parties failed to gain much ground. The two major parties remained, as they had been before, conglomerate parties with catchall programs. It is true that the Republicans and Democrats often seemed to have different centers of gravity. The Republican center of gravity was business; in the Demo-cratic party it was the white South and increasingly the great urban political machines based on the immigrants and the poor. But because businessmen were in a minority, as they always are, the Republicans could not win elections without the support of farmers and even of urban workers. White Southerners were, as had been obvious to their sorrow for generations, also in a minority; hence Democrats could not win presidential elections without support in the North and West, that is, among farmers and urban workers.

In the twentieth century political conflicts have not been fought across any single and constant socioeconomic boundary. For example, it is virtually impossible to find any sizeable economic stratum in the United States whose opinions on political questions are violently at odds with those of the rest of the population. Thus if we classify Americans according to whether the head of the household is a professional man, a businessman, a clerical worker, a skilled worker, an unskilled worker, or a farmer, we invariably find that whenever Americans in general disagree on some question, then people within each of these occupational groups will also disagree among themselves. This is not to say that opinion is uniform among all occupational groups; it is not, and the differences are of great importance. What is striking is not how much variation there is from one group to another, but how little.

For example, a survey in 1964 by Free and Cantril tapped attitudes on five key issues of public policy—federal aid to education, Medicare, the federal housing program, urban renewal, and the government's responsibility to do away with poverty. According to the extent to which respondents supported policies requiring positive federal action to deal with these problems, they were classified into five categories. Table 22.6 clearly confirms the first two of the three observations just made. Dif-ferences in occupations do matter: blue-collar workers are more in favor than the other major groupings of intervention by the federal government on the issues represented in this table; indeed, as other surveys show, on a great variety of economic issues they hold inter-ventionist attitudes. Yet the differences are on the whole rather modest. If we assumed that a high degree of polarization means, say, that more

11. Cf. Chapter 26.

Table 22.6
Attitudes Toward Federal
Action on Five Public
Policy Issues, by
Occupations, 1964

Occupation	Strongly Favor- able[a]	Predom- inantly Favor- able	Mixed	Predom- inantly Against	Strongly Against
Professional, business	33%	21%	22%	11%	13%
White-collar workers	39	20	29	5	7
Farmers	34	24	21	12	9
Blue-collar workers	51	23	18	5	3
Nonlabor[b]	44	19	20	9	8

[a] The authors labeled their categories ''liberal'' and ''conservative'' where I have used simply ''favorable'' or ''against'' federal action.

[b] Consists primarily of households headed by retired people, and, to a lesser extent, by housewives, students, or the physically handicapped.

Source: Free and Cantril, *Political Beliefs of Americans*, p. 216.

than two out of three persons in one group hold attitudes in marked conflict with two out of three persons in another group, then what is striking about Table 22.6 is the absence of any significant polarization. In fact, a majority in each of the five occupational categories strongly or predominantly favors government intervention on economic issues.

Free and Cantril also constructed an ''ideological spectrum'' from responses to five statements[12] that were designed to tap general political perspectives rather than attitudes toward the kinds of specific policies represented in Table 22.6. Depending on the extent to which they agreed or disagreed with the five statements, respondents were classified as ''completely conservative,'' ''predominantly conservative,'' ''middle-of-the-road,'' ''predominantly liberal,'' and ''completely liberal.'' One highly interesting finding is the discovery of a second dimension of ''liberalism-conservatism.'' On specific economic issues, as Table 22.6 indicates, preponderant majorities support interventionist policies that would ordinarily be identified in the United States as on the 'liberal' side of the liberal-conservative spectrum. Yet Table 22.7 reveals that at a more general or abstract level preponderant majorities give responses that would usually be identified as on the 'conservative' side. I shall come back to this finding later on. Meanwhile, what is as striking about Table 22.7 as about Table 22.6 is the absence of marked differences in outlook among the major occupational categories.

These differences of opinion within occupational groups, and the similarities of opinion from one group to another, mean that conflict

12. The five statements were: ''1. The Federal Government is interfering too much in state and local matters. 2. The government has gone too far in regulating business and interfering with the free enterprise system. 3. Social problems here in this country could be solved more effectively if the government would only keep its hands off and let people in local communities handle their own problems in their own way. 4. Generally speaking, any able-bodied person who really wants to work in this country can find a job and earn a living. 5. We should rely more on individual initiative and ability and not so much on governmental welfare programs'' (Free and Cantril, *Political Beliefs of Americans*, pp. 31–32).

Table 22.7
Ideological Attitudes by
Occupations, 1964

Occupation	Completely or Predom- inantly Liberal	Middle of Road	Predom- inantly Conser- vative	Completely Conser- vative
Professional, business	19%	33%	17%	31%
White-collar workers	17	29	17	37
Farmers	9	28	20	43
Blue-collar workers	18	37	22	23
Nonlabor	10	30	18	42

Source: Free and Cantril, *Political Beliefs of Americans*, p 221.

rarely if ever occurs along clear-cut occupational lines of cleavage. A political leader who favors active government intervention in the economy will draw both his supporters and his opponents from all occupational groups. He cannot therefore make his appeal exclusively to the laboring classes, lest he lose his support among business and professional men and farmers. And by the same token, a conservative who opposes government intervention in economic life will gain supporters from a great variety of economic groups, including skilled laborers and farmers.

SOCIAL CLASSES   *Problems of definition.* Social classes are not much more significant. In fact, although differences in status unquestionably exist in the United States and are highly important in the lives of many Americans, class lines are so blurred that it taxes the ingenuity of social scientists to provide justifiable methods for classifying Americans according to their social class. In sample surveys, the problem is generally solved in two ways. The individual respondent himself may tell the interviewer what class he thinks he belongs to; social scientists often call this his 'subjective' status or self-identified 'class' identification. Alternatively, the social scientist may himself assign an individual to some set of classes— two, three, five, six, or whatnot—according to so-called objective criteria, such as the amount of education he has, his occupation, and his income. The product of this method is often called his 'objective' status or class.

Distribution of class identification. Earlier surveys in which respondents were asked to choose between the upper, middle, or *lower* class resulted in nearly everyone placing himself in the middle class and thereby encouraged the illusion that few Americans identified themselves with the working class. Once the option of "working class" was offered in addition to "lower class," the proportion in the "middle class" declined to a minority. In fact, in a study of nine nations undertaken in 1948, using the question, "If you were asked to use a name for your social class, would you say you belong to the middle class, working class, or upper class?" the proportion who identified themselves with the working class was higher among Americans than among Australians, Frenchmen, Germans, Italians, and Norwegians:[13]

	Middle	Working	Upper	Don't Know
Australia	50%	47%	2%	1%
Britain	35	60	2	3
France	44	46	6	4
Germany	52	41	3	4
Italy	54	42	4	0
Mexico	45	51	2	2
Netherlands	33	60	4	3
Norway	43	45	1	11
United States	42	51	4	3

In 1956 the Survey Research Center of the University of Michigan put the following question to a national sample of Americans: "There's quite a bit of talk these days about different social classes. Most people say they belong to the middle class or to the working class. Do you ever think of yourself as being in one of these classes?" One out of every three respondents said no. These people who did not spontaneously put themselves in any class were then asked, "Well, if you had to make a choice, would you call yourself middle class or working class?" With the aid of still another question, all the respondents were ultimately sorted out as follows:[14]

Middle Classes		
Upper	7%	
Average	29%	36%
Working Classes		
Upper	9%	
Average	52%	61%
Don't Know		3%
		100%

In 1964, Free and Cantril asked: "In the field of politics and government do you feel your own interests are similar to the interests of the propertied class, the middle class, or the working class?" A majority of Americans identified their interests with the working class:[15]

13. Buchanan and Cantril, *How Nations See Each Other*, p. 13.

14. Key, *Public Opinion*, p. 140. Similar results were found by Richard Centers, *The Psychology of Social Classes* (Princeton: Princeton University Press, 1949), p. 77.

15. Free and Cantril, *Political Beliefs of Americans*, p. 206.

Propertied	5%
Middle	37%
Working	53%
Don't know	5%

Thus, Americans are not, as is sometimes thought, a people who all think of themselves as belonging to the middle class.

FINDINGS   *Class feelings are moderate.* The two principal methods we use to assign Americans to social classes seem to show several things. In the first place, class identity seems to be very weak. One adult American out of three, as we have seen, says that he does not ever think of himself as being in the middle class or the working class. Even among those who identify themselves with one or the other, class feelings seem to be tepid. It is illuminating, in fact, to look beyond the bare statistics to the kinds of things the respondents say to the interviewers who ask them what "class" they belong to. Happily, some of the responses made to a survey in 1956 have been summarized by V. O. Key, and reveal, as he says, "the tenuous quality of class identification":

> . . . A Nebraska farm housewife on class: "I suppose it would be working class as that is about all we do." A North Carolina gift shop proprietress when asked if she had to make a choice: "That's a new one to me. I just want to say I'm as good as any of them." An Ohio skilled worker when faced by the choice problem: "I wouldn't say. (Why?) Well, what is the middle class and working class?" A South Carolina housewife: "I think middle class and working class come under the same heading." A Los Angeles housewife: "I can't say. I just wouldn't know." The wife of a New Mexico miner: "I don't quite understand the difference. I guess we work so we must belong to the working class. I don't quite see it." An Idaho lady: "I'm retired but used to be working class." A Pennsylvania steelworker: "When you're in a mill you're workin'." A North Carolina retail grocer had never thought of herself as being of a class: "I think that class talk is just political talk. Here the Republicans are called the rich man's party, and they run a man who came up from just plain people, and the Democrats say they are the little man's party and they run a millionaire." Wirer in California radio factory: "Well I work for a living so I guess I'm in the working class." Retired Ohio worker: (Ever thought of yourself as being in one of these classes?) "Never gave that a thought, missus." The wife of a Kentucky brewery salesman: (Ever thought of self in class?) "I never thought of that." An interviewer noted: "I've had more trouble with R's (respondents) in regard to this class thing. Where the distinction is, no one seems to know."
>
> The schedule also contained a question whether the respondent's family when he was growing up was working class or middle class. A Connecticut respondent: "Middle class after '29. Upper class before '29." An Iowa farmer: "I've always been just average — no upper class stuff for me or my family." A Texas widow reported that her family had been upper middle: "We didn't have a college education but we tried to keep ourselves with good characters and things like that." The wife of an Ohio skilled

worker: "No, just average people; don't know if we came in any class." A retired hospital orderly said his father had been middle class: "Upper part. My father owned a saloon." A Texas lady: "We always had plenty but what class I don't know."[16]

In the Buchanan and Cantril study in 1948, few Americans seemed to see people in classes other than their own as implacable enemies. In response to the question, "Do you think you have anything in common with fellow countrymen not in the working class?" seven out of ten Americans who had identified themselves with the working class answered yes.[17]

Subjective class is not identical with objective class. To confuse the role of social class even further, there are persistent discrepancies between "subjective" status—the class with which a voter identifies himself—and "objective" status defined by occupation or other measures. Some blue-collar workers say they belong to the middle class; a considerable number of white-collar workers say they are in the working class. Given the vagueness of class boundaries in the United States, these anomalies are scarcely surprising. But what is highly significant is that if two people whom an observer would put in the same social class nonetheless put themselves in different social classes, they are likely to make rather different judgments about political matters. A skilled worker who tells you that he belongs to the middle class is also likely to look at political questions with the kinds of values, biases, and aspirations that tend to prevail among people with distinctly middle-class occupations—business and professional men, for example. A skilled worker who says that he belongs to the working class, on the other hand, is likely to consider political choices more nearly from the same viewpoint as other workers. To be specific, if we take a group of citizens from the same broad occupational category, those who identify themselves as belonging to the working class are much more likely to have a 'liberal' outlook on economic issues than those who say they belong to the middle class.

Class provides a basis for cleavages: in attitudes. Despite its weakness as a divisive factor, status or social class does of course provide some basis for political cleavages in the United States. "The extensive modern literature on social class and political behavior has shown persistently

---

16. Key, *Public Opinion*, p. 141 fn.

17. In most of the countries, the percentages were considerably higher among middle-class and upper-class respondents than among working-class respondents (Buchanan and Cantril, *How Nations See Each Other*, Appendix D, Report of Survey Agencies, pp. 125 ff). Among working-class respondents only, the percentage answering yes to the question "Do you think you have anything in common with fellow countrymen not of your class?" were: United States, 70%; Australia, 70%; Norway, 66%; Great Britain, 60%; France, 58%; Germany (British zone of occupation), 53%; Mexico, 46%; Netherlands, 45%; Italy, 37% (*ibid.*, pp. 17, 18).

Table 22.8
Attitudes Toward Federal
Action on Five Public
Policy Issues, by Self-
Identified Classes, 1964

Class Identification	Strongly Favorable	Predominantly Favorable	Mixed	Predominantly Against	Strongly Against
Propertied class	20%	20%	34%	12%	14%
Middle class	36	21	24	10	9
Working class	50	24	17	5	4

Source: Free and Cantril, *Political Beliefs of Americans*, p. 216.

Table 22.9
Ideological Attitudes, by
Self-Identified Classes,
1964

Class Identification	Completely or Predominantly Liberal	Middle of Road	Predominantly Conservative	Completely Conservative
Propertied class	4%	33%	18%	45%
Middle class	13	32	20	35
Working class	21	35	20	24

Source: Free and Cantril, *Political Beliefs of Americans*, p. 221.

that individuals of higher status (subjectively or objectively) tend to give 'conservative' responses on questions of economic policy and tend as well to vote Republican; individuals of lower status respond more 'radically' and vote Democratic."[18] The relationship is, however, not very strong. That is, we find once again that a sizeable proportion of people with higher status are not conservative whereas a large fraction of voters in the lower status group are. Thus Free and Cantril found that respondents who identified their interests with the working class were more favorable toward the idea of active federal intervention on key questions than were those who identified themselves with the middle class—and both were markedly more than the self-styled propertied class (Table 22.8). Differences also showed up on the liberal-conservative ideological spectrum constructed by Free and Cantril; but what is even more obvious from Table 22.9 is how modest the ideological differences were between working class and middle class. Only the tiny propertied class stands out very sharply in its conservatism.

In voting. As had already been indicated, like occupational differences class differences also show up in voting. If we arbitrarily divide the population into working and middle classes by using the "objective" indicator of manual versus nonmanual occupations, or if you like blue-collar versus white-collar, we would expect to find members of the working class giving more support to the Democratic party than does the middle class. And of course they do. But a comparison of public

18. Campbell et al., *The American Voter*, p. 346.

Figure 22.1
Class Voting in the
Anglo-American Countries,
1936-62

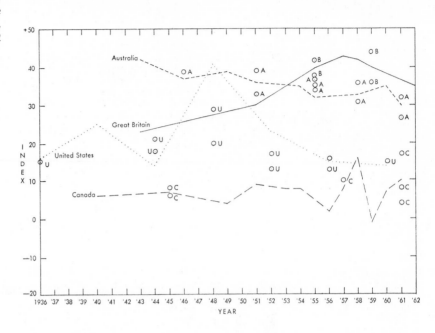

Source: Alford, *Party and Society*, pp. 102–103. "The index of class voting was computed by subtracting the percentage of non-manual workers voting for 'Left' parties from the percentage of manual workers voting for 'Left' parties. For Great Britain, the Labour party was used; for Australia, the Australian Labor party; for the United States, the Democratic party; for Canada, the CCF (or NDP) and Liberal parties. Where two parties were classified as 'Left,' their votes among each strata were combined. For a discussion of the index, see Chapter 4. See Appendix B for the exact questions asked in each survey, the occupational divisions used, the dates of polls, and the numbers of cases in manual and non-manual occupations. The surveys were taken at various times between 1952 and 1962. All questions referred to voting intention or past vote in a national election."

opinion surveys from 1936 to 1962 showed that the difference in party preference between people in manual and nonmanual occupations was markedly less in the United States than in Britain or Australia (though higher than in Canada, where class voting was almost negligible). In the United States during that period a third to nearly a half of the nonmanual strata voted Democratic. And, with the exception of 1948, from a third to nearly a half of the manual strata voted Republican (Figure 22.1).

As Figure 22.2 shows, the relationship is also not very steady. That is, the extent to which one's status seems to have a bearing on one's political views seems to fluctuate. In the presidential election of 1944, which took place in the midst of a great war of survival, the relationship between one's status or class and the way one voted in the election was quite weak. Franklin Roosevelt, the wartime president, drew his support from all social strata. After the war, however, economic questions again

Figure 22.2
Class Voting in the
United States, 1936-60

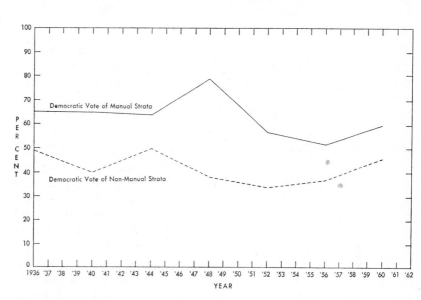

Source: Alford, *Party and Society*, p. 227.

became highly controversial, as they had been before the war. Seizing upon economic discontents in his 1948 campaign, President Truman employed much of the New Deal ideology of the 1930s, attacked the Republicans as the party of wealth and business, challenged his opponent with an ambitious reform program, his Fair Deal, and castigated the Republican-dominated Congress for rejecting his proposals. In that election, the relationship between status and presidential vote rose to a postwar peak. From that high point it receded in subsequent elections. General Eisenhower's appeal transcended class; like FDR in 1944, Eisenhower in 1952 and 1956 attracted support among all segments of the population.[19]

The net impact has been to give something of a class tinge to the two major parties. Thus Free and Cantril found that nearly two out of three Republicans identified their interests with the middle or propertied classes, whereas two out of three Democrats identified their interest with the working class (Table 22.10). The two parties, then, have different centers of gravity, and their leaders can generally be counted on to respond somewhat differently to these diverging gravitational pulls.

19. See also *ibid.*, p. 347.

Table 22.10
Class Identification
by Party

Identify Interests with	Republicans		Independents		Democrats	
Propertied class	11%	} 61%	5%	} 46%	2%	} 31%
Middle class	50		41		29	
Working class	35		46		65	
Don't know	4		8		4	
	100%		100%		100%	

Source: Free and Cantril, *Political Beliefs of Americans*, p. 142.

RACIAL, ETHNIC, AND RELIGIOUS CLEAVAGES

It was long thought—and widely hoped—that the United States was truly a melting pot of races, religions, and ethnic groups all of whose members would rapidly shed their distinctiveness in the process of Americanization. Recently, however, the melting pot has come under severe attack both as ideal and as fact. As an ideal, the melting pot is often seen nowadays as a discreditable process of compulsory homogenization during which successive waves of immigrants were expected to abandon their own cultural heritage and, at great cost to their own identities and sense of self-respect, adapt so far as possible to the predominant culture of the white Anglo-Saxon Protestant American.

However one may evaluate the moral and psychological gains and costs of the melting pot ideal, the extent to which homogenization has occurred is now much more debatable than a few decades ago. For evidence accumulates that earlier announcements of the end of political and social cleavages related to racial, ethnic, and religious differences were premature. Thus after studying the major ethnic groups in New York City a decade ago, Glazer and Moynihan concluded:

> Religion and race seem to define the major groups into which American society is evolving as the specifically national aspect of ethnicity (i.e., the specific nation from which one's ancestors came) declines. In our large American cities, four major groups emerge: Catholics, Jews, white Protestants, and Negroes.[20]

Like many other prevailing American social and political ideals, the melting pot tacitly excluded the Afro-American. Today, differences between whites and blacks produce what is almost certainly the most distinguishable political cleavage and very likely the highest degree of polarization existing in American society. Evidence from the survey by Free and Cantril in 1964, before more widespread militancy developed among black activists in the last half of the decade, was conclusive on this point: in attitudes toward government intervention on public-policy matters, the proper extent of government power, a conservative-liberal

20. Nathan Glazer and Daniel Patrick Moynihan, *Beyond the Melting Pot* (Cambridge: M.I.T. Press and Harvard University Press, 1963), p. 314.

Table 22.11
Attitudes Toward the
Role of Government,
by Race, 1968

Government Role	Whites	Blacks
Active	27%	73%
Passive	50	9
Other, don't know	23	18
	100%	100%

Source: Survey Research Center, University of Michigan, 1968 Election Survey.

spectrum, the two major parties, and practically everything else tapped by the survey, differences between blacks and whites outdistanced those of every other category. By comparison, differences according to occupation or class appeared to be of piddling importance.[21]

A survey in 1968 continued to show large differences in attitudes of blacks and whites. Thus on the proper role of government, nearly three out of four blacks favored an active interventionist role compared with only about one out of four whites (Table 22.11). A study of the 1968 election found that "while some 97% of black voters in the nation cast their ballots for Hubert Humphrey, less than 35% of white voters did so. Thus," the authors observed, "the presidential vote must have been as sharply polarized along racial lines as at any time during American history."[22]

The extent of political polarization along the white-black plane of cleavage is, however, atypical. With this important exception, ethnic and religious loyalties are rather like region, occupation, class, and other cleavage lines: differences among groups do persist, but within any given group there is also a very considerable amount of heterogeneity. Ethnic origins and religion, then, continue to have significant impact on American political life long after they should, according to the melting pot theory; yet the impact of ethnic and religious identification is as moderate as that of the other factors discussed earlier. The impact is, indeed, often reduced by the crosscutting effects of these other factors.

The major religious categories—Protestants, Catholics, Jews—are as much ethnic as religious. In any case, differences persist in political attitudes and party identifications. In general, Protestants have been the most "conservative" on national affairs, Jews the most "liberal" (Table 22.12). Among white ethnic groups, Americans of English, German, and Scandinavian origin have been more "conservative" than Americans of Irish, Eastern or Central European, or Italian origins (Table 22.13).

The extent to which religious differences cut across 'class' differences is revealed in a very general way by data on voting. In national

---

21. Free and Cantril, *Political Beliefs of Americans*, Appendix F, Tables 1, 2, 3, 9.
22. Converse et al., "Continuity and Change in American Politics," p. 1085.

Table 22.12
Political Attitudes, by
Religion, 1968

	Protestant	Catholic	Jewish
For active role of government	33%	37%	55%
For desegregation	36	41	57
For foreign aid	39	42	60

Source: University of Michigan, Survey Research Center, 1968 Election Survey.

Table 22.13
Attitudes Toward
Government Intervention
by Ethnic Groups (Whites
Only), Five Issues, 1964

English	30%
German	34
Scandinavian	39
Irish (Catholic)	54
Eastern or Central European	54
Italian	57

Source: Free and Cantril, *Political Beliefs of Americans*, p. 152.

elections over the past generation, among both manual workers and nonmanual workers, Catholics have voted Democratic in considerably higher proportions than Protestants. The differences between Catholics and Protestants were least in the elections of 1952 and 1956, when General Eisenhower was the Republican candidate, and, as might be expected, greatest in 1960 when John F. Kennedy, a Catholic, was the Democratic candidate. The biggest discrepancy in 1960, incidentally, was between 'middle-class' (nonmanual) Catholics and Protestants; many Catholics who had moved into nonmanual occupations maintained their traditional loyalties as Democratic voters.

To look at the same data in another way, Protestants split most sharply along class lines in 1936 in the midst of the Great Depression, when Franklin Roosevelt was running for a second term. Catholics split most sharply in 1952 when many middle-class Catholics succumbed to the appeal of Eisenhower; in 1960, on the other hand, Kennedy all but obliterated the appeal of class among Catholics by his appeal as a fellow Catholic.[23]

Thus religion or ethnic identity may either amplify the effects of class and status on voting, as in the case of the blacks or working-class Catholics; or conversely, religion or ethnic identity may depress the significance of class and status by providing a crosscutting cleavage, as in the case of middle-class Catholics and Jews or white working-class Protestants. Moreover, just as the impact of occupation and economic position on voting may vary, depending on the state of the economy,

23. See Table 11, pp. 92–94, in Seymour Martin Lipset, "Religion and Politics in the American Past and Present," in *Religion and Social Conflict*, eds. Robert Lee and Martin Marty (New York: Oxford University Press, 1964).

so the impact of religion and ethnic identity is not a constant but a varying factor, depending on current issues and on the candidates themselves.

IDEOLOGIES: DEMOCRACY

Americans are frequently portrayed by foreigners and by themselves as a supremely pragmatic and un-ideological people. This is, at best, a half-truth.

For Americans are a highly ideological people. It is only that one does not ordinarily notice their ideology because they have, to an astounding extent, all agreed on the same ideology.

As we have already seen, perhaps more than any other people in the world, Americans have been united in expressing faith in a democratic ideology, even if they often have not acted on what they claimed to believe. Since their ideology is a source of unity rather than cleavage, the moment in which to observe the American as an ideologist is not when he talks about domestic politics but when he talks about international politics, and especially when he talks about America in relation to the rest of the world. Here we find the ordinary American looking at political problems in a distinct ideological framework.

In a world conference of average citizens, who could fail to guess what the American would say? He would tend to see all changes as movement toward or away from 'democracy' and 'freedom.' He would have no difficulty judging which systems were the best, which should be praised, which should be emulated; for the best would be 'democratic' and 'free.' The ideology of democracy, then, has tended to unite Americans; it has not sharply divided them.

IDEOLOGIES: "LIBERAL" VERSUS "CONSERVATIVE"

Nonetheless, Americans have often disagreed as to what democracy means both as an idea and in practise. They have disagreed as to how far democracy and equality should be extended, how widely the advantages enjoyed by elite groups should be distributed throughout the general population, how much equality of opportunity and of power is desirable. The controversy among the Founders between those who wanted an aristocratic republic and those who wanted a democratic republic was just such an ideological cleavage. Further, these two ideological viewpoints have reappeared in various guises ever since the Constitutional Convention. It will do no great harm if, for the moment, we call the one that stresses equality and democracy 'liberalism' and the other 'conservatism.' Most of the time, no doubt, people of wealth, property, and high status have tended to be 'conservative,' while the less well-to-do have tended to be 'liberal.' Moreover, throughout long periods liberals have probably been more numerous in one party while conservatives have been more often drawn to the other. Thus the Federalists, the Whigs, and the Republicans were more attractive to well-to-do conservatives, while the Democratic-Republicans and the Democrats gained the loyalities of the liberals of more modest circumstances.

Of course one must be exceedingly cautious in placing too much confidence in these historical hypotheses, for the data with which one could test them properly are almost entirely lacking except for recent years. Fortunately, however, for the most recent period, from the 1930s, survey data have demonstrated beyond any reasonable doubt that voters of higher status tend to be conservative in ideology and are likely to vote Republican, while voters of lower status tend to be more liberal in ideology and are more likely to vote for Democratic candidates.[24]

Conceivably, a three-way relationship between status, ideology, and party might divide Americans into two rather sharply polarized groups. A single line of cleavage might separate people according to status, ideology, and party, as follows:

	Camp I	Camp II
Status	Upper	Lower
Ideology	Conservative	Liberal
Party	Pro-Republican	Pro-Democratic

But the tendency in this direction is restrained by numerous exceptions. Each of the tendencies is important; yet none is strong enough to exert a dominant pull on American political life.

As our discussion of occupations and social class has already shown, the connection between status and party is highly imperfect. Likewise (as we saw, for example, in Tables 22.7 and 22.8) in every large occupational or status group, a significant minority hold opinions ideologically diverse from the prevalent views; a considerable number of manual workers are as conservative as nonmanual workers, and many nonmanual workers are as liberal as the majority of manual workers. Even the link between ideology and party is not overwhelmingly powerful. Both parties have been supported by conservatives and liberals. Finally, one relationship often dilutes the purity of another: For example, low-status Republicans are evidently about as likely to be highly liberal on domestic issues as are low-status Democrats. Conversely, high-status Democrats tend, like high-status Republicans, to be conservative.[25]

---

24. ". . . This triangle of relationships [has been] replicated in dozens of empirical studies. . . . Obviously, the facts presented by these relationships cannot be soberly questioned" (Campbell et al., *The American Voter*, p. 203).

25. *Ibid.*, pp. 207–208, including fns. 7 and 8 and Figure 9.1.

Why Liberalism and Conservatism
Do Not Produce A Sharp Cleavage

Why, you might ask at this point, aren't liberalism and conservatism more powerful in stimulating a clear-cut cleavage? There are at least three reasons: these two ideologies are vague; they consist of several different dimensions; and in any case coherent ideological thinking is highly uncommon among American voters.

Vagueness. Neither liberalism nor conservatism is a clear-cut, thoroughly worked out statement of principles and programs so much as a hodgepodge of ideas, ideals, and policies. Because of their generality and vagueness, liberal and conservative ideologies do not provide a clear-cut guide for a citizen who has to make up his mind on a single issue. On concrete questions liberals disagree among themselves, and so do conservatives. For example, many liberals who support welfare measures such as federal aid to education, which unquestionably requires federal expenditures, nonetheless want to cut taxes. Indeed, the Survey Research Center uncovered the paradox that in 1956 among voters who favored school aid, more were in favor of lower taxes than among those who opposed federal aid. One's attitudes toward tax cuts seemed to be only remotely connected to one's liberal or conservative ideology. Whether a voter wants taxes cut evidently depends more on the size of his income than on his general economic ideology. It will be astounding to some and perfectly reasonable to others to learn that "even among persons of equal education or with similar occupations, it is the high-income people who are relatively *more* willing to pay taxes than have the government postpone doing things that need to be done. It is the low-income group that demands a tax reduction even at the expense of such postponement."[26]

Dimensions. In truth, the terms *liberal* and *conservative,* which we have been using without apology up to this point, cover a wide assortment of views. What we have been calling 'liberalism,' no doubt to the irritation of some people who think of themselves as 'true' liberals, is a favorable view of government intervention in economic and social problems to aid citizens who suffer from the effects of an unregulated economy and unequal distribution of incomes and opportunities. Yet there are other dimensions of 'liberal' and 'conservative' ideologies that often crosscut views on government intervention. Let me suggest several.

1. *Concrete versus abstract.* One of the most interesting findings from the study by Free and Cantril which I have been drawing on is

---

26. *Ibid.,* p. 196.

that many Americans hold one set of attitudes when they consider *concrete* or specific policies involving government intervention and another set when they are responding at a more general or *abstract* level. The first of these Free and Cantril called the "operational spectrum of liberalism-conservatism," the second the "ideological spectrum." To avoid confusion, in the tables I have labeled the first simply what it is: attitudes toward government intervention on specific policies. The "ideological spectrum" was constructed from responses to statements such as, "The federal government is interfering too much in state and local matters," "The government has gone too far in regulating business and interfering with the free enterprise system," "We should rely more on individual initiative and ability and not so much on governmental welfare programs," etc. Free and Cantril discovered that while a preponderant majority of respondents (65 percent) were "liberal" on the more specific operational or interventionist spectrum, on the ideological spectrum the largest group, exactly half, were "conservative"! It turned out that nearly half the ideological conservatives were interventionist on concrete issues, while among those most in favor of government intervention on specific matters, slightly more (29 percent) were ideologically "conservative" than "liberal" (28 percent), and among those moderately in favor of government intervention, 46 percent were "conservative" in their general views as compared with only 14 percent who were "liberal."[27]

2. *Economic matters versus political and civil liberties.* A person who is concerned about reforming the economic institutions that were created by industrial capitalism need not be particularly concerned about political and civil liberties. These two concerns, which in America are often put together under the label of liberalism, are logically and ideologically distinct. Indeed, the proof, if one were needed, is the classic nineteenth-century English liberal who combined his belief in political liberty with an equally fervent belief in the virtues of a laissez-faire economy; in twentieth-century continental Europe, those who call themselves liberals often have had more in common with their nineteenth-century counterparts than with the present-day liberals of the English-speaking countries. It would serve no good purpose to argue here over the meaning of the terms *liberal* and *conservative*. What is important is to recognize that these loose ideologies comprise several different dimensions; political libertarianism and economic reformism may go together, but they equally well may not.

It is an exceedingly important fact that, in the United States, people who are in favor of economic reforms are frequently anti-libertarian on

27. Free and Cantril, *Political Beliefs of Americans*, p. 37, Table III-4; and p. 222, Table 3, Appendix.

questions of civil and political rights.[28] Conversely, some citizens who oppose government intervention in the economy nonetheless support government intervention on behalf of civil and political rights. As a good example, we may take the question of racial integration. Do people who believe that the government ought to intervene actively on such matters as federal aid to education, medical care, public housing, urban renewal, unemployment, and the like also believe that the government should intervene in the question of whether white and black children go to the same school? Not necessarily. Free and Cantril found that 44 percent of those who strongly favored active government intervention on economic matters thought the pace of integration was too fast; 21 percent thought that Negroes should have less "influence in government and political matters than they have now." Respondents were also asked whether they agreed or disagreed with the statement, "Most of the organizations pushing for civil rights have been infiltrated by the Communists and are now dominated by Communist trouble-makers." Among those most strongly in favor of government intervention on economic issues, 39 percent agreed; among those predominantly interventionist, just under half agreed.[29]

3. *Internationalism versus isolationism.* Historically, the philosophy of liberalism has been associated with internationalism; conservatives are often more nationalistic than liberals. Among Americans, then, does economic reformism go with internationalism and economic conservatism with isolationism? To some extent, but not entirely. In a 1956 survey the relationship was practically nonexistent. The proportion of internationalists was nearly as high among economic conservatives (50 percent) as among economic liberals (58 percent); likewise the proportions of isolationists were about the same among economic liberals and conservatives—in fact, in this particular survey there were a few more isolationists among the liberals.[30] In 1964, however, Free and Cantril found a somewhat stronger relationship, perhaps because of differences in the questions they used (Table 22.14). Yet what is most salient about the data in this table is not the amount of disagreement but the rather high consensus.

It follows, then, that the foreign policies forged after the Second World War commanded the support of both liberal voters and conservative voters, and at the same time these policies were opposed by both liberals and conservatives. Or to put the matter in another way, a relatively liberal leader like President Truman could generally count on support for his foreign policies from citizens who opposed his domestic policies, while some citizens who supported his domestic policies were

28. Lipset, "Working Class Authoritarianism," in *Political Man,* pp. 97–130.
29. Free and Cantril, *Political Beliefs of Americans,* pp. 122, 124–125.
30. Key, *Public Opinion,* p. 158.

Table 22.14
Percent Internationalist
of Liberals and
Conservatives

	Internationalist
Those who qualified on the Operational Spectrum as	
Completely liberal	71%
Predominantly liberal	66
Middle-of-the-road	63
Predominantly conservative	58
Completely conservative	50
Those who qualified on the Ideological Spectrum as	
Completely or predominantly liberal	76%
Middle-of-the-road	71
Predominantly conservative	67
Completely conservative	51
Those who identified themselves as	
Liberal	73%
Middle-of-the-road	69
Conservative	57

Source: Free and Cantril, *Political Beliefs of Americans*, p. 68.

lukewarm or hostile to his foreign policies. The same thing held true with a more conservative president like Eisenhower: he drew support for an internationalist foreign policy from liberals who opposed him on domestic issues.

4. *Innovation versus tradition.* There is still another dimension to liberalism and conservatism, or at least so it is commonly supposed. This dimension (or set of dimensions) consists of attitudes toward change, innovation, tradition, custom, and conventional morality. Considered along this dimension, we might say that conservatives tend to resist change as undesirable and often unnecessary, while liberals accept it more sympathetically as inevitable and desirable. Drawing upon the writings of political philosophers like Edmund Burke, Herbert McCloskey has devised a scale for 'conservatism' in this broad sense.[31] Yet curiously enough, in 1956 among the general population there was no significant relationship between this sort of conservatism and the political party with which people identified themselves, even outside the South. Moreover, this species of conservatism seemed to be almost unrelated to the economic policies a voter would support.[32]

The ideologies of conservatism and liberalism, then, are made up of a number of different dimensions. We have seen that one of these, economic interventionism, is by no means highly related to four others—general or abstract political views, political and civil liberties, foreign policy, and attitudes toward change. There may be—and very likely are—still other dimensions. Consequently, two people who find them-

---

31. See McCloskey, "Conservatism and Personality."
32. Campbell et al., *The American Voter*, p. 211.

		Total Sample	Voters
	Table 22.15		
	Ideologues and Non-Ideologues Among American Voters		
I.	Ideologues	2½%	3½%
II.	Near-ideologues	9	12
III.	Group interest	42	45
IV.	Nature of the times	24	22
V.	No issue content	22½	17½
		100%	100%

Source: Campbell et al., *The American Voter*, p. 249.

selves close together along one dimension of liberalism-conservatism are likely to find themselves very far apart along another dimension. Thus the different dimensions of liberalism and conservatism divide Americans one way on one kind of issue but quite another way on another kind of issue.

THE LIMITS OF IDEOLOGICAL THINKING

Most Americans (like most people everywhere) simply do not possess an elaborate ideology. It is difficult for political philosophers accustomed to manipulating abstract ideas to realize how slight and fragmentary is the analytical framework most people bring to bear on political problems. There is some evidence on this subject from surveys in 1956 and 1960 that is of unusual interest, for these two surveys represent the first serious attempt to use survey methods to examine the level of ideological thinking among a national sample of American voters. In 1956 the respondents were asked whether there was "anything in particular that you like about the Democratic party," or anything "that you don't like." The same questions were asked about the Republican party. They were also asked whether there was "anything in particular about Eisenhower (Stevenson) that would make you want to vote for him," or "against him." The answers some people gave indicated that they thought in terms of a liberal-conservative continuum of some sort, even if an exceedingly vague one. In fact, this continuum was almost the only dimension that could be discovered in the data.[33] Others responded by citing possible benefits or dangers to this or that group—to farmers, workers, doctors, big business. A third group simply made comments about the goodness or badness of the times—peace or war, prosperity or recession. A fourth group made no comments at all on any political issues under debate (see Table 22.15). Even though the liberal-conservative dimension was about the only one that seemed to exist at all, less

33. Philip E. Converse, "The Nature of Belief Systems in Mass Politics," in *Ideology and Discontent*, ed. David E. Apter (New York: Free Press of Glencoe, 1964), pp. 206–261.

than one voter in six seemed to appraise the 1956 election in terms of liberal or conservative ideologies. An example of an 'ideologue' might be the woman residing in a Chicago suburb who responded to the question of what in particular she didn't like about the Democratic party:[34]

> Well, the Democratic Party tends to favor socialized medicine—and I'm being influenced in that because I came from a doctor's family.
>
> *(Like about Republicans?)* Well, I think they're more middle-of-the-road—more conservative. *(How do you mean, "conservative"?)* They are not so subject to radical change. *(Is there anything else in particular that you like about the Republican Party?)* Oh, I like their foreign policy—and the segregation business, that's a middle-of-the-road policy. You can't push it too fast. You can instigate things, but you have to let them take their course slowly. *(Is there anything else?)* I don't like Mr. Hodge. *(Is there anything else?)* The labor unions telling workers how to vote—they know which side their bread is buttered on so they have to vote the way they are told to!
>
> *(Dislike about Republicans?)* Mr. Hodge! *(Is there anything else?)* I can't think of anything.

A 'near-ideologue' is represented by a man in upstate New York:

> *(Like about Democrats?)* Well, I like their liberalness over the years. They certainly have passed beneficial legislation like social security and unemployment insurance, which the average man needs today.
>
> *(Dislike about the Democrats?)* The Communists linked to Roosevelt and Truman. Corruption. Tax scandals. I don't like any of those things.
>
> *(Like about Republicans?)* I also like the conservative element in the Republican Party. *(Anything else?)* No.
>
> *(Dislike about Republicans?)* No, not at present.

Slightly under half the voters seemed to evaluate the two parties and the two candidates according to the benefits or harm they might confer on particular groups, as with the Ohio farm woman who said:

> *(Like about Democrats?)* I think they have always helped the farmers. To tell you the truth, I don't see how any farmer could vote for Mr. Eisenhower. *(Is there anything else you like about the Democratic Party?)* We have always had good times under their Administration. They are more for the working class of people. Any farmer would be a fool to vote for Eisenhower.
>
> *(Dislike about Democrats?)* No, I can't say there is.
>
> *(Like about Republicans?)* No.
>
> *(Dislike about Republicans?)* About everything. *(What are you thinking of?)* They promise so much but they don't do anything. *(Anything else?)* I think the Republicans favor the richer folks. I never did think much of the Republicans for putting into office a military man.
>
> *(Like about Stevenson?)* I think he is a *very smart* man. *(Is there anything else?)* I think he will do what he says, will help the farmer. We will have higher prices. *(Anything else?)* No.

34. These quotations are from Campbell et al., *The American Voter*, pp. 228–248.

> *(Dislike about Stevenson?)* No. But I have this against Stevenson, but I wouldn't vote against him. In the Illinois National Guards he had Negroes and Whites together. They ate and slept together. I don't like that. I think Negroes should have their own place. I don't see why they would want to mix.
> *(Like about Eisenhower?)* No.
> *(Dislike about Eisenhower?)* Yes. He favors Wall Street. I don't think he is physically able, and he will step aside and that Richard Nixon will be president. *(Anything else?)* To tell the truth, I never thought he knew enough about politics to be a President. He is a military man. He takes too many vacations and I don't see how he can do the job.

One quarter of the people explained their preferences and dislikes, as a woman in Louisville did, by referring in one way or another to good times or bad times:

> *(Like about Democrats?)* Well, I really don't know enough about politics to speak. I never did have no dealings with it. I thought politics was more for men anyway. *(Well, is there anything you like about the Democratic Party?)* I like the good wages my husband makes. *(It is the Republicans who are in now.)* I know, and it's sort of begun to tighten up since the Republicans got in. *(Is there anything else you like about the Democratic Party?* No.
> *(Dislike about Democrats?)* No, I couldn't think of a thing.
> *(Like about Republicans?)* Well, truthfully, the Republican Party just doesn't interest me at all. *(There isn't anything you like about it?)* No—I just am not particularly interested in either one.

About one in six said nothing at all about political issues; they simply preferred one party to the other, or one candidate to the other, or virtually could not respond at all. Thus a Massachusetts man replied:

> *(Like about Democrats?)* I haven't heard too much. I don't get any great likes or dislikes.
> *(Dislike about Democrats?)* I hate the darned backbiting.
> *(Like about Republicans?)* No.
> *(Dislike about Republicans?)* No.
> *(Like about Stevenson?)* No, I don't like him at all.
> *(Dislike about Stevenson?)* I have no use for Stevenson whatsoever. I had enough of him at the last election. I don't like the cut-throat business—condemn another man and then shake hands with him five minutes later.
> *(Like about Eisenhower?)* As a man I like Eisenhower better. Not particularly for the job of President, but he is not so apt to cut your throat.
> *(Dislike about Eisenhower?)* No.

In 1960 the people in the sample classified in Table 22.15 were reinterviewed. This time they were asked: "Would you say that either one of the parties is more *conservative* or more *liberal* than the other?" Respondents who said yes were asked which party seemed the more conservative and, then, "What do you have in mind when you say that the Republicans (Democrats) are more conservative than the Democrats (Republicans)?" Thirty-seven percent of the respondents "could supply no meaning for the liberal-conservative distinction." Slightly more than

50 percent of the respondents furnished evidence that they could identify the meaning of these terms correctly, more or less. To a majority of these people, however, liberalism was simply equated with government spending and conservatism with economy.[35]

Obviously then, a great many people have only weak traces of a liberal or conservative ideological framework within which to judge political issues, candidates, and parties. This does not mean that they are necessarily making foolish or uninformed choices. It does mean that they have to find some framework for judgment, other than a liberal or conservative ideology. What seems to happen in a great many cases is that as a voter moves from indecision to decision, he bypasses his ideology and takes a much more direct route. Somehow ideology is short-circuited. In some cases it is short-circuited by immediate consideration of self-interest or group interest that do not require ideological analysis and that may, in fact, lead to support for policies that a full-blown ideologue would oppose. The fact that the less well-to-do segments of the population favor tax cuts, for example, has very little or nothing to do with their other economic policies: here primitive self-interest short-circuits ideology. Party loyalties also short-circuit ideology. Once a voter has developed a firm attachment to a party, he can bypass the painful task of appraising policies and candidates according to ideological criteria. Having concluded long ago that the Democratic party or the Republican party was better for him, for his group, or for the nation, he now supports the party's candidates and the party's general policies (so far as he is familiar with them) without much further thought. Attraction or hostility toward a candidate because of his personal qualities also helps to short-circuit the more complex route of ideological thinking. It has been estimated that in 1956 the personal appeal of Eisenhower in comparison to Stevenson gave the Republicans a net advantage of nearly 8 percent of the votes. In 1964, on the other hand, highly adverse reactions to Goldwater's personal attributes combined with a more favorable view of Johnson among the electorate is estimated to have given the Democrats a net advantage of 5 percent of the votes. Thus, the difference between Eisenhower in 1956 and Goldwater in 1964 probably cost the Republicans in the neighborhood of 13 percent of the vote.[36]

Are we then to conclude that liberal and conservative ideologies in their various manifestations and multiple dimensions are unimportant in American politics? Such a conclusion is surely unwarranted for two reasons. First, while the great bulk of the people can often bypass ideological considerations, they cannot always do so. In a complex world,

---

35. Converse, "Nature of Belief Systems," pp. 219–222.

36. Donald E. Stokes, "Some Dynamic Elements of Contests for the Presidency," *American Political Science Review,* 60 (March, 1966), 19–28, especially pp. 22–23 and Figure 4, p. 23.

even the connection between self-interest and national policies is often so obscure that it cannot be traced out by an uninformed mind; ideology, however vague it may be, may sometimes help to establish the connection. On international policies in particular, the commitment of Americans to democracy and political self-determination perhaps serves as a guide, even if a vague one, to some citizens.

Second, some people are much more ideologically minded than others. As might be expected, the more active a person is in political life, the more likely he is to think in ideological terms.[37] In all that we have been saying so far, we have been describing ordinary voters, the rank-and-file citizens. But ideologies have always been the special property of political activists. In American political life, as elsewhere, political activists are very much more ideological than the great bulk of the population. Thus liberal-conservative differences that are absent, blurred, confused, or contradictory among ordinary citizens, and particularly among citizens who are least involved in politics, are much sharper among the politically active strata.

The greater salience of ideology among activists and leaders produces the paradox that while activists are in greater agreement than ordinary citizens in their adherence to a democratic and libertarian ideology, they are more divided ideologically on questions of government policy. The explanation for both the greater ideological unity and greater ideological disagreement among the activists and leaders is evidently the same: ideological considerations are much more salient among activists than among ordinary citizens. Hence, to the extent that the perspectives of the general American democratic and libertarian ideology are salient among activists, they are united by their common ideology; but to the extent that liberal and conservative ideologies are salient, they are divided by their differing ideological perspectives. And since it is these very people, the activists and leaders, who more than any others shape not only policies, party platforms, and nominations but constitutional and political norms, democratic, liberal, and conservative ideological perspectives do have a significant effect on American political life.

CONSEQUENCES   The pattern of ideological divergencies in the United States is roughly the pattern that ordinarily prevails with respect to geographical, socio-economic, ethnic, and religious differences. Conflicts do not accumulate along the same lines of cleavage. On the contrary, different conflicts seem to involve rather different lines of cleavage. As a result, citizens who hold similar views on one issue are likely to hold divergent views

37. Key, *Public Opinion*, p. 440; Campbell et al., *The American Voter*, p. 258; Converse, "Nature of Belief Systems," pp. 226–231.

on another—or no views at all. How this general pattern bears on the way party coalitions are formed during elections and in Congress is not only complex but rather obscure; it is reasonable to suppose, however, that the general effect is to attenuate the severity of any particular electoral and legislative conflict. If you think that among your opponents in today's contest are some potential allies for tomorrow's, you are likely to be conciliatory and unlikely to press extreme demands that could eliminate the possibility of winning recruits from the other side for a new contest another day.

Obviously, unless attitudes are highly polarized, it is impossible to divide a population into two like-minded collections of people. No matter what criterion is used for dividing people, within each of any two categories, there will be many conflicting views. Given the existence of a two-party system, it follows that unless attitudes are highly polarized, each of the two parties can hope to win only by constructing an electoral coalition made up of people whose views coincide on some questions but diverge on others. This is exactly what happens most of the time in the United States. As long as (1) political attitudes are not polarized, and (2) only two major parties exist, there can be no escape from two parties with heterogeneous followings.

Although we have surveys and election studies for only the past quarter century, there is substantial reason for thinking that low polarization has been the usual condition of American politics, and that the reasons for low polarization have been about the same in the past as they are now: large socioeconomic groups have generally been heterogeneous in political attitudes, and persons who agree on one question disagree on others.

There have been historical fluctuations; undoubtedly the tide of polarization ebbs and flows. But extreme polarization is rare in American politics, and it has never persisted over long periods. Most of the time political life displays the characteristics of moderate conflict that have been examined in the last two chapters. Whether the pattern of overlapping cleavages and relatively low polarization will prevail in the future depends on the extent to which the American polyarchy is able to deal effectively in the 1970s with the issues that began to fragment American cohesion in the 1960s. Because polarization hovers like a dark cloud over the future of the American polyarchy, we now turn from the normal patterns of American politics to the deviant and dangerous patterns of polarization.

Comprehensive Change and
Severe Conflict

23

It is often supposed, not only by foreigners but by Americans themselves, that except for the Civil War the American political system has managed to avoid severe conflicts. Americans, it is often said, are a moderate people; they display their moderation even in their conflicts, most of all in their political conflicts. How much truth does this view contain?

In Chapter 21 it was suggested that we define the severity of conflict along these lines: the more one side looks upon the other as an enemy to be destroyed by any means available, the more severe the conflict is. Unfortunately it is not easy to translate this definition into a precise and satisfactory way of measuring the relative severity of different conflicts. However, if one accepts as signs of the severity of a conflict such indicators as threats or moves to disrupt the constitutional system, or threatened or actual violence against or on behalf of national policies, or expressions by sober and informed observers or participants that a given conflict will lead to disruption, revolution, or civil war—if one accepts these as portents, then the weight of historical evidence does seem to offer solid support to this proposition: from the very first years under the new Constitution, American political life has undergone *about once every generation* a conflict over national politics of *extreme severity*.

THE RECURRENCE OF INTENSE CONFLICT

To suggest the evidence for this proposition, let me review some familiar historical episodes.[1]

Before the Constitution had completed its first decade, the Alien and Sedition Acts (1798)—which threatened the very existence of any

---

1. This section draws heavily on my essay "The American Oppositions: Affirmation and Denial," in Dahl, *Political Oppositions in Western Democracies*.

organized political opposition—were challenged by the legislatures of Kentucky (1798) and Virginia (1799) in resolutions that hinted for the first time (but definitely not the last) that a state government might deliberately refuse to enforce a federal law which its legislators held to be unconstitutional. The specters raised by the Alien and Sedition Acts on the one side, and by the Kentucky and Virginia resolutions on the other, were temporarily banished by what Jefferson called "the Revolution of 1800."

Within hardly more than another decade, New England Federalists, driven to desperation by the embargo policies enforced by the Republicans, assembled at Hartford (December, 1814) in a convention that not only adopted a set of resolutions calling for extensive constitutional changes but issued a report asserting among other things that "in cases of deliberate, dangerous, and palpable infraction of the Constitution, affecting the sovereignty of a State and liberties of the people; it is not only the right but the duty of such a State to interpose its authority for their protection, in the manner best calculated to secure that end."[2]

Less than another score of years went by before the United States approached civil war over the tariff. In 1828, the legislature of South Carolina adopted a set of eight resolutions holding the newly passed "Tariff of Abominations," which ultimately hit cotton exporters with what seemed to them undue harshness, unconstitutional, oppressive, and unjust; in an accompanying document written by John C. Calhoun the legislature espoused the view that in such cases a single state might "nullify" an unconstitutional law (1828). Four years later when the South Carolinians were still chafing under the protective tariff, a convention called by the state legislature adopted an ordinance that "nullified" the tariff acts of 1828 and 1832, prohibited the collection of duties within the state, and asserted that the use of force by the federal government could be cause for secession. The state legislature passed laws to enforce the ordinance, to raise a military force, and to appropriate funds for arms. President Jackson thereupon sought and gained from Congress the legal authority to enforce the tariff laws, by military means, if necessary. A compromise tariff was worked out in Congress, South Carolina rescinded her Ordinance of Nullification, and civil war was avoided—or rather postponed for thirty years.

Thereafter, the middle years of the century were occupied with various aspects of the controversy over slavery, particularly whether slavery should be permitted in the great unsettled areas of the West, a question that touched the most sensitive interests of Northerners and

2. Morris, *Encyclopedia of American History*, p. 153.

Southerners. Finally, as everyone knows, the issue no longer could be contained; and for four terrible years men died of wounds and disease to settle the question—or so it was supposed.

Although it does not quite fit our list of severe conflicts, there occurred in the decade before the Civil War a curious political phenomenon that is worth marking. In the 1840s European immigration, chiefly from Ireland and Germany, greatly increased. A nativistic, antiforeign, anti-Catholic, superpatriotic reaction began to set in. In the early fifties, political tickets consisting of antiforeign candidates appeared in New York, Pennsylvania, and New Jersey. Soon a party began organizing secretly; it called itself the American party. Because its members refused to divulge their secrets, their enemies called them Know Nothings. The party showed some promise of replacing the Whig party. As it turned out, however, the life of the American party was brief and unsuccessful, for it was consumed in the struggle over slavery. Had it prospered, the whole course of American history would have been different.

The issue of slavery was settled only in part by the Civil War: slavery was abolished, to be sure, but the freed Negroes were not long permitted to enjoy equal political rights—to say nothing of economic, educational, or social privileges. Ten years after Appomattox, the election of 1876 brought the country to the verge of another civil war, but as so often happened before and after, the outcome was compromise rather than war; yet a compromise that tacitly allowed the restoration of white supremacy throughout the South and thus adjourned the whole problem of effective citizenship for Negroes until the middle of the present century.

This adjournment allowed economic questions to take over. During the last third of the century, discontented farmers and urban workers formed a pool of recurring opposition to the policies of a national government which responded less and less to their demands than to those of the new men of business, industry, and finance. Out of economic dissatisfaction, radical and reformist movements developed: Socialist Labor, the Greenbackers, the Farmers' Alliance, Populism, the Socialist party, the IWW. The trade union movement also had its turbulent beginnings: the Knights of Labor, the AFL, the railway unions. Strikes, lockouts, and protest meetings frequently led to severe violence.[3]

---

3. For example, in 1886 during a demonstration near the McCormick Reaper Works in Chicago, six strikers were killed by the police and many more were wounded. The next day two thousand persons attended a protest meeting in Haymarket Square; policemen ordered the meeting to disperse; a bomb was thrown, killing a policeman; in the ensuing battle, seven more policemen and four workers were killed, sixty policemen and fifty workers were wounded. Six men who had addressed the meeting were sentenced to death; four were hanged the following year.

In 1894, Grover Cleveland, the first Democrat elected to the presidency since 1856, then in his second term as president, called out federal troops in order to break a great nationwide strike of railway workers against the Pullman Company.

In the presidential elections of 1896, William Jennings Bryan, a man of primitive intellect and beguiling eloquence, whom Democrats and Populists had jointly nominated as their candidate, and who in his simple and confused protests against the "domination of Eastern Capital" evidently evoked support among a considerable number of farmers and some urban workers, was defeated by McKinley after a campaign period of unusually high tension.[4]

Sixteen years later, a new Democratic president, the second since the Civil War, was elected; under Wilson's leadership many of the specific reforms that had been demanded earlier by Populists and Socialists were carried out. Although these reforms were sharply opposed, the conflicts seem to have lacked some of the earlier intensity; the country was not widely viewed as approaching another civil war.

The next generation witnessed the Great Depression, mass unemployment, extensive discontent, the election of the third Democratic president since the Civil War, new outbreaks of violence, the rise of quasi-democratic or anti-democratic political movements on both right and left, and extensive changes in national policies, changes that from 1935 onward were fought with increasing bitterness. Driven to extreme measures by a Supreme Court dominated by conservatives who steadily rejected the major items of the New Deal as unconstitutional, President Roosevelt in 1937 even tried to 'pack' the Court. It was his first important move to prove unpopular, and he was defeated. From about 1937 until the bombing of Pearl Harbor in 1941, political leaders were bitterly divided over the question whether it was better to meet threats of military aggression by 'isolation' or 'intervention.'

Less than thirty years later a new crisis began to develop, quite possibly one of the most serious in the nation's history. In the early 1960s, the ancient, unsolved problem of securing equal rights and opportunities for Afro-Americans, a consequence of the most persistent and most profound failure of the American polyarchy to adhere even approximately to widely proclaimed standards of political equality and consent, produced a new eruption of open discontent among black Americans, this time greater than ever before. Though this new demand that the United States live up to its proclaimed values first manifested itself in the South (initially, often, under both black and white leadership), it soon appeared also and in even more militant form in the black ghettos of large Northern cities. Passage of the Civil Rights Acts of 1964 and 1965 marked the beginning of a historic shift in the South when at long last Southern blacks began to gain and, what is more, to use the suffrage

---

4. Bryan won 47 percent of the two-party vote and carried twenty-one states—all of them, however, agricultural states of the South, Midwest, and West.

they had once held only briefly during Reconstruction. Yet the enduring burden of oppression and inequality was far too monumental to be removed even by a change that, had it come decades earlier, might truly have been epochal.

Before the country's leadership had moved decisively to deal with the increasingly tense domestic situation, in a tragic historical development, the United States became deeply involved in the Vietnam war. Although presidential policies and actions in Vietnam were initially supported by a large majority of the public, they were bitterly and increasingly opposed by a growing minority. The swelling bitterness and violence stemming from an accumulation of frustration with both domestic and international causes produced a level of intense conflict that some observers believed had not been seen in the United States since the Civil War.

After years of opposition that ran the gamut from peaceful persuasion to organized and disorganized violence, and as the failures of American intervention became more and more apparent, majority support for the war in Vietnam rapidly crumbled and President Nixon began to withdraw American troops. Meanwhile, however, war-induced inflation combined with a high rate of unemployment fanned further discontent. Thus the crisis in American life that had begun in the 1960s still persisted during the early 1970s.

Whoever supposes, then, that American politics has been nothing more than a moving consensus, a sort of national Rotary Club luncheon, has not sufficiently reflected on the regularity of intense conflict, crisis, and violence in American history.

THE PATTERN OF SEVERE CONFLICT

Like massive hurricanes that sweep in from the Atlantic, brief, violent, and devastating tornadoes of the Middle West, or earthquakes along the West Coast, great conflicts in American political life are long remembered by the survivors, much discussed, and imperfectly understood. Yet it is possible to discern some elements in the pattern.

If we take as our point of departure a period of moderate conflict that adheres to the pattern described in the last chapter, then the development of a severe conflict is marked by the kinds of shifts suggested in the paradigm presented in Table 21.1.

Divergence of Attitudes

Leaders of rival coalitions diverge more and more in their attitudes on key political questions. This growing divergence may come about in a variety of ways:

☐ Older leaders may change their original views. This is probably the least likely development.

□ Previous issues that would have divided leaders had they been more significant earlier—and perhaps did divide them at times—may become much more salient and urgent than before.

□ New issues emerge on which the views of leaders had not previously crystallized.

□ Older leaders may be replaced by newer leaders with different views. For example, the generation of the Revolution and the Constitutional Convention virtually disappeared from active political life after Madison's second term, and a whole new generation—John Quincy Adams, Clay, Calhoun, Jackson, Van Buren, Webster—took its place. This new generation had in turn largely disappeared by the 1850s, when still another generation, that of Lincoln and Douglas, took over.

Even when the views of political leaders are known, it is difficult to speak with confidence about the development of 'public opinion' in a severe conflict. The most reasonable assumption is, however, that the 'public' responds to the divisive issue slowly and in diverse ways. At one extreme the apoliticals remain untouched even at the peak of tension (or right up to the time when political conflict turns into organized slaughter from which even the apoliticals cannot escape—as happened in 1861). Thus a recent examination of "letters from the 1850s and 1860s, which had been preserved by old families in the various attics of a small Ohio community" revealed that "no references to abolition were ever found in any of the letters"![5]

At the other extreme, the political actives are heavily involved. Indeed, it is mainly the actives who determine the course of the conflict; severe conflict means a growing intensity of conflicting views among the actives; it is they who settle or fail to settle a dispute.

What of the in-between group, the ordinary voters? For the most part they intervene only in one way: by voting. But that one way can be important. Although most voters continue to vote their traditional party loyalties, without regard to the course of a dispute that seems to be polarizing the country, some do change. Ironically, they may change for reasons that have nothing to do with the conflict: a farmer in 1860 might have voted against the Democrats because his crops were poor or his prices were low and he felt that the Democrats were responsible because they had held the presidency. The perception the ordinary voter has of what is at stake when *he* votes need not have much to do with what political leaders think is at stake. Nonetheless, political leaders do interpret the election returns; they must perforce interpret an election in terms of their own perspectives, which may not be those of the voter.

---

5. Converse, "Nature of Belief Systems," in Apter, *Ideology and Discontent,* pp. 206–261, quote on p. 251.

Hence political leaders often interpret an election as favoring or disapproving this or that policy. As a result their own enthusiasm for one alternative may wax or wane. In politics nothing succeeds like success.

Moreover, whatever the voters may intend, an election has consequences for the balance of power among the contesting groups. One party, for example, may sweep the Congress and the presidency, while the other is reduced to a legislative minority. Probably we shall never know much about what was in the minds of voters when they went to the polls in 1860. But the consequence of their votes was to reduce the spokesmen for Southern slaveholders to a clear minority in Congress, and to confront that minority with a president who would not yield on the key issue of whether slavery was to be allowed in the territories. The message of the election was, then, that slave owners were a political minority without enough safe allies in the rest of the country; that they would remain forever a minority; more, that they would henceforth be a diminishing minority. Thus, though most voters North and South almost certainly did not intend it, the indirect consequence of the election was to encourage Southern leaders to embark on the fatal course that led to secession and civil war.

From Crosscutting to Cumulative Cleavages

As a conflict intensifies, ties which have held the politically active strata together and made it relatively easy for them to negotiate disputes begin to snap; their views have less and less in common. As social and ideological ties begin to snap and overlapping cleavages diminish, great fault lines begin to separate the country, or at any rate the most active and articulate elements in the political life of the country. If there is a single giant fault line, as slavery in the territories became before the Civil War, then we may speak of a growing *polarization* of the nation as the country is divided into two ever more hostile camps and as neutrals and moderates begin scrambling to clear out of the no-man's-land between them. If there are several fault lines, then we speak of *fragmentation*. In the historic crises in this country, what appears to be polarization was probably accompanied by some fragmentation; but since polarization into two enemy forces presents the greater danger, I shall focus mainly on this pattern. Polarization can be both a consequence of conflict and an additional factor exacerbating the conflict.

In most of the severe conflicts listed earlier, the process of polarization did not go very far: if it had, the Revolution of 1776 might not have been our last revolution, nor the Convention of 1787 our last full overhauling of the Constitution, nor the Civil War our last civil war. But in the years just before the Civil War the process of polarization into two camps went much further than at any other time in history. Here is how the ties snapped in three major kinds of nationwide institutions:

- ☐ Several major religious groups split into separate Northern and Southern churches over the issue of slavery:[6]
  1844: the Methodist Episcopal Church
  1845: the Baptist Church
- ☐ The political parties fell apart or split:
  1850–6: disintegration of the Whigs
  1854–60: formation and rise of the Republican party as a sectional party with no Southern wing
- ☐ Splitting of the Democrats in 1860:
  Northern Democrats nominate Douglas
  Southern Democrats nominate Breckenridge
- ☐ The Federal Union split:
  1860, December: South Carolina secedes
  1861, January: Florida, Alabama, Mississippi, Georgia, Louisiana
  February: Texas
  April: Virginia
  May: Arkansas, Tennessee, North Carolina

High Stakes

In all the conflicts described at the beginning of this chapter, the stakes were high (or, what amounts to the same thing, seemed to be high) for one side or both. Often a conflict was interpreted by one side or the other as allowing no satisfactory compromise because gains by one side entailed losses by the other; this was the case, for example, in the tariff dispute of 1828 to 1832 when Southern leaders argued that any protective tariff imposed for the benefit of Northern industry caused a corresponding loss to Southern exporters of cotton. In fact, in each of the severe conflicts mentioned above, leaders on one side—and sometimes on both sides—believed that the way of life to which they and their constituents were attached was seriously threatened by the goals pursued by their opponents. Whether or not their views were 'rational' or even factually correct is irrelevant: people hate and fight no less if what they believe to be true happens to be false.

Each of these severe conflicts could also be interpreted as a situation in which leaders of strata whose way of life was supported by the status quo now saw themselves threatened at the foundations by the aspirations and policies of other groups whose expanding influence, if unchecked, would destroy or at the very least seriously impair their way of life. At the outset of a conflict, the 'conservative' strata may have enjoyed enough influence with national policy-makers—the president, the Congress, and the Supreme Court—to insure their own protection,

6. After the outbreak of war in 1861, the Presbyterian Church and the Protestant Episcopal Church also split.

Table 23.1
The Stakes of Conflict:
Ways of Life

Spokesmen for the Following Groups or Strata:	Were Perceived by Spokesmen for the Following Groups or Strata as Threatening Their Way of Life:	Thus Producing Severe Political Conflict and These Crises:
Small farmers, Southern planters, Democratic-Republicans	New England commercial interests, Federalist 'aristocracy'	1798-9: Alien and Sedition Acts; Va. and Ky. Resolutions
Northern and Western whites; manufacturers; Western farmers; abolitionists	Southern whites	1828-32: Tariff, So. Car. Nullification 1840-60: Slavery in the territories 1860-77: Civil War and Reconstruction
Immigrants, Catholics, Irish, Germans	Native Protestants	1850-60: Know-Nothingism
Farmers and urban laborers	Businessmen, bankers	1880-1900: new parties, Greenback, Socialist, etc.; strikes, violence 1892-6: Populism as major force 1933-7: New Deal
Southern blacks	Southern whites	1865-75: Reconstruction 1954-present: integration, civil rights, violence
Northern blacks	Northern urban whites	1960s-present: equal opportunities, violence— Harlem, Rochester, Chicago, Los Angeles, etc.

even if insurance against defeat required vigilance and unremitting struggle. But as leaders of the 'conservative' strata began to believe that their influence was diminishing and that soon they might be unable to stem the tide, they more and more perceived their opponents as implacable enemies who must be destroyed lest they be destroyers.

How the conflicts described fit this interpretation is shown in Table 23.1.

AMERICAN POLITICAL INSTITUTIONS AS MANAGERS OF CONFLICT

What of the fourth factor in our paradigm of conflict: political institutions? In times of moderate conflict, American political institutions encourage compromise, consensual decisions, and incremental changes. But what is the effect of the political institutions when proposals for more comprehensive changes inspire severe conflicts? Political institutions continue to provide stubborn and well-organized groups numerous opportunities to veto, modify, or delay the passage or enforcement of policies that would entail comprehensive change. Hence even in the face of proposals for more far-reaching changes, and even in the presence of increasingly severe conflict, the tendency of the political institutions is to handle severe conflicts along the same lines as moderate conflicts. American political institutions, then, encourage political leaders to respond to severe conflicts in three ways:

1. By forming a new political coalition that can overpower the opposition. But this, as we shall see, is a difficult solution.
2. By incremental measures that postpone comprehensive change.
3. By enduring compromises that remove the issue from serious political conflict.

Overpowering the Opposition

A severe conflict is sometimes moderated or even terminated when one political coalition gains enough power to overcome the resistance of its opponents. Instead of compromising, the winning coalition enacts its policies despite the opposition of the defeated coalition. If the opposition fights back, as it is likely to do, it finds itself too weak to prevail. Unable to reverse the main direction of policy imposed by the winning coalition, the opposition may in time accept the major policies enacted by the winners and settle down to bargaining for incremental adjustments; thus severe conflict gives way to a period of moderate conflict.

Probably the only effective way in American politics for one coalition significantly to reduce the bargaining power of an enemy coalition is to turn it into a visible and even isolated political minority by defeating it in national elections. However, because of the large number of positions where an embattled minority, unable to win the presidency or a majority in either house of Congress, can dig in and successfully continue to challenge the policies of the majority coalition, a single electoral victory is ordinarily not necessarily enough, particularly if the contest is close. The victories of the winning coalition may have to be large, thus visibly demonstrating the weakness of the opposition, and repeated in a series of presidential and congressional elections, thus demonstrating for all to see that the minority coalition has little chance of regaining its power and must come to terms with the victors.

In at least three instances, severe conflicts seem to have been moderated or terminated in this way:

1. Republicans overwhelmed Federalists in the elections of 1800 and

continued to do so for a generation. By 1814 when the Federalists at the Hartford Convention talked disunion, their leaders gained little national support. After 1814 Federalism disappeared as an effective political movement, though old Federalist leaders constituted a kind of feeble opposition until they died or despaired.[7]

2. From the midterm elections of 1894 onward, and particularly after the presidential election of 1896 when Republicans overwhelmed the coalition of Democrats and Populists that supported William Jennings Bryan, a severe conflict over economic policies was thereby moderated (and postponed). The defeat of the Populists meant that neither of the two major parties would develop into a farmer-labor coalition with an ideology and program comparable to those of the British and European Labor and Socialist parties. A major challenge to unregulated capitalism was turned back and a socialist alternative was effectively removed from American political competition (Chapter 26).

3. After 1932 when elections temporarily destroyed the power of the Republican coalition centered on the policies of business, it became possible for most of the New Deal proposals of FDR to be enacted. By the time the Republican opposition was able to regroup, it could no longer *undo* the New Deal except in minor ways. However, it entered into a coalition with Southern Democrats, which by bargaining in Congress impeded or prevented further reforms until the power of both the Republicans and the Southern Democrats was temporarily smashed by the presidential and congressional elections of 1964.

Yet elections are often indecisive; neither Truman's reelection in 1948 nor Kennedy's election in 1960 enabled the victorious president to enact the major policies he and his party had advocated in the campaign, despite the fact that both presidents had Democratic majorities in Congress. Truman presented to Congress an extensive Fair Deal program involving a number of social reforms. But only a few of these had been enacted when he went out of office.[8] Why are elections so infrequently decisive? Why, people often ask, don't elections settle things one way or the other? Why is it so difficult for a president and Congress ostensibly of the same party to terminate a severe conflict by overriding the objections of their opponents, carrying through their legislative program, and letting the country decide at the next election whether it likes the changes or disapproves of them?

---

7. Livermore, *The Twilight of Federalism.*

8. Congress passed legislation providing for housing and slum clearance, and an expansion of Social Security coverage. It failed to pass "Fair Deal" proposals for federal aid to education, health insurance, a new Department of Health, Education, and Security, repeal of the Taft-Hartley Act, a reorganized farm plan providing direct production payments to farmers, a fair employment practises commission, and eliminating the poll tax. Most of these proposals have since been enacted, mainly under President Johnson.

By now it must be clear that American political institutions were never designed to operate in this fashion; nor do they. The pattern of partitioned power which has been carried about as far in the United States as in any polyarchy in the world simply prevents elections from being decisive except under the most extraordinary circumstances. Moreover, because Americans predominantly believe in the desirability of partitioning power, and, in particular, approve of the main institutional arrangements that partition power and authority in the United States, there is little support for changes that might make elections more decisive.

American political institutions, then, do not ordinarily endow the candidates or parties who receive a majority of votes in an election with enough power to carry out their policies over the opposition of the defeated minority. And American political beliefs do not endow the winning majority with overarching and unambiguous legitimacy; nor do they deprive the defeated minority of grounds on which to argue that its policies and not those of the majority must be allowed to prevail.

Consequently, while a severe conflict is sometimes terminated by an overwhelming victory for one side in a congressional and presidential election, the American political system and American beliefs make this solution somewhat difficult and uncommon.

Postponing Comprehensive Changes

American political institutions are excellently designed for making incremental changes. But they also foster delay in coming to grips with questions that threaten severe conflict. It is true that delay may provide precious time during which a seemingly severe problem may change its shape, become more manageable, even disappear. But postponement may also inhibit leaders from facing a problem squarely and searching for decisive solutions—solutions that may be forced upon them many years later when they can no longer delay.

Policies of economic reform which were barely more than marginal have sometimes taken decades or even generations to accomplish. When the Democrats won the presidency and majorities in Congress in 1892 that enabled them to pass an income tax law, the Supreme Court, rightly foreseeing that the income tax could be the foundation for redistribution at the expense of the rich, struck it down; it required sixteen years and the Sixteenth Amendment to make it possible for Congress to enact an income tax again. The regulation of child labor, as we saw, was held up for a generation by a Supreme Court unwilling to yield to Congress and the president. In 1948, President Truman, acting on recommendations from his advisory committee on civil rights, recommended federal legislation against lynching, the poll tax, segregation in public transportation, and discrimination in employment. Although mild civil rights legislation was passed in 1957 and 1960, no major legislation on civil rights cleared Congress until 1964, almost two decades after President Truman's recommendations. Passage of American welfare and social security laws has followed the enactment of comparable laws in most European democracies by one to several generations. A national medical care program has been advocated for generations. In 1945, President Truman proposed to Congress a comprehensive medical insurance program for persons of all ages. The first law establishing a national system of medical insurance was not enacted until 1965, and it was restricted to the elderly.

Compromise

The existence of innumerable fortified positions from which an embattled but well-organized minority can fight off and wear down an attack, combined with the absence of any *single* rule for making legitimate decisions on which the political activists are agreed, means that it is difficult to terminate a conflict by the clear-cut victory of one side over another. Hence severe conflicts are sometimes handled by reaching a compromise. Occasionally the result is a long-lasting compromise. Two of the most enduring compromises of this kind in American history both involved Afro-Americans; both sought to eliminate the black as a source of severe conflict among whites; both succeeded in doing so for long periods; both were at the expense of the blacks; and by present-day standards in all civilized countries, both were unjust. One dealt with the blacks as slaves, the other with blacks as freed slaves.

The first was the Missouri Compromise of 1820 which, by providing that slavery would be permitted south but not north of the line 36°30′ across the vast territory acquired in the Louisiana Purchase, promised to maintain a balance between the numbers of free and slave states and thereby preserve to each side a veto over future national policies. This compromise kept the problem of slavery in the territories and the future of slavery itself within manageable bounds for thirty years. Then the new land acquired as a result of the Mexican war added territories not covered by the old compromise and, as we shall see in the next chapter, triggered the decade of severe conflict that eventuated in the Civil War.

The second great compromise was arrived at in 1877, after the long crisis produced by the contested presidential election of 1876. We shall also return to it in the next chapter. Briefly, however, the effect of this settlement was to bury Reconstruction and to permit white Southerners to restore white supremacy. Once again the fate of the Negro was removed as a source of severe conflict—once again by whites at Negro expense. This shameful compromise endured for seventy years. The beginning of the end for the Compromise of 1877 was the legislation on civil rights and employment introduced by President Truman. His proposals split the Democratic party and strengthened the coalition of Southern Democrats and Northern Republicans in Congress; hence it was not until the passage of the Civil Rights Acts of 1964 and 1965 that the Compromise of 1877 finally came to an end.

These two experiences say something about the limits of compromise. First, there are moral limits; by the standards of the contemporary civilized world, both of our great national compromises went beyond these limits. Second, it is obvious that one necessary condition for any such compromise is that the contestants can somehow discover an alternative that vastly reduces the threat from the other side, particularly by eliminating or markedly decreasing the dangers to the way of life defended by one or more contestants. Such a solution may not exist, or —what amounts to pretty much the same thing—it may not be discovered. The Compromises of 1820 and 1877 were possible only because Afro-Americans had no voice in arranging them. If spokesmen for the slaves had enjoyed the same veto power over national policies that spokesmen for slaveholders possessed until 1860, the Compromise of 1820 would have been impossible. If the freedmen had been as influential in 1877 as white Southerners, that compromise too would have been impossible.

A Tentative Conclusion

One effect of all these factors is to impede decisive action through the ordinary processes of presidential leadership and congressional law-making. The consequences of this are twofold and not lacking in paradox. The system encourages presidents who wish to be decisive to draw on their reservoir of powers that lie outside the control of Congress or Court; hence in these domains, most visibly in foreign policy, the president is more and more his own master and the normal processes are more and more displaced by executive decision. Yet side by side with presidential decisiveness in areas where he cannot be closely controlled, the system operates to inhibit decisive action. Thus while incremental changes can be bargained for, large reforms that elsewhere have been enacted in a single session of parliament hard on the heels of a single election in the United States must await many elections and many sessions of Congress. To make the point once more, the system encourages incremental changes; it discourages comprehensive change. It facilitates the negotiation of moderate conflicts.

But what is the effect of American political institutions on severe conflict? Do they intensify conflict by preventing early, if drastic, changes in policies? Do they prolong and exacerbate severe conflict? Although the evidence we have examined in this chapter lends itself to this interpretation, the evidence is murky and allows other arguments. Yet it would be hard to deny that the danger is there.

POSSIBLE CONSEQUENCES OF SEVERE CONFLICT: POLITICAL INTEGRATION, ALIENATION, CIVIL WAR

The Constitutional Convention, we saw, did not decide whether the United States was to be an aristocracy or a polyarchy. That decision was made by the Americans who came after, who affirmed their commitments to a polyarchy rather than a more aristocratic republic.

The outcome depended upon widespread acceptance among Americans of the legitimacy of a polyarchy as a system of government for Americans, and on the legitimacy of certain procedures for arriving at political decisions—procedures, in the case of Americans, largely but not wholly fixed by the Constitution.

Severe and prolonged conflict may cause one or another of the antagonists to reject the system itself. If rejecting the system produces nothing more than apathy, the structure may nonetheless survive. But if rejection leads to revolution or civil war, the structure may be destroyed. The twentieth century has seen this happen: in Italy between 1919 and 1924, in Germany between 1929 and 1934, in Spain between 1935 and 1938. In each of these cases the costs of conflict, rejection, and revolution were staggering.

Each of the conflicts mentioned at the beginning of this chapter and recapitulated in Table 23.1, endangered the solution that Americans had arrived at by about 1800: a polyarchy operating within the institutional and procedural limits set by the Constitution. If leaders and citizens in the conflicting groups were to reject this solution, then the American polyarchy very likely could not survive.

As it turned out, some alienation, some rejection of the American polyarchy did occur side by side with political integration. In the early years, the victory of the small farmers doubtless sped their political integration and strengthened their loyalty to the republic. Yet the other side of the coin is that many of the defeated New England Federalists rejected it; the importance of their rejection was mitigated only by the fact that they were few in numbers. Many of them remained alienated from the more democratic aspects of polyarchy, hostile to the very idea of democracy and wide sharing of power. From his conversations in the United States (May, 1831–February, 1832), Tocqueville observed that

> . . . when the democratic party got the upper hand, it took exclusive possession of the conduct of affairs, and from that time the laws and the customs of society have been adapted to its caprices. At the present day the more affluent classes of society have no influence in political affairs; and wealth, far from conferring a right, is rather a cause for unpopularity than a means of attaining power. The rich abandon the lists, through unwillingness to contend, and frequently to contend in vain, against the poorer classes of their fellow citizens. As they cannot occupy in public a position equivalent to what they hold in private life, they abandon the former and give themselves up to the latter; and they constitute a private society in the state which has its own tastes and pleasures. They submit to this state of things as an

irremediable evil, but they are careful not to show that they are galled by its continuance; one often hears them laud the advantages of a republican government and democratic institutions when they are in public. Next to hating their enemies, men are most inclined to flatter them. . . .

But beneath this artificial enthusiasm and these obsequious attentions to the preponderating power, it is easy to perceive that the rich have a hearty dislike of the democratic institutions of their country. The people form a power which they at once fear and despise. If the maladministration of the democracy ever brings about a revolutionary crisis and monarchical institutions ever become practicable in the United States, the truth of what I advance will become obvious.[9]

The old Federalists did not change by much; rather they died out and were replaced by a younger generation with more flexible notions.

The conflict between Northerners and Westerners on the one side, and Southern slaveholders on the other, was accompanied in its last stages by an increasing rejection of the American polyarchy by spokesmen for the slavocracy. The rejection was long lasting: the full political integration of the South into a polyarchy with universal suffrage was retarded for a century after the Civil War by the refusal of Southern whites to concede political equality to Negro citizens. Only now, and painfully, is that long alienation from democracy crumbling.

The conflict between immigrants and native Protestants never expanded politically beyond the limits of Know-Nothingism. Hostilities remained and often had political consequences. For one hundred seventy years no person not of Anglo-Saxon Protestant stock was elected president. The parties feared even to nominate presidential candidates of immigrant origins or Catholic faith. In 1928 the Catholicism of Alfred E. Smith was a factor in the election. No Catholic was elected president until 1960. Despite all this, the immigrants and their children, who could easily have remained a large politically unintegrated element in the population, were quickly absorbed into the political system and soon came to accept the ideology and institutions of the American polyarchy. Indeed, in few countries in the world have so many people been so fully integrated into a polyarchy in so short a time. Thus the conflict between immigrants and native Protestants never erupted on a nationwide scale; though it persisted, it was contained.

In many other countries, the conflict between labor and capital—to use two vague labels—led to the alienation of one stratum or the other. Nearly everywhere in Europe the rapid expansion of the working classes posed a severe problem of political integration. For if the spokesmen of capitalism had their way, the revolutionary spirit was likely to spread among working-class groups and organizations. And if the spokesmen of the working class appeared on the verge of gaining power, then the

---

9. Tocqueville, *Democracy In America*, vol. I, pp. 186–187.

defenders of the economic status quo might be alienated and withdraw their support for democratic institutions. Unlike every European polyarchy, in the United States workers did not develop a separate working-class political movement. Unlike many of the most stable and highly developed European polyarchies, in the United States a labor-socialist party did not gain office, introduce extensive reforms, consolidate the commitment of workers to the notion of peaceful change by means of democratic procedures and institutions. Yet in following another route, the American working classes were politically integrated into the American polyarchy: and in the process their economic antagonists, businessmen, were not permanently alienated. The development was long, however, and often disturbed by sharp conflict. We shall return to it in Chapter 26.

The failure of white Americans to allow equal political, economic, educational, and social opportunities to black Americans produced among many Negroes a kind of rejection that took the form of political apathy, hopelessness, and indifference. Then as Negroes began to exchange apathy for new forms of political action, and as they gained federal protection for their rights, many whites, especially in the South, fell back on the old, anti-democratic, aristocratic ideology and constitutional doctrines to justify resistance to equality. Perhaps at no time since the years just before the Civil War was conflict more intense than in the declining decade of Southern white power from 1954 to 1964. Meanwhile, in the depressed black ghettos of the great Northern cities, where slum dwellers were moved by a spirit of alienation and despair, violence began to erupt. Northern whites now began to feel threatened. The peaceful political, social, and economic integration of the American black remains perhaps the greatest internal problem of our time.

Thus conflicts and rejection of polyarchy ebb and flow in American political life. For a time moderate conflicts prevail. Then the tides of antagonism begin to surge, and political conflict grows more deadly. Yet even during bitter conflicts, the pattern of moderation is never *totally* transformed into the pattern of severe conflict. When by one means or another the antagonisms diminish, the pattern of moderate conflict reappears. But it, too, is impermanent. The high tide of conflict has almost always risen within the span of about one generation.

Yet in one case, as every American knows, the tide of conflict rose angrily until it swept the nation into the carnage of civil war, destruction, disease, suffering, and death. Because of the extraordinary importance of that violent breakdown in the American polyarchy when overlapping cleavages were displaced by extreme political polarization, we shall examine it in more detail in the next chapter in order to clarify the process of political polarization that could lead to civil war.

SUMMARY   1. Although crosscutting cleavages and moderate conflict are the normal pattern of American politics, political life in the United States has undergone a conflict over national policies of extreme severity about once every generation.

2. The development of a severe conflict is marked by the kinds of changes indicated in the paradigm on page 311:

☐ *Divergence of attitudes:* Leaders of rival coalitions diverge more and more in their attitudes on key political questions. This change may come about as:

Older leaders change their original views.

Previous issues become divisive as they become more salient and urgent than before.

New issues emerge.

Older leaders are replaced by newer leaders with different views.

☐ *From crosscutting to cumulative cleavages:* As conflicts accumulate along one or two major fault lines, the country is increasingly polarized or fragmented into enemy camps.

☐ *High stakes.* The outcome of the conflict is increasingly seen as involving very high stakes, perhaps even a way of life, for a large segment of the country.

3. American political institutions tend to handle severe conflicts along the same lines as moderate conflicts. The result may be to exacerbate rather than to reduce the conflict. American institutions encourage political leaders to respond to conflicts by:

☐ forming a new political coalition that can overpower the opposition. But the institutions, practises, and beliefs in extreme partitioning of power and authority make this rare and difficult.

☐ incremental measures that postpone comprehensive change. Thus deeper causes of severe conflict may be dealt with too slowly, or not at all.

☐ securing long-lasting compromises that remove the issue from serious political conflict. But in some situations, such compromises may be impossible, immoral, or sow the seeds of future discontent.

4. Severe conflicts involving extensive polarization or fragmentation may lead to greater political integration and support on the part of some of the contestants, apathy or alienation among others, and, in the extreme case, the possibility of civil war.

Political Polarization and Civil War

In the disputes that thrust this country into civil war, American experience offers a compelling and tragic illustration of severe conflict. It is the course of this conflict, the greatest failure in the history of American polyarchy, that we examine in this chapter.

Whether any polyarchy could have arrived at a peaceful solution to any issue as monumental as slavery had become in the United States, no one can say with confidence. What we do know—what no American can forget—is that the American political system was unequal to the task of negotiating a peaceful settlement to the problem of slavery. Violence was substituted for politics. Yet even civil war, the supreme mark of political failure, did not solve the issue, which was now transformed from slavery to the question of whether Negroes were to acquire full and effective citizenship.

The Civil War did not answer this question. Nor did Reconstruction. The unresolved issue was passed down from one generation to the next, until it exploded for all the world to see, a century after the outbreak of the Civil War.

SYMPTOMS OF RISING CONFLICT

In May, 1856, John Brown and a small party of antislavery Kansans massacred five proslavery men in the Pottawatomie region of Kansas. Over the next few years, violence frequently broke out between pro- and antislavery forces in what came to be popularly called Bleeding Kansas. At almost the same time as the Pottawatomie Massacre, Senator Charles Sumner of Massachusetts delivered a vehement attack on slavery in the Senate; his speech was not free of personal invective; shortly afterward a Southern Congressman entered the Senate and beat Sumner furiously over the head with a heavy cane. In both houses of Congress there were other outbursts of violence involving antagonisms over slavery. In the course of a debate about Kansas in 1858, proceedings in the House became riotous. On other occasions, too, the House and Senate verged on open physical violence.[1]

At a time when intemperate language was commonplace, public figures frequently invoked threats of secession, disruption of the Union, violence, civil war. In letters, in the press, even in Congress, the more radical Southerners began to speak of secession as the only alternative if the North could not be brought to terms. As the election of 1860 approached, Southerners frequently reiterated the threat that the South would secede if a Republican were elected president. Seward stoked the fires of controversy by his famous statement in Rochester in October, 1858: "It is an irrepressible conflict between opposing and enduring forces, and it means that the United States must and will, sooner or later, become either entirely a slaveholding nation or entirely a free-labor nation." Just one year later, John Brown staged his futile raid at Harpers Ferry in a vain, ill-organized, and half-insane attempt to free the slaves of Virginia. On the heels of the news of Harpers Ferry, the legislature of Alabama met and authorized the governor to call a state convention if a Republican should be elected president in 1860. In the summer of 1860, a number of conservative South Carolina Democrats, hitherto opposed to the 'fire-eaters' who advocated secession, declared that if the Republicans were to win the election in November, South Carolina would secede. If this was Southern bluster and bravado, in November the bluff was called. It was not a bluff. On December 20, 1860, the state of South Carolina seceded from the Union. Within six months ten other Southern states had followed. Lincoln, backed by a substantial share of articulate Northern opinion, refused to permit the Southern states to secede and thereby disrupt the Union. The result was civil war.

'Explanations' of the 'causes' of the Civil War abound. Yet in the best of circumstances—under laboratory conditions—causal analysis is not easy. Causal interpretations of complex, multi-faceted, and almost certainly multi-causal historical events are particularly uncertain and vulnerable. It would therefore be absurd in this brief chapter to introduce another causal theory about the origins of the Civil War. All the following analysis is intended to show is that the events of 1850–61 closely conform to the expected pattern indicated by the paradigm on page 311. Conditions which encourage moderation gave way to conditions that would be expected to eventuate in a more severe conflict. Probably never

1. For historical details this chapter relies heavily on Roy Nichols' exceptionally important study of the Democratic Party from 1856–1860, *The Disruption of American Democracy* (New York: Macmillan, 1948); and his *The Stakes of Power, 1845–1877* (New York: Hill & Wang, 1961); C. Vann Woodward, *Reunion and Reaction: The Compromise of 1877 and the End of Reconstruction* (Boston: Little, Brown, 1951); *The Burden of Southern History; The Strange Career of Jim Crow* (New York: Oxford University Press, 1957); and "Seeds of Failure in Radical Race Policy," *Proceedings of the American Philosophical Society,* 110, no. 1 (February, 1966), 1–9.

before or since in American history has the pattern of moderate conflict been so fully transformed into the pattern of severe conflict.

First Condition: Divergence of Views

During the course of the 1850s, events and new perspectives posed the issue of slavery in the territories in such a way that compromise became increasingly difficult. As the decade wore on, the issue of slavery was more and more bound up with a second major question—union or secession.

The slavery issue. At the start of the decade, there was an exact balance in the Senate between the slave states and free states. Slavery already existed in fifteen Southern states and it was prohibited in fifteen Northern states. The balance in the Senate could be maintained or disrupted by what happened in the Western territories. Should slavery be protected in the territories, or prohibited? If it were protected, would there not be, in due course, more slave states than free states? If it were prohibited in the territories, could there ever again be an additional slave state? Would not the South become an ever smaller minority in the nation, and in the Senate, finally perhaps too small to prevent the free states from abolishing slavery by constitutional amendment and, if need be, by coercion?

In principle, the policies adhered to by the federal government on slavery required an answer to a single question applied to three different regions. The question was this: Should slavery be prohibited or protected? The regions were these: the existing free states of the North and Northwest, the slave states of the South, and the territories of the West.

Revolutionary opposition: abolition. Consider the alternatives. An abolitionist would prohibit slavery in all three regions. His position demanded a revolution in Southern life and institutions. If enough Americans had supported the abolitionist position in 1800, the attempt to perpetuate slavery and the tragedies caused by that evil anachronism might never have occurred. Although we shall never know how many Americans held the abolitionist position before the Civil War, the membership of the Anti-Slavery Society amounted to only 3 or 4 percent of the adult population outside the South.[2] Discrimination against Negroes was commonplace in the North; Northerners who were prepared to accept the Negro as their equal were evidently a minority, and probably a very small

---

2. Converse, "Nature of Belief Systems," in Apter, *Ideology and Discontent,* p. 250. "This figure is for 1840, and it undoubtedly advanced further in the next decade or two, although one deduces that the expansion of membership slowed down after 1840. Our estimates do not take into account, however, the standard inflation of membership (intentional or unintentional) that seems to characterize movements of this sort" (p. 260, fn. 46).

minority.[3] It is clear that until the outbreak of war the abolitionists remained a tiny opposition whose views were widely thought to be extreme —as revolutionary views generally are.

Radical opposition: prohibit slavery outside the South. A less revolutionary position, though in the perspectives of the 1850s a radical one nonetheless, was taken by Lincoln, Seward, and the Republican party. Like all the other major protagonists to the great controversies of the 1850s, with the exception of the abolitionists, Lincoln and most leading Republicans assumed that although the free states would continue to prohibit slavery, slavery might be left intact in the South. In fact, as the price of Union, the South might even be given additional guarantees that its peculiar institution would be protected from the abolitionists. In this view, the institution was so deeply rooted in the South that it could not be abolished in the near future; hence Southern slavery would be protected until such time as the South itself would peacefully yield it up. What was immediately at stake, however, was not slavery in the South or the prohibition of slavery in the North; it was the question of whether slavery was to be permitted in any of the Western territories.

As early as 1846, David Wilmot, a Democrat from Pennsylvania, had introduced a resolution that would have barred slavery in all the territories. Although the Wilmot Proviso was never adopted, it became a rallying point for a number of northern congressmen. The view of Lincoln and some of his fellow Republicans was essentially that of the Wilmot Proviso: the federal government should prohibit slavery throughout the length and breadth of the territories; hence it would be all but certain that when these territories finally came into the Union, they would enter as free states, not slave states. Although Lincoln and Seward were willing to compromise on many points in order to reassure the Southern slavocracy—compromises often thought to be serious blemishes on Lincoln's overblown reputation as the Great Emancipator—on this issue they never budged. And the frantic efforts to forge another great compromise during the tense months as the year 1860 closed and the new year began all failed because neither Lincoln nor the leaders of the South would alter their positions on the crucial issue of slavery in the territories.

Limited opposition: local option. A considerably more limited opposition to slavery provided better grounds for compromise in the early 1850s than was offered by the Wilmot Proviso. This was the policy of 'popular sovereignty' embodied in the famous Compromises of 1850 and 1854.

---

3. "The fact was that the constituency on which the Republican congressmen relied in the North was a race-conscious, segregated society devoted to the doctrine of white supremacy and Negro inferiority. . . . Ninety-three percent of the 225 thousand Northern Negroes in 1860 lived in states that denied them the ballot, and seven percent lived in the five New England states that permitted them to vote" (Woodward, "Seeds of Failure in Radical Race Policy," p. 1).

The solution was outwardly democratic and simple: let the people of the territories choose whether they wish to protect or to prohibit slavery.

Confronted by the problem of providing government for the territories acquired from Mexico (land to which the old Missouri Compromise of 1820 did not apply), the aging veteran Henry Clay and the new senator from Illinois, Stephen Douglas, had in 1850 engineered the solution of popular sovereignty for California, New Mexico, and Utah. Then in 1854, when the vast unorganized remnants of the Louisiana purchase were given territorial government, Douglas piloted through Congress another compromise on the same basis; but under pressure from Southerners to put slavery on an equal footing, the venerable Missouri Compromise was repealed outright. At its national convention in Cincinnati in 1856, the Democratic party proclaimed popular sovereignty as its official doctrine.

Douglas's solution suffered from two disadvantages common to compromise proposals in times of profound controversy. First, it was ambiguous, since it did not specify clearly *when* the people of a territory were to decide about slavery. (Opponents of slavery favored an early decision; spokesmen for the slavocracy wanted it as late as possible, only when the territory was ready for admission as a state. Presumably, both were operating on the assumption that slave owners would move into a territory much more slowly than free farmers.) Second, and more important, popular sovereignty became increasingly less acceptable to the major antagonists. Lincoln, Seward, and a sizeable number of other leaders rejected popular sovereignty because they favored the total exclusion of slavery in the territories.

Radical defense: protect slavery in the territories. Spokesmen for Southern slaveholders also found local option more and more unacceptable. Many of them came to espouse a view that was, in its own way, as radical a break with the past as Lincoln's policy. This was the view that only the people of a *state* had the power to prohibit slavery. Hence the federal government had no constitutional power to prohibit slavery in the territories, nor did the people of the territories, until (or just prior to) their admission as a state. It was the duty of the federal government, then, to protect the rights of slaveholders throughout all the territories. Between this position and Lincoln's, there was no room for compromise.

Although numerous minor variations on these main themes can be detected, they did not change the alternatives in any significant way. The five principal alternatives are summarized in Table 24.1.

The secession issue. As the decade wore on, the question of slavery in the territories (and with it the ultimate future of slavery in the South) more and more required an answer to a second question: Was the Union

		Type of Action Proposed for		
Stand on Slavery	Free States	Territories	Southern States	Spokesmen and Proposals
Revolutionary opposition	Prohibit	Prohibit	Prohibit	Abolitionists
Radical opposition	Prohibit	Prohibit	Protect	Wilmot Proviso, Lincoln, Seward, Republicans
Limited opposition	Prohibit	Protect or prohibit: People decide	Protect	Advocates of Popular Sovereignty: Clay, Douglas—Compromise of 1850, 1854, Cincinnati Platform of Democratic Party
Limited defense	Prohibit	Protect *and* prohibit: Congress decides		Advocates of extending Missouri Compromise; Crittenden
Radical defense	Prohibit	Protect	Protect	Taney: Dred Scott, Calhoun, Constitutional Democrats, Breckenridge

to be preserved at all costs, or was secession a permissible solution? Is one particular combination of human beings into a single polity more right than any other combination? If so, why? If one of the main ends of a democracy is to secure the consent of all citizens, should not citizens who no longer consent to the basic principles of their government be allowed to depart in peace? Why must the integrity of the Union not be broken by secession? Although the Civil War settled the matter by establishing the principle that secession from the United States is impermissible, the questions themselves are among the most troublesome in the whole domain of political theory.

Lincoln's answer, as everyone knows, was a profound commitment to the Union. In part, his view reflected the nonrational and almost unanalysable nationalism that forms a vital prerequisite for the modern nation-state all over the world. Nationalists may disagree about boundaries; but they do not doubt that, once the nation has been defined, the nation must be preserved. In addition to Lincoln's nationalism, which was doubtless widely shared in the North (and in the South as well), there was also his deep commitment to the importance of the American polyarchy, founded on principles of liberty and equality, as an example for all mankind. If the South should secede, then the greatest living evidence for the proposition that a polyarchy could survive the challenge of dissident minorities would no longer serve as "proof of the impossi-

Table 24.2
Slavery and
Secession, 1850-61

Stand on Slavery	Stand on Secession	
	Pro-Union	Pro-Secession
Revolutionary opposition	Most Abolitionists, Radical Republicans	Some Abolitionists
Radical opposition	Lincoln, Seward, most Republicans	Some Republicans
Limited opposition	Clay, Douglas	—
Limited defense	Crittenden, Buchanan, Alexander Stephens	—
Radical defense	Taney—Dred Scott	Calhoun, Yancey, Jefferson Davis

ble." "If the minority will not acquiesce, the majority must, or the government must cease," Lincoln said in his first inaugural address. ". . . If a minority in such case will secede rather than acquiesce, they make a precedent which in turn will divide and ruin them. . . . Rejecting the majority principle, anarchy or despotism in some form is all that is left." As he said at Gettysburg, the Civil War was a testing of whether any nation conceived in liberty and dedicated to the proposition that all men are created equal could long endure.

Nearly every one of the groups listed in Table 24.1 contained both Unionists and those who advocated or accepted secession. Some abolitionists who despaired of developing a free society as long as the South was in the Union were not unhappy at the prospect of a separation. There were even Republicans who took this pragmatic view of the matter and did not share Lincoln's passionate belief that the Union must be preserved. At the other extreme, some Southerners who advocated radical defense of slavery were, throughout most of the decade, opposed to secession; many of these fell in line only during the last months before Fort Sumter. In the election of 1860 the Constitutional Union party, which had only two planks—support for the Constitution and loyalty to the Union—gained much of its support from Southern Whigs. Its presidential candidate, Senator John Bell of Tennessee, together with the pro-Union candidate of the Democratic party, Senator Douglas, carried eight of the fifteen slave states against Breckenridge, the candidate of the secessionist Democrats. In the fourteen slave states where presidential electors were chosen by the voters (characteristically, the anachronism of choosing electors in the state legislature still existed in South Carolina), Breckenridge received only 570,000 votes to his opponent's 705,000.

If we put the two dimensions of policy together—slavery and secession—a new pattern emerges (Table 24.2).

Among the spokesmen and leaders who helped form public opinion, discussed and debated the alternatives, and made the decisions, the events of the 1850s thinned out the center and pushed leaders more and more toward the northwest and southeast corners of Table 24.2. The presidential election of 1860, in which no advocate of any of the principal positions won a majority of popular votes, provided the final polarizing thrust that gave Lincoln and the Republicans in Congress enough control to insure that their views would prevail, and encouraged Southern leaders to unite upon the view that only secession would protect slavery in the South. Between these two radically opposed alternatives, it proved impossible to find any compromise.

Second Condition:
A Zero-Sum Contest with High Stakes

By the spring of 1861, leaders had exhausted the major possibilities of compromise between the two radical positions. No compromise could be acceptable so long as Republicans and Southerners held to their positions. Yet neither would yield, for in the 1850s the issue of slavery was converted into a zero-sum contest in which the stakes were different ways of life.

In the perspectives of the principal contestants, either slavery had to be prohibited in all the territories or it had to be allowed in all the territories. And the stakes in the contest (if we interpret them as the contestants claimed to see them) had come to be nothing less than this: a society based on slavery or a society based on free farmers and free labor.

Southern stakes. These alternatives were most sharply visible in the perspectives of Southern leaders. From the Constitutional Convention onward, it had been reasonably obvious that the South could maintain slavery only under a Constitution that insured protection for the rights of slaveholders in the Southern states; the South had, in fact, gained such a Constitution in 1787; and the South could maintain it as long as slave states had enough power to veto a change in the Constitution. If the time were to come, however, when the growth of population and free states permitted the North and West to override the opposition of the South and to alter the Constitution, then the institution of slavery, and with it the whole structure of the planter society, would be imperiled.

This was the shape of the future which Southern leaders more and more vehemently insisted they saw in every solution not guaranteeing a full opportunity for slaveholders to implant their institutions in the territories; hence not only in the Wilmot Proviso and the Republican commitment to free territories but even in popular sovereignty. Quite possibly even an outright constitutional guaranty would not insure that slavery would in fact be exported to the Western territories. If not, then surely the only solution was secession. If slavery could be introduced in the West, however, then another solution might be acceptable to Southerners: this was nothing less than the principle announced by Taney in the Dred Scott case, that Congress has no power to prohibit slavery in the territories.

Northern stakes. The alternatives may have seemed less stark in the free states than in the South. Nonetheless, from 1856 onwards, Northern politicians who were unwilling to commit themselves to halting the expansion of slavery by federal legislation were to an increasing degree challenged and defeated by opponents who were prepared to put a definite and permanent end to the spread of slavery beyond its existing boundaries. Not only were individuals voted out; whole parties were defeated. The Whigs disintegrated; the Democrats split; the Republicans surged.

The evidence suggests, then, that even if the perspectives for the future were not so grim in the North as in the South, among Northerners a variety of views helped to crystallize the belief that the territories should be preserved exclusively for free farmers. Among these precipitating factors was a loathing for slavery that went far beyond the abolitionists; many people who were not ready to accept Negroes as their equals nor willing to bear the costs of abolishing slavery where it was already entrenched were, like Lincoln, sickened by all proposals, even those in the name of compromise, that would let slavery expand one inch beyond its existing limits. Then, too, the states of the North and Northwest were still populated predominantly by farmers—free farmers—some of whom had themselves wrested land out of the wilderness; of the others many, perhaps most, must have shared the deeply ingrained expectation, then well over a century old, that the great rich lands to the west were open to them, their neighbors, their sons, or other white farmers like themselves. The spread of slavery would violate that interest, destroy that dream. (It is relevant as a symbol that the first act of the Republicans after secession began was to admit Kansas as a free state.) There were also economic issues on which the veto of the Southern slaveholders prevented solutions favored by many Northerners: the admission of Kansas, the tariff, federal expenditures for internal improvements, railroads to the West. Early in 1861, as soon as enough Southern states had seceded to make the Republicans a majority in Congress, Republicans together with a handful of Northern Democrats rushed bills through Congress that admitted Kansas, raised the tariff, and by ending a mail subsidy for steamships to the Pacific Coast eased the way for the construction of a railroad to California.[4] Within a few years, other major

---

4. Nichols, *Disruption of American Democracy,* pp. 476 ff.

Table 24.3
Election of 1860:
Percentage of Votes Won,
by Major Regions

	North and West	South	Total
Lincoln	98.6%	1.4%	100%
Douglas	88	12	100
Breckenridge	33	67	100
Bell	13	87	100

Source: Computed from data in Walter Dean Burnham, *Presidential Ballots, 1836–1892* (Baltimore: Johns Hopkins Press, 1955), pp. 78, 246.

policies were enacted that the South had long opposed: the Homestead Law, land grants for agricultural colleges, subsidies for two transcontinental railroads, a Contract Labor Law permitting agents to contract abroad for labor, and, under the pressure of war, even an income tax.

Thus slavery in the territories was no narrow issue. In the waning years of the 1850s, it was interpreted by more and more leaders (and presumably by many involved citizens) as a matter that posed two alternative ways of life, two kinds of society, two visions of man's fate and man's hope.

Third Condition:
Decline of Overlapping Cleavages

In the course of the 1850s, the issue of slavery in the territories was like a wall rising between neighbors. At the beginning of the decade the wall could still be climbed; but as it grew higher, it became more and more impassable to traffic of all kinds. A pattern of crosscutting cleavages which had prevailed through the Compromise of 1854 was transformed into a pattern of nonoverlapping or cumulative cleavages.

To be sure, total polarization was never reached. But, like Mercutio's wound, it was enough.

From fragmentation. Between 1850 and 1860, the Whig Party, one of the two national parties which had leaders and constituents in both North and South, disintegrated into a weak rump party in the South, and thereafter vanished.

Between 1854 and 1860, a new party took the place of the Whigs. The Republican party was exclusively a Northern and Western party. If we discount the Federalists in their declining years, for the first time in the history of American parties one of the two major parties did not spread across both sides of the Mason and Dixon line. In the election of 1860, Lincoln won only 1.4 percent of the total vote in the fifteen slave states (Table 24.3). In ten slave states Lincoln did not gain so much as a single vote!

In 1860, the Democratic party, which for more than sixty years had been the great nationwide party, whose leaders had worked with unflag-

	N (000)	%
Table 24.4		
Election of 1860:		
Votes Won		
Republicans: Lincoln	1,866	40
Democrats: Douglas	1,383	30
Constitutional Democrats: Breckenridge	848	18
Constitutional Union: Bell	593	12
Total	4,690	100%

Source: Burnham, *Presidential Ballots*, p. 246.

ging zeal to knit the sections together, split apart on the issue of slavery in the territories. One wing, the Constitutional Democrats, became a predominantly Southern party. The other, Douglas's party, barely retained any Southern following at all in the elections of 1860 (Table 24.3). Southern Whigs and other unionists organized a new party, the Constitutional Union party; its platform was "The Constitution of the Country, the Union of the States, and the enforcement of the laws." But it, too, proved to be a sectional party.

Thus in 1860, for the first (and, so far, last) time in American history, four, not two, major parties sought the presidency. No party came close to winning a majority of popular votes (Table 24.4) and each was wholly or almost wholly either a Southern or non-Southern party (Table 24.3).

To polarization. Congress, hitherto the forum of compromise, became in the late 1850s a battle ground where almost every issue split the membership into the same two camps. In 1858–9, Congress had lengthy deadlocks on almost every issue: the admission of Kansas, transcontinental railroads, rivers and harbors appropriations, a homestead bill, the tariff. Deadlock and conflict so much dominated the session that the Congress was not even able to agree on the annual appropriation for the Post Office, and at the end of the session, the Post Office Department was left without funds. In the Congress that met in the winter of 1859–60, no party had a majority in the House; it took two months and more than forty ballots simply to elect a speaker. During all this time the legislative business of the House was at a complete standstill.

In the 1840s and early 1850s, political leaders who might have quarreled over slavery agreed on so many other key questions that they were impelled toward a compromise on slavery. In Congress, in politics generally, and, it seems, in the country, attitudes North and South of the Mason-Dixon line were not so distinct as to prevent coalition, agreement, mutual concession, and compromise on many issues. An opponent on one issue was not necessarily an opponent on all issues. By the late

1850s, however, the chances were that a Northerner and a Southerner not only disagreed about slavery; they disagreed about a great many other key questions as well. The political leaders of the country were increasingly polarized into two opposing sides. More and more, then, one's enemies today would be one's enemies tomorrow and the day after. The North-South fault line split the country not only on slavery in the territories and the admission of Kansas, but on the tariff, government aid for roads, harbors, and other internal improvements, the need for and the route of transcontinental railways, federal land grants for educational institutions, homestead laws, banking laws, constitutional theory, and ideological views on aristocracy and democracy. By the spring of 1860, a year before Fort Sumter, a Senator from South Carolina privately observed: "There are no relations, not absolutely indispensable in the conduct of the joint business, between the North and South in either House. No two nations on earth are or ever were more distinctly separate and hostile than we are here."[5]

Limits of polarization. It would be easy, nonetheless, to exaggerate the point. Among political leaders the cleavage was never total. As to the views of the people themselves, one cannot be certain how much they ever became polarized. Then as now the views of ordinary citizens must have been more fragmented, less coherent, less clearly formed than the views of men whose daily lives were wrapped up in the great public controversies. To many citizens, perhaps to most (though one cannot be sure), the issues of slavery probably seemed more remote, less distinct, perhaps even less important than the preoccupations of daily life.

Perhaps the North-South fault line was weakest on the very issue that moved to the forefront in 1860–1: union or secession. Not all those who supported or were willing to go along with secession were Southerners; and by no means all Southerners supported secession. Without question the secessionists were a minority in the nation. Very likely they were a minority even in the South. Of the four candidates in the presidential election of 1860, none advocated outright and immediate secession. Three were flatly opposed to secession. Although Breckenridge was the candidate of the secessionists, he said he did not favor it as a solution. Breckenridge won only 18 percent of the national vote (Table 24.4) and he won considerably less than a majority—38 percent—of the votes in the South. In fact, Breckenridge received absolute majorities in only eight of the fifteen slave states. Moreover, it appears that even in these states a considerable number of his supporters were opponents of secession who were loyal Southern Democrats, supporting, as they thought, the candidate of their party. Later, in voting on candidates for

5. Nichols, *The Stakes of Power*, p. 287.

the conventions called in the seven states that seceded before Fort Sumter fell, the issue of union or secession was made clearer. In these elections many of the counties that had voted *for* Breckenridge voted *against* secessionists in favor of Union candidates. Support for secession was concentrated most heavily in the counties with large numbers of slaves, where the vote was about 7–3 for secessionist candidates. In counties where slaves were few, the proportions were reversed: voters supported pro-Union candidates by about 2–1.[6] Even in the states that led the movement to secede, the secessionists barely outnumbered their Unionist opponents; in Mississippi in the election of candidates for the convention that was to vote on secession, the ratio of votes cast for secession versus cooperation was 4–3; in Alabama, 9–7; in Georgia, 5–4. As late as March, North Carolina voted decisively against secession.[7] Tennessee and Arkansas did not vote to secede until after the outbreak of war. Four other slave states remained in the Union: Maryland, Delaware, Kentucky, Missouri; and West Virginia split off from Virginia rather than secede.

Triumph of a minority. Thus it is probably no exaggeration to say that it was a small minority of slaveholders who, together with their retainers, followers, and spokesmen, engineered secession and thereby precipitated civil war.[8] It seems altogether possible that if a plebiscite had been held during the week before Fort Sumter, and perhaps after, it would have revealed the secessionists to be a minority in the South. Yet with skill, energy, and luck, secessionist leaders gained control in seven states in the deep South, and in the end brought four additional but more reluctant slave states along.

Fourth Condition:
Negotiation without Decision?

How, if at all, did the operation of American political institutions affect the course of the controversy over slavery?

That the institutions and the ways of thinking which men brought to these institutions provided powerful inducements for negotiation and compromise on the issue of slavery is hardly open to question. In the first half of the century, the issue which was to tear the country apart during the second half was handled by one compromise after another: 1820, 1850, 1854. The inertial forces of the system continued to operate until May of 1861. During the final year of peace, or cold war, there were

---

6. Lipset, "The Emergence of the One-Party South," in *Political Man*, pp. 344–356, Table II, p. 349.

7. See Nichols, *Disruption of American Democracy*, pp. 418, 435, 499.

8. Cf. Burnham's comment, ". . . it was probably a rather small minority which engineered secession in a good many Southern states" (*Presidential Ballots*, p. 83).

frantic and unceasing efforts to arrive at a compromise that would head off the event that so many saw and feared: the Conference Convention; the Crittenden Compromise; the Committee of Thirty-three in the House; the Committee of Thirteen in the Senate; proposals by Toombs, Jefferson Davis, Stephen Douglas, and countless other political leaders; the constitutional amendment proposed by the House and backed by Seward and Lincoln which would have preserved slavery in the states where it already existed. (The amendment, incidentally, passed both House and Senate as—height of irony—the *Thirteenth* Amendment, but its ratification was consumed by war.)

By 1860, however, events were too advanced for these compromises. Did the political institutions encourage compromise too much and too long? Did they inhibit political leaders and citizens from squarely confronting the alternatives?

It is impossible to provide a confident answer. Human rationality has distinct limits. Because history has unfolded its answer to us, we can now discern those who in 1820 already divined correctly the shape of the future. But wrong guesses about 1860 could not be proved wrong in 1820.

The Southern veto. Nonetheless, it seems clear that the political institutions provided both Southerners and Northerners with sound reasons for believing that slaveholders—or the political representatives of the South—could prevent national laws directed to the peaceful abolition of slavery. So long as the South was in the Union, then, the alternatives were either revolution or some sort of compromise, for no decision on slavery could be reached without the assent of the South.

The power of the South was protected by federalism and the Constitution, for slavery could not be abolished in Southern states except by amending the Constitution. The power of the South was further protected by the Senate, where numbers of states counted, not numbers of people. The South might also seek protection from the Supreme Court, as it did in the case of Dred Scott.[9] The South gained further

---

9. *Dred Scott v. Sandford*, 19 How. 393 (1857). The Court, incidentally, has never been more knowingly and deliberately a political and legislative body than in that case. One of the justices, Catron, kept his old friend Buchanan, the incoming president, closely informed of what was happening; Buchanan was thus able to compose his Inaugural Address in the confident expectation that Taney and four other members of the Court would relieve Buchanan of the need for making a statement in his Inaugural on the controversial matter of slavery in the territories. On March 4, Buchanan announced in his Inaugural that the forthcoming decision of the Court had made the question of slavery in the territories "happily, a matter of but little practical importance." Rather disingenuously, since he knew what the decision was to be, he also pledged: "To their decision, in common with all good citizens I shall cheerfully submit, whatever this may be." Within a few days, the Supreme Court, as Buchanan expected, announced its decision. A bare majority of five members of the Court—four of whom were Southerners—declared the Missouri Compromise unconstitutional; four, all Southerners, declared that Congress could not prohibit slavery in the territories. Although their lack of foresight is scarcely credible, Buchanan and Taney evidently believed that the Dred Scott decision would actually solve the most burning issue of contemporary politics by judicial declaration. Never has the fragile basis of the Court's power over political questions been made so obvious. (For these details, see Nichols, *Disruption of American Democracy*, pp. 60–73.)

political advantage, as it was to do for the century following the Civil War, by the professionalization of politics and the long continuity in leadership that enhanced the influence of her spokesmen. A historian has written:

> The control of the Federal government by the South during the fifties had been almost complete. While the Presidents were of Northern origin they had been nominated by national conventions dominated by Southern leaders. The Cabinets had generally had four of the seven members from the South. In Congress the most important committees were chaired by Southerners. At one time the President pro tempore of the Senate and the chairmen of the Foreign Relations, Finance, and Judiciary committees were experienced representatives from the South. When the Democrats were in control, the Speakers of the House were Southern. Five of the nine members of the Supreme Court were from that section. These men controlled both legislation and the fortunes of statesmen. . . .[10]

The political parties. Finally, the very merits of the political parties as instruments for settling moderate conflict may have disabled them during severe conflicts. The parties, both Democratic and Whig, were un-ideological, conglomerate, nationwide, crosscutting parties avid for compromise on an issue that their leaders accurately foresaw would, if inflamed, destroy them. The small parties, like Free Soil, that tried to pose the issue of slavery clearly were crushed by the great giants. For many years, the efforts of the parties succeeded; they were able to compromise the issue and thereby keep the peace. In 1836 they had even pushed through a 'Gag Rule' in the House, which prevented the House from taking up "petitions, memorials, resolutions, propositions or papers relating in any way or to any extent whatsoever to the subject of slavery or the abolition of slavery."[11] The rule or others even stricter endured until 1844. By these and other means the oldest, largest, and most clearly national party—the American Democracy as it called itself —managed to maintain a compromise between Northern and Southern wings until 1860.

Yet the hypothesis—it can be no more than that—is defensible: If the American system had been based more fully on the principle of majority rule at the national level, and if the parties had been more concerned with ideological issues, they might have presented a clearer picture of the alternatives much earlier than they did. Southern slave-holders would have seen quite early that slavery was subject to a decision by the representatives of a majority of voters. As a distinct minority in the nation, their bargaining power would not have been amplified as it was by the innumerable devices of the American Constitution that reinforce minorities against majorities.

---

10. Nichols, *The Stakes of Power*, p. 76.
11. Morris, *Encyclopedia of American History*, p. 179.

If slavery had been ended earlier, without disrupting the country, the gains would have been incalculable; for a problem would have been solved while it was still manageable in the ways of peace. But would a political system less responsive to minority power only have led to secession earlier, when the republic was still young? If the Republic had split earlier, what would have been the fate of Southern and Northern Negroes? Compared with what actually transpired, would their lot have been worse—or better?

This much seems clear: the political institutions encouraged compromises that preserved in the South a system based on slavery for so long that this peculiar and anachronistic but deeply entrenched way of life was not likely to be revolutionized by peaceful negotiations.

CHANGE, COMPROMISE, RECONCILIATION

Only the immediate question was settled by Civil War: slavery was forever barred not only in the territories but in the old slave states as well.

Unimpeded by the political opposition of the Southern slavocracy, the Republican coalition of North and West carried through a program of comprehensive changes that insured the expansion of industry, commerce, and free farming. I have already mentioned the main items. Instead of a Thirteenth Amendment that would have preserved slavery, another Thirteenth Amendment abolished it. Instead of the policies of economic laissez faire that the slavocracy had demanded (side by side with a rigid and meticulous governmental intervention to protect slavery), the Republicans substituted the doctrine that the federal government would provide assistance for business, industry, and farming: the protective tariff, homesteads, land subsidies for agricultural colleges, transcontinental railways and other internal improvements, national banks. When the defeated South came back into the Union, it had to accept the comprehensive alteration in government policy and economic institutions that the historian Charles A. Beard was later to name the Second American Revolution.

Yet the revolution in the South that might have liberated the freed Negro slave, a revolution sought by some abolitionists and Radical Republicans, was never carried out. The only hope that black Americans might commence their march to full equality depended upon the prospects for a social, economic, and political revolution. But the freed black was securely provided with neither land nor education nor civil rights.

The Prospects for Revolution:
Change in the South

How could the domination of politics by a small white oligarchy be ended? For this was the central pattern of political life in the South in the pre–Civil War period. As in many developing nations of the world today, one hopeful possibility lay in land reform. If a large body of prosperous, independent, free farmers (as in the North) could be created by redistributing land holdings, then political power might come to rest with coalitions of free farmers, white and black, and the dominance of the great landowner might be destroyed. Education and civil rights would also be required. In time, the system would be able to sustain itself without protection from the outside.

It was some such strategy that a few Radical Republicans such as Thaddeus Stevens seem to have had in mind during Reconstruction. Even if hesitantly and from a variety of motives, the Radical Republicans in Congress took steps to reorganize the Southern economy, society, and polity. In 1866 they passed the Southern Homestead Act; although it was weak and never implemented, it provided that in five Southern states where federal lands remained, all public lands (constituting one-third of the total area of these five states) were reserved exclusively for homesteaders. Like many whites, most Negroes needed education; this was a major aim of Reconstruction government in creating public school systems in the Southern states. Above all, Negroes needed political influence, which first of all meant the ballot. Neither the Civil Rights Act of 1866 nor the Fourteenth Amendment, which the Southern states were required to accept before being readmitted to Congress, provided for Negro suffrage. However, the Military Reconstruction Act of 1867 organized the South into five military districts and instructed the commanding general of each to register Negro voters and to protect their right to vote by stationing soldiers at polls and registration places. By the end of 1867, 703 thousand blacks (and only 627 thousand whites) had been registered.

The Revolution that Failed

Yet the revolution so boldly envisioned by a few was never completed. As we have seen during the present century, it is extraordinarily difficult for outsiders to impose a lasting revolution on a country. Without support from people inside a country, policies imposed entirely from outside are likely to produce only shallow changes.

By blacks? Freed slaves could not make a revolution unaided. They were a black minority amidst a national and even a regional majority of whites. In its awful destruction of pride, self-reliance, and family—that tiny island of human solidarity which has sometimes withstood, elsewhere, a thousand years of oppression—slavery left its scars.[12] If

---

12. A lively debate goes on among historians as to whether American slavery was the most—or least—inhuman in the Western hemisphere. The most devastating interpretation is by Stanley M. Elkins, *Slavery* (New York: Grosset's Universal Library, 1959–1963). See also Kenneth M. Stampp, *The Peculiar Institution* (New York: Vintage Books, 1956). For a different interpretation, see Marvin Harris, *Patterns of Race in the Americas* (New York: Walker & Co., 1964).

there was to be a revolution after the Civil War, it had to be made by white citizens for black citizens. But the North was too irresolute, too infirm, and too divided in its aims to persist in the revolutionary reconstruction of Southern institutions that might have liberated the freed man. The white South and its traditional leaders were much more easily mobilized to resist that revolution.

By whites? How many Northern citizens, or even Northern leaders, ever eagerly embraced the idea of making a revolution in Southern society remains uncertain. There is strong evidence that few Northerners who supported Reconstruction in the South were ready to accept Northern blacks as their equals. After the Civil War, as before, Northerners remained notably unenthusiastic about extending civil rights to the blacks in their midst. Except for Minnesota and Iowa—neither of which had many blacks—no Northern state in the postwar period voluntarily granted the suffrage to blacks; efforts to do so were steadily defeated.[13] As the obstacles to reconstruction in the South became more evident, support dwindled in the North. The reforming spirit flagged. "One is driven by the evidence," C. Vann Woodward has written, "to the conclusion that the radicals committed the country to a guarantee of equality that popular convictions were not prepared to sustain."[14] Their leaders also wearied. Men like Charles A. Dana, editor of the influential *New York Sun* and once a Radical, used his newspaper to proclaim throughout Grant's second term: "No force bill! No Negro domination!" Old antislavery men like William Cullen Bryant, editor of the *New York Evening Post,* James Russell Lowell, and Robert Ingersoll all foreswore Radicalism and Reconstruction. Edwin L. Godkin in the columns of the *Nation* (a journal that had been in the vanguard in opposing the subjugation of the Negro) now steadily attacked the notion that the evils of the South could be cured by outsiders.[15]

Neither the people nor their leaders were prepared to commit themselves to the long, persistent, and often disagreeable tasks of reconstructing an alien society—nor, for that matter, their own. The old and often decent impulse to compromise and conciliate was strong. Equality of the Afro-American had little to attract white citizens other than the

---

13. By 1869, nine northern states permitted Negroes to vote. In addition to the five New England states, Minnesota, and Iowa, these included "Nebraska, which entered the Union with Negro suffrage as a congressional requirement, and Wisconsin by decision of her Supreme Court" (Woodward, "Seeds of Failure in Radical Race Policy," p. 7). The Republican platform of 1868 proclaimed: "The guaranty by Congress of equal suffrage to all loyal men at the South was demanded by every consideration of public safety, of gratitude, and of justice, and must be maintained; while the question of suffrage in all loyal [i.e., northern] States properly belongs to the people of those states" (*ibid.,* p. 6).

14. Woodward, *The Burden of Southern History,* p. 83. See also his comments at pp. 79–83, 90–93.

15. Paul H. Buck, *The Road to Reunion, 1865–1900* (New York: Vintage Books, 1959), p. 101.

weak appeal of abstract justice—and, for a time, the prospect so alluring to the radical politicians, a Republican South founded upon Negro votes. A policy of reconciliation (at the expense of the black) made a strong appeal not only to the spirit of compromise so deeply ingrained in Americans, but to history, tradition, identity, race, and economic interest, North and South. Revolution was tiresome; in any case by 1876 all the signs showed that the revolution was failing.

Restoration of white supremacy. In the defeated states where Negroes were a minority, whites used a mixture of votes and intimidation to restore their control. In states like Mississippi where Negroes were a majority, for whites to win elections required an even stronger dose of intimidation and Ku Klux Klan. In one state after another, reconstruction governments that fully protected the rights of Negro voters in the old slave states were displaced by 'conservative' governments: Tennessee in 1869, Virginia and North Carolina in 1870, Georgia in 1872, Alabama and Arkansas in 1874, Mississippi in 1876. By the time of the elections of 1876, Republican governments controlled only three Southern states, South Carolina, Louisiana, and Florida. Two sets of actions symbolized what was happening and foreshadowed the full restoration of white supremacy. In 1873 a minority, and in 1876 a majority, of the Supreme Court announced in language plain enough for all to understand that it was stripping the Negro of the protections he was presumed to have under the Fourteenth Amendment; instead, the Court would use the Amendment to protect business enterprise from government regulation.[16] In July, 1876, Southern congressmen won enough support among their Northern colleagues to gut the Southern Homestead Act of 1866: land reform, half-hearted at best, was ended.

Return to Subjection: The Compromise of 1877

In November, 1876, the presidential contest led to a disputed outcome in which both candidates, backed by their parties, claimed victory. The bitter and inflamatory dispute went on through the fall of 1876 and the winter of 1877 and was finally settled only a few days before the date for the new president's inaugural (March 4). This compromise permitted the Republican candidate to take office and marked the end of Reconstruction in the South.

The leading historian of that episode has summed it up:

> The Compromise of 1877 marked the abandonment of principles and of force and a return to the traditional ways of expediency and concession. The compromise laid the political foundation for re-union. It established a new sectional truce that proved more enduring than any previous one and

16. In *The Slaughter House Cases* (1873); *United States* v. *Reese* (1876); *United States* v. *Cruikshank* (1876).

provided a settlement for an issue that had troubled American politics for more than a generation. It wrote an end to Reconstruction and recognized a new regime in the South. More profoundly than Constitutional amendments and wordy statutes it shaped the future of four million freedmen and their progeny for generations to come. It preserved one part of the fruits of the "Second American Revolution"—the pragmatic and economic part—at the expense of the other part—the idealistic and humanitarian part. . . .

The Compromise of 1877 did not restore the old order to the South, nor did it restore the South to parity with other sections. It did assure the dominant whites political autonomy and nonintervention in matters of race policy and promised them a share in the blessings of the new economic order. So long as the Conservative Redeemers held control they scotched any tendency of the South to combine forces with the internal enemies of the new economy—laborites, Western agrarians, reformers. Under the regime of the Redeemers the South became a bulwark instead of a menace to the new order.[17]

After the compromise, troops were withdrawn in the states where they still remained. All serious efforts at reconstruction ceased. The attempt to create an independent yeomanry of white and Negro farmers failed utterly:

In spite of the low price of land and the small acreage in which it could be acquired, few Negroes or white farmers were financially capable of purchasing farms and becoming actual owners. The split-up of the plantation did not result in a land-owning, independent and sturdy yeomanry. A system of tenancy, in which the laborer worked assigned tracts and shared the produce with the owner, developed and became permanent. It can be demonstrated that the increase in the number of small farms was a barometer for measuring the increase in tenantry. By 1880 forty-five per cent of all the farms of Georgia were operated by tenants. . . .

The abounding poverty depressed the tenant into a status approximating peonage. Lacking sufficient savings to live through a season of growing crops without borrowing, he discovered that credit was an expensive luxury. Banking facilities in rural areas fell sadly short of the demand. Even where they existed, the only security the tenant had to offer the bank was a lien placed on his share of the anticipated crop. The village merchant with whom he traded for food, clothing, and other supplies perforce became his banker, giving credit in return for a crop lien. By 1880 approximately three fourths of the agricultural classes in the South were chronic debtors, and the merchants through their control of credit were the dominant factor in the new economic structure.[18]

White supremacy was restored. The South became the one-party region it remained for almost a century. For white Southerners not only abhorred the Republican party as responsible for inflicting civil war on their soil, freeing the slaves, and attempting to push through the policies

17. Woodward, *Reunion and Reaction*, pp. 245–246.
18. Buck, *The Road to Reunion*, pp. 151, 152.

of Reconstruction; they also saw that whites could unite to maintain white supremacy in a single party, whereas they would be dangerously weakened if they divided into two competing and conflicting parties.

The Supreme Court of the United States, as it must do sooner or later, adhered to the terms of the compromise: it undertook the long and sordid process of whittling down the meaning of the Fourteenth and Fifteenth Amendments—and converting the Fourteenth into a protection for business enterprise against state regulation. As the Court and federal government stood aside, blacks were, in time, disfranchised throughout the South. In 1896 in *Plessy* v. *Ferguson* the Court wrapped the Constitution around the doctrine of segregation.

"Capitulation to racism," as Woodward has called it, now became complete. During the years that followed *Plessy* v. *Ferguson* a new wave of segregationism fastened the yoke of Jim Crow and Negro disfranchisement firmly upon the South,[19] a system into which most white (and many black) Southerners were to be so thoroughly inducted by indoctrination and overwhelming social pressure backed by violence that they received it as a precious and unalterable way of life to be protected against all change and all interference. It was not until after the middle of the present century that this way of life—one of the greatest anachronisms, surely, of the twentieth century—finally came under an attack from outside and from within so powerful and so steady that the hallowed ways began to yield, at last, to new ways that for the first time in the nation's history might someday be reconciled with the democratic promises of American polyarchy.

SUMMARY   The developments leading to the Civil War conform in the main to the paradigm of extreme conflict represented on page 311 and discussed in the last chapter:

1. In the course of the 1850s two issues came to the forefront on which views diverged so widely that compromise became increasingly difficult. These were slavery and secession.

2. The conflict over these issues came to be increasingly perceived by the contestants as a zero-sum contest with high stakes, involving, indeed, alternative and irreconcilable ways of life.

3. The pattern of crosscutting cleavages that had prevailed until about 1854 was transformed into a pattern of nonoverlapping or cumulative cleavages. The effect was initially to fragment political parties and other institutions of reconciliation and finally to polarize the contestants into two camps. However, even by the outbreak of the Civil War polarization of attitudes was far from complete, particularly among the general

---

19. Woodward, *The Strange Career of Jim Crow.*

public. Secession was engineered by a small minority of slaveholders and their retainers, followers, and spokesmen.

4. Negotiations could no longer produce acceptable solutions. The existence of what was in effect a veto in the hands of Southern leaders on decisions about slavery, the heterogeneity of the parties and their inability to act cohesively, and the extreme partitioning of political authority all made elimination of slavery through ordinary political processes virtually impossible throughout the whole period from 1787 to the Civil War.

Yet despite enormous human cost, the Civil War did not lead to equal political rights for the freed slaves, much less equal opportunities for Afro-Americans generally. The revolutionary change in Southern landholding patterns that might have created a body of prosperous, independent free farmers, black and white, was not carried through. Freed slaves could not bring about changes unaided, and Northern whites finally proved unwilling to enforce changes over the opposition of Southern whites. The Compromise of 1877 permitted the restoration of white supremacy in the South.

Reflections
On
Political
Action

part

5

Influencing the Conduct of Government: An Overview

25

Whether he is aware of it or not, the daily life and the long-run chances, opportunities, advantages, and handicaps of each citizen are powerfully shaped by the actions and inactions of American governments. If you doubt it, perform any one of the following mental experiments: imagine that the American governments abolish public education; triple the tax rate; equalize incomes; abolish police and judiciary; prohibit divorce on any grounds; repeal all laws having to do with property; prohibit strikes and trade unions; nationalize all private businesses; suppress all political parties except one; sell all highways to private owners; make it a criminal offense to go to church. That these are extreme possibilities is irrelevant; that these are *possible* emphasizes what American governments actually do by showing what they might do.

American governments, then, like most other governments exercise great influence over the lives of their citizens. Only governments can legally punish a citizen who refuses to send his children to school, to treat them humanely, to have them vaccinated against smallpox. Only governments can lawfully seize a citizen's property without his consent and compel him to pay taxes. Governments have the legal authority to coerce; they can fine, imprison, or even kill citizens who disobey their rules. American governments add to their legal powers a very large measure of legitimacy: most citizens feel that it is not only dangerous to disobey the laws but also wrong to do so. Armed with legality and legitimacy, American governments can and do acquire vast resources. They can and do use these resources not only to punish but also to reward; they allocate jobs, salaries, grants, contracts, payments, and other benefits in infinite variety. Cash expenditures by the federal government alone amount to about 20 percent of the gross national product, state and local expenditures, more than 10 percent; thus government spending is equal to about one-third of the gross national product.[1]

Because governments are extraordinarily influential, they are inevitably the objects of influence. To influence the conduct of government is to influence the way it uses its powers of compulsion, coercion, punishment; its capacity to render actions legal or illegal, legitimate or illegitimate; its ability to allocate rewards, benefits, privileges, handicaps, wealth, incomes, influence, and power itself. It is easy to see, then, why few things are fought over with more persistence, vigor, and bloodshed than the conduct of government. But how, specifically, can and do Americans influence the conduct of their governments? This is the question that will concern us in this chapter and the next. To answer it will require, first, drawing together a number of matters that have already been treated in previous chapters.

PROSPECTS FOR SUCCESS

All societies regulate the ways in which people may attempt to influence the government. Only in a Hobbesian state of nature is everything permissible; and a state of nature in which everything is permissible would surely be as unbearable as Hobbes insisted it must be.

Like other systems, polyarchies regulate attempts to influence government. Thus they try to rule out efforts to gain influence and power over government officials by coercion, violence, and corruption. More than other systems, they also try to disperse influence widely to their citizens by means of the suffrage, elections, freedom of speech, press, and assembly, the right of opponents to criticize the conduct of government, the right to organize political parties, and in other ways.

Even so, it is obvious that citizens do not enjoy perfectly equal chances of getting the government to do what they want it to do. Why not? At least four kinds of factors affect the chances that a citizen or a group of citizens can secure favorable action from the government. These are: one's own situation, the situation of one's allies, the situations of one's opponents or potential opponents, and the amount of change one seeks.

Own situation. If one reflects on his chances of influencing the government, he will readily see that his chances depend on his own situation, that is, his political resources, his political skills, and his incentives.

Allies and opponents. Because no one is alone in a political system,

1. See "Federal cash expenditures as a percentage of Gross National Product, 1869–1964," in D. J. Ott and A. F. Ott, *Federal Budget Policy* (Washington: The Brookings Institution, 1965), p. 42, Figure VI. For state and local expenditures, see Maxwell, *Financing State and Local Governments*, p. 22.

chances of success will also depend upon the situation of one's allies and opponents. All that has been said about resources, skills, and incentives applies equally to them. Allies may enable you to multiply resources and skills and hence improve your chances of success. Conversely, the greater the resources, skills, and incentives of your opponents, the worse your prospects are. Indeed, one of the characteristics of political systems is the frequency of *mutual escalation:* if you and your allies begin to invest your skills and resources in order to change the conduct of government, your political activity activates your opponents. They, too, mobilize their skills and resources; they seek allies. In response, you now mobilize more skills and resources and search for additional allies. Yet your reaction once again provokes your opponents to respond. Fortunately, legal limits and accepted norms vastly reduce the likelihood that mutual escalation will finally proceed to the level of violence, although that possibility is never wholly out of the question—as the American Civil War illustrates. Another restraint on mutual escalation results from its *anticipation.* If you are quite sure your opponents will respond by escalating, you may decide that the potential gain from political action is not worth the cost. People sometimes think that politics is a cheap game to buy into, but it can be a costly game to win. This is one reason why many people with sizeable resources nonetheless remain aloof from politics or confine their actions to some specific aspect of the conduct of government that they care most about—schools, taxes, foreign policy, civil liberties, racial integration, agricultural subsidies, or one of a thousand other possibilities.

Amount of change required. In addition to the resources, skills, and incentives of you, your allies, and your opponents, your chances of gaining a favorable action from the government depend on still another factor: *how much change* you require in the behavior of other people in order for the government to do what you want it to do. The greater the amount of change required, the less your chances of success—other things being equal, of course.

How do we determine or measure "the amount of change required"? If there were time to explore it here, the concept would prove to be a highly complex one of many dimensions; but it is convenient, and sufficient for the purpose of this chapter, to think of the amount of change required as having two dimensions: the number of persons who must change their minds, and the costs to each person involved in changing his mind. Obviously, chances of success are much better if it involves persuading only one key member of a congressional committee rather than all the members; winning over a majority of only one committee rather than a majority of a whole chamber; or 10 percent of the electorate rather than 51 percent, etc. In Southern states, a Republican candidate for office would ordinarily have to change the minds of many more voters than his Democratic opponent in order to win. In presidential elections, the two major parties each begin with a hard core of millions of supporters; to win, a candidate needs to change the minds of only a minority of the electorate. But third-party candidates, who begin with only a tiny hard core of support, might have to change the minds of a third or more of the electorate in order to win.

As we all know, changing one's mind may be very easy or extraordinarily difficult. You find it easier to change your mind when you see only small differences between the alternatives than when you see large differences; thus if you are a Republican it is ordinarily easier for you to switch to another Republican when your preferred candidate fails to gain the Republican nomination than to switch to the Democratic candidate. It is easier to change your mind on matters you consider unimportant than on important matters. It is easier to change recently acquired or superficial views than long-standing, deeply rooted views. It is easier to change consciously held opinions than unconscious attitudes, easier to change your opinions than your personality, loyalties, identifications—in short, yourself.

If you want to get other people to change their views, it appears that the greater the amount of change in other people's behavior you require for success, the more resources and skills you will need to use, the greater your incentives will have to be, and the more you need allies. It will be easier for your opponents, on the other hand, to block the change. Conversely, the less the amount of change in other people you require, the less resources and skills you need, the lower your incentives may be, and the less you may have to depend on allies. These elements are summarized in Figure 25.1.

THE KEY GOVERNMENTAL ACTOR In a concrete sense governments are made up of officials. To influence the conduct of government one must sooner or later influence the conduct of officials. Far and away the most important government official is the president. The president's extraordinary influence follows from his extraordinary resources, skills, and incentives.

As we have already seen, among the president's resources, unmatched by any other official, are:

☐ His preeminence in legal authority, the duties, privileges and powers which by law and Constitution no one else can legally perform: e.g., his veto, the need for his signature on laws, his right to act as commander in chief of the armed forces.
☐ The exceptional legitimacy, respect, and deference endowed on his office during the course of its historical evolution.

Figure 25.1
Successful Efforts to
Influence Government

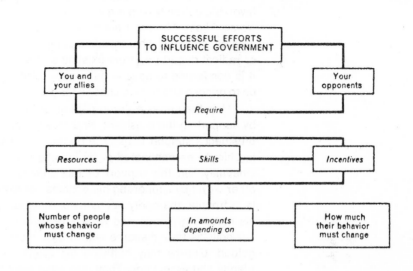

Figure 25.1
Successful Efforts to
Influence Government

☐ His widespread popularity, partly resulting from the factor just mentioned, partly a result of his election, partly a prerequisite to being
elected.
☐ His command of public attention, and thus his influence on the content
of the mass media.
☐ His influence over appointments and promotions to key posts in the
national government.
☐ His unparalleled access to expertness, knowledge, secret information.
☐ His influence over the executive and administrative agencies of the
national government, and hence the way they allocate rewards and
punishments.

Not only does the president have exceptional resources; any man
who wins that office is likely to have acquired exceptional political skills
before he enters the White House, skills that will be further refined by
the manifold challenges of the presidency. Then, too, the president has
stronger incentives than most people for using his skills and resources as
effectively as possible, for few people can see more clearly than the man
in the White House how much hangs on his success and failure.

Because the presidency is the repository of more influence than any
other office, the president becomes the most important object of political
influence. All politically active groups tend to gravitate toward the White
House. It is difficult and often impossible for any group to affect the
conduct of the national government over continued and active presiden-

tial opposition. Even with presidential support, a group may fail to secure favorable action from the government; without it, their chances are much worse. Those who most need the president's aid are those who seek the greatest changes, who advocate comprehensive alterations, innovations, or radical departures from existing policies. But even for conservatives, it is comforting to have an ally in the White House who can be counted on to oppose attempts to change the status quo.

How then does a group gain presidential support? Most commonly, by supporting the president. Probably the most effective way to gain the president's support is to be in on the process of choosing him: by helping him to be nominated or by helping him to get elected or reelected. One may win the support of the president by giving him support in other ways: by supporting his policies, for example, particularly when he is in trouble and badly needs help. Allies of the president may also win his present gratitude and his future support by refraining from criticizing policies they disagree with: in the metal of politics, silence can be golden. Groups may cultivate his friendship or the friendship of his friends and associates. They may even seek to win him over by persuasion. Rational persuasion—or at any rate semirational persuasion—may be more important in winning presidents over to proposed policies than is commonly supposed. Failing these and other friendly ways of winning presidential support, one may turn to the public, the citizen body, the voters, in the hopes that if one can write the handwriting on the wall in letters large enough, the president will read it.

OTHER ACTORS   Congress

Even if a group has access to the president, it may also need to influence the Congress or some part of Congress. A group that lacks presidential backing may need to cultivate support in Congress all the more. The techniques that are used to win presidential support are also used to acquire support among senators and representatives. But senators and representatives are ordinarily closer and more accessible; it is easier to approach one's congressman than to gain a hearing from the president.

While an individual, a group, an organization, a movement that seeks comprehensive change or a major innovation in government policies must turn toward the White House for leadership, groups with less ambitious goals may gain all they seek with little more than the cooperation of a handful of congressmen. They may use Congress to veto, delay, or amend a hostile measure advanced by the president. Strategically placed support in Congress may be enough to provide the marginal changes in existing policies that a group considers critical: a loophole opened up, an appropriation increased or cut, standards weakened or tightened, an agency rebuked by an appropriations subcommittee, an investigation launched, a speech on the Senate floor. One's senator or representative can also serve as an ambassador to one of the administrative agencies.

Lobbies. A persistent organization may—and sooner or later probably will—establish a Washington representative to lobby for its interests in Congress. Retired senators and representatives—retired, usually, by the voters—are available. Between 1946 and 1965, twenty former senators and seventy-six former representatives registered themselves as lobbyists under the Federal Regulation of Lobbying Act passed in 1946.[2] Each year several hundred groups report a total of about 4 million dollars for lobbying in Congress; unreported lobbying would doubtless swell the totals to figures considerably larger.

Administrative Agencies

With or without the aid of lobbyists, groups may also seek to gain their ends directly through the administrative agencies themselves. The American Medical Association doubtless seeks to maintain good working relations with the Department of Health, Education, and Welfare; the National Association of Electric Companies with the Federal Power Commission; the Transportation Association and the Association of American Railroads with the Interstate Commerce Commission; the National Small Business Men's Association with the Department of Commerce and the Small Business Administration; the National Milk Producers Federation, the National Association of Farmer Cooperatives, and the American Farm Bureau with the Department of Agriculture; the AFL-CIO with the Labor Department; and so on. These relationships are sometimes antagonistic ones; occasionally, on the other hand, the private group may virtually capture the government agency. Thus a student of interest groups describes the relationships between the Farm Bureau Federation (a private association of farmers) and the federal agricultural agencies under the New Deal as follows:

> In addition to the advantages which accrued to the Farm Bureau by reason of the policy of the Agricultural Adjustment Administration, a tightly drawn web between the administrative structure of the government agency and that of the private association produced a coalition of monopolistic proportions. The source of the Farm Bureau foothold in administering the Agricultural Adjustment Act lay in its long-standing affiliation with the Extension Service. The county farmers association, having the responsibility of assigning quotas and insuring compliance was a basic part of the AAA program. Since the Extension Service was already operating in the field, it was the logical agency to administer the program. While the AAA machinery was being established, the Farm Bureau, working through the Extension Service, actually supervised the establishment of local units. Farm Bureau

---

2. *Congress and the Nation*, vol. 1, pp. 1572–1576.

representatives performed the task of delivering benefit checks to farmers, which symbolized the organization as a dispenser of the public largess and, on occasion, deducted organizational dues before final transmittal. After the initial organizational phase of the AAA, the Farm Bureau–Extension administration continued to be the center of reliance for the farmer. The parent organization confined its operation to central review in Washington.[3]

Supreme Court

An individual or a group may also turn to the Supreme Court for help. Sometimes the Court will extend the protection of the Constitution to an otherwise defenseless person. However, for reasons already explored in Chapter 16, a group in outright opposition to the dominant national coalition of the day is unlikely in the long run to secure striking success in the Court. Even such an opposition group may nonetheless win delaying actions—and sometimes the delay can go on for a very long time, as in the defeat by business interests of child-labor legislation. A group stands a better chance of winning the Court's support and protection if the national coalition is divided, or if the group itself represents one segment of the national coalition; or, in some cases, if the group stands outside the national coalition, neglected or overlooked. The Court is an awkward, uncertain, unreliable, and rarely used instrument for bringing about major changes in national policies; it is better for veto than for positive innovation. Yet as we have seen, it was neither the president nor the Congress but the Supreme Court, responding not to outside pressures but to the sense of justice and ideological commitments of the justices themselves, that launched the United States on the road to integration and civil rights. It was the Court, as we have seen, that altered the existing balance of political power among cities, suburban, small town, and rural areas by forcing the states to reapportion their legislatures. In both these cases, however, the action of the Court was directed to state governments; particularly in the case of civil rights, the Court's action was not particularly effective until the Executive Branch, and ultimately Congress, backed it up with new and positive policies to replace those struck down by the Court.

State and Local Governments

The state and local governments are in many ways duplicates of the national government on a local scale. Individuals and organizations may succeed in achieving at these lower levels what they could not gain at the national level. They may even use the states to defy the national government. Within the state itself, the same process goes on. Groups who lack influence with city governments may turn to the state legislature; urban groups unable to gain what they want at the state level may concentrate

---

3. Harmon Zeigler, *Interest Groups In American Society* (Englewood Cliffs: Prentice-Hall, 1964), p. 191.

on the city administration, and city administrations themselves may bypass the state government and acquire allies, funds, and legal backing in Washington.

THE MULTIPLICITY OF CHECK POINTS When one looks at American political institutions in their entirety and compares them with institutions in other polyarchies, what stands out as a salient feature is the extraordinary variety of opportunities these institutions provide for an organized minority to block, modify, or delay a policy which the minority opposes. Consequently, it is a rarity for any coalition to carry out its policies without having to bargain, negotiate, and compromise with its opponents; often, indeed, it wins a victory in one institution only to suffer defeat in another.

The president, the House, and the Senate are separate institutions. Each reposes on a separate and different system of elections with different terms of office and different electorates. Groups weighty in a presidential election may be much weaker in House and Senate elections. The policies of a particular group or coalition may be supported in one institution and opposed in another. In many areas of policy, each of these major institutions has a veto over the others. Each has a reservoir of legal, constitutional, and *de facto* power.

Neither the executive, the House, nor the Senate is monolithic. A group may be strong in one executive agency, weak in another; strong in a particular House or Senate committee, weak elsewhere. A group may have individual spokesmen and opponents located at various places in the executive agencies, the regulatory commissions, the House, the Senate, the standing committees, a conference committee.

The political parties themselves are coalitions. Nominations are not centrally controlled. National party leaders have limited resources for influencing their members in Congress. A minority may be defeated at the presidential nominating convention, yet retain its strength in state and local party organizations; it cannot be pushed aside.

Again and again in the history of the Supreme Court, a minority coalition that could not win the presidency or majorities in Congress has preserved a majority within the Supreme Court to fight a rear-guard delaying action. Chief Justice John Marshall fought Thomas Jefferson. In the Dred Scott case, Chief Justice Roger B. Taney, fearing what future majorities might do, fought to preserve dead or dying ones. Embattled minorities entrenched in the Court knocked out the income tax in 1894, child-labor laws in 1918 and 1922, New Deal reforms from 1935 to 1937. In its epochal decision on school integration in 1954, the Court pronounced policy that could not possibly have passed through Congress at that time. Even if they rarely win their wars in the Congress, minorities well represented on the Court can win some impressive battles.

Even when minorities lose in national politics, they still may win in the states. Although defeated in the Civil War, the white South nonetheless forced the North to concede white supremacy, thanks in considerable measure to the institutions of federalism. In the North, trade unions and advocates of factory reform, abolition of child labor, workmen's compensation, shorter hours, and protection of women workers won in the state legislatures what they could not win nationally without the agreement of president, Congress, and Court. The principle holds even within the states, where legislative, executive, and judicial institutions follow the pattern of the national government, though often with greater fragmentation. Local governments provide still other checkpoints.

If in constitutional theory there is no hierarchy of legitimate authorities, then fact, as we have seen, conforms with theory. That the president is no mere agent of the Congress; that the Congress is not subordinate to the president; that neither the federal government nor a state is subordinate to the other on all matters—these are facts of political life, facts doubly resistant to change because fact corresponds to constitutional doctrine and American ideology.

The institutions, then, offer organized minorities innumerable sites in which to fight, perhaps to defeat, at any rate to damage, an opposing coalition. Consequently, the institutions place a high premium on the strategies of compromise and conciliation, on a search for agreement. They inhibit and delay change until there is wide support; they render comprehensive change unlikely; they foster incremental adjustments. They generate politicians who learn how to deal gently with opponents, who struggle endlessly in building and holding coalitions together, who doubt the possibilities of great change, who seek compromises.

SOME POLITICAL AXIOMS What conclusions can be drawn from this somewhat general and abstract discussion? Let me list some axioms—most of them rather obvious—suggested by the discussion so far:

☐ Other things being equal, a full-time professional politician is more likely to influence the conduct of government than a part-time amateur, a rich man than a poor man, an educated person than an uneducated person, a newspaper editor than a newspaper reader, a celebrity than an obscure citizen, etc.

☐ Other things are rarely equal, however, and a citizen who has less of one resource than another citizen may nonetheless gain greater influence because he has other resources. Though he has less money, he may have more time, more energy, greater popularity, stronger ethnic ties.

☐ A citizen who is weak in resources may gain allies and thereby increase the total resources, skills, and incentives mobilized for his policies.

☐ Probably no resource is uniformly most effective in American politics. A variety of resources therefore is generally a greater political asset than a very large amount of only one kind of resource.

☐ It is generally easier to maintain old programs than to initiate new government policies. To maintain an existing program usually requires less change in the behavior and views of the people. What is more, once a program exists the program itself is likely to generate resources—time, money, organization, information—that can be used to win support for it; and the people employed in the program will ordinarily have strong incentives to preserve it. Nothing is harder to create than a new institution, nothing harder to destroy than an established one.

☐ Modifying a law is easier than changing the attitudes that give rise to a law.

☐ You have more chance of gaining favorable action if you have to influence only one segment of government rather than several. The greater the number of obstacles on the course, the better the chance that you will fall on your face.

☐ The less a proposal deviates from prevailing ideas and ideology, the better its chance of success. Hence marginal changes stand a better chance than comprehensive changes.

☐ Advocates of a change usually try to make it appear smaller than it is; opponents try to make it appear larger. Advocates portray their proposal as conforming with the prevailing practises, ideas, and institutions; opponents are more likely to portray it as an attack on prevailing practises, ideas, and institutions. If opponents succeed in portraying it as un-American, they have won more than half the battle.

☐ In general, it is easier to veto a change than to initiate one, easier to preserve the status quo than to change it, easier to make technical changes than ideological changes, easier to make incremental changes than comprehensive or revolutionary changes.

☐ It follows that supporters of the status quo usually need fewer resources, less skill, and lower political incentives to prevent changes than opponents of the status quo need in order to make changes. Reformers and radicals, then, require more resources, skills, and incentives than conservatives. Revolutionaries require even more.

These observations are valid in a general way, but one must be cautious in drawing further conclusions that would be invalid. Since people who benefit most from the status quo and thus have the greatest resources of wealth, income, and social standing are likely to support the status quo most strongly, it might appear that conservatives who defend the status quo would always be in an impregnable position. Not only is this conclusion historically incorrect; it does not follow from what we have said. For those who benefit most from the status quo are often fewer in *numbers* than those who expect to benefit by a change; moreover, well-to-do defenders of the status quo may be more out of touch with other citizens and hence lack political skills and popularity. Critics of the status quo may greatly outnumber defenders; by combining and organizing they may mobilize greater total resources; they may possess greater skills; they may even have stronger incentives and a greater willingness to use what resources they have to bring about change. Thus if the defenders of the status quo often win a great many skirmishes, persistent and untiring critics of the status quo sometimes win the big battles.

SUMMARY   1. In general, prospects for success in influencing the government depend upon one's own resources, skills, and incentives, those of one's allies, and the amount of change required in the behavior of others. The amount of change includes both the number of persons who must change their behavior and the costs each person incurs by changing his mind.

2. In the American polyarchy the key governmental actor is the president.

3. Yet gaining the support of the president is often not enough to secure the policy you want. Thus you may need to turn to the other important actors: Congress, the administrative agencies, the Supreme Court, state and local governments.

4. Perhaps the most distinctive general condition bearing on the problem of influencing the government, a characteristic not shared by all other polyarchies, is the existence of a multiplicity of check points that offer organized minorities innumerable sites in which to fight and perhaps to defeat an opposing coalition.

5. These observations reinforce the following conclusions:

☐ The tendency for influence on government to be distributed unequally is strong.

☐ It is often possible, however, to compensate for weaknesses in some resources (e.g., money) by strength in others (e.g., numbers or energy).

☐ At any given time, supporters of the status quo are likely to exercise greater influence in proportion to their numbers than advocates of change.

☐ Those who seek incremental or piecemeal changes stand a better chance of succeeding in the American polyarchy than those who seek comprehensive change.

Alternative Strategies for Political Activists

26

Suppose that a group of American citizens wishes to bring about changes in the conduct of the government—changes in policies, personnel, or structure. In view of the characteristics, operation, and processes of the American polyarchy that have been described in this book, how should such a group proceed?

RISE UP AGAINST THE GOVERNMENT? In a polyarchy that was the fruit of a revolution, one should hardly forget Lincoln's sentences quoted earlier in this book: "This country, with its institutions, belongs to the people who inhabit it. Whenever they shall grow weary of the existing government, they can exercise their constitutional right of amending it, or their revolutionary right to dismember or overthrow it."

Our group of citizens, then, would need to make a crucial preliminary judgment: Should they choose to exercise "their revolutionary right to dismember or overthrow" the American polyarchy? Or, alternatively, should they use the peaceful processes that are available, or potentially available, in a polyarchy?

After the United States entered into its latest cycle of severe political conflict in the mid-1960s, as fragmentation and polarization increased and the crises in American society intensified, there was, not surprisingly, a corresponding increase in the advocacy of revolution as a way out.

By the end of the decade, in fact, the term *revolution* had become so stylish that even President Nixon could safely use it to refer to his programs. As often happens when serious terms become modish, what the term *revolution* gained in popularity it lost in meaning. To some people revolution evidently had no specific political content: it meant speeding up cultural and attitudinal changes—about race, poverty, war, sex, drugs, life-styles, or whatnot. To others it simply meant bringing about comprehensive changes in government policies, pretty much by legal means: ending the war in Vietnam, vigorously attacking the crisis of the cities, eliminating poverty, unemployment, and inflation, insuring greater opportunity for racial minorities, the economically disadvantaged, women. To some it meant the use of what had once been thought of as unconventional—hence "revolutionary"—ways to achieve specific changes: e.g., mass marches or civil disobedience to end the war or to call attention to racial injustices. To a few the term meant little more than a justification for random, anomic violence—"trashing," killing "the pigs," hurling Molotov cocktails. To a few others, it meant a political strategy aimed at bringing down the government, overthrowing it by force, replacing it with another kind of regime, different leaders, different aims and policies. To these persons, analogous events were the French Revolution of 1789, the Russian Revolution of 1917, Mao and the Chinese Communists, Castro's victory in Cuba, and the like. (It is important to note, incidentally, that none of these revolutions had occurred in a polyarchy.)

Revolution in this strict sense—overthrowing the existing government by force and replacing it with a new and different type of regime—offers, as Lincoln pointed out, a genuine political alternative to achieving changes by means of the processes available in a polyarchy. In my view, it is an alternative with such scant prospects of succeeding in the United States that I find it difficult to weigh it with the seriousness its advocates, who are sometimes deeply committed and self-sacrificing persons, would insist is appropriate. Since 1787 there has probably never been a time when some Americans have not advocated over-throwing the existing government by force, somehow, and replacing it by a new and better regime. Probably their numbers have waxed during periods of severe conflict and polarization and waned during the lengthier intervals of moderate conflict and crosscutting cleavages. These revolutionaries have always been a tiny minority of the population, impotent to do much more than bring down upon them the often crushing weight of social, economic, and physical sanctions, both legal and illegal. In the United States it has been the fate of revolutionaries—using the term still in its strict sense—to be well supplied with incentives, but inept, pitifully weak in all political resources, and lacking wholly what is most needed by revolutionaries to overcome their scant resources: allies who are powerful either because of sheer numbers or superior organization or for other reasons.

The operation of the American polyarchy in the 1960s was, if not exactly typical in this respect, at least familiar. Like their predecessors, active revolutionaries were an infinitesimally small proportion of the adult population, even among young people, where they were assumed to be most numerous. What is more important, despite evidence of fairly rapid changes in attitudes on a number of cultural, social, and political matters, the overwhelming proportion of Americans of all ages and races remained unsympathetic to revolution as a political strategy. As usual, violence by or attributed to revolutionaries alienated more persons than it won over.[1] And as usual, social, economic, and political sanctions, legal and illegal, decimated the ranks of revolutionaries, discouraged many, confused others, and caused a few leaders to rethink questions of strategy and tactics.[2]

The political revolutionary, in the narrow sense used here, faces an implacable dilemma in a long-established polyarchy where the people tend to adhere to a democratic ideology. If revolutionaries could win a majority of the people to their program, it will be said, they would have no need to overthrow the government by force: they could gain office by elections. If they are unable to gain enough support among the people to accomplish their program through the processes of polyarchy, they suffer not only from a shortage of political resources but also from illegitimacy in the eyes of the population: for on that moral basis can these modern advocates of aristocracy justify their claim to rule over a preponderant majority unwilling to support them?

There are, of course, ways of dodging the horns of this dilemma. To anti-democrats who believe in elitist, aristocratic, or meritocratic ideologies, the dilemma is false. It is a revealing fact that the only major instances in which revolutionaries have overturned polyarchies in modern countries involved weak, fledgling polyarchies that were barely struggling to exist in the midst of protracted crises and that were destroyed by revolutionaries who openly proclaimed anti-democratic programs and ideologies. In a society where polyarchy has been functioning long and well enough to be fairly deeply rooted, and where the people substantially agree on an ideology that accords legitimacy only to "government by the people," the dilemma is much harder to dodge. The effort to dodge it is more likely to be an exercise in revolutionary dialectics than a

---

1. The preceding propositions are supported by a substantial amount of data. "Researchers have agreed since 1968 that only about 10 per cent of the students are alienated or politically radical, and of these perhaps one-third have revolutionary views" (Lipset, "Youth and Politics," in Merton and Nisbet, *Contemporary Social Problems*, p. 755).

Based on interviews with 4,000 young people, Yankelovich found that 87 percent of the students agreed with the statement that the "American system of representative democracy can respond effectively to the needs of the people" (Yankelovich, *Generations Apart*, p. 24).

Among the population at large, revolutionary sympathies are so scarce that they hardly show up in national surveys. Even nonrevolutionary but simply new and unconventional attitudes are often confined to an astoundingly small percentage of the population. Thus in 1968, "those who opposed Vietnam and were sympathetic to Vietnam war protestors make up less than 3 percent of the electorate—even if we add comparable blacks to the group—and law and order were not unpopular with the 97 percent" (Converse et al., "Continuity and Change in American Politics," p. 1088).

2. Thus in 1971, Huey Newton, a leader of the Black Panthers, a self-styled revolutionary organization, announced that henceforth the Panthers would avoid violence and cultivate the support of religious and other groups within the black community.

successful strategy for seizing power. In fact, in every polyarchy where widespread suffrage and the other main institutions of polyarchy have been in existence for a generation or more, the polyarchy has so far proved invulnerable to being overturned by strictly internal forces. Experience shows that long-established polyarchies are extremely tough and resilient and have a remarkable capacity for riding out severe crises.

A prolonged failure to cope satisfactorily with issues that a large proportion of citizens regarded as urgent could, of course, so undermine the legitimacy of polyarchy as to generate widespread support for some alternative to polyarchy. Well-established polyarchies may be sturdy but they are surely not invulnerable.

USE THE PROCESSES AVAILABLE IN POLYARCHY? If you conclude for the reasons set out above that revolution in the strict sense is not a serious alternative strategy in the American polyarchy, the question that opens this chapter still remains unanswered. Putting to one side for the moment questions of *tactics*—whether in a given situation to support a particular candidate, to appeal to friends and neighbors at the local level, to engage in mass demonstrations in Washington, or whatnot—a political movement that rejects the path of revolution, and seeks to use the processes constitutionally available or potentially available in the American polyarchy, has open to it, roughly speaking, four strategies:

1. The movement can organize a separate political party of its own.
2. The movement can form a new coalition party by combining with another group or movement that has similar, overlapping, but not identical objectives.
3. Although it remains neutral between the two major parties, the movement can act as a pressure group to secure favorable legislation and the nomination and election of sympathetic candidates.
4. By entering into one of the existing parties, the movement can become an element in a major party coalition; it can then use its bargaining power to gain influence for the movement within the party.

Each of these alternatives has its own inner logic, its special advantages and disadvantages. Perhaps this is why all four strategies have been tried so often. The first strategy has been tried by Free Soilers, Socialists, Greenbackers, Communists, Prohibitionists, Single Taxers, America Firsters, Vegetarians, and the Church of God party, among others. The first strategy enables a movement to maintain its ideological purity and avoid compromising its goals. Yet the usual price is political isolation, defeat, and ineffectuality. The second strategy helps a movement break out of its isolation; but in doing so the movement may lose at least some of its purity and still fail to become a major party. The second strategy was that of the Populists, until they went all the way in 1896 and backed the Democratic candidate, Bryan. It was also the strategy of Progressive movements in 1924 and 1948. The third strategy may yield high payoff if the goals of the movement are narrow and group-oriented. But as a price, the movement must do nothing to alienate the major parties. This is the strategy of most pressure groups; in some states and localities it has also been the strategy of third parties, like the Liberal party in New York. The fourth strategy may yield a movement more influential over a greater range of goals than the third strategy, a better chance of winning elections than the second strategy. The price, however, is a willingness to negotiate, to bargain, to compromise in order to form a winning coalition, and to run the risk of turning members of the other party into opponents. This is the strategy that some unions have adopted at the state level, like the United Automobile Workers in Michigan. It was also the strategy the Populists were moving toward when they supported Bryan in 1896.

Weighing the advantages and disadvantages of the four alternatives is a recurrent task in American politics. Few choices are so important to the destiny of a political movement. It is instructive, therefore, to examine the experience of a movement that has had to face these four alternatives. An obvious candidate is the American labor movement, for from its earliest years down to the present day the labor movement has debated the pros and cons of the various strategies. As in so many other cases, Americans once again chose a path different from that taken in most European countries. Yet the debate over alternatives is not yet ended; perhaps it never will be.

DEMOCRACY AND THE PROLETARIAT   Not only in the Western world but throughout much of the globe, industrialization has gone hand in hand with the growth of cities and the rapid expansion of the urban working classes. A nation of traders and farmers, as Britain still remained in the eighteenth century, was already well on the road to becoming a nation of urban employers and urban workers before the end of the nineteenth century. If the United States began as a nation of farmers and if, as a result, Americans have not yet wholly given up a romantic assessment of the virtues of rural life, the country was nonetheless destined to become a nation of urban workers, white-collar employees, technicians, and businessmen.

The Civil War not only stimulated the growth of Northern industry but liberated economic development from the dead hand of Southern slavocracy. In the last half of the nineteenth century, the proportion of Americans employed in commerce and industry rose steadily as the proportion in farming declined. By 1880 farmers and farm workers out-numbered nonfarm workers. By 1930 the urban population exceeded the rural population. Between 1910 and 1920 the absolute number of farmers reached its peak and thereafter the total number of farmers steadily declined. By 1960, farmers and farm workers were only about 8 percent of the gainfully employed.

The workers who were employed in urban industries represented a new class. It was all too obvious that they were not farmers, even if they might once have been farmers, farm laborers, or peasants who had come to the cities from an American or European countryside. They were not middle class. They were not, at least to any great extent, property owners. They were definitely not employers. Nor were they small businessmen. Huddled in the cities, often living in execrable slums, working long hours with little or no protection from the hazards of unemployment, illness, injury, and old age, they constituted a new and separate interest in society, a social and economic class. On this point, Marx said no more than what was widely assumed in his time.

In the nineteenth century, not only Marx but many other observers took it for granted that the relative expansion of the industrial working classes would continue more or less indefinitely. A few observers like the German socialist critic of Marx, Eduard Bernstein, foresaw that industry and commerce might also expand the size of the white-collar classes. Bernstein, it turned out, was closer to the truth than Marx. The proportion of blue-collar workers, the authentic proletariat, would rise less rapidly than the proportion with white-collar occupations. Between 1910 and 1920 this trend showed up markedly in the most advanced industrial nation, the United States, though the full political significance of the development is far clearer in retrospect than it was to most observers at the time. In the mid-1950s, the white-collar strata began to outnumber the historic 'working class.'

Nonetheless, during the half century or so following the American Civil War, it was not unreasonable to hold that urban working classes constituted a distinct political, social, and economic stratum with interests antagonistic to much of the rest of industrial society. To many people in both Europe and America it was an open question whether these two strata, the working classes and the newer business classes—employers, industrialists, bankers, traders, investors, and executives and professionals of many sorts—could live at peace in the same political system. Anyone concerned with the future of polyarchy might well have wondered whether the allegiance of both strata could be won to polyarchy and to an agreed set of constitutional principles. For how could either of the two strata peacefully accept the principles of majority rule and constitutional decision-making if this meant that spokesmen for the other stratum, apparently their natural enemies, might determine policy?

**PATTERNS OF
REFORM:
EUROPE VERSUS
AMERICA**

In some countries, democratic ideas and the institutions of polyarchy failed to win enough allegiance from both strata; from a democratic point of view, the results were disastrous. One of the most advanced industrial countries in the world, Germany, and two of the least industrialized in Europe, Italy and Spain, plummeted into violence, dictatorship, and war. In France, the urban proletariat developed into a country within a country, hostile, resentful, alienated, and after the Second World War predominantly Communist.

Yet in most countries with sturdy traditions of constitutionalism and representative government, the conflict eventuated in a victory for polyarchy. These countries include a number of north European nations like Britain, Norway, Sweden, Denmark, Holland, and Belgium, and the English-speaking polyarchies of Australia, Canada, New Zealand—and the United States.

There were conflicts, often severe, over economic issues. Yet these conflicts were settled peacefully, and in the end the allegiance of the population to polyarchy was held or won.

Conflicts

In the United States, as in the north European countries, conflicts over economic issues were often harsh and brutal. "Violence in labor disputes," a leading student of the subject has said, "is more common in the United States than in any other industrial nation."[3] Not only was violence more common; in the United States labor conflicts took on a ferocity seldom equaled in Europe. An authority on both the French and American labor movements has remarked that "American workers had to fight bloodier battles than the French for the right of unions to exist and to function."[4] Nonetheless, despite occasional setbacks and fierce opposition from employers, union membership grew from 447 thousand in 1897 to over 2 million in 1904.[5]

Government and employers frequently formed a coalition against workers. State governments, and on occasion even the federal government, were brought into industrial disputes. In the strike of the American Railway Union against the Pullman Company in 1894, U.S. Attorney General Richard Olney who had formerly been a railroad lawyer sought an injunction in federal court against Eugene V. Debs and other strike leaders on the ground that the strike interfered with the mails and interstate commerce and violated the Sherman Anti-Trust Law. The federal court issued a sweeping order against the strike leaders. When the

---

3. Philip Taft, "Violence in American Labor Disputes," *The Annals of the American Academy of Political and Social Science*, 364 (March, 1966), 127–140, especially p. 128.

4. Val R. Lorwin, "Reflections on the History of the French and American Labor Movement," *Journal of Economic History*, 17 (March, 1957), 37.

5. Philip Taft, *Organized Labor in American History* (New York: Harper & Row, 1964), p. 162.

U.S. marshall claimed that he was unable to enforce the court order, Olney persuaded President Cleveland to send federal troops to Chicago, although neither the mayor of Chicago nor the liberal governor of Illinois, Altgeld, had requested federal help and both protested against the presence of the troops. Extensive rioting erupted. The strike failed. "It was not the soldiers that ended the strike," Debs concluded ". . . it was simply the United States courts." Debs was sentenced to six months in jail for contempt of court, and three other strike leaders to three months.[6] Later, Debs was to run five times as candidate for president on the Socialist ticket. It is altogether likely—and fitting—that Debs became a Socialist while he was serving his prison sentence.[7]

Reforms

In the United States and the north European countries, reforms in capitalism tended to come in bunches, usually as a result of elections that put reform administrations in office. In the United States the main waves of reform came about twenty years apart: Wilson's New Freedom from 1913 to 1916, Franklin Roosevelt's New Deal from 1933 to 1937, and the Kennedy-Johnson program from 1961 onward and particularly after the overwhelming Democratic sweep in the 1964 election.

By the beginning of the final third of the twentieth century, the results of reforms were in many ways similar in both the United States and Europe: a good many levers of economic control in the hands of governments; a mixed economy regulated by a vast variety of different instruments—trust-busting, competition, regulatory commissions, public corporations, government contracts, government ownership, fiscal measures, monetary controls; extensive expenditures for a broad range of welfare purposes; large national organizations of employers, farmers, workers, and countless numbers of more specialized interests; and strong interest-group organization and participation in policy-making. There were differences, too, and some of these were important. Thus by 1960 the distribution of incomes was much closer to equality in Australia, New Zealand, Britain, and Norway than in the United States— whereas the distribution of wealth was somewhat more equal in the United States than in Britain.[8]

In none of these countries, however, did unregulated, politically uncontrolled, laissez-faire capitalism exist. Nor, on the other hand, were

---

6. See *Ibid.*, pp. 148–158, for a description of the strike, and the statement by Debs.

7. On Debs's conversion to socialism, see Ira Kipnis, *The American Socialist Movement, 1897–1912* (New York: Columbia University Press, 1952), p. 47.

8. On income distribution, see Russett, *World Handbook of Political and Social Indicators,* Tables 71, 72, pp. 245–246. On property distribution in Britain and the United States, see H. F. Lydall and D. G. Tipping, "The Distribution of Personal Wealth in Britain," *Bulletin of the Oxford University Institute of Statistics,* 13 (1961), 97; and Robert J. Lampman, *The Share of Top Wealth Holders in National Wealth 1922–1956* (Princeton: Princeton University Press, 1962), pp. 210–215.

these economies 'socialist.' The economies were politicized, oriented toward welfare and high consumption, but a major share of production and distribution was not carried on by government-owned enterprise. Indeed, by 1960 the democratic socialist parties of Western Europe had abandoned nationalization of industry as a goal and advocated concrete programs distinguishable only in details from platforms adopted at their national conventions by the Democratic party in the United States.

Differences in Strategies

If by midcentury working-class movements in the United States and in many parts of Europe had reached a rather similar destination, they had arrived by distinctly different routes. In Europe the typical path led to the first and second strategies: formation of a separate and independent labor or socialist party that ultimately became one of the major governing parties and helped to bring about extensive reforms. The American labor movement deliberately and with full awareness that it was deviating from the path of European labor chose a different route. It explicitly and self-consciously rejected the first and second strategies. For many decades it favored the third strategy, political neutrality. Then from the time of the New Deal onward, the fourth alternative has more and more become the policy of key labor unions and the unofficial policy of the AFL-CIO.

U.S.: Home of Unsuccessful
Working-Class Parties

Surprising as it may seem, the first authentic party of the urban working classes was born not in Europe but in the United States. Called the Working Men's Party, it was organized in Philadelphia in 1828 and lasted about three years.[9] After the Civil War, a number of American socialists affiliated themselves with the First International. Socialist parties proliferated with what now seems a bewildering profusion of names, programs, and ideologies: in 1875 the Social-Democratic Party of North America dominated by followers of Lassalle, the German socialist and rival of Marx; in 1875 the Working Men's Party of the United States, a coalition of Lassalleans and Marxists, which the following year became the Socialist Labor Party of North America; in 1883, the International Working People's Association, a union of militant revolutionary socialists and anarchists; in 1897 the Social Democracy of America; in 1901, the Socialist party. In every presidential election since 1892 voters in most states have had an opportunity to vote for socialist candidates for the presidency. But the socialist vote never went beyond 6 percent of the total votes cast (1912), and finally all but died out.

---

9. Taft, *Organized Labor in American History*, pp. 15–20.

THE PATTERN OF CONFLICT Why did the first strategy, adopted by labor movements in many European polyarchies, fail in the United States?

Similar Levels of Conflict

It was not for lack of conflict over capitalism, the role of government, and the power of labor and business in society and the economy. As we have already seen, the relations between workers and employers frequently displayed the most visible symbol of severe conflict—violence. Moreover, two more of the principal conditions of severe conflict were also present: *conflicting views* on matters involving *high stakes*.

In describing the conflict between labor and business we are handicapped, as we were with slavery, by the lack of good data on attitudes and views among the general public or among urban laborers and businessmen. What we have instead are expressions by leaders in politics, speeches and party platforms, statements in the press, demands presented by interest groups such as the AFL, the Farm Bureau Federation, the National Association of Manufacturers.

In the conflicts between these spokesmen, the stakes have never been insignificant and often they have been high. Who is entitled to control decisions on wages, working conditions, and personnel? According to what standards? How and by what standards are prices and employment to be regulated? How shall incomes be distributed? Who is to be protected and who harmed by government intervention? Whose freedom is to be expanded or reduced? These are the weightier if not always visible stakes involved in disputes over the role of labor unions, regulation of business, antitrust, the forms and incidence of taxes, welfare measures, monetary, fiscal, tariff, and agricultural policies.

At times, important blocs of national leaders have diverged widely on these issues: in the 1890s, certainly, and again in the 1930s. From all the evidence at hand, both decades were periods of severe conflict. During both periods there was a sharp divergence of views; and during both periods the stakes were high. (To repeat a point made earlier, the leaders involved obviously *thought* the stakes were high, and for our purposes that is all that matters.)

Yet the conflict was never successfully pressed by a distinct labor party nor a party bearing a classic socialist ideology and program. The political conflicts occurred between and within parties that were conglomerate coalitions, coalitions that lacked ideologies as distinct as European socialism was from European liberalism or conservatism.

No doubt the absence of a labor party with a socialist ideology and program as a major competitor of the other parties helped to keep down the size of the stakes involved in American politics. The absence of a powerful socialist party also meant that political views did not diverge so sharply as in the north European polyarchies. Yet it is worth noting again that even if the northern European countries took a different route they arrived at roughly the same place as the United States. Their socialist parties gradually abandoned much of the distinctively socialist ideology they had begun with; they turned pragmatic and reformist; they gave up the classic socialist instrument: nationalization of industry, and they became, or tried hard to become, conglomerate catchall parties uniting urban labor with rural labor, white-collar workers, farmers, fishermen, government employees.

The United States did not, then, avoid sharp and sometimes severe conflicts over economic issues; yet it did skip a transitional stage that was universal among the northern European polyarchies and quite possibly essential to their success in winning over business and labor to polyarchic institutions and a common set of constitutional procedure. Why did the United States and Europe diverge? Why did labor-socialist parties fail to thrive in the United States?

Divergent Strategies: Causes

Economic growth? One part of the answer is perhaps to be found in the fact that while the stakes were high in the United States, the contest was not "zero-sum." An expanding economy created an ever-available surplus to be distributed.[10] Gross national product and personal consumption grew faster than population; from 1839 to 1959 they increased at the rate of about 1.6 percent a year per capita. These seemingly modest rates amounted to a doubling about every forty years, a fivefold increase in a century. Working-class hostilities were vastly weakened by rising living standards; it took major depressions, as in 1893–4 and the Great Depression after 1929 to deepen hostilities to a point where the working strata could be mobilized to support extensive reforms.

Yet the European economies were also expanding. And it is often argued with persuasive evidence that revolutionary movements prosper most when improving conditions stimulate hope and confidence. Hence to call on the expanding American economy to explain the inability of a labor-socialist party to grow in the United States is not a wholly satisfactory explanation. Was it then because the fruits of economic growth came earlier in the United States than in Europe? Possibly, but there were other differences.

To what extent is the explanation, or a part of it, to be found in the other two sets of factors described in Chapter 21 as influencing the course of political conflict: the pattern of cleavage and the political institutions?

---

10. David Potter, *People of Plenty* (Chicago: University of Chicago Press, 1957).

Cleavages. It seems clear that a pattern of overlapping cleavages was never fully displaced by a pattern of superimposed cleavages cumulating along a single faultline. One cannot be dead sure that the overlapping cleavages were greater in the United States than in the European democracies, but there is an impressive amount of evidence suggesting that they were, and that in any event neither workers nor businessmen were sharply cut off from one another or from the rest of American society.

Three factors helped to maintain a pattern of overlapping cleavage lines even during times of considerable stress. One of these was the extraordinary consensus among Americans on a number of basic ideological issues. In Europe, the socialist parties often battled for polyarchy against their 'bourgeois' opponents; it was the socialists, often, who fought for parliamentary government, cabinet responsibility, and an equal and universal suffrage. In Norway and Sweden, for example, in the early stages, socialist and middle-class parties fought more over polyarchy than over socialism. In the United States this ideological, institutional, and constitutional conflict had been pretty well settled before the urban laboring population began to expand. The American labor movement of the 1880s and 1890s did not have to fight for polyarchy; the institutions of polyarchy were already here and a democratic ideology widely accepted. To be sure, the constitutional structure was at stake in the Civil War, but it was never again seriously contested. The labor movement joined in the broad consensus on democratic ideas and the institutions of polyarchy that have been such a pronounced aspect of American life. What is more, the labor movement never mounted a strong opposition even to the traditions of private property and competitive self-advancement.

Another factor that helped to maintain overlapping cleavages was the fact that in comparison with Europe, other cleavages were stronger than class. The "solidarity of the working classes" predicted by Marx was weakened in the United States by ethnic differences, language, religion, and region. In many cities where the socialist parties drew most of their proletarian strength from the foreign born, the very parties that most strongly stressed the importance of working-class solidarity had to establish separate branches to accommodate their different and sometimes unfriendly ethnic groups.

Finally, the course of American economic development doomed both labor and business, like all other economic interests, to remain minorities. Until 1880, urban workers were outnumbered by farmers. Yet when the number of farmers began to decline, the number of white-collar workers rose. Hence a party that drew its support exclusively or even mainly from urban labor could not hope to win majorities in national elections. Businessmen were equally condemned to minority status. Owners and executives of business firms were bound to be outnumbered by their employees. Hence they too could not hope to win majorities in national elections with a party that appealed only to businessmen.

OPERATION OF THE POLITICAL INSTITUTIONS

The political institutions also offered a powerful and quite possibly a decisive resistance to the creation of a successful labor-socialist party or even a labor-farmer coalition.

Impact of Federalism

First of all, the institutions of federalism made it risky for the labor movement to identify itself exclusively with a single party. The failure of the Working Men's Party of Philadelphia in the early 1830s taught labor leaders the disadvantages of a workingmen's party.[11] For in a federal system many of the specific aims of labor could be achieved more quickly through state action than by federal laws. A separate party which ran candidates against those of the major parties would antagonize state legislators otherwise responsive to demands made on them by workingmen's organizations. A leading student of American labor history has written:

> Only a state legislature could compel defaulting employers to pay wages earned, impose safety rules on hazardous occupations, and define minimum sanitary standards in work places. The state legislatures prescribed standards for schooling, voting, and minimum age for working, the employment of women, and limitations of hours of labor in certain occupations. . . . Union representatives appealing for legislative concessions understood that frequently only a beginning in the reform of a given problem could be made, and they were usually confident that additional improvements could be subsequently introduced. They also knew that the great majority of legislators were not ideologically committed to or opposed to many pieces of legislation sought by organized labor, and the members of legislative assemblies would respond to the pleas and pressures at slow or rapid rates depending upon the problem and the forces arrayed against labor on a particular issue. Promotion of an independent labor party would have necessitated the severance of relations with many members of the legislatures, who, assured of organized labor's political hostility, would have been more reluctant to support the bills labor annually or biennially presented to the legislatures.[12]

Thus the strategies of the American labor movement were shaped, during its formative years, by the political realities of the federal system.

---

11. Taft, in *Organized Labor in American History*, says: "According to Professor Frank T. Carelton, the Working Men's Party of New York made an important indirect contribution to future labor tactics. 'When in 1833–1837, the strong trade union movement arose, the fate of the Working Men's Party was accepted as a conclusive argument against direct political effort. Hence the trade unions kept aloof from party politics and merely questioned candidates as to their position on measures which were regarded as affecting the interests of labor.' Frank T. Carelton, 'The Working Men's Party of New York City,' *Political Science Quarterly* (September, 1902), p. 415" (p. 19).

12. Philip Taft, "Labor History and the Labor Issues of Today," *Proceedings of the American Philosophical Society*, 106 (August, 1962), 306. See also Taft, "On the Origins of Business Unionism," *Industrial and Labor Relations Review*, 17 (October, 1963), 20–38.

Impact of Winner-Take-All Elections

In the second place, there was the sobering matter of the election system, the effects of which we have already explored. In no country in Europe did the labor-socialist parties ever manage to gain a majority of popular votes. But they did obtain the introduction of systems of proportional representation, which reduced or eliminated the multiplier effect of the winner-take-all system. In the United States, not only in national but also in state elections, the single-member district and the winner-take-all system had depressing consequences for a third party trying to make its way against the two existing giants. The evidence of American experience was clear enough to anyone who cared to examine it: for a third party to cross the magic threshold to major party status was a formidable, discouraging, and probably hopeless task.

It is true that in Britain, which was also a two-party country, the Labor party in the 1920s became the main opposition party; and though it never acquired an absolute majority of popular votes in subsequent elections, thanks to the winner-take-all system it has gained a majority of seats in the House of Commons on four occasions—1945, 1950, 1964, and 1966. The majority it won in 1945 enabled the Labor party to carry out most of the program it had developed since 1918. However, by the time the successful experience of British Labor became available as an example to encourage the advocates of a separate labor party in the United States, that strategy had long since been firmly rejected by the American labor movement.

Impact of Already Existing Parties

In any event, another aspect of American political life greatly reduced the relevance of British experience with the Labor party. This was the fact that the urban workers had already been won over to the two existing parties before the American labor movement itself developed.

As the number of urban workers multiplied rapidly after the Civil War, there were already on the scene two major parties accustomed to assimilating workers into their organizations. In Europe, in Britain, in the Scandinavian countries and elsewhere working men faced existing parties—Liberals, Conservatives, and the like—which were run by members of the middle classes and the aristocracy. These middle-class parties had little or no grass-roots organizations extending down to the wards and precincts. They lacked the kind of organization that was created for American parties during Jefferson's presidency, perfected during Jackson's, and adopted as a matter of course by the newly organized Republican party in the late 1850s. In Europe the middle class and aristocratic parties could ignore the urban workers, for workers were deprived of the suffrage.[13] But in the United States, where the working classes had enjoyed the franchise from the early decades of the nineteenth century, to ignore these potential voters would have been political stupidity of a sort alien to party politicians. The urban machines of the Democratic party were particularly adept at using primitive social welfare devices to gain the votes and often the permanent loyalties of immigrants. Thus, unlike Europe, in the United States there was no vacuum into which a labor party could rush.

The Democratic and Republican parties not only had the advantages of organization; they also profited from the crushing inertia of established party loyalties. A successful labor party would need more than a program or an ideological appeal to workers; to be successful a labor party would first have to break down well-established attachments to one of the existing parties. There was nothing peculiar to the mentality of a worker (despite the romantic notions of some socialists) that inhibited him more than other citizens from incurring emotional ties to the Democratic or the Republican party.

A realistic appraisal of the American political scene, then, would lead inexorably to the conclusion that the two major parties could not be thrust aside by a labor party organized by the labor movement.

DIFFICULTIES IN THE SECOND STRATEGY

There was, however, another possibility: a coalition party drawing its strength from both farmers and urban workers. This strategy was doubly tempting, for, oddly enough, the farmers of South and West were much more responsive than labor itself to new parties that advocated labor-socialist programs. Even the Socialist party, although organized and led mainly by urban socialists, gained more electoral support in the agricultural states than in the industrial states. In 1912 at the high-water mark of the Socialist vote, Eugene V. Debs, the Socialist candidate for president, received 5.9 percent of the national vote. The highest percentage he won in any state was 16.6 percent which he won in—of all states—Oklahoma. The five other states in which Debs won more than 10 percent of the vote were Nevada, Montana, Washington, California, and Idaho—none at this time a highly industrial state.

The greatest success for the strategy of a farmer-labor coalition—and the most consequential failure—was achieved by the Populists in

---

13. In Britain, a substantial proportion of urban working-class householders were enfranchised in 1867–8; further reforms enlarged the franchise in 1884; virtually universal male suffrage came in 1918. It has been estimated that "perhaps one in twelve adult males could vote before 1832, one in seven thereafter, one in three after 1868, and three in five after 1884" (Allen Potter, "Great Britain: Opposition with a Capital 'O'," in Dahl, *Political Oppositions in Western Democracies*, p. 3). The dates for universal equal manhood suffrage in some other European countries were: Norway, 1898; Sweden, 1909; Denmark, 1901; The Netherlands, 1917; Belgium, 1919; France, 1848; Prussia, 1919; Germany, 1867; Italy, 1912.

the 1890s. As we have seen, the period from 1892 to 1896 marked a series of critical elections in which party loyalties were realigned for over three decades. The defeat of Bryan in 1896 amounted to a profound defeat not only for Populism but for the prospects of a new third party that would unite farmers with labor in a powerful national coalition.

Even though industrial labor and farmers constituted a shrinking proportion of the electorate, proponents of the farmer-labor strategy did not wholly die out. Both farmers and urban wage earners were injured in the economic turbulence of the usual cycle of inflation and depression that followed the First World War. In 1920 a combination of socialists, trade unionists, and liberals organized a Farmer-Labor party that nominated a presidential slate; however it gained only 265 thousand votes— less than a third of the perennial Socialist party total and barely more than the Prohibition party.

Although "the Farmer-Labor Party did not attract many top labor or agricultural leaders,"[14] during the next few years a far more serious effort was launched, mainly on the initiative of trade-union leaders, and these chiefly in the railway unions. Their instrument, the Committee for Progressive Political Action, nominated Senator Robert M. LaFollette, a nationally known Progressive Republican, as their presidential candidate; as his vice-presidential running mate the Committee selected a well-known progressive Democrat from Montana, Burton K. Wheeler. Despite the fact that the American Federation of Labor had not sponsored the Committee for Progressive Political Action nor proposed the nomination of a third-party slate, in a departure from standing policy the executive board of the AFL publicly endorsed the election of LaFollette and Wheeler.[15]

Although LaFollette and Wheeler carried only LaFollette's home state of Wisconsin, they won 4.8 million votes, or 16 percent of the total, and they ran second in eleven states. As in the past, the Progressive candidates won their biggest share of the votes in rural, not industrial, states. In 1925 the Committee for Progressive Political Action was dissolved.[16]

In 1948, a group of liberals and communists organized the Progressive party and nominated as its presidential candidate the well-known New Dealer, the one-time secretary of agriculture and ex-vice-president, Henry Wallace. The Progressive party was a sad caricature of the authentic farmer-labor parties that had preceded it. The national labor movements opposed it. The AFL maintained its traditional policy of neutrality, though in fact its leaders were hostile. The head of the CIO's political organization announced that it had been "the policy of the CIO Political

---

14. Taft, *Organized Labor in American History*, p. 384.
15. *Ibid.*, p. 387.
16. *Ibid.*, p. 388.

Action Committee not to support a third party." The CIO Executive Board decided by 33–11 that "it was politically unwise to inject a third party into the political scene of 1948."[17] In late August, the CIO Executive Board endorsed the Democratic presidential slate of Truman and Barkley. Deprived of trade-union support and leadership, the Progressive party and Wallace's candidacy became little more than an instrument of the Communist party. In the election of 1948, Wallace was crushed; not only did he fail to carry a single state but he actually won fewer votes than a dissenting group on the right, the States' Rights party, managed to pick up in the South.

With the passage of time, the prospects for a separate farmer-labor party have been dimmed beyond hope by the facts of economic growth. In 1964 less than one person out of four in the total United States working force was a member of a trade union; only four persons out of ten in the working force were farmers, farm laborers, or blue-collar workers. No party that attended exclusively or even primarily to the interests of labor and farmers, and ignored the claims of service and white-collar workers, could hope to become a majority party.

THE THIRD AND FOURTH STRATEGIES   It was not from want of a fair trial, then, that the first two strategies were rejected. Nor was it from any failure to consider the pros and cons of each alternative. For decades, in fact, socialists and others who advocated comprehensive social and economic reforms and an independent labor or farmer-labor party put their case before the annual meetings of the AFL. The discussions were highly sophisticated; it is doubtful whether working-class leaders in any other country more thoroughly canvassed the consequences of the various alternatives. The first leader of the AFL, Samuel Gompers, a social radical in his native England in his youth, knew the arguments for third-party action; he heard them again and again, but he rejected them as inapplicable to the American scene.

The Traditional Strategy of the AFL: Neutrality and Local Autonomy

At the first conventions of the AFL in the late 1880s and the 1890s, the question was argued out. The AFL then adopted the position from which it has never deviated:[18] it rejected an independent party of workers and instead chose to be neutral as between the major parties, to endorse candidates favorable to the labor movement, and to secure favorable legislative and administrative action by pressure-group activities.[19] As

17. *Ibid.*, p. 612.

18. Even in 1924 the AFL endorsed LaFollette and Wheeler by name and made clear that it did not endorse any party as such.

19. Taft, *Organized Labor in American History*, pp. 230 ff., and *passim*. See also Taft, *The AFL in the Age of Gompers* (New York: Harper & Brothers, 1957), pp. 289–301.

the controversy over Populism approached its peak in 1895, the annual convention of the AFL declared that "party politics, whether they be democratic, republican, socialist, populistic, prohibition or any other, should have no place in the convention."[20]

The AFL adopted one more position of some importance: it permitted complete autonomy on political matters to the constituent unions and to state and local federations. These departed more frequently than the parent body from the practise of political neutrality, but even they were politically neutral more often than not.

Although leaders of the labor movement pretty consistently found the Democratic party more sympathetic to their demands than the Republicans,[21] so long as the Republicans were the dominant party in the North, where trade unionism, industrialization, and urbanism were strongest, while the strength of the Democrats lay in the least industrialized region, the South, the Democratic party did not appear to be a particularly good risk for the labor movement.

As we have seen, however, the critical presidential elections from 1928 to 1936 saw a realignment of party loyalties. This time the balance in national support tilted decisively toward the Democrats. Urban workers, North, South, and West, flocked to Democratic candidates and identified themselves as Democrats. If it was by no means a labor party or even a farmer-labor party, the Democratic party was nonetheless highly dependent on and highly responsive to urban labor in general and to organized labor in particular.

Challenges to the Traditional Strategy

Organized labor made great gains under the New Deal. The National Labor Relations Act guaranteed the right of workers to join unions. For the first time, the powers of the national government were now definitely on the side of unionism, not against it. From 1935 to 1941 trade-union membership expanded from 3.6 million to over 10 million. Unemployment insurance, old age annuities, and other New Deal measures gave benefits to blue-collar workers. Then in 1947, a Republican Congress passed the Taft-Hartley Act over President Truman's veto; this act banned the closed shop, which was prized by many AFL union leaders, allowed employers to sue unions for broken contracts, and imposed other restraints on unions. Perhaps the most offensive provision to the labor movement was Section 14b, which dealt with the closed shop and the union shop, both highly prized among various unions. The closed shop—where union membership is a condition for obtaining a job—was banned outright by 14b. The union shop—where union membership is a condition for hold-

---

20. Taft, *Organized Labor in American History*, p. 232.
21. For the period from 1900 to 1920, see *Ibid.*, pp. 241–245, 372–382.

ing a job—was not banned directly; but 14b permitted states to outlaw the union shop if they chose. The Democrats pledged themselves to repeal the Taft-Hartley Act.

Support for Democrats. Confronted with Democratic leaders more friendly to labor than the Republicans, the AFL-CIO became more and more deeply involved in partisan politics despite its formal neutrality. It established a Committee on Political Education to press for policies favorable to labor, promote the registration of voters, and support specific candidates. During the 1960 campaign, COPE spent almost 800 thousand dollars and in 1964 almost 1 million dollars in behalf of various candidates, mostly Democrats. In 1964 it also spent around 250 thousand dollars on voter registration.[22] In that campaign, two experts on campaign finance report, "organized labor, as always, ranked among the Democratic party's most openhanded allies. . . . Thirty-one different labor committees were active at the national level, disbursing a reported total of $3.7 million. . . . Four-fifths of it was paid out as contributions or transfers to other committees or candidates—mostly Democratic."[23] Organized labor's expenditure at the national level was, in fact, larger than that reported by the Democratic National Committee (3 million dollars) and almost two-fifths the size of the expenditures reported by all Democratic national campaign committees (11 million dollars).[24]

Support by Democrats. In pursuing its traditional strategy, the AFL-CIO also lobbied in Congress, not only for bills directly bearing on unionism, such as the attempt to repeal the Taft-Hartley Act, but also to promote Medicare, federal aid to education, civil rights, and other measures. Since the Second World War the AFL and CIO have reported expenditures of 125–150 thousand dollars a year for lobbying in Congress —in some years, a good deal more. In terms of reported expenditures, the AFL-CIO is generally among the half-dozen largest lobbyists in Congress.[25] Legislation supported by the AFL-CIO has frequently been backed by a majority of Democrats and opposed by a majority of Republicans. Thus the labor movement has often found that even in pursuing the third strategy, acting as a pressure group in Congress, it is more dependent on Democrats than Republicans.

22. Herbert E. Alexander, *Financing the 1960 Election* (Princeton: Citizens' Research Foundation, 1962), p. 42; and *Financing the 1964 Election* (Princeton: Citizens' Research Foundation, 1966), p. 64; *The New York Times*, December 3, 1965, p. 39 M.
23. Herbert E. Alexander and Harold B. Meyers, "The Switch in Campaign Giving," *Fortune* (November, 1965), 216.
24. Alexander, *Financing the 1964 Election*, p. 43, Table 4.
25. In addition, subdivisions of the AFL-CIO—international unions, the AFL-CIO Industrial Union Department, etc.—generally spend sizeable amounts. Cf. *Congress and the Nation*, "Top Lobby Spenders, 1964–1968," vol. 2, pp. 926–927.

A de facto part of the Democratic party. More and more, then, in spite of its official policy of neutrality, the labor movement has become one of the major coalition partners in the Democratic party. In fact, the CIO (which was separate from the AFL until 1955) began life under the aegis of the New Deal and rejected the notion that the labor movement must necessarily remain outside the Democratic party. In 1944 the CIO Political Action Committee openly worked for the renomination by the Democrats of FDR and Henry Wallace and for the election of Franklin Roosevelt and his vice-presidential candidate, Harry Truman. In 1948, the CIO Executive Board officially endorsed Harry Truman for president. In a number of industrial states and cities, the main leaders of organized labor became deeply involved in Democratic party politics—nominations, campaign finances, elections, policies. Opinion poll after opinion poll revealed that trade-union members were among the staunchest Democratic voters in the North. Then in 1964 when the labor movement was offered a choice between a Democratic presidential candidate who supported most of its goals, including the repeal of Section 14b of the Taft-Hartley Act, or an avowedly conservative Republican who opposed practically all of the existing laws and new legislation which the labor movement most ardently supported, the general board of the AFL-CIO rejected neutrality and publicly endorsed the election of President Johnson and Vice-President Humphrey.

Despite its endorsement of Democratic candidates in 1964 and its *de facto* involvement with the Democratic party, however, the AFL-CIO did not officially reject its classic position: the labor movement may have embraced the Democratic party—but it did not officially endorse the party. Nonetheless, that possibility was weighed more and more favorably by leaders of the AFL-CIO. In 1965, in fulfillment of his campaign promises President Johnson sought to persuade Congress to repeal Section 14b of the Taft-Hartley Act. The Republican majority leader in the Senate, Senator Dirksen, mounted a filibuster that contributed mightily to the defeat of the repeal measure. President Johnson thereupon pledged that he would again fight for repeal in 1966. The president of the AFL-CIO, George Meany, announced to his fellow unionists that "If they [the Republican leaders] are going to conduct their business on the basis of absolute bias against the organized trade-union movement . . . then I think labor, itself, is going to take a new look at this entire question of our relationship with the political parties."[26] However, after President Johnson failed again in 1966 to persuade the Democratic majority in Congress to unite behind the repeal of 14b, Meany's ardor for the Democrats cooled. The AFL-CIO did not "take a new look at . . . our relationship with the political parties"; instead it

---

26. Political Memo from COPE, November 29, 1965.

remained, as before, technically neutral but *de facto* an element of the Democratic coalition.

Every group, every organization, every movement that seeks changes in government policies faces the same alternatives as the labor movement. Weighing the pros and cons of alternative strategies is no easy task. Ideologues are drawn toward the first or second strategy; pragmatists toward the third or fourth. A strong desire to maintain the purity of its aim beckons a movement toward independent political action; a strong desire to be effective beckons a movement toward negotiation and coalition. Idealism cries: Reject compromises! Realism asks: Of what value is ideological purity when it leads merely to political futility?

Difficulties and Failures of the First Strategy

If success is measured by the ability to win elections, then historically the first strategy has been the least successful. The history of the first strategy is, in plain fact, a record of very nearly total failure. Why this is so should by now be self-evident. The first strategy is likely to appeal most to a movement committed to goals which are unacceptable to either of the two major parties. Yet, if the goals of the movement are unacceptable to either of the existing parties, is there not good reason to think that these goals will also be unacceptable to the followings of the major parties and hence to most voters? If one goal of a political movement is to win elections, the first strategy will work only if at least one of the two major parties has fallen down badly on the prime job of the politician: to find out what appeals to voters and to act accordingly. The one clear historical instance of atrophy among the existing parties and the emergence of a new major party is furnished by the birth of the Republican party; the newborn Republican organization rapidly acquired the support of dissident Whigs and Democrats throughout the North and West. Yet this example remains the only case in which a third party has attracted enough support from discontented followers of the major parties to develop into a major party in its own right.

Doctrine of the hidden majority. If this is so, why does the first strategy have any appeal at all? Partly, no doubt, because its advocates ignore the historical regularities in American politics; partly because a movement with goals unacceptable to the major parties may simply have no other alternative open to it; and partly, one suspects, because of faith in the 'doctrine of the hidden majority.' The doctrine of the hidden majority, which is sometimes propounded by movements on both the extreme right and the extreme left, is the belief that a majority of like-minded citizens already exists waiting only to be mobilized, since the

Figure 26.1
The Vicious Cycle
of Political Alienation

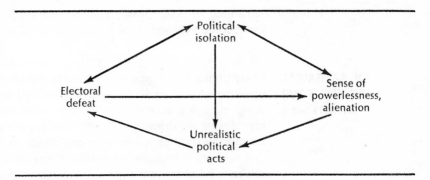

two major parties are for some reason ignoring and frustrating that latent majority. Belief in the doctrine of the hidden majority is not always confined to people on the most extreme fringes; in 1964 Senator Goldwater seems to have assumed the validity of the doctrine and to have fashioned his campaign accordingly with disastrous results.[27]

The vicious cycle of political alienation. Choice of the first strategy by a movement that is already divorced from the main currents of American opinion may establish a vicious cycle of political alienation: defeat, political isolation, and powerlessness reinforce a sense of political alienation and lack of realism in the movement, while alienation and lack of realism in turn increase the likelihood that the movement will be badly defeated in elections and will remain politically isolated and powerless.

Difficulties and Failures
of the Second Strategy
The second strategy has been, at least in national politics, no more successful than the first. The second strategy has some of the appeal of the first, for it enables a group to adhere to most of its goals even though it enters into a coalition with one or two other groups with slightly divergent (but in the main overlapping) goals. The strategy reached its zenith of success in the Populist party; but the needed majority was not forthcoming. Neither 'labor' nor 'farmers' constituted a homogeneous body of like-minded citizens, and the combination of the two groups created an even more heterogeneous coalition. Bryan and the Populists gained a good deal of support in some farming areas, especially in the South and West. But they lost badly in others and failed to win urban

---

27. Cf. Converse et al., "Electoral Myth and Reality: The 1964 Election." See also, however, the comment by William C. Baum, "On Electoral Myth and Reality," *American Political Science Review, 59* (September, 1965), 693.

labor. If the American citizen body was already highly heterogeneous in the 1890s, it is probably even more heterogeneous today.

Doctrine of the pure and simple coalition. Just as the appeal of the first strategy may lie in the doctrine of the hidden majority, so the appeal of the second may be drawn from the 'doctrine of the pure and simple coalition': a belief in the possibility of forming a majority coalition that is *pure,* in the sense that the coalition partners do not need to modify their goals in order to create or maintain a coalition, and that is *simple,* in the sense that it can be formed from only two or three groups, movements, classes, strata, each of which is internally homogeneous. Hence the appeal of a pure and simple coalition of workers and farmers; of the civil rights movement and the peace movement; of conservatives and property owners.

Yet if the interpretation set out in Chapter 22 is roughly correct, the doctrine of the pure and simple coalition must also be largely mythical. For where are these two or three internally like-minded groups that can combine to form a majority? Blue-collar workers are a minority of the working force, and a declining minority at that. Trade-union members are an even smaller minority—a fifth to a quarter of the employed population. The white-collar strata constitute a complex of occupational minorities, from clerical workers to professional men and employers. Professional men and women are a small minority of the working force; doctors are a minority of professionals; psychiatrists, a minority of doctors. The poor are a minority, but so are the rich; the middle-income strata are only a statistical category, not a homogeneous group. Blacks are a minority; so are white Southerners; so are Southerners, white and black. Jews and Catholics are minorities; the Protestant 'majority' is largely a fiction, for it is a congeries of minorities as different as Southern Baptists, Lutherans, Episcopalians, and Quakers. What is more, none of the categories just mentioned are, in fact, collections of like-minded people—blue-collar workers, trade-union members, white-collar workers, professionals, doctors, psychiatrists, the poor, the rich, the middle-income strata, blacks, white Southerners, Northerners, Jews, Catholics, Protestants, Democrats, Republicans, liberals, conservatives. No major category of the population defined by a single criterion, whether occupation, income, religion, ethnic group, region, or any other, consists altogether of like-minded voters.

Limits and Possibilities
of the Third Strategy

The third strategy offers a fair chance of success for any group smaller than a majority, when the members of the group agree on relatively narrow or specific goals that do not run sharply counter to

Table 26.1
Four Factors Relevant to
the Choice of Political
Strategies by a Group

A. GOALS	Goals of the group are:	
1. Breadth	1a. Oriented to NARROW objectives	1b. Oriented to COMPRE-HENSIVE objectives
2. Acceptability	2a. ACCEPTABLE to both major parties	2b. UNACCEPTABLE to either major party

B. MEMBERS	Members of the group are:	
3. Number	3a. FEW in number	3b. NUMEROUS
4. Homogeneity	4a. HOMOGENEOUS in political outlook	4b. DIVERSE in political outlook

widely prevailing beliefs. The third strategy is the strategy of the pressure group. For limited purposes it can be highly successful. Farm organizations, representing at most a small and diminishing minority, have used it with enormous success. So, in varying degrees, have literally thousands of other organizations, representing or claiming to represent trade unionists, veterans, businessmen, industrialists, taxpayers, bankers, oil companies, copper importers, doctors, women's clubs, nature-lovers, stream pollutionists, conservationists, foreign policy groups, old people.

But a movement that seeks something more than its own group interests may conclude that as a pure pressure group it will exert too limited an influence over the policies of the American republic. If a movement also has a numerous following of prospective voters, like the labor movement, it may find the fourth strategy more reasonable than the third.

**Limits and Possibilities
of the Fourth Strategy**

Is the fourth strategy perhaps the 'best' all round strategy? Not necessarily. A very small and well-organized group without many votes behind it may retain more influence as an independent pressure group. A large group whose members are divided among people loyal to both parties would run the risk of splitting its following if it adopted the fourth strategy. A group with narrow goals more or less acceptable to both parties may succeed better as a pressure group. A group whose goals diverge widely from those supported by both parties could not find a home in either party.

Thus each strategy has its advantages and disadvantages. Since enthusiasts are prone to believe that they can have the advantages of a strategy without its disadvantages, a choice among the four strategies is often a somewhat irrational process colored more by hope and faith than by hard-headed analysis.

Table 26.2
Appropriate Strategies for
Four Kinds of Groups

Thus if a group's Goals are	Members are	An appropriate strategy would be to:
I. Comprehensive, acceptable to neither party	Few, homogeneous	Form an independent party.
II. Comprehensive, acceptable to neither party	Numerous, diverse	Form a new coalition party.
III. Narrow, acceptable to both parties	Few, diverse	Form a pressure group.
IV. Comprehensive, acceptable to one party	Numerous, diverse	Form a coalition with an existing party.

FOUR FACTORS RELEVANT TO CHOOSING A STRATEGY

It is probably impossible, and in any case not very useful, to lay down a set of hard and fast rules according to which one strategy or the other would always be the most 'rational' in the American political system. Instead, let me try to draw the discussion together by pinpointing four factors that seem relevant in choosing among strategies (Table 26.1).

Theoretically, these factors can be combined in a number of different ways. For many combinations it might be difficult or impossible to say that one strategy was more 'rational' than another. For others, however, one strategy does seem more appropriate than the others. Table 26.2 shows one type of group for which a particular strategy seems appropriate.

Why is it that every strategy seems to have certain disadvantages? The main source of trouble is an apparently inescapable fact: *In the United States, any group of people who have virtually the same views on political questions, the same political loyalties and identifications, is certain to be a minority.* Whether the group is microscopic or relatively numerous, it will be a minority of the total body of citizens, even a minority of voters, and a rather small minority at that. To make the same point in another way, every aggregate of American citizens large enough to constitute a majority of voters is necessarily a rather heterogeneous collection of individuals and groups who may agree on some matters but are sure to disagree on others. No group of like-minded citizens can ever win a national election merely by mobilizing themselves and others who think exactly the way they do. To win national elections, even to win influence over national policies, every group must participate somehow in the politics of coalition building. To be sure, it can pursue its own goals; and it must engage in conflict; but it must also conciliate, compromise, negotiate, bargain—and in the process often forego its lesser goals for its greater objectives. In this sense, no single group *can* win national elections—only a heterogeneous combination of groups can.

Some people, particularly if they happen to be highly confident of their own political virtue, the rightness of their own goals, and the evils of compromise, find this a most repugnant interpretation of American political life. Either this interpretation is false, they say, and the strict, undiminished pursuit of the goals held by the group, the movement, the cause will one day eventuate in political success uncontaminated by compromise, or if the view is true, then politics is a dirty and evil business.

This, I think, is too crabbed, too inhuman a view of political life. For it seems obvious that, in a polyarchy, freedom and diversity lead inexorably to conflict. Yet they need not lead to inexorable conflict. For among a people guided, even in their conflicts, by a talent for conciliation and a commitment to the principles and institutions of a polyarchy, both freedom and diversity might flourish.

SUMMARY

1. A group of American citizens who wish to bring about changes in the conduct of the government have the option of adopting a revolutionary strategy, in the sense of trying to overthrow the government by force and replacing it with a different kind of regime, presumably not a polyarchy. In long-established polyarchies where the people tend to adhere to a democratic ideology, as in the United States, this strategy has regularly failed. However, chances for success might rise in the face of a prolonged failure to cope satisfactorily with issues that a large proportion of citizens regard as urgent.

2. If a group rejects the revolutionary option and chooses to use the processes available in the American polyarchy, it faces four general alternatives:

☐ The movement can organize a political party of its own.
☐ The movement can form a new coalition party by combining with another group or movement that has similar, overlapping, but not identical objectives.
☐ Although it remains neutral between the two major parties, the movement can act as a pressure group to secure favorable legislation and the nomination and election of sympathetic candidates.
☐ By entering into one of the existing parties, the movement can become an element in a major party coalition.

3. An examination of the choice among these strategies made by the American labor movement reveals that unlike labor movements in many European countries, the American labor movement rejected strategy 1. An explanation for the difference is found mainly in:

☐ The pattern of overlapping cleavages in the United States.

☐ The operation of American political institutions, particularly federalism, the winner-take-all system of elections, and the existence of two well-organized national parties before the American labor movement itself developed.

4. The labor movement also experienced severe difficulties with strategy 2: efforts to form a labor-farmer coalition proved unsuccessful.

5. The AFL adopted strategy 3. It came out against an independent labor party and opted for neutrality vis-à-vis the two major parties and for seeking political goals by pressure-group activities. It did, however, permit complete autonomy on political matters to the constituent unions and to state and local federations. However, under the impact of the New Deal and the development of goals more in line with the policies of Democrats than Republicans, the AFL-CIO has often found political neutrality difficult and has de facto, if not officially, become a part of the Democratic coalition.

6. An appraisal of the experience of the labor movement and other experience suggests that none of the four strategies is in all cases the one best. Which strategy is best depends upon at least four factors:

The breadth of a group's goals.
The acceptability of their goals to the parties.
The size of their following.
The homogeneity or diversity of their following.

7. Each of the four strategies may be the most appropriate for a different combination of these factors (Table 26.2).

8. The main reason why every political strategy has some drawbacks is that in the United States any group of people who have virtually the same views on political questions, the same political loyalties and identifications, is certain to be a minority.

The Uncompleted Agenda of
The American Polyarchy

27

In 1787 the Founders, we saw, left an uncompleted agenda for Americans to finish. The constitutional system they prescribed could have foundered completely, as constitutions have done so often since in so many countries. Or the constitution they proposed could have been adapted to rule by a narrow elite, an oligarchy, or a meritocracy. Or it could, as we now know, help form the framework of a polyarchy based on a broad suffrage.

The Founders themselves did not, nor could they, close off the options. That the political system moved, with astounding speed, toward polyarchy rather than toward the narrow oligarchy that was still to prevail in Britain for some generations or toward the breakdown of the new constitutional order and the rise of dictatorship that was to happen in France within one generation depended on circumstances and events mainly, though not wholly, beyond the capacity of the Founders to influence.

Today's uncompleted agenda contains matters that were, in a larger sense, on the agenda as far back as 1787. I have in mind the audacious attempt to develop a political system that would achieve a satisfactory level of political equality and consent. How satisfactory we judge the performance of the American polyarchy to be, when it is measured against these criteria, forms the subject of this final chapter.

DESCRIPTION, EXPLANATION, AND APPRAISAL

With such a task we move to matters where my own biases, values, and subjective perceptions are certain to have a larger impact than they have had, I hope, on the previous parts of this book.

To be sure, it would be claiming too much to insist that all the descriptions and explanations set forth up to now have the same degree of objective validity as, say, a biologist's description and explanation of the performance of a frog's circulatory system. One critical test for objectivity is whether other well-trained observers concur. I take it that over a very considerable domain biologists agree on their descriptions and explanations. It is on the frontiers of theory, data, and research that they begin to diverge. Although I would not claim to have achieved the biologists' level of objectivity throughout, that is what I have aimed for in all the details, descriptions, and explanations in Parts II, III, and IV of this book. In Part V, particularly the last chapter, my assessment of complex alternatives was, I have no doubt, more subjective and more debatable.

We are on even less firm ground when we try to make judgments on the broader matters discussed in Part I, especially when we try to decide among alternative theoretical or philosophical perspectives of the kind described there. No doubt some of you, particularly those for whom the exploration of theoretical alternatives is a new and unsettling experience, will be troubled to learn as you approach the end of this book that the interpretation of the American political system as a polyarchy, while conclusive for me and no doubt acceptable in its fundamentals to most observers, will be challenged by others, some of whom at the one extreme will contend that the system is much closer to majority-rule democracy and others of whom at the opposite extreme will insist that the system is closer to unfettered rule by elites than is thought to be valid in the perspective of polyarchy advanced in this book. Yet even if alternative perspectives are debatable, they are also open to a considerable amount of objective testing. Data and findings may not be—evidently are not at present—so conclusive as to eliminate dispute resulting from basic differences in perspectives. But data and findings are relevant. As findings multiply they increase or decrease the plausibility of one interpretation or the other. A young reader might appropriately regard reading this book as only the beginning of a lengthy process of testing alternative perspectives against additional data and experience.

When we turn to the task of *appraising* a system as vast and complex as the American polyarchy, as we do briefly in this chapter, the element of objectivity is likely to be even more elusive. Appraisal requires standards of judgment or values; it requires a comparison of actual performance, or what is believed to be actual performance, with the standards; and it requires a judgment on the significance or meaning of the discrepancy between actual performance and standards. Factors inherent in the very process of evaluation, difficult if not impossible to remove in practise, insure that one person's appraisal will contain judgments with which other observers can disagree, and where differences in judgments cannot be resolved easily or perhaps not at all.

Nonetheless, appraising a political system need not be, as is sometimes thought, a purely arbitrary decision to which objectivity and data are irrelevant. Criteria of performance may be arbitrary or subjective in their ultimate grounds, as many modern philosophers have contended. Yet choosing appropriate and relevant criteria for judging the American polyarchy need not be *wholly* arbitrary, if only because history, tradition, and public ideology give us some guidelines. Moreover, once standards of performance have been chosen—arbitrarily or not—comparing the actual performance with the standards need not, and obviously should not, be wholly arbitrary; for unless it is intended as pure daydreaming, such a comparison requires and depends on data about actual performance.

CONSENT AND POLITICAL EQUALITY AS STANDARDS

Among the standards most clearly available and relevant for judging the performance of the American polyarchy are the historic goals that have for so long been so central to American public values: political equality and consent. These are by no means the only standards that might be used; a truly comprehensive appraisal of the American polyarchy would require a very large book (a task, so far as I know, that has never been attempted—not even by Tocqueville). Nor is an appraisal of the American polyarchy equivalent to appraising the performance of American society. Many specific problems confronting American society do, of course, depend on the way the polyarchy performs: problems involving the environment, health, the cities, transportation, the quality of education (as distinct from the distribution of educational opportunities), the control of nuclear energy, and so on. But while satisfactory solutions to problems like these could enormously improve the quality of American life and society—hence they are unquestionably important and even urgent problems—they would not necessarily reduce gaps between the achievement and the performance of the American polyarchy, measured against standards of political equality and consent.

In Chapter 3 I suggested that continuing (as against once-and-for-all) consent combined with political equality would require that every full citizen must have unimpaired opportunities:

1. to figure out, discover, and formulate his goals or preferences: to find out what he really wants;
2. by acting individually or in concert to indicate his goals or preferences to his fellow citizens and to the government; and
3. to have his preferences weighted equally in the conduct of the government—that is, weighted with no discrimination because of *what* he wants or *who* he happens to be.

So our question now is: How well does the American polyarchy measure up to these standards?

FIVE PERSPECTIVES FROM WHICH TO EVALUATE PERFORMANCE

Before coming directly to grips with that question, let me first suggest five different perspectives from which we might try to evaluate a political system.

1. Absolute. We might estimate the gap between actual performance and what would be a perfect or ideal attainment of a standard if it were adopted quite literally. Important as this step is, however, it is at best only preliminary. For most of us know that ideal standards are practically never achieved; we may even think them unattainable. Their very distance is one reason we retain such standards as ideals. To discover that a gap exists between perfection and reality is often disillusioning for adolescents; but for any mature person it is hardly novel information. Consequently, we want to know not only about the existence and general magnitude of the gap between ideal and actual: how far short the performance of this system is from ideal or perfect performance; we also want to decide how *satisfactory* or unsatisfactory such a gap is. Knowing that any actual performance is almost bound to be less than ideal, is the gap too great, or small enough to be satisfactory? If we decide that performance is satisfactory, we can afford to turn our attention to another problem. But if it is unsatisfactory, we should want to explore how we might close the gap further.

2. Optimal. One difficulty with choosing a particular set of goals or standards—the three listed above, for example—is that they are sure to be a subset of a larger universe of goals, ideals, values, standards. If perfect achievement of some goal in our subset would conflict with attaining a valued goal we happen to have left out, we may want to bring the excluded goal to bear in order to see whether the price of perfect achievement of the one goal may not be too high measured by others. If so, we should not expect or even want to attain the absolute level of any single standard—one single goal—but rather an optimal mix according to a number of standards.

A good example is furnished by the possibility of conflict between the goal of political equality, which democratic theory emphasizes, and the goal of competence or specialized knowledge in public decisions, which has since Plato's time been so heavily emphasized by philosophers who advocate aristocracy or meritocracy, as we saw in Chapter 3. Of course, no democratic theorist has ever totally ignored the problem of competence, or denied its relevance. To take what looks like a trivial example, yet one which is chock full of implications, no one to my knowledge has ever seriously proposed that in order to pursue the democratic ideal children should be granted exactly the same rights as adults to participate in public affairs. Whether a boundary is arbitrarily fixed at age 21 or 18 or elsewhere, every theorist assumes that it should be drawn at an age that accords in a rough way with a minimum level of competence. Yet to the extent that one puts a value in decision-making on competence, expertness, technical knowledge, reliability, availability, and so on, what one regards as the most desirable or *optimal* goal of political equality will fall short (as in the exclusion of children from equal political rights) of achieving the absolute goal. The absolute goal, it turns out, is not really perfect after all; paradoxically, the optimal may appear less than 'perfect'—yet it is clearly more desirable!

3. Comparative. In trying to arrive at a judgment about what is optimal, we might find it reasonable to compare the performance of one political system with the performances of other systems. In the case of polyarchy, it might look promising to compare the performance of the United States with the performance of all other polyarchies. There are, however, two problems in such an exercise. First, all polyarchies might fall short of the optimal, for want of commitment to democratic ideals, or for other reasons. Second, one country's potential achievement at any given time might be higher or lower than that of another.

4. Potential. Hence one might want to look at potentials. For example, individual differences in human skills, incentives, and resources persist even in societies that are earnestly trying to reduce such differences by expanding the opportunities available to disadvantaged persons. A historical accumulation of inequalities is not eradicable overnight. The burden of past history will reduce the potential for political equality below the absolute level in the short run, and even perhaps below the long-run optimal level. Potentials often vary from one historical epoch, society, or country to another. The potential for democratizing the polity of Britain, Sweden, or Japan in the fifteenth century was surely vastly lower than it is today. The potential for achieving high levels of consent and political equality in a country just emerging from centuries of despotic or oligarchic rule, as is true in many of the developing countries, can hardly be as great as the potential of a country that has enjoyed several centuries of orderly constitutional rule and long experience with polyarchy. Hence it seems reasonable to insist on a higher level of performance in the second country than in the first.

5. Historical. Considerations of potential achievement suggest that we might also want to look at a particular system historically, in order to take into account the trend of its development. A country at a low absolute level of achievement that is moving steadily to enlarge the domain of equality and consent might be judged as closer to its present potential, and thus more satisfactory in its achievement, than a country at a fairly high level of achievement that is static or regressing.

Figure 27.1
The Cycle of Defeat

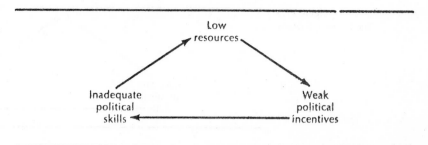

Low
resources

Inadequate   Weak
political   political
skills   incentives

DEFICIENCIES IN THE PERFORMANCE OF THE AMERICAN POLYARCHY

Judged from any one of these perspectives there are, I believe, some serious and persistent deficiencies in the performance of the American polyarchy. The American polyarchy has not only failed to achieve political equality and consent in an absolute sense, but its performance is unsatisfactory, in my view,[1] even when we judge American performance on the basis of optimality, comparative achievements, potentiality, or historical trend. Let me list the most important of these deficiencies.

1. Traditional Institutionalized Inequalities

In Chapter 7 I emphasized that one of the distinctive characteristics of the American polyarchy is its long history of discrimination against certain racial minorities: not only Afro-Americans, but also Indians, Chicanos, Orientals. While a few racial minorities, most notably Japanese-Americans, have in recent years substantially overcome these inequalities and appear to have attained full political equality, and while there has undoubtedly been more progress since the mid-1950s with respect to the others than during the whole prior history of this country, traditional and institutionalized inequalities have left some minorities with such limited political resources, skills, and incentives that it is impossible for them to achieve equality unaided by lifting themselves up by their own bootstraps, as many white Americans evidently feel they should.

Traditional institutionalized inequalities tend to create all the conditions needed for a perfect self-fulfilling prophecy: political weakness leads to continued political weakness, and strength to continued strength. Where a long history of inequality creates a group with few resources—wealth, income, status, education, official position—the prospects of successful political action are so meager that incentives to act politically are low: as a consequence, political skills are not acquired. So the cycle tends to be perpetuated (Figure 27.1). Conversely, groups with large

---

1. Since I have made clear the subjective aspect of these judgments, I omit the qualifier hereafter.

Figure 27.2
The Cycle of Success

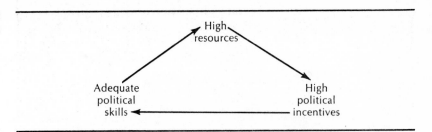

resources are likely to have both their incentives and their skills reinforced by success (Figure 27.2).

To break out of the cycle of defeat is particularly difficult if a group
is a small minority and lacks even the potential resource of large numbers—a resource, as we saw in Chapter 26, of great historical importance
to labor movements. With activity and skill, however, a minority may be
able to concentrate its numbers so as to maximize their impact: for
example, to win local elections and to count heavily enough in nominations and elections for state and local offices so that minority views and
leaders gain influence. In this respect, the increasing dispersion of the
black population throughout the country is both an advantage and a
disadvantage: they have become a smaller minority in the South but they
have become larger minorities elsewhere (Table 27.1). Meanwhile, too,
the Civil Rights Acts of 1964 and 1965 opened up the possibility, for the
first time since Reconstruction, of large numbers of blacks gaining entry
into the South's political system. As a result, since 1965 Southern blacks
have gradually been bringing an end to the South's old dual system—
a polyarchy for whites who collectively exercised hegemony over blacks.
And in the North the awakening of the ghettoes and the increasing
proportion of blacks, especially in the central cities, have given blacks
an increasing political voice, particularly within the Democratic party.
Though still much underrepresented in political life, by 1971 there were
1,860 black elected officials in the United States (Table 27.2).

Yet the movement toward political equality—which requires higher
levels of resources, skills, and incentives—is slower than it would be
with a greater commitment by whites. After the historical breakthrough
achieved by the Civil Rights Acts of 1964 and 1965, commitment to further
progress, at best never a very strong one, weakened.[2] Meanwhile,
spokesmen for other groups suffering from traditional institutionalized
inequalities in political resources, skills, and incentives—Puerto Ricans,
Chicanos, American Indians, and (though statistically a majority, not a
minority) women—have demanded that the American polyarchy begin

2. See, for example, the data in "The Troubled American, A Special Report on the White
Majority," *Newsweek* (October 6, 1969), 28–73.

Table 27.1
Distribution of Black
Population in the
United States

Region	Percentage of black population			
	1970	1960	1950	1940
United States	11.2%	10.6%	10.0%	9.8%
Northeast	8.9	6.8	5.1	3.8
North Central	8.1	6.7	5.0	3.5
West	4.9	3.9	2.9	1.2
South	19.2	20.6	21.7	23.8

Source: U.S. Census Bureau data published in *The New York Times*, March 4, 1971, p. 20C.

Table 27.2
Black Elected Officials
in the United States,
March, 1971

	South	Non-South	Total
Total	635	1,222	1,857
Congress			
Senators		1	1
Representatives		13	13
State			
Senators	6	30	36
Representatives	34	128	162
Statewide elected offices		2	2
County			
Commissioners, supervisors	36	50	86
Election supervisors	16*		16*
Others	11	7	18
City			
Mayors, vice-mayors	28	53	81
Councilmen, aldermen	284	369	653
Others	5	46	51
Law enforcement			
Judges, magistrates	26	122	148
Constables, marshalls	37	21	58
Justices of the Peace	50	7	57
Others	8	3	11
Education			
College trustees		9	9
School board members	94	361	455

* All Mississippi.
Source: *National Roster of Black Elected Officials* (Washington, D.C.: The Joint Center for Political Studies, 1971), March, 1971.

to achieve political equality and consent much more fully than it has ever done up to now.

Until performance has eradicated these traditional institutionalized inequalities, the American polyarchy will continue to exhibit a large and palpable gap between the standards of performance Americans have long publicly proclaimed as desirable and the level of performance their polyarchy has actually attained.

Table 27.3
Shares of Income Received
by United States Families,
1968

Families and individuals ranked lowest to highest	Money income (unadjusted)		Total income (before tax and transfer payments)*	
	Money income range	Percent of income rec'd	Total income range	Percent of income rec'd
Lowest fifth	Under $3,150	3.7	Under $3,800	3.0
Second fifth	$3,150–$6,100	11.1	$3,800–$8,200	9.5
Middle fifth	$6,100–$8,800	16.5	$8,200–$12,100	16.5
Fourth fifth	$8,800–$12,500	26.2	$12,100–$17,500	23.0
Highest fifth	Over $12,500	42.5	Over $17,500	48.0
Top 5 percent	Over $19,700	16.8	Over $29,700	22.0
Top 1 percent	Over $32,000	4.9	Over $60,000	9.3

* Total income includes adjustments for underreported income, capital gains, retained corporate earnings, and so on.
Source: Herriot and Miller, "Who Paid the Taxes?", Table 2. Miller was chief of the Population Division, U.S. Census Bureau, and the computations are from census data.

2. Inequalities in Wealth and Income

Many of the Founders assumed, as previous political theorists like Aristotle, Locke, Rousseau, and Montesquieu, that a democratic polity could be attained only if the society could avoid extremes of wealth and poverty. For they believed that extreme differences in wealth and income would produce extreme differences in power, extreme class conflict, extreme hostility, fear, and resentment, and a high probability of rule by either an oligarchy of the wealthy or a dictatorship of the poor.

Polyarchies, nonetheless, have managed to survive in the presence of considerable inequality. In the United States, the distribution of income is highly unequal both before and after taxes and government assistance. The lowest two-fifths of the families receive about one-eighth of the total income. At the other end of the scale, the top fifth receive nearly half the total income, and the top one-twentieth, more than one-fifth the total income (Table 27.3). Moreover, despite a widely held popular belief to the contrary, taxes, including the income tax, do very little to change the distribution of income. In fact, as a percentage of income the sum total of all taxes, federal, state, and local, bears more heavily on the very poor than on any other income group. The very poor pay 50 percent of their income in taxes, the rich 45 percent, and the in-between 29–35 percent (Table 27.4). It is true that the very poor receive various forms of financial assistance from federal, state, and local governments, and these may more than offset their taxes. In 1968 families and individuals with incomes under $2,000 had their money incomes increased by 56 percent when *both* taxes *and* government assistance (transfer payments) are included; those with incomes in the range $2,000–$4,000 had a net

Table 27.4
Government Taxes as a
Percent of Total Income:
1968

Adjusted money income levels	Total taxes	Federal taxes				State and local taxes		
		Total	Income tax	Corporate profit tax	Social Security tax	Total	Property tax	Sales tax
Tax and transfer rates, total	31.6%	21.7%	9.5%	4.7%	5.1%	9.9%	3.7%	2.8%
Under $2,000	50.0	22.7	1.2	6.0	7.6	27.2	16.2	6.6
2,000– 4,000	34.6	18.7	3.5	4.3	6.5	15.7	7.5	4.9
4,000– 6,000	31.0	19.0	5.3	3.6	6.7	12.1	4.8	4.1
6,000– 8,000	30.1	19.4	6.5	3.2	6.8	10.7	3.8	3.6
8,000–10,000	29.2	19.1	7.4	2.9	6.2	10.1	3.6	3.3
10,000–15,000	29.8	19.9	8.7	2.9	5.8	9.9	3.6	2.9
15,000–25,000	30.0	20.7	9.9	3.9	4.6	9.4	3.6	2.4
25,000–50,000	32.8	25.0	12.9	7.5	2.5	7.8	2.7	1.8
Over 50,000	45.0	38.4	19.8	15.4	1.0	6.7	2.0	1.1

Source: Herriot and Miller, "Who Paid the Taxes?", Table 7.

gain of 14 percent in incomes.[3] But the effect on income inequality was still slight; a family with an income of $2,000 and net income supplements of 56 percent would still have received only about $3,100, an amount well below the poverty level.[4]

If polyarchies have survived in spite of inequalities in wealth and income, as is the case in the United States, there can hardly be any doubt that these inequalities generate a gap between ideal democracy and the actual performance of polyarchies. For wide differences in access to economic resources—and these are mainly a result of differences in wealth and income—are associated with and contribute to inequalities in political influence. Economic resources are often directly convertible into political resources, as is obvious with campaign expenses, for example, as well as publicity, propaganda, corruption, economic pressure, and so on. Economic resources also are indirectly converted into political resources because economic advantages significantly increase the probability of acquiring additional kinds of political resources: education, for example, or higher status, or available time, or even psychological resources such as confidence and optimism, which have profound consequences for incentives and learning new skills. Here again we find a strong statistical tendency (to which, of course, there are important individual exceptions) toward the reinforcement and perpetuation of inequality in influence (Figure 27.3).

3. Roger A. Herriot and Herman P. Miller, "Who Paid the Taxes in 1968?", presented at a meeting of the National Statistical Conference Board, March 18, 1971, pp. 10–11 and Table 7; published in *Conference Board Record* (May, 1971) under the title "The Taxes We Pay."

4. The official poverty line in 1969 was $3,550 for an urban family of four.

Figure 27.3
How Economic and
Political Inequalities
Tend to Reinforce
One Another

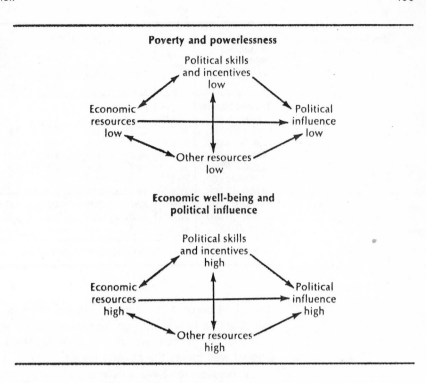

Figure 27.3
How Economic and
Political Inequalities
Tend to Reinforce
One Another

The distribution of wealth and income is not inevitable or fixed by nature. As Table 27.4 shows, the way net incomes are distributed depends partly on the policies of federal, state, and local governments with respect to taxes and transfer payments. The federal income tax is somewhat progressive; social security, property, and sales taxes are regressive. One result of tax policy (and other factors) is that the distribution of income is more unequal in the United States than in several other polyarchies where goverments have sought to reduce inequalities, such as Norway, Britain, and Australia.[5]

In general, inequalities in the distribution of economic resources help to produce drastic inequalities in opportunities to discover and communicate political preferences and have them taken into account equally when governments make decisions.

3. Inequalities in Education

It has always been a central assumption of democratic philosophers and advocates that a satisfactory achievement of democratic goals would require that opportunities for education be widely dispersed and generally taken advantage of among the vast body of citizens. Modern

5. Russett, *World Handbook of Political and Social Indicators*, Tables 71, 72, pp. 245, 247.

social science confirms this traditional view; in study after study social scientists have found a relatively high correlation between education and a variety of factors on which political influence depends: political participation in its various forms, organizational memberships, political knowledge, confidence, sense of political efficacy, etc. Probably no other single factor shows up so steadily in so many different studies as being so highly related to political effectiveness.

In a more general sense, it is obvious that education tends to enhance the three basic opportunities used here to characterize political equality and active consent: opportunities for discovering what one wants, for communicating to others what one wants, and for acting effectively to insure that these wants are taken into account equally with those of others when government decisions are to be made. Looking at the matter in a different way, it is again obvious that by providing knowledge and skills and ways of acquiring new knowledge and skills, education facilitates the acquisition of resources useful in gaining influence. It also helps one to develop the special skills that are particularly relevant to political life—skills in the arts of communication and organization, for example. For what are doubtless highly complex reasons, education also tends to be associated with and probably contributes to the development of the kinds of incentives that make it more likely that an individual will direct his energies toward political action and will persist in political action over comparatively long periods.

Education, then, has a powerful channeling or screening function. Thus a person with only an elementary-school education is very much less likely to be highly involved in politics than a person who has gone to college. In every polyarchy, consequently, and more emphatically in the United States than in some, elected officials are rarely recruited from the ranks of blue-collar workers; full-time politics is distinctly a monopoly of the white-collar strata.

Until recently, the United States led most other countries in the distribution of educational opportunities to its citizens. In recent decades the differences have diminished between the United States and other countries with a comparatively high level of per capita income. For many reasons, including inequalities of the kinds discussed earlier, many Americans are wretchedly educated. As a consequence, they are severely disadvantaged in politics. Decisions in the American polyarchy are likely to be made, therefore, without taking their preferences into account, certainly not as fully as the criterion of political equality implies—and without their active consent.

4. Inequalities in Discretionary Authority

Finally, a gap exists between ideal standards and actual performance that would very likely persist even if the inequalities described so far were drastically reduced. This is the difference in influence on government decisions that exists because of the opportunities available to government officials, elected and nonelected, to exercise discretionary authority.

In a political order in which the preferences of every citizen were weighted equally, at least in the final say, the individual preferences of a public official would have exactly the same weight as those of an ordinary citizen, no more, no less. In a country with a hundred million adult citizens, then, the purely individual preferences, values, and goals of the president, like those of any other *single* citizen, would have negligible influence on decisions. As an elected official the president would undoubtedly exercise a good deal of delegated authority. For his authority to be acceptable from a democratic perspective, however, he would have to exercise it by attempting to satisfy the dominant goals, values, or wills of the citizens, weighting each citizen as the equal of every other.

Admittedly this highly abstract notion is not without problems of interpretation and justification, but it enables us to focus on one simple but important point: while an elected official *qua* official may have a large measure of authority delegated to him, in exercising that authority he has no special right, *qua* citizen, to give extra weight to his own goals as an individual citizen.

This principle is only a special application to officials of the third of the theoretical requirements for political equality and active consent listed earlier. That it is an exceptionally difficult, perhaps impossible, criterion to satisfy is obvious. What citizens want, and what they would be likely to want if adequately equipped with technical advice, are in all polyarchies frequently unknown, obscure, self-contradictory, vague, or unexpressed. For a variety of reasons, in all polyarchies officials have a good deal of discretionary authority. Consequently they have opportunities to give undue weight to their own private or individual preferences in making decisions. They may sometimes exploit these opportunities for personal aggrandizement, including material gains obtained through graft and corruption. That many officials do act primarily in their own interests has long been one of the pessimistic convictions of the common man. In this case, the common man is moderately realistic.

In a large country, however, the problem goes far deeper than personal aggrandizement and material gains. For with more than a hundred million adult citizens, a close connection between the preferences of citizens and the decisions of officials sometimes becomes very difficult to maintain. In Chapter 13 we saw that a gap exists between constituents and members of the House of Representatives; for senators and the president, the difficulties are compounded by sheer numbers of constituents. Nor can the president and Congress exercise tight control over the administrative agencies. State and local government duplicate the problem in greater or lesser degrees. The upshot is that throughout the American polyarchy many officials, elected and non-elected, make decisions in which their own individual preferences, including, be it said in all fairness, their own particular conception of the public good, carry far more weight than those of any other citizen, or at least any ordinary citizen.

The problem has become particularly acute, as we saw in Chapter 11, when the president draws on the cornucopia of discretionary authority that has become available to him in foreign affairs, particularly on matters involving military decisions during crises or pseudocrises. Since by virtue of his constitutional, political, and psychological position the president can exercise exceptional influence on public opinion, he often leads on foreign and military decisions while the bulk of the citizens obediently follow. It may be technically correct to argue that because a majority of citizens support his policies, he is acting in accordance with their policy preferences; the crucial point, however, is that he is in a position to determine in considerable measure what their overt policy preferences will be. In such situations it is not the president who is the agent of the people so much as the people who are the agents of the president.

While a greater measure of supervision and control exercised by Congress, the press, and informed publics might reduce the president's discretion on foreign and military affairs and thus make him more an agent and less a manipulator of the public in this specific sector of public affairs, the *general* problem is bound to persist in a very large nation confronted by complex decisions on policies of all kinds. It is easy to see why, historically, democratic philosophers originally envisioned democracy as appropriate to very small units, no larger than a city, where practically everyone might know what was going on and where officials and citizens would be so close to one another that the problem of discretionary authority could hardly arise, or if it did, abuses could be quickly stopped. It is easy to see, too, why Rousseau denied that representative governments could ever be legitimate. For he saw, rightly, that the individual, personal, private, or collective interests of elected officials might—in his view certainly would—cause them to override the broader public good for their own narrower goals. It is also easy to see why early American advocates of representative democracy like Jefferson believed that the crucial locus of decisions ought to be at the smaller, more manageable local levels rather than the more remote level of the federal government.

In the present world and what can be foreseen of its shape for an indefinite future, total decentralization to completely independent city-states is plainly out of the question. A vast range of crucial problems,

from the rising tide of pollution to the continuing threat of nuclear anni-
hilation, make vast numbers of human beings interdependent over vast
territories; in some cases the limits of interdependence are reached
only with the earth itself. For this reason, it is also illusory to think that
all important decisions can be decentralized to local or state governments operating within a federal system in which the national government would be little more than a night watchman. Indeed, even the
governments of large nation-states are too small to cope successfully
with some acute problems. In a slow-motion race against the cascading
sands of time, transnational units like the European Common Market
are evolving. Mankind, it seems, is likely to survive long into the future
only by yielding up illusions of national sovereignty and subjecting the
lawlessness of international life to a constitutional order. Americans and
the American polyarchy will hardly be able to sit out this decisive turning point in the evolution of human society.

It is difficult to imagine how an international order could emerge
unless the United States and most other nation-states remain as units
of considerable autonomy and power. Yet a federal system of grander
dimensions than the United States would require the delegation of more,
not less, authority to more, not less, distant officials. Thus the problem
of discretionary authority and its possible abuse is certain to persist
well into the foreseeable future. Indeed, one price of human survival
may prove to be that this problem becomes more, not less, difficult
to solve.

It may seem irresponsible if I only state these problems and fail
to suggest solutions. But to investigate solutions responsibly would
take me far beyond the limits of this book into what would have to be
another and quite different volume. By calling attention to these four
problems I complete my purpose, which has been to describe, to explain,
and in this final chapter to appraise, in small part, the performance of
the American polyarchy, employing the public standards Americans long
ago adopted as suitable criteria for judging their political system.

Index

tive in, 125, 139; class identification in, 324, 326n; labor reforms in, 406–07; socialist parties in, 410; suffrage in, 413n
NRA, 202

Officiality factor: as political resource, 32; inequalities of, 437–40
Offsetting social power, principle of, 72, 73
O'Hara, Rosemary, 281n
Oligarchy: as rule by the people, 29, 31; Michels's theory of, 30
Olney, Richard, 405–06
Opportunism, 294
Ordinance of Nullification. See South Carolina
Orientals, and racism, 431
Ostracism, as political resource, 25
Ostrogorski, Moisei, 278n; on political parties, 284–85
Ott, A. F., 388n
Ott, D. J., 388n

Padover, Saul K., 59n, 120n
Pareto, Vilfredo, 29, 34; defines elite, 30
Parliamentary-cabinet government. See Cabinet government
Partitioned authority: in U. S., 50–53, 57; Founders' concepts of, 65–67, 71–74, 149–58; doctrine of, 109; suffrage related to, 111; and polyarchy, 113–14; in policy-making, 175–86; in local governments, 227, 239; affects elections, 356
Paterson, William, 80, 81
Peace Treaty of World War I, 136
Pearl Harbor, 348
Pennock, J. Roland, 163n
Pennsylvania, colonial government in, 119
People's party, 273
Perloff, H. S., 319n
Philippines, polyarchy in, 41 (table)
Pickering v. Board of Education, 205n
Pierce, William, 67–69 passim, 74, 78
Pinckney, Charles Cotesworth, 59, 61, 71, 91, 153, 248n; on equality,

87–88; suggests class stratification, 154
Pitkin, Hanna Fenichel, 163n
Pitt, William, the Younger, 268n
Plato, 20, 429; The Republic, 19
Plessy v. Ferguson, 383
Polanyi, Karl, 299n
Political agreement. See Consent
Political alienation, vicious cycle of, 420
Political change: in U. S., 294–301 passim; location factor of, 296; magnitude of, 296–97; incremental, 297–98; revolutionary, 298; sources of, 298–301; participation and apathy in, 301–02; resulting conflict of, 302–03; citizen power in, 387–98 (incl. tables); labor's efforts for, 405–19; appraisal of problems of, 419–24 (incl. tables)
Political equality. See Equality
Political influence: of resources, 31; inequality in, 435–37 (incl. table)
Political institutions: and conflict, 5, 309–12 passim (incl. table), 353–60 passim (incl. table), 375–78; acceptance of, 49–50, 53, 57, 112, 113; affect coalitions, 51; aid change, 353, 396; aid minorities, 395–96; affect labor movement, 411. See also Political parties
Political participation and apathy, 94–97 (incl. tables); in local governments, 231–39 (incl. tables); in political changes, 301–02; education related to, 436–37
Political parties: popular modern views of, 240–42 (incl. tables); Constitutional Convention's concepts of, 242–44 passim, 250; initial opposition to, 244–46, 250; old versus modern definitions of, 244; growing acceptance of, 246; engendered by polyarchy, 246–47; early history of, 247; institutional development of, 248–50; third party strength, 251–52 (incl. table), 255–57 (incl. table), 258 (table); and ideology, 252, 261–65, 275;

consent and conflict related to, 252, 274; PR versus winner-take-all systems of, 253–55 (incl. table), 274; and loyalties, 255–57, 262–64 (incl. table), 274, 284–88, 289–90; effective competition related to, 257, 274; control factor of, 257–60, 274, 276–78, 281, 288–89; cohesiveness in, 260–61, 274; socially stratified membership in, 265–67 (incl. table), 275; durability of, 267–68, 275; varying support of, 269–75 (incl. table), 275; aid polyarchy, 276, 288–89; conflict management by, 276, 288, 290; internal oligarchy of, 278–80, 289; offsetting oligarchy of, 280–81, 289; rationality factor of, 281–84, 289; severe-conflict actions of, 306; rise of radical and reform, 347; labor's affiliation with, 412–13. See also Elections; parties by specific names
Political resources: inequality related to, 31–33, 431–40 passim (incl. tables); time factor, 31–32; legitimate authority, 32; officiality, 32; political skill, 32; incentives, 32–33; institutional guarantees, 44; mass media, 107, 145; citizen power of, 388–91 (incl. table), 396–98
Political skill: as resource, 32; inequality related to, 94, 113, 431–36 passim (incl. tables); citizen power in, 388–91 (incl. table), 397–98; education related to, 437
Polk, James K., 133
Polsby, Nelson, 314n
Polyarchy: theory of, 35–36, 46–47; democracy versus, 36–37; 1971 existence of, 39–41 (incl. table), 86; majority rule versus, 41–43, 47; hegemony versus, 43, 47; Mosca on, 45; policy making in, 175–86; engenders political parties, 246–47; party systems in 251, 274; aided by political parties, 276–90; conflict in, 293–94, 302–03; government control in, 387–88; citizen power in

PRINTED IN U.S.A